anus Hyperboreus

Balor regio

Nublius lacus

Oechardes fl.

SERICA
regio

Isfedon

Ottorocoras

CATHAY

Quinfai

MANGI

INDIA
ltra Gãgem

Sinarũ regio

Marcotta   Rhanda

Cyamba

Ambaſtæ

Chientij

Archipelagu
7448 inſular

Sindi

Pego

Regio aurea

Malaqua

Porne

Gilolo
Vel

Iaua minor

Moluca

Tarinata

Inſulæ p̃donũ

Iaua maior

The Light of Asia

The Light of Asia

A History of Western Fascination with the East

CHRISTOPHER HARDING

ALLEN LANE
an imprint of
PENGUIN BOOKS

ALLEN LANE

UK | USA | Canada | Ireland | Australia
India | New Zealand | South Africa

Penguin Books is part of the Penguin Random House group of companies
whose addresses can be found at global.penguinrandomhouse.com.

First published in Great Britain by Allen Lane 2024

001

Set in 12/14.75pt Dante MT Std
Typeset by Jouve (UK), Milton Keynes
Printed and bound in Great Britain by Clays Ltd, Elcograf S.p.A.

The authorized representative in the EEA is Penguin Random House Ireland,
Morrison Chambers, 32 Nassau Street, Dublin D02 YH68

A CIP catalogue record for this book is available from the British Library

ISBN: 978–0–241–43444–4

www.greenpenguin.co.uk

For my children

Contents

Contents

PART THREE

INWARD: DWELLERS ON THE THRESHOLD (1910S TO 2000)

List of Illustrations

Photographic Acknowledgements

Every effort has been made to contact all rights holders. The publishers will be pleased to amend in future editions any errors or omissions brought to their attention. Photographic sources are shown in italics.

Endpapers

The endpapers show a map of Asia from Sebastian Munster, *Cosmographia*, Basel, 1550. *Photo: Barry Lawrence Ruderman Antique Maps, Inc.*

Text Illustrations

Page x: Swami Vivekānanda at the World's Parliament of Religions, Chicago 1893. From *Vivekananda: A Biography in Pictures*, pub. Advaita Ashrama, Kolkata, 1966.

Page 10: Map of the world according to Herodotus. *Photo: CPA Media/Alamy.*

Page 20: Alexander encounters the 'naked philosophers'. Illustration from Augustine, *City of God*, c. 1480. Bibliothèque municipale, Mâcon, MS I, fol 73 (detail).

Page 34: The Temptation of Adam and Eve and Expulsion from the Garden of Eden. Woodcut, workshop of Michael Wolgemut, from the *Nuremberg Chronicle*, c. 1493. *Photo: Cornell University Library, Division of Rare and Manuscript Collections.*

Page 188: *A Hiogo Buddha*. Illustration from Isabella Lucy Bird, Unbeaten Tracks in Japan, Vol II, *c.* 1878. National Library of Scotland, Edinburgh (AB.2.98.2). *Photo: NLS.*

Page 204: Madame Blavatsky, undated photo. *Photo: Science History Images / Alamy.*

Page 224: *Hotei Yawning*, by Sengai (1750–1837). Gitter-Yelen Foundation and Art Study Center, New Orleans. *Photo: Artefact / Alamy.*

Page 242: Alan Watts, *c.* 1970. *Photo: Pictorial Parade / Getty Images.*

Page 256: Mountain peaks around Kurisumala, Kerala, South India. *Photo: Antographer / Alamy.*

Page 272: Erna Hoch at Nur Manzil. *Photo: Gosteli-Stiftung Foundation (AGoF 657 : 1:142-004).*

Page 290: Alan Watts, Timothy Leary, Allen Ginsberg and Gary Snyder, 1967. *Photo: Alamy.*

Page 304: George Harrison, John Lennon, Cynthia Lennon, Jane Asher and the Maharishi at Rishikesh, India, February 1968. *Photo: Pictorial Press Ltd / Alamy.*

Page 324: Bede Griffiths at Shantivanam. *Photo: copyright Adrian Rance.*

Page 346: Bird on a Branch. Hanging scroll by Unkei Eii, inscribed by Daiko Shōkaku, early sixteenth century. Metropolitan Museum of Art, New York. Mary Griggs Burke Collection, Gift of the Mary and Jackson Burke Foundation, 2015. Acc. No. 2015.300.59. *Photo: Met, NY.*

Swami Vivekānanda, pictured fourth from the right at the
World's Parliament of Religions, Chicago 1893.

Introduction

11 September 1893. At thirty years of age, this was Swami Vivekānanda's first attempt at public speaking. Wearing a saffron-coloured turban above robes of crimson and orange, he rose to face an audience of 4,000 people, split between the floor and gallery of the brand-new Hall of Columbus.[1]

A couple of years before, this part of the Lake Michigan shoreline, just south of Chicago, had been nothing but scrubland. Then 12,000 labourers had set to work: dredging, filling, and laying railway tracks. Locals paid a fee to enter the awe-inspiring construction site, looking on as the sort of iron and steel technology used in Chicago's skyscrapers was riveted and raised into place. Off these towering frames was hung a mix of white plaster, horsehair and hemp, moulded into colossal structures intended to complement the plazas, fountains and statues all around in recalling ancient Greece and Rome.[2] A classical paradise, but with American backbone.

The occasion for all this was the 400th anniversary of Christopher Columbus' famous journey west. The World's Columbian Exposition was a year late in opening. But in all other respects, a continent in whose existence Columbus himself had resolutely refused to believe – convinced until the end that his voyages had taken him to Asia – was pulling out the stops to make him proud. There were columns and porticoes, a gilded statue of the Goddess of Liberty, and murals and inscriptions celebrating everything from Isaac Newton to steamship technology. There was Stars and Stripes drapery, electric floodlights and a grand archway inscribed with the words: 'Ye Shall Know The Truth, And The Truth Shall Make You Free'.[3] Here was a country entering its pomp: New Rome and New Jerusalem rolled into one, propelled into the future by Enlightenment values, scientific know-how and the kind of prosperity and optimism without which an undertaking on this scale would be inconceivable.

Today's event was the opening session of a 'World's Parliament of Religions'. Its aim was to bring to an exposition heavily focused on material accomplishments – from engineering to finance – a touch of the transcendent. Proceedings began with the echo around Lake Michigan of the 'Liberty Bell', tolling once in honour of each of ten major world religions: Shinto, Taoism, Confucianism, Buddhism, Hinduism, Jainism, Zoroastrianism, Judaism, Christianity and Islam. Sixty or so speakers from around the world processed solemnly into the hall, cassocks and robes of all colours swishing along together as national flags fluttered above. An organ was fired up and a psalm sung, before everyone took to their seats for the speeches of introduction.[4]

A devoted biographer later remarked of Vivekānanda that he remained in sage-like meditation as all this unfolded. The man himself remembered things differently: 'My heart [was] fluttering and my tongue nearly dried up.' When his turn came to speak, in the morning session, he had had to decline. Now, he was ready to greet the gathered throng and, via the media clustered near his feet, to present Hinduism to a Western world which, across many centuries, had largely failed to understand it. It was a truly historic moment. And Vivekānanda hadn't prepared anything to say.[5]

'Sisters and brothers of America', he began – and was forced to stop there, as raucous applause took hold of the hall. Vivekānanda went on, when the audience allowed him, to make an outline case for Hinduism. The 'mother of all religions' had 'taught the world both tolerance and universal acceptance'. 'We believe', he added, 'not only in universal toleration, but we accept all religions as true'. To an audience consisting primarily of American Christians, familiar with the claim, attributed to Jesus of Nazareth, that 'No one comes to the Father except through me', Vivekānanda offered a contrasting line from the *Bhagavad Gita*: 'Whosoever comes to Me, through whatsoever form, I reach him; all men are struggling through paths which in the end lead to me.'[6]

By the time the World's Parliament wrapped up its proceedings seventeen days later, Vivekānanda's charismatic contributions had turned him into a minor celebrity. Invitations came in to lecture across the United States and Great Britain. Rumour – or possibly hagiography – had it that extra security had been installed at the Hall of Columbus, after people surged forward on one occasion, trying to touch his robe.[7]

Vivekānanda no doubt benefitted from largely negative Western impressions of Hinduism up to this point, thanks in no small part to Christian missionary reports about life in rural India that read like grisly dispatches from the front-lines of a war on despair. Against this backdrop, Vivekānanda was a revelation. But perhaps the biggest reason for his success was that Vivekānanda richly deserved his new name, given to him shortly before departing for America by his disciple and sponsor the Mahārāja of Khetri: 'Vivekānanda' meant 'bliss of discerning knowledge'. What he discerned in America, and in the wider West, was a blend of fascination and hunger.

The fascination was old. Colourful stories about India had circulated in Europe as far back as the fifth century BCE, joined later by news of China, Japan and their Asian neighbours. Here was a region of the world – 'the East', in European eyes – that appeared rich in gold, jewels, spices and silk. There was monstrosity, too, from strange creatures rumoured to roam India's plains to the supposedly cannibalistic Japanese. From the early modern era, Asia's fascination as a place of wealth and wonder was complemented by its promise as colonial and Christian mission territory, and later as a source of fresh wisdom for the West.

The light of Asia appeared, for a time, to shine especially brightly in China. Europeans like Voltaire were thrilled to discover an ancient and successful society, built and maintained on learning and merit rather than clerical privilege. By the time that Swami Vivekānanda arrived in Chicago, Western attention had shifted to India's exalted poetry and philosophy – drawing in Goethe and Samuel Taylor Coleridge, amongst many others – and interest in Asia had become infused with a sense of lack and longing. Christianity's biblical foundations were being shaken by geological discoveries, Darwinian evolution and new forms of scholarship. More than a few Christians found that their religion asked too much of them, in terms of doctrine and an exclusive claim to truth, while offering too little of what they needed in return: love, peace, spiritual experience – reassurance that the universe was not just Newtonian mechanism, but spirit and fire as well.

America had particular problems of its own. The constellation of fine structures that made up the World's Columbian Exposition acquired the nickname 'White City', and not just on account of the building materials. Black America was largely missing from this celebration of the United States, a fact condemned by Ida Wells and Frederick Douglass. The latter listed all the things that he would love to share with visitors coming in from around the world, about the condition of his country almost thirty years on from the abolition of slavery:

> The moral progress of the American people has kept even pace with their enterprise and their material civilization . . . two hundred and sixty years of progress and enlightenment have banished barbarism and race hate . . . the people of the United States are a nation in fact as well as in name.[8]

Douglass could not share any of this, he said, because none of it was true. The exposition was, 'morally speaking . . . a whited sepulcher'. Especially egregious was the use of plazas, walkways and exhibits to portray the cultures of the world according to favoured Western taxonomies of savage, half-civilized, and civilized. Douglass regarded an ethnographic exhibit comprising people from the west African kingdom of Dahomey (now southern Benin) as a calculated insult: they were 'here to exhibit the Negro as a repulsive savage'.[9]

Vivekānanda had only been in the United States for a few weeks, arriving from Bombay via Nagasaki and Vancouver.[10] But he understood enough about the broader worries of the western world to be able to tailor his talks accordingly. He was generous in lauding

America's virtues, and on matters spiritual he attended to the anxieties of the age almost point by point. Religious truths are an attempt to describe something real, he assured his listeners. They are not imaginary, metaphorical, or relative. But doctrine ought to be treated as a means to truth, not truth itself. Science, meanwhile, is an ally, not a threat: his own tradition, Vivekānanda claimed, had anticipated recent and future findings of the natural sciences by millennia, from the conservation of energy to the impossibility of dead matter giving rise to mind.[11]

Greater roles for women in society? Some of the sages to whom the Vedas, India's oldest texts, had been revealed, were women. A lesser role for priests? Vivekānanda barely mentioned them, casting the spiritual life as a relationship between a human being and the divine. What about the problem of evil? Karma: a fair and rational arrangement, in which bodies may suffer but a person's soul journeys on towards union with 'the Almighty and the All-merciful' – at once father, mother, and friend, and worshipped primarily in love. Why, though, did the cosmos have to be this way – so complicated, so painful? Hindus do not know, admitted Vivekānanda – a thoroughly disarming response for anyone who had become weary, of late, with certitudes and platitudes, whether religious or scientific.[12]

Vivekānanda's appearance at the World's Parliament of Religions marked a turning point. In two and a half millennia of Western fascination with Asia, he was the first Asian religious leader to lecture widely in the West. Many more followed in his wake, and Vivekānanda's thousand-year-old Advaita Vedānta tradition – which inspired T. S. Eliot to remark that India's philosopher-poets made their European counterparts 'look like schoolboys' – was soon joined by Japanese Zen as one of Asia's most popular exports. Western enthusiasm grew rapidly from there, passing through the Beatles and flower-power, the New Age, and into the twenty-first century's mindfulness and wellness movements.

Garlands and gurus. Incense and chanting. Gnomic one-liners and quiet restraint. Had he lived to see the speed at which Asian cultures would – in some quarters, at least – become mired in misrepresentation and cliché, Swami Vivekānanda might briefly have wondered why he had bothered boarding the boat in Bombay. In the early twenty-first century, his beloved discipline of yoga – which Vivekānanda introduced to small groups of admirers while in America – found itself beset by accusations that an ancient spiritual practice was being reduced to a glorified workout. The fact that billions of dollars was changing hands in the process, with little of it finding its way to India, raised questions about stolen property. It compounded a sense of anger amongst people with Asian heritage at having precious practices or ways of looking at the world subjected to crude and potentially lasting manipulation – sometimes just for the sake of an #uplifting Instagram post.

Disappointed Vivekānanda might have been – but probably not surprised. In his final address to the World's Parliament of Religions, he observed that Westerners' interest in Hinduism appeared to be tinged by a desire for 'the exclusive survival of [their] own religion'. He had in mind not just Christianity but the broader culture of which it was a part in the modern West. The parliament had convened amidst the most extraordinary architectural display of wealth, creativity and success. Yes, people sensed something lacking – otherwise Vivekānanda would have been speaking to an empty hall. But how much was the average person prepared to risk in addressing that lack? When it came down to it, were they in search of wisdom or window-dressing?

Any spiritual leader worth their salt knows how deep such difficulties run, and how mixed people's motivations may be. What is real? Who says? How should I live? These three questions have often been at the heart of Western fascination with 'the East', all the way from ancient authors for whom India's fabled beasts and riches marked an extension of reality's range through to the intense, even salvific allure of Asian philosophy and spirituality for their modern counterparts. The result has been an extraordinary fusion of hope, struggle, astonishment and adventure with avarice, racism, fear of new and radical notions and the desire to apply to the duller parts of life a splash of 'Oriental' colour. Pop culture has played its own powerful, confounding role: supplying potentially transformative ideas with unprecedented momentum via music and film, even while its rapid churn threatens to drain them of their drama and banish them to a safe, ironic remove. *Star Wars* surely retains, for some fans, its Asia-inspired fascination: 'Luminous beings we are,' says Yoda to Luke Skywalker in *The Empire Strikes Back* (1980), 'not this crude matter.' Others will have grown up with the parodies and the second-rate imitations.

The Light of Asia sets out to explore this rich weave, focusing on India, China and Japan and on the highs and lows of 'fascination'. Global politics and economics have, for some time, been moving us away from the notion of two cultural zones confronting one another – 'West' and 'East'. But it would be a brave commentator who claimed that those three animating questions – What is real? Who says? How should I live? – have been settled to general satisfaction. On the contrary: as institutional religion wanes in parts of the West and people sift an array of alternative worldviews, both religious and secular, fascination remains evergreen. How it plays out, in individual lives and across whole societies, feels as pressing now as ever.

Part One of the book – 'Outward: Discovering Asia' – traces the evolution of early Western knowledge about Asia, from Greek rumours of fantastical creatures to the eastward journeys of Alexander the Great, Roman traders, Marco Polo and travel writers like the Englishman Thomas Coryate (nickname: the 'Legge-Stretcher'). Part Two – 'Downward: Fathoming Asia' – traces a deepening but highly selective Western understanding of how people in India, China and Japan saw the world, beginning with the Jesuits and running through to the late Victorian era's enthusiasm for Buddhism and the occult.

Across the twentieth century, increasing numbers of Westerners looked to Asia for solutions to empty lives and faltering societies. Part Three – 'Inward: Dwellers on the Threshold' – explores this intimate concern with the East by homing in on three people who launched themselves on spiritual odysseys of a kind, touching the lives of many others in the process. The English writer Alan Watts (1915–73) was one of his era's pre-eminent popularizers of Asian wisdom, and a leading light in America's counter-culture. His fellow Englishman Bede Griffiths (1906–93) spent the second half of his life in south India, living as a *sannyasin* – religious ascetic – and working out a blend of Christianity, Hinduism and modern science that earned him the title 'Father of the New Age'. The Swiss psychiatrist Erna Hoch (1919–2003) moved to the Indian city of Lucknow to run one of the country's first mental health clinics. There, and later in the Himalayas, she brought her love of the Stoics and her ebbing Christian faith into conversation with Indian thought and the emerging worlds of psychotherapy and transcultural psychiatry.

Our epilogue – 'Onward' – returns to the three big questions that have driven and shaped Western fascination with the East, surveying the successes and failures of the past and looking to the future. The personalities and technologies are changing, but the challenges and joys seem set to remain: of encountering fresh ideas and facing the invigorating prospect – conveyed so vividly by Vivekānanda in the cavernous Hall of Columbus – that the world can yet be re-imagined, all the way down.

PART ONE

Outward: Discovering Asia
(Antiquity to 1600)

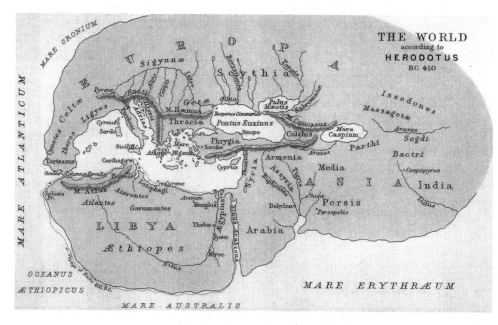

Map of the World according to Herodotus, (*c.* 450 BCE).

I.

Barbaroi, Agrioi

The great Olympian games were at hand, and Herodotus thought this the opportunity he had been hoping for. He waited for a packed audience to assemble, one containing the most eminent men from all Greece; he appeared in the temple chamber, presenting himself as a competitor for an Olympic honour, not as a spectator; then he recited his *Histories* and so bewitched his audience that his books were called after the Muses, for they too were nine in number.

Lucian, Herodotus and Aetion[1]

If the ancient Greek historian Herodotus of Halicarnassus (c. 484–c. 425 BCE) really had recited his *Histories* in its entirety at the Olympics, then not only he but his audience too would have been in line for a medal – or rather an olive-leaf wreath, for such were the prizes given out at the quadrennial games. An account of Greek relationships with eastern *barbaroi* ('barbarians') from the mid-sixth century through to Herodotus' own era, the *Histories* ran to more than twice the length of the *Iliad* or *Odyssey*. It would have taken somewhere in the region of fifty hours to perform.[2] This anecdote, penned centuries later by the notoriously mischievous satirist Lucian, is probably even less reliable than a rival version that has Herodotus waiting for some cloud cover at Olympia before beginning his recitation – only for his audience steadily to disperse, leaving him with no one to speak to.[3]

Elements of the story are plausible nonetheless. It may be that as few as 10 per cent of adult citizens in the Greek city-states were literate in this period. Theirs was an overwhelmingly oral society, in which great writers 'published' their works by performing them at festivals or in wealthy homes.[4] With that in mind, the ancient Greek equivalent of a literary agent might have regarded the Olympics as a very good gig if you could get it: the Panhellenic event par excellence, up there with the poetry attributed to Homer, the Greek language, the pantheon of gods and goddesses found in the writings of Hesiod, and latterly the Graeco-Persian Wars (499–449 BCE), as both source and ongoing expression of a proud shared culture.

If Herodotus, whom Cicero famously dubbed the 'Father of History', did indeed read portions of his great work at the Olympics, one can imagine him choosing his passages with care. Despite suffering defeat at Thermopylae in 480 BCE, along with the subsequent burning of a hastily abandoned Athens, the Greeks had managed to see off the mighty Persian Empire a year later at Plataea. This presented ideal material for Olympic spectators willing to put aside traditional city-state rivalries and consider themselves 'Greeks' for the day. And yet it is hard to imagine an audience hungering for Greek heroism or clamouring for Persian blood offering more than polite, slightly perplexed applause for Herodotus' observation that 'Everyone believes his own customs to be by far and away the best'. Ditto the revelation that amongst those who respected the Olympic ideal – competing for honour, not reward – was none other than arch-villain Xerxes. Herodotus' lauding of hardiness and austerity was a guaranteed crowd-pleaser, but only if he left out the parts where Persians, too, were shown to possess those qualities. Even the celebrated climax of the *Histories* would have required some judicious editing: Herodotus counselled that 'Soft lands are prone to breed soft men' – but he places this wise observation not in a Greek mouth but on the tongue of Cyrus II.[5]

The cliché of plucky democratic Westerners wiping the floor with lazy, despotic Orientals, often read back into Herodotus and his account of the Graeco-Persian Wars, was largely an invention of a later era – deployed with particular force by colonial-era Englishmen and women writing about Mughal India. Herodotus did indeed contrast the free, courageous and law-abiding people of Sparta with Persians living in fear of an unfettered autocrat. But his foundational work of history-writing and ethnography was less concerned with ideology and jingoism than with evidence, nuance and the highs and lows of human behaviour across the known world.[6] When Plutarch dubbed Herodotus the 'Father of Lies', his complaint was not a fetish for falsehood, but rather Herodotus' stubborn unwillingness to arrange his facts into the form of a morality tale.[7]

So much for the near, known world. What of the world's farther reaches, in Herodotus' day? Many Greeks understood the earth to be a cylinder, floating in space and surrounded by other celestial objects including the sun and moon. The world's landmass lay atop the cylinder, divided into three continents: Europe, Asia and Libya. From the Greek city-states, more or less at the centre, this world spread outwards in concentric circles. First came the lands of non-Greeks (lumped together as *barbaroi*), where people knew little of the language, customs and institutions of the *polis*. They did not worship, treat women or raise children in the right way. Next came the wild people (*agrioi*), beyond whose inhospitable lands lay only the perpetually circulating river – and god – Oceanus, marking the very edge of the world.[8] Epic poems like the *Odyssey*, telling the story of Odysseus' journey home from the Trojan War, played on and deepened this sense of a safe and secure centre versus perilous peripheries.

Herodotus refused to accept the idea of a River Oceanus, on the basis of a lack of evidence. And only grudgingly did he follow what he described as the 'conventional' tripartite division of land.[9] In this scheme, Europe dominated the northern half of the world. Asia was imagined as running from Asia Minor and the River Nile all the way eastwards to India. And Libya was pictured running westwards from the Nile. The word 'Libya', noted Herodotus, was said to derive from a woman of that name who had lived there in the distant past. 'Asia' was the name of a goddess-nymph: daughter of Oceanus, and wife of Prometheus. 'Europe', meanwhile, was thought to be named after the goddess Europa, one of the consorts of Zeus. For

Herodotus, all this suggested that when it came to how Greeks imagined the earth, stories passed down over time were taking precedence over reliable geographical knowledge.

What about the people spread out across these continents? Here, the dividing line between stories and evidence was less closely considered by Herodotus. Instead, the power of the strange and the fantastical – over writer and reader alike – was given free rein. Working with the testimony of informants from various parts of the world, with whom he communicated in Greek, Herodotus set out to describe nearby peoples: the Lydians of Asia Minor, the nomadic Scythians to the north and east of the Black Sea, the Egyptians – whom the Greeks associated, amongst other things, with ancient and mysterious wisdom – and of course the Persians.[10]

Should one risk venturing north of the Scythians, Herodotus suggested, monstrous peoples lay in wait. The Sauromatae were known for their warlike womenfolk, refusing to take a husband until they had killed a man on the battlefield. Then there were the lawless, cannibalistic Androphagi, alongside other groups who were variously bald, possessed goat's feet, slept for six months of the year (Herodotus didn't believe this particular story), turned into wolves on occasion, ate lice and held funerary feasts at which diced flesh from the corpse was mixed with cattle-meat. Herodotus suspected that, insofar as they might be true, these horrors of the far north were attributable to a poor climate: rocky or arid land prevented the living of settled, civilized lives. The local wildlife was said to be equally inhospitable, ranging from golden griffins (here again, Herodotus had his doubts) through to gorgons.[11]

Herodotus was not the only Greek writer of his era to ponder the relationships between climate and culture. A treatise called *Airs, Waters, Places*, possibly authored by Hippocrates (c. 460–370 BCE), concluded in the wake of Greek victories over the Persian Empire that Asia's moderate climate was ideal for growing crops and raising healthy livestock but was terrible for human development. Such a happy climate resulted in too great an emphasis on pleasure. Only where the weather varied wildly and kept human beings on their toes could virtues such as 'courage', 'industriousness' and 'spiritedness' truly flourish. Many Asian peoples had the additional disadvantage of living under monarchies, which the author of *Airs, Waters, Places* saw as an additional reason for passivity and for Persia's recent defeats – who, after all, would willingly fight a war in defence of someone else's sovereignty?[12]

★

The vast Persian Empire was important to Greeks, not just as an adversary but as a conduit for news of what lay still further eastwards: a land through which, Herodotus claimed, a great river ran, called the Indus. One could travel no farther eastwards than this: beyond lay only sand and the rising sun. Herodotus recorded that after Darius I brought this region under his control, he sent an Ionian explorer named Scylax of Caryanda on a thirty-month expedition sailing down the Indus River to find out where its crocodile-infested waters went. If an ancient reconnaissance mission of this kind did indeed take place – and excavations, alongside a range of authors, attest to one – it would make Scylax the first recorded Western visitor to India.[13]

Herodotus' writings about the region around the Indus were a potent and uncertain blend of fantasy and hearsay. The latter most likely comprised a blend of what someone, somewhere along the line had actually observed, with material drawn from India's mythological oral literature – stories of gods, kings and fabulous beasts. Greek literature surely played a role too, its love of marvel informing the way that Herodotus imagined his readers and their expectations.[14]

There were, claimed Herodotus, 'many nations' amongst the Indians, 'none speaking the same language'.[15] Some were vegetarians, others sailed the seas in boats fashioned from a single piece of cane, catching fish and eating them raw. Still others consumed animal flesh, and even human beings who had fallen ill or grown old. This last was a fairly standard form of behaviour, in Greek thinking, for people who lived close to the edge of the inhabited world. 'Volubly though he may protest his good health,' wrote

Herodotus, 'they will not pay him the slightest attention, but kill him anyway and make a feast of him.'[16] The creation of life was scarcely more decorous than its destruction: it was said to be common for men and women to have sex in public.[17]

Herodotus had heard from Persian sources that India was a place of great wealth in gold. Some parts of north India supposedly consisted of sandy desert, inhabited by giant ants, somewhere between a fox and a dog in size. These ants dug holes, returning sand to the surface that was full of gold dust. Indians gathered this bounty into sacks during the blistering heat of the day, while the ants were taking refuge underground. They then raced out of the desert on the backs of camels that were as swift as Greek horses, outpacing irate ants who would catch their scent and give chase.[18] Herodotus seemed relatively convinced of this aspect of Indian life: he had heard of it from a Persian informant to whose superiors some of the gathered gold was paid in tribute. (The story perhaps has origins in Rajasthan's Thar Desert, though one theory for the gold-digging ants is a type of Himalayan marmot, which does indeed dig holes in gold-bearing soil.)[19]

Alongside geography and wildlife, Herodotus introduced his readers – or listeners – to a natural product which would one day be of great interest to Europeans. It was a kind of wool, 'more beautiful and excellent than the wool of sheep', which was said to grow on trees.[20] Unlike the giant ants, this material – cotton – had actually been seen with Greek eyes: in the form of woven fabric, on the bodies of Indian warriors fighting for the Persian Empire. Indian infantry, armed with reed bows and reed arrows tipped with iron, were said to have fought at the Battle of Plataea. Some may have ended up in Athens, as slaves.[21]

Herodotus was not the only means by which news or rumours of India reached the Greek-speaking world. Scylax is thought to have penned an account of his travels in the Indus region – since lost to posterity – amongst whose memorable and stubbornly long-lived claims was that India was home to various strange groups of people. One, the Skyapods (shadow-feet), possessed only one leg, on the end of which was a foot so enormous that they deployed it as a sun-shade at noon. Another group, the Otoliknoi (winnowing-ears), were said to have ears so big that they could wrap them around their bodies. As with parts of Herodotus' account, so too with Scylax; some of these notions probably had origins in Indian storytelling – becoming mixed up, perhaps, with fantastical elements in Greek poetry.[22]

The first known Western work devoted to India came in the fifth century BCE. The *Indika* survives now only in fragments – fittingly, perhaps, since it was torn to shreds by its critics. It was the work of Ctesias of Cnidus who, having been captured as a prisoner of war, went on to serve as court physician to the Persian emperor in Persepolis for some seventeen years at the end of the fifth century. This position would have given him access both to ideas circulating about India at the heart of the Persian Empire and to Indian diplomats and merchants in person.

Despite these advantages, and while going out of his way to condemn Herodotus as a liar, Ctesias produced a series of claims that baffled and enraged his later critics – who, in seeking to define themselves as new and more serious sorts of commentators, depicted Ctesias by contrast as a charlatan. India, insisted Ctesias, was a place where liquid gold flows from springs, and single-horned wild asses roam the land – the origin, most likely, of a Western belief in unicorns. Howling dog-headed men loom over 'pygmies', little more than two feet tall, who let their hair and beards grow long to conceal their modesty. Most fearsome by far was the *martichora* ('man-eater'), one of which Ctesias claimed to have seen with his own eyes when it was brought to the Persian court. Red and lion-like, with a human face incorporating blue eyes and three rows of teeth in each jaw, it had a scorpion tail that was capable of firing foot-long stingers at its enemies.[23]

Not all the criticism levelled at poor Ctesias was fair. He claimed that the *martichora* were hunted by Indians riding enormous monsters capable of uprooting trees and smashing city walls. Fluttering around above were birds with crimson faces, black beards and dark blue plumage, who would speak to you in Greek if you taught them how. Better still, some Indians possessed supernatural swords that could withstand harsh monsoon weather undamaged. Lies, lies, lies. Until, that is, Westerners encountered elephants, parrots and craftsmen who had found a way of adding phosphorous to wrought iron to create a rust-resistant alloy.[24]

★

One of the first Greeks to write at length about elephants was Aristotle (384–322 BCE). One of the first to fight them was his pupil Alexander (356–323 BCE), son of Philip II of Macedon. Alexander may have imbibed from his polymath tutor the idea that from atop the 'Asiatic Parnassus' (Hindu Kush), you would be able to see the great River Oceanus itself.[25] To cross the Kush would, in other words, bring you close to a full conquest of the eastern portion of the world.

The influence of Aristotle was certainly at play after Alexander succeeded his father and completed his conquest of the Greek-speaking world. Rather than sit back and relax, he gathered a retinue of geographers, historians, botanists and zoologists, alongside an army of around 40,000 men,[26] and in 334 BCE crossed the Hellespont into Asia – in search of glory, riches and the Oceanus.

Alexander and the Indian 'Gymnosophists', a.k.a. 'naked philosophers'.

2.

Into India

Since you are a mortal, why do you make so many wars? When you have seized everything, where will you take it?

Attributed to Dandamis, one of the 'naked philosophers'[1]

In just a handful of years after crossing the Hellespont, Alexander's armies managed to prise from Persian hands an astonishing amount of territory, spanning Asia Minor, the Mediterranean coast, Egypt and Mesopotamia. Babylon fell, followed by the Persian capital Persepolis. Built by Darius I and his successors over many generations, it was plundered and partially destroyed. On the armies went, crossing the Hindu Kush mountain range and storming through the Swat and Gandhara regions before crossing the Indus and entering the city of Taxila in 326 BCE.

The king in Taxila made peace, but a ruler named Porus, whose kingdom lay the other side of the River Jhelum, chose to fight. Alexander's hardened, highly mobile cavalry and flaming arrows won the day against Porus' ponderous elephants.[2] But his journey east ended soon thereafter: not at the River Oceanus, as planned, but at the River Beas (Hyphasis, in Greek), still only in the northwest of the Indian subcontinent. A portion of his forces sailed down the Indus and followed the coast to Mesopotamia, while Alexander led a contingent overland to Babylon, where he fell ill and died in 323.

Quite why Alexander did not push on, no one knows. Most likely an exhausted soldiery, missing their families and with armour and clothes so worn that some had exchanged them for Indian dress, saw no point in pressing beyond the Beas into a country that was larger and better-defended than expected.³ A history of his campaigns by the Greek historian Arrian, written in the second century CE, has Alexander at the Beas trying to convince his sceptical soldiers that the River Ganges is not too far away. The Ganges, Alexander assures them, is part of 'the great sea that encircles all land' – Oceanus.⁴

The reasons why the Beas became a turning point, literally and historically, are shrouded not just in mystery but in legend. Alexander's arrival in India did not so much dispel previous fantasies about the country as generate new ones, and place him at the centre of them. One of many myths that grew up around the memory of 'Alexander the Great' was that his forces did in fact travel as far east as the River Ganges. At this point they were greeted by a river 4 miles wide and 100 fathoms deep, on whose farther bank waited an Indian army consisting of 200,000 foot soldiers, 80,000 cavalry, 8,000 chariots and 6,000 war elephants – their trumpeting calls and powerful odour wafting across the water.⁵

Other stories about Alexander's short time in India, found in various ancient sources alongside versions of the largely legendary *Alexander Romance*, tell of encounters in idyllic surroundings with the country's so-called 'naked philosophers' ('gymnosophists'):

[Alexander] saw great forests and tall trees, beautiful to look at and bearing all kinds of fruit. A river ran round the land, with clear water as bright as milk. There were innumerable palm trees, heavy with fruit, and the vine stock bore a thousand beautiful and tempting grapes . . . the philosophers themselves [were] entirely without clothing and living in huts and caves. A long way off from them he saw their wives and children, looking after the flocks.⁶

According to legend, the king of the naked philosophers was a man named Dandamis (in some sources, 'Mandamis'). He asked Alexander about his endless war-making. Alexander replied by pleading the power over him of the 'divine will': 'I would like to stop making war,' he said, 'but the master of my soul does not allow me.' He then asked questions of his own. Did the philosophers have graves? Were the living or the dead greater in number? Was life or death stronger, earth or sea greater? And which was the wickedest of creatures? With this last enquiry, Alexander appeared to have set a trap for himself. 'Learn from yourself the answer to that', he was told: 'you are a wild beast'.[7]

Although some of these accounts were bound up with later European reappraisals of Alexander, and the destruction wrought by his armies, it is probable that he did indeed encounter a number of Indian ascetics. By the fourth century BCE, the subcontinent's earliest known sacred literature had been developing for around a thousand years (that of the preceding Indus Valley civilization has been lost). Its foundations lay in four 'Vedas': Sanskrit texts, understood to have been divinely revealed to sages and transmitted orally thereafter. The oldest of the Vedas was the Rig Veda – literally 'praise knowledge'. Dating back to around 1500 BCE, it included hymns and mantras, discussion of rituals, and lines of poetry. The concept of dharma (approximating to 'righteous conduct', or 'right living') made its appearance in this early Vedic era, as did karma, the cycle of rebirth, and a number of powerful gods including Agni, Indra, Sūrya and Vishnu.

Since the sixth century BCE, small numbers of people in north India's increasingly urbanized polities had chosen to abandon everyday life in favour of seeking religious knowledge via renunciation (*sannyasa*): living simply and remotely, and engaging in various sorts of ascetic discipline. Two of the best known of these renunciates were Siddhartha Gautama and Mahavira, who may have lived around the time of Herodotus and whose Buddhist and Jain monastic communities, respectively, were growing in influence during Alexander's era. Historians have speculated that the Greek philosopher Pyrrho (360–270 BCE), who travelled in Alexander's entourage, may have met and been influenced by Buddhists while in India. What we know of his renunciate lifestyle, his 'suspension of judgement' on ultimate questions, and his teachings on *apatheia* ('freedom from suffering') and *ataraxia* ('untroubledness') bear striking resemblance to Buddhist ideals.

Most of the *sannyasi* in north-west India, however, came from the priestly Brahmin caste, and remained within the Vedic tradition (or 'Brahmanism', as it came to be called). These *sannyasi* contributed to India's Vedic literature some of the subcontinent's first and most profound philosophical speculations, known as the 'Upanishads': a Sanskrit word comprising *upa* (near), *ni* (down) and *shad* (sit), giving the sense of sitting down near a spiritual teacher to receive wisdom. Over time, these philosophical passages became detached from their respective Vedas and incorporated into the Vedānta schools of philosophy. 'Vedānta' indicated the 'end-point' or 'essence' of the Vedas, helping to suggest to Westerners in the far future that these passages represented the highest point of Indian wisdom.

The historical basis of the back-and-forth dialogue attributed to Alexander and the naked philosophers is unknown, but it has the ring of the sort of public question-and-answer sessions sometimes found in the Upanishads and similar Sanskrit texts. Onesicritus, one of the historians who travelled in Alexander's entourage, wrote about these men after meeting some of them, it seems, near Taxila. He noted their frugal and natural living, receipt of alms, vegetarianism and knowledge of the natural world.[8] Here was India moving, in the Western imagination, from a fantastical place – of little real concern beyond being a source of good stories – to one inhabited by people with complex ideas and respectable practices. No wonder that traditions later emerged, running right into the modern era, that Greek wisdom owed something to ancient India. Some claimed that this influence had come via Egypt; others argued that the likes of Pythagoras (*c.* 570–495 BCE) might actually have travelled to India.

It was soon clear, too, that India was home not just to wise but to wealthy and powerful men. Amongst the generals left to scrap amongst themselves for pieces of Alexander's short-lived empire was Seleucus Nikator. In the course of consolidating his territory – the Seleucid Empire, which ended up spanning much of Asia Minor and Mesopotamia – he and his army made their way towards the Indus River. There they encountered forces commanded by Chandragupta Maurya (350–295 BCE). He had seized control of the prosperous kingdom of Magadha, including its enormous capital Pataliputra on the southern bank of the Ganges, and was in the process of turning it into the earliest known pan-Indian empire. Seleucus was one of the first people to get in Chandragupta's way, resulting in war and the latter's victory in 303 BCE.

More important than the fighting, for Western understandings of India, were the terms of the peace. Seleucus withdrew to the Hindu Kush, Chandragupta lavished 500 war-elephants on him, and the two men agreed to exchange ambassadors. Selected as Seleucus' man in Pataliputra was Megasthenes (c. 350–290 BCE). For the first time, the Greek-speaking world gained an on-the-spot amateur ethnographer. His four-volume study *Indica* (c. 300 BCE), which survives in fragments reproduced in the writings of later authors including Strabo, Pliny the Elder and Arrian, represented a first attempt – deeply influential through to the Roman era and beyond – to make sense of Indian culture and geography for a Western audience.[9]

At its most ambitious, *Indica* attempted to find a place for India in the cosmos as Megasthenes understood it. He claimed that this had once been a land of nomads given to eating raw animal flesh and the bark of trees. Then, one day, Dionysus, a son of Zeus, had arrived, bringing civilization with him: seeds and settled agriculture, architecture, law, weapons and wine. He taught people how to worship the gods, himself included, with cymbals and drums. The heroic Heracles, another son of Zeus, followed some fifteen generations later, taking a great many wives and leaving behind a large number of sons – alongside a single daughter by the name of Pandaea, who became a queen and ruled over an area of India beyond the Indus, which came to be named after her.

India's philosophers could be divided, thought Megasthenes, into mountain-dwelling devotees of Dionysus and plains-dwelling worshippers of Heracles. He noted that some of these philosophers were women – he was perhaps encountering members of the Buddhist *sangha* here. And to the description offered by Onesicritus he added that the philosophers were interested in the soul, death and the illusory ('dream-like') nature of life.[10]

What looked like an audacious mythological land-grab on the part of Megasthenes, turning two famously adventurous Greek gods into founding figures for India, had origins in recent history. Alexander was convinced, during his Indian campaign, that he was following in the footsteps of Dionysus and Heracles. A tradition grew up around the idea, encouraging Megasthenes to discern both gods in India's festivals and sacred literature. He was probably introduced to the latter by Brahmin priests who passed it on by word of mouth (nothing was written down until centuries after Megasthenes' death). 'Dionysus' may have been Shiva or possibly Indra, a warrior-god and bringer of settled agriculture, at whose festivals wine was drunk.[11] Some Indian festivities involved cymbals and drums, which again were associated in Greek mythology with Dionysus and his merry band of dancers, nymphs, and satyrs.[12] Evidence for Heracles was probably found, by Megasthenes and others, in worship of Krishna, an avatar (incarnation) of Vishnu.[13]

Megasthenes also furnished Westerners with their first inkling of social or professional categories in India, reporting that there were seven divisions within society. 'Philosophers' were at the top (most likely meaning priests and *sannyasi*) followed by farmers, and then shepherds and hunters. Workers and traders were placed on the fourth rung down, followed by warriors on the fifth, government inspectors on the sixth, and then advisers and counsellors at the very bottom.

Quite how strict Megasthenes thought this hierarchy was, and whether he was reporting here on something approaching caste, is unclear. His idea of seven stratifications may have been borrowed from Herodotus, who suggested something similar of Egyptian society. But his general impression was one of strong social order in India, rather than conflict. Indians struck Megasthenes as honest and trusting, with theft, lawsuits and guards for houses all reported to be rare. People ate rice and seasoned meat, and dressed in sometimes brightly coloured cotton, complemented by ornate jewellery. They were generally healthy and long-lived. India was more broadly, in Megasthenes' telling, a place of plenty: great rivers; elephants, tigers and monkeys; two harvests per year; gold and silver.[14]

For all that Megasthenes was able to write on the basis of experience in India, and of access to people in the know, he followed in the footsteps of predecessors like Ctesias in frustrating his readership with what looked like tall tales. Many of these had origins in Indian stories about gods, kings and far-away people, which Megasthenes picked up – probably quite imperfectly, given barriers of language – during his time in India. So it was that alongside providing matter-of-fact discussions of Pataliputra, Megasthenes also wrote about mouthless people who survived on the aromas of fruits, flowers and roasted meats (and who could be killed by bad smells). Other peoples apparently missing key bits of anatomy included the 'Noseless Ones' and the 'One-eyes'.[15]

It may be that in this era a certain amount of cultural influence began to run the other way, too. Greek-speaking communities had emerged in the north-west of India and Central Asia, comprising veterans of Alexander's army who had taken local wives and were now living in garrison towns like Alexandropolis (which via 'Iskander' later became known as Kandahar). They crop up in ancient Indian texts as *mlecchas* (barbarians), who don't keep the rules and are not generally considered an asset to the area. This was not entirely fair, however. Greek medicine spread in the region, and Greek words connected with astronomy found their way into Sanskrit.[16]

Artistic exchange from the second century BCE onwards produced a mixed 'Gandhara' style, whose Graeco-Roman elements were clear in images of the Buddha looking rather like the god Apollo.[17] Suggestive parallels – albeit lacking evidence of actual connections – have been found between two sets of epic poems: the *Iliad* and *Odyssey*, set down in writing around the sixth century BCE, and India's *Mahābhārata* and *Rāmāyana*, both composed between around 300 BCE and 300 CE. The *Iliad* and the *Mahābhārata* are military adventures. Both involve gods and men, both include an archery contest, and both feature a hero – Achilles and Krishna, respectively – sustaining a fatal wound to the heel. The *Odyssey* and the *Rāmāyana* meanwhile depict journeys home to loved ones, the latter work including a war to rescue a beloved woman (Sita) who bears comparison to Helen of Troy.[18]

★

The empire that Chandragupta built made its way, in 262 BCE, into the hands of his grandson, Ashoka, one of the most celebrated figures in Indian history. Ashoka expanded the Mauryan Empire until it stretched from the Hindu Kush in the west across to the Bay of Bengal in the east, and down to Mysore in the south, leaving only the southern tip of the subcontinent beyond its borders. Filled with remorse at the cost in blood of all this success, Ashoka famously committed himself to ruling according to the Buddhist dharma as he understood it: with honesty, compassion, mercy, tolerance, benevolence and non-violence. He carved these teachings into rocks and pillars located across the land, sent emissaries across his empire and beyond to places like Burma and Sri Lanka, and even preached the dharma personally on royal tours. He taught respect for all religions, but was recalled with particular warmth by Buddhists, as a powerful and effective patron.

Whatever the blend of piety and pragmatism at work in Ashoka's rule – the unifying potential of the dharma, across a large and diverse empire, must not have escaped his notice – the result was a realm that required precious little from abroad. Everything from agrarian produce to raw materials to finished crafts of all kinds was available via overland and riverine trade routes that came to span the subcontinent. These routes remained long after the Mauryan Empire declined and finally collapsed in 185 BCE, maintaining connections across what became a patchwork of kingdoms and republics. Cities began to gain reputations for particular products: Varanasi in the north for sandalwood and muslin; Madurai in the south for cotton goods.[19] Traders ventured beyond India's borders too, some of them heading out into South-East Asia in search of jewels and spices.

It may have been thanks to a shipwrecked Indian sailor that maritime trade got going between the Graeco-Roman world and India. In 118 BCE, a sailor is said to have been rescued from the Red Sea and brought before Ptolemy II of Egypt. He was somehow taught Greek, and in that language he began to divulge the secrets of the monsoon winds. This made it possible for a Greek navigator by the name of Eudoxus of Cyzicus to be sent by Ptolemy on a successful journey to India and back.

Whether or not the story of the Indian sailor is true, Eudoxus' journey is well-attested, usually dated to around 116 BCE.[20] A trading route between Egypt and India, across open ocean, was soon established, although only modest use of it was made at first. That changed with the rise of the Roman Empire. Within a few years of Octavian's defeat of Mark Antony and Cleopatra at the Battle of Actium (31 BCE), the trade began to boom. Strabo (*c.* 64 BCE–24 CE) estimated the number of ships heading out to India every year from the Red Sea port of Myos Hormos at 120. Trade with south Indian kingdoms on the Malabar Coast was especially significant, marking the entry of the southern portion of the subcontinent into Western consciousness – where previously 'India' had meant the Indus Valley region, along with territory eastwards towards the Ganges.[21]

Octavian – granted the honorific title 'Augustus' in 27 BCE – received up to four separate embassies from Indian rulers.[22] They came bearing gifts, which two authors of the era (Strabo and Dio Cassius) claimed included tigers, a boy with no arms and a holy man who burned himself alive in front of Augustus while he was visiting Athens. Receiving embassies from as far afield as southern India was enormously significant for Rome's first emperor. The reference point for Graeco-Roman culture, when it came to the East, was Alexander the Great and his extraordinary achievements, and not even he had succeeded in making such distant contacts. A few decades later, Emperor Claudius (reigned 41–54 CE) received an embassy from Sri Lanka, which was known at the time as 'Taprobane'.[23]

Trade between the Graeco-Roman world and India was no doubt helped along by warm diplomatic relations at the top, but it relied principally on networks of merchants spread across the route: Indians, Egyptians, Romans and Greeks, perhaps alongside Arabs and Ethiopians too.[24] By Pliny's reckoning, the trade with India 'drained' the empire's economy of 50 million sesterces every year – though quite where he got his figures from, and what he meant by them, remains unclear.[25]

The trade was not without its risks. An important maritime manual of the era, the *Periplus of the Erythraean Sea*, estimated the journey time to India at six months. The two key ports were on India's western coast: Muziris in the far south, part of the Malabar region, and Barygaza in the north. Alongside the inherent risk involved in riding the strong monsoon winds, even in the sturdy Arab vessels that are thought to have been used, piracy off the eastern coast of the Red Sea during the journey became enough of a problem that some Roman freighters began putting to sea in small fleets for the sake of collective security – some, reported Pliny, with companies of archers aboard.[26]

Such was the seasonal nature of the south-west monsoon that ships tended to arrive in India around early September and then depart in early November. This left plenty of time for doing deals. Roman traders brought with them slaves, wine, Spanish olive oil, terracotta jars (amphorae), bronzeware including mirrors and lamps, unworked glass and glassware, and large quantities of silver and gold coins. Local rulers were plied with gifts, and Roman mercenaries sometimes sold themselves into service with Indian princes: as soldiers, or as bodyguards. Amongst the goods coming the other way were perfumes, precious stones and woods, cardamom, turmeric, cinnamon, Kashmiri wool, ivory, pearls, Indian and Chinese silk, parrots and the occasional tiger or leopard. Indian slaves may have formed part of this trade, too.[27]

The most important commodity by far featured in a Tamil poet's description of the arrival of the 'Yavana' (Greeks, or perhaps people from the west in general) at the port of Muchiri (Muziris):

Here lies the thriving town of Muchiri, where the beautiful large ships of the Yavana come, bringing gold, splashing the white foam on the waters of the [River] Periyar, and then return laden with pepper. Here the music of the surging sea never ceases, and the great king presents to visitors the rare products of sea and mountain.[28]

Pepper had been known in the Mediterranean world since the second millennium BCE, and was probably first imported by the Phoenicians. But the availability of spices in the early decades of the Roman Empire was unprecedented, and the Roman appetite for pepper prodigious.[29] Some in south India, where it was brought to the coast from forests in Kerala, began to refer to it as *Yavana-priya*: 'passion of the Yavana'. Pliny the Elder (c. 23–79 CE), who used Greek sources to write about India in his *Natural History*, regarded Rome's emerging pepper passion as indulgent folly.[30] He worried, too, about Roman women's love of silk. The material was sometimes reworked in Syria and Egypt after import from India, creating a diaphanous final product that gave its wearer, according to Pliny, the appearance of near-nakedness.[31] Seneca (c. 4–65 CE) concurred, denouncing both the figure-hugging qualities of silk and the immodesty of Roman women who were prepared to wear it.[32]

The Roman poet Martial (c. 40–103 CE) took a slightly different view. Writing to a friend by the name of Flaccus, he cautioned against having anything to do with the kind of woman 'who values herself at no more than half a dozen jars of pickle'. His own mistress demanded of him 'the most precious perfume' and 'green emeralds'. Nor was that all:

[She] will have no dress except of the very best silks from the Tuscan Street [in central Rome] . . . Do you think that I wish to make such presents to a mistress? No, I do not: but I wish my mistress to be worthy of such presents.[33]

Here, in early form, was an example of the contradictory takes on Asia that would recur down the centuries in the West. Sometimes luxury, laziness and vice were the keynotes, in contrast to hardy and high-achieving Westerners. At other times, a variety of virtues were discerned, or imagined: great refinement, as suggested by high grades of silk; or a purity of heart and conduct, of a sort that had been lost or squandered in the West. Cicero (106–43 BCE) was one of the earliest to write in this latter vein, praising the endurance of India's ascetics and offering the practice of *sati* – a widow's self-immolation on her husband's funeral pyre – as evidence of the admirable fidelity of Indian women.[34] The poet Propertius (*c.* 50–15 BCE) took up a similar theme. He contrasted, in one of his poems, the materialism of silk-loving Romans with an imagined scene playing out in India:

> When the last torch has been thrown onto the funeral pyre, the dutiful crowd of widows stands with flowing hair, and hold a deadly competition as to which of them will, living, follow her husband: it is a source of shame not to have had the chance to die.

'We', Propertius went on, 'have a faithless race of brides.'[35] Strabo too, working with information supplied by Megasthenes, emphasized the 'simplicity and thrift' of Indians, though elsewhere – and rather randomly – he chided them for eating alone and not keeping regular hours for their meals.[36]

In other writings of this era, India remained simply a byword for the very ends of the earth. Since the time of Plato and Aristotle, the earth had increasingly come to be understood as spherical rather than cylindrical in shape. Eratosthenes (*c.* 276–194 BCE) had offered an estimate of its circumference, speculating that were it not for the 'enormity of the Atlantic Ocean . . . we would be able to sail from Iberia to India'.[37] The practical impossibility of making such a journey strengthened the Graeco-Roman sense of a civilized centre versus barbarous and mysterious peripheries. The poet Catullus (*c.* 84–*c.* 54 BCE) wrote of 'far-flung India' in one direction, and 'the formidable Britons, furthermost of people', in the other.[38] Missing from this global picture was a great silk-producing civilization to India's east, of which the Romans had – as yet – only the very faintest sense.

The Temptation of Adam and Eve, and Expulsion from the Garden of Eden.

3.

Silk, Spice, Paradise

At the northernmost point, where the sea ends somewhere on the
outer fringe, there is a very great inland city called Thina from which
silk floss, yarn, and cloth are shipped by land . . . and via the Ganges
River . . . It is not easy to get to this Thina; for rarely do people come
from it, and only a few.[1]

With these words, the maritime manual *Periplus of the Erythraean
Sea* (first century CE) provided the Graeco-Roman world with an
early inkling of a place known already to speakers of Sanskrit as
'Cīna'. The name came from 'Qin': a feudal state located on the Wei
River, far to the east of India, which in 221 BCE emerged victorious
from a long period of war. Its leader declared himself 'emperor',
becoming founder of China's first imperial dynasty.

It was the China of the succeeding Han Dynasty (206 BCE–220
CE) with which the Graeco-Roman world first came into contact.
The two cultures shared a high regard for their own way of life –
family, farming, worship, bureaucracy – as the happy norm.
Nomadic peoples, by contrast, were inherently suspect. For Herodotus, that had meant the Scythians: inhabitants of the western end
of the Eurasian steppe, north of the Black Sea. Uppermost in Chinese minds was a loose grouping of tribes and nations at the other
end of that steppe, known to them collectively as the Xiongnu.

The Records of the Grand Historian (c. 85 BCE) depicted these
Xiongnu as living in 'northern wastelands', keeping 'strange animals'
including camels, and lacking literature, ritual and righteousness.
Their 'heaven-endowed nature' was to wage war, flee when it went
badly, and live solely for material profit.[2] Apprehension fuelled these

depictions: the Xiongnu were formidable horsemen, whose lightning raids into northern areas of imperial China had necessitated the building of the first Great Wall, complete with watchtowers and signalling beacons. The Xiongnu were also traders. They were part of a diverse range of communities running westwards from China through Central Asia's mountains and deserts and then into Mesopotamia and South Asia, all taking part in a great commodity relay. Contrary to the modern image of 'the Silk Road', with caravans trundling along the Asian equivalent of the Appian Way, this was in fact a network of routes, which most people would travel only in part. Nor was silk the only commodity on the move. It took its place alongside goods including chemicals, metals and paper.[3]

Ever concerned with security to their north-west, by around 100 BCE the Han Chinese had secured control over the first leg of the relay, running along the Gansu corridor as far as Dunhuang. Beyond this point, they were aware of around fifty Central Asian kingdoms – many little more than the size of a city – whose rulers sent envoys bearing gifts to the Chinese emperor.[4] Quite how much Chinese traders sending bolts of silk westwards knew of their Roman customer base some 5,000 miles away remains a mystery. But by the end of the first century CE, something of Rome's reputation had clearly reached the Chinese court. *The Book of the Later Han* reports that in 97 CE, a man named Gan Ying was sent to see this far-off place for himself. He travelled, it seems, through the vast Parthian Empire – which had displaced the Seleucids in a region running from the Euphrates to the Hindu Kush – before arriving at the shores of the Persian Gulf.

Another forty days of journeying would have brought Gan Ying into the Roman Empire – but he turned back. Perhaps fearing competition in maritime trade, local sailors exaggerated the length and difficulty of the sea crossing that lay before him, warning of great homesickness and possibly death. 'When Ying heard this', says *The Book of the Later Han*, 'he gave up his plan.'

Gan Ying returned to China, probably with a stock of second-hand stories about the empire that he had failed to reach. These

combined with existing Chinese notions about the far West to produce a picture of a place where the people were tall and honest,
lived in towns with stone walls, shaved their heads, wore embroi-
dered clothes and made interesting products, including glassware.
The 'seat of government' was said to be home to five palaces, whose
pillars and tableware were made from crystal. These palaces were
occupied, presumably on a rotating basis, by a king who was selected
on the basis of his worthiness. All this was deemed similar enough
to the Chinese way of life that this mysterious country, at the other
end of the known world, was dubbed Daqin – 'Great China'.[5]

Just a few decades later, China received a visit from some of the
inhabitants of Daqin. *The Book of the Later Han* records that in
166 CE: 'King Andun of Daqin sent envoys to present ivory, rhino
horns, and the shells of hawksbill turtle, and they arrived from places
beyond Rinan. Thus began the communications between the Han
and Daqin.'[6] 'King Andun' was most likely either the Roman Emperor
Antoninus Pius or his adopted son and successor Marcus Aurelius
Antoninus. And the 'envoys' were probably mere merchants, hur-
riedly promoting themselves and turning trade goods into 'tribute'
after landing at the southern Chinese military outpost of Rinan and
receiving a cooler welcome than they might have hoped for. This
would explain why no Roman records exist of any such mission.

In Rome, meanwhile, there was only a vague awareness of 'Thina',
thanks to the *Periplus*, alongside references to the 'Seres', or Silk
People, who were believed to live in the far east of the world. This
Roman sense of product and place would have been rendered hazier
still by the fact that some of the silk in Roman markets was manufac-
tured in India and on the Greek island of Cos, not in China at all.

Ptolemy's *Geography* (c. 150 CE) offered a step forward in Roman
awareness of the world. Remarkable for his use of longitudes and
latitudes measured in degrees, to indicate key locations, Ptolemy
speculated about the distance to 'Sera', the presumed capital of the
Seres. In doing so, he drew on what he claimed was a merchant's
report. A man named Maes Titianus, possibly a Macedonian, had
apparently sent an expedition through Central Asia, as far east as

the 'Stone Tower' near the border with the Seres. Here was evidence, perhaps, of Roman trade with China, though the absence, so far, of Roman coins found buried in Chinese soil – whereas whole hoards have been dug up in India – suggests limited direct dealings at best. Likewise, at the diplomatic level, it seems that Han China and the Roman Empire came tantalizingly close to making contact – but never quite close enough.

*

The Han Dynasty collapsed in 220 CE. One hundred and fifty years later, the Huns, possibly related to the Xiongnu, began to move westwards from their lands on the western fringe of the Eurasian steppe. As they did so, they pushed another group who were likewise regarded by Rome as barbarians – the Goths – across the River Danube, and into the western Roman Empire. There followed a Herodotean fever dream, as rival groups of barbarians, from places about which he had warned readers of his *Histories* many centuries before, fought with one another and also with a Roman Empire so weak that it was forced to employ barbarians in its own military ranks. Rome's leaders tried to keep the Gothic King Alaric out of their city by offering him goodies including 4,000 silk tunics and 3,000 pounds of pepper. It didn't work. Rome was sacked in 410, Alaric got all the tunics and pepper he could ever want, and the last Western emperor was deposed little more than half a century later.

The Western appetite for Eastern luxuries survived the extinguishing of Roman power, and across the Middle Ages pepper, ginger, cinnamon, saffron, cloves and nutmeg continued to flow into Europe. They were valued less for their ability to preserve meat or disguise a failure to do so – it was generally cheaper to just buy fresh meat – than for their contribution to adventurous cuisine. Visual display was highly prized, alongside interesting aromas and the taking of even educated palates by surprise. A lucky guest might find pureed peas on the menu, fried in bacon fat with chicken, ginger and saffron. Or chessmen crafted from sugar and spices, standing atop a chessboard fashioned from spiced sweetmeats.[7]

Physicians, influenced by Greek humoral theory, touted the health benefits of spices. Some of them, they noted, possessed purgative properties: a messy but vital means of maintaining inner equilibrium. People suffering with melancholy or sexual dysfunction might be prescribed a pick-me-up combination of foreign spices and local herbs such as rosemary and thyme.[8]

Certain religious rites would smell wrong without a little frankincense. Some of the early Christian communities had associated exotic fragrances with Roman pantheism, self-indulgence, decadence and dirt (used, as they sometimes were, to mask the urban stink of rubbish and faeces). But in the Bible, spices frequently mark sacred moments. The air is heavy with fragrance when bride encounters bridegroom in the Song of Solomon, a poetical celebration of human and divine love. At the beginning of his life, Jesus is offered frankincense and myrrh by the Wise Men of the East; at the end, his followers are poised to anoint his body with spices before finding it gone. Writing to the people of Corinth, the apostle Paul (c. 5–64 CE) referred enigmatically to the 'aroma of Christ'. From the reign of Emperor Constantine (306–337 CE) onwards, as purpose-built churches began to replace the use of private homes for worship, it became common to burn incense – usually frankincense. Spices were used, too, in the ceremonies commissioning new members of the Church's hierarchy, from humble priests right up to the Pope.[9]

The Bible appeared to offer hints as to the origin of these spices, though there was disagreement about how its various books ought to be read. Following in the footsteps of ancient Greek thinkers grappling with Homer, and Philo of Alexandria interpreting Jewish scripture, the Christian theologian Origen (185–254 CE) explored the role played by allegory in sacred texts. Sometimes, he was blunt:

Now what man of intelligence will believe that the first and the second and the third day, and the evening and the morning, existed without the sun and moon and stars . . .? And who is so silly as to believe that God, after the manner of a farmer, planted a paradise eastward in Eden, and set in it a visible and palpable tree of life, of such a sort that anyone who tasted its fruit with his bodily teeth would gain life?[10]

Large parts of the Old and New Testaments could, thought Origen, be read in the way that one might read Herodotus: as history. Some passages, however, including accounts in Genesis of the Creation and of Adam and Eve, contained elements that should not be read literally.[11] These were part of scripture's more important purpose: conveying spiritual realities, which were hidden by the Holy Spirit from the unready but would nourish those who were suitably prepared.

Augustine of Hippo (354–430 CE) took varying views of Genesis over time, but he tended to regard the story of Adam and Eve as containing reliable historical and geographical information. According to that account, Eden was to be found to the east of Asia. It was watered by a great river, which split into four earthly headwaters as it left the Garden. These 'rivers of paradise' were named in Genesis as the Tigris, Euphrates, Pishon and Gihon. Pishon came to be identified with the Ganges (or sometimes the Indus), and Gihon with the Nile. Augustine sought to reconcile this information with the secular cartography of his day, according to which a shared source for these four rivers was implausible, by suggesting that the rivers of paradise must run, for part of their course, underground.[12]

This general view of the world was taken up by European mapmakers across the Middle Ages, rendering spices, along with a hazily conceived 'India' as their point of origin, all the more special. Their powerful odour and taste were taken as signs that they were blessed by proximity to the Garden of Eden. Perhaps, some speculated, spices actually grew on trees in Eden, and were carried on breezes into the rivers of paradise, from where they made their way into the ordinary world. This idea gained a degree of plausibility from the observed fact that precious stones and metals did indeed flow within river currents.[13] But it also showed just how marginal Europe was, in these centuries, to a global spice trade whose supply centred on India, Indonesia and Indochina, and whose customer base ranged from small European countries in the west through the vast expanse of Asia.

The main result of being peripheral to proceedings was that Europeans paid an inordinately high price for spice.[14] By 750, an Islamic caliphate extended from Spain, across north Africa, through Persia and as far east as the Indus. It was no longer straightforward for Europeans to get ships through to Asia, and they were forced to rely on Arab traders acting as middlemen. Unable to visit India, they dreamed of it instead. A particularly cherished prospect, which first emerged in the mid-1100s during preparations for the Second Crusade, was that of 'Prester John': a powerful Christian king, who was believed to reside somewhere in 'India'.[15] This Asian saviour, destined to help restore Europeans' fortunes, had even been kind enough to send them a letter:

> If indeed thou desirest to know wherein consists our great power, then believe without hesitation, that I, Prester John, who reign supreme, surpass in all virtue, riches and power all creatures under heaven.
>
> I am a zealous Christian and universally protect the Christians of our empire, supporting them by our alms. We have determined to visit the sepulchre of our Lord with a very large army, in accordance with the glory of our majesty, to humble and chastise the enemies of the cross of Christ and to exalt his blessed name . . .[16]

The 'Letter of Prester John' began circulating in Europe in the 1160s, around twenty years after the first rumours of his existence. In addition to announcing Prester John's power and crusading intentions, the letter told of a truly extraordinary kingdom. A river flowed through it, directly from Paradise, chock-full of emeralds, sapphires and more. There were pepper forests, gems capable of rendering the wearer invisible, and a spring whose eminently potable waters could fix a person's age at thirty-two. There were no thieves or liars in this land: 'We all follow truth and we love one another.' Most impressive of all was a consecrated mirror, guarded day and night by 12,000 soldiers, in which Prester John could see everything that went on in his great kingdom.[17]

Here was vivid testament both to the imaginative powers of medieval Europeans and the flimsiness of their understanding of actual goings-on in Asia, across the long centuries that followed the fall of the western Roman Empire. An accurate map of the world around the year 1000, focused on global flows of trade and wealth, would have had the subcontinent at its centre. From Gujarat, Konkan and Malabar on India's western coast, trade routes ran across to the Arab world and east Africa. From its eastern coast, particularly the Bay of Bengal in the north and Coromandel in the south, ran routes into the Malay Peninsula, South-East Asia and southern China. India's reputation for great wealth, including from international trade, began to attract Turkic-Afghan Muslims in the 1100s: first as raiders, and then as settlers in parts of north India. Delhi was captured in 1193, and in 1206 Qutb-ud-din Aybak proclaimed himself sultan there. He became founder of India's first Islamic empire, which in time spread a Persianized Islamic culture across much of the northern Gangetic plain.[18]

Europeans knew little of these developments, but the fantasy of an Indian Christian king seems to have been inspired by snippets of information making their way through from Asia into Europe. The earliest roots of the legend dated back to the third century, with the *Acts of Thomas*. This text, heavily laden with romance and fantasy, purported to describe the later life of one of Jesus' disciples: 'doubting Thomas', famous for seeking physical proof that the risen Jesus was real. The disciples, claimed the *Acts of Thomas*, had divided the world between them, and it had fallen to Thomas to serve as apostle to India. Arriving at the port of Muziris, he had commenced a highly fruitful twenty-year Indian ministry. It ended with his martyrdom in Mylapore, on India's south-east coast, in 72 CE.

Parts of the legend of Thomas may be true. Stone crosses found in the south-west of the subcontinent suggest a Christian presence in India dating back at least as far as the early second century. Connections were established in later centuries with the Church of the

East, also known as the Nestorian Church.[19] The outcome, on India's Malabar Coast, was a collection of Christian communities, many of them involved in the pepper trade, whose liturgy was conducted in Syriac and whose affairs were overseen by a bishop sent out from Persia. Hazy European knowledge about these communities is reflected in the ninth-century *Anglo-Saxon Chronicle*, which reports that in 883 King Alfred sent two Englishmen – Sighelm and Aethelstan – to take alms to the tomb of St Thomas in India, perhaps in hope of securing divine help against the Danes. Thomas's tomb features in the Letter of Prester John, too. It describes the great king's lands as 'extend[ing] from farthest India, where the body of St. Thomas the Apostle rests, to the place where the sun rises, and returns by the slopes of the Babylonian desert near the tower of Babel'.[20]

European hopes of salvation at the hands of Prester John were bolstered by rumours, in the early 1200s, about Mongol victories over Muslim rivals in Central Asia. A powerful force was clearly rousing itself in Christianity's favour. This was not quite how Genghis Khan saw it. But what he lacked in pious intention, his armies made up for by carving out a vast empire that made it possible, for a few short decades, for people to pass overland from the Crimea to China. It was with just such a journey in mind that, in the late thirteenth century, one of Europe's most celebrated travellers packed his bags.

Marco Polo being received at the Great Khan's palace.

4.

Esploratori: *Polo and Columbus*

Honoured emperors and kings, dukes and marquesses, counts, knights and townspeople, and all who want to know about the various races of mankind and the peculiarities of the various regions of the world, take this book and have it read to you! Here you will find all the greatest wonders and chief curiosities of Greater Armenia and Persia, of the Tartars and India, and of many other lands. Our book will lay them out for you in the proper order as related by Messer Marco Polo, a wise and noble citizen of Venice, who has seen them with his own eyes.[1]

Roll up, roll up . . . When recited aloud, as they were intended to be, the opening lines of *The Description of the World* – better known as *The Travels of Marco Polo* – have the feel of a stallholder hawking his wares. And well they might: this was retail of a kind, part of a broader commercial revolution. By the time of Marco Polo's birth in 1254, his home city of Venice had gone from being a client state of the Byzantine Empire to a formidable maritime and trading power in its own right, dominating much of the Adriatic and Aegean and capable of capitalizing on Byzantine weakness and the upheaval of the Crusades.

Polo's co-author, Rustichello, was a romance writer from a second maritime republic, Pisa, and the two men met in a jail located in a third: Genoa. These were the three greatest of a handful of Italian maritime republics which, alongside cities such as Marseille and Barcelona, were by this time sending merchants to spice markets including those of Alexandria. Where the maritime republics had grown rich trading everything from spices to slaves, Polo and

Rustichello's product was stories – *true* stories, mind you: by far the most detailed and (they insisted) trustworthy account of eastern lands and peoples ever to be offered up to European eyes and ears.[2]

Europeans setting out for the East in this era did not need to begin their journeys with a trudge through eastern Europe. One could sail the Mediterranean Sea, pass through Constantinople to cross the Black Sea, and from there continue overland either north or south of the Caspian Sea. This would bring you to one of the starting points for the trans-Asian routes opened up by Mongol conquests. According to the *Travels*, this was how Marco Polo's father Niccolò and his uncle Maffeo made it all the way to the court of Kublai Khan around 1260 – located perhaps, at this point, in his emerging capital Daidu (present-day Beijing). Having interrogated the pair, Kublai sent them back to Europe as his emissaries to the Pope, demanding that they return to his court along with one hundred Christian scholars and a vial of holy oil from the Church of the Holy Sepulchre in Jerusalem. Niccolò and Maffeo did their best, arriving at Kublai's summer palace in northern China in 1273 or 1274, not with one hundred scholars but with two friars sent by the Pope – plus Niccolò's seventeen-year-old son Marco.[3]

The three Polos supposedly remained in Asia until the early 1290s. Marco spent around seventeen years serving as an administrator and emissary for Kublai Khan, developing a good claim to be the first European to travel widely in China and the first ever to see Indochina. Afterwards, during the three men's long journey home, they became the first known Europeans to visit Sumatra, some of the first in many centuries to visit India – alongside the Italian Franciscan missionary John of Monte Corvino, who spent a year in south India around the same time that the Polos were there – and the first to report the existence of a great number of small spice-producing islands. Marco Polo arrived home in 1295, but three years later he was captured in a sea battle fought between the Venetians and the Genoese. He used his jail time to dictate to his fellow inmate Rustichello some of the details of what he had spent the past twenty-five years doing and seeing.[4]

Not everyone in Europe believed what they read when manuscript copies of *The Travels* began to do the rounds. Some of Polo's
own friends apparently urged him, on his deathbed, to recant any
lies or exaggerations while he still had time.[5] And for a long while
after it emerged, the book was regarded as a romance rather than a
travel account.[6] News of a far-distant Chinese civilization possessing postal services, paper money and complex and populous cities
seems to have unnerved people who, in the face of a potential
Mongol threat, increasingly regarded themselves as 'Europeans' not
merely in a geographical but also in a cultural sense, tinged with
pride.[7] They were upset, too, by Polo's debunking of cherished
ideas. Unicorns, he claimed, were not magical beasts who would let
themselves be caught by virgins; in fact, they were 'very ugly', with
hair like buffalo, and they loved to wallow in mud (Polo seems to
have been describing a rhinoceros).[8] There were no pygmies in
India, as some liked to imagine, just some 'very small monkeys with
a face like a man's'. Polo even did away with Prester John. He had
been a Mongolian warlord, claimed Polo, who was scornful of the
Great Khan and paid the ultimate price in battle.[9]

Well into the modern era, Polo had his doubters. How could you
go to China and fail to mention the Great Wall, chopsticks or tea?
Why do the Chinese histories contain no mention of a man named
Marco Polo? Polo undoubtedly gilded the lily, abetted by Rustichello. He almost certainly did not serve as governor of a Chinese
city, as the *Travels* claimed. Nor did he supply foreign engineers to
create siege-breaking trebuchets – the siege in question was long
over by the time he arrived at Kublai's court.[10] But the Great Wall
was not a noteworthy, imposing structure in Polo's day. And too
much discussion of Chinese customs might have been considered
improper when Polo's boss, Kublai Khan, had just brought the Song
dynasty to an end and was busy creating a new, Mongol dynasty
(the Yuan) in its place.[11]

Most now agree that Polo did indeed go to China, travelling far
and wide and furnishing his audiences with generally reliable
information – if sometimes exaggerated – about its rivers and canals,

natural resources, architecture and industries.[12] Polo described at length the wonders of Xingzai (Hangzhou): an immense trading city, of wide and airy streets, squares and canals. To its markets, people brought fish, deer, rabbits, partridges, ducks and geese, alongside vegetables and fruits of all kinds. Nobles and magistrates built their homes on the banks of a 'crystal-clear freshwater lake'. In the centre of that lake lay two islands, on each of which stood 'a truly marvellous and sumptuous palace with more rooms and apartments than can be imagined'. Parties were held there, sometimes a hundred at once, while in the surrounding waters people enjoyed pleasure-cruises on boats and barges, large and small.

There is no reason why Polo's account of travelling in India, too, ought not to be believed, at least in outline. His travels there were facilitated, it seems, by a combination of Mongol and Muslim maritime power, alongside the Arabic and Persian languages: Polo made heavy use of Arabic place names in his *Travels*, and while he spoke no south Indian languages he could probably get by in Persian. This would have allowed him to pick up stories and explanations about India from Muslim interlocutors.[13]

In other ways, Polo's relative lack of formal education, having left Europe while still a very young man, may have played in his favour. Rather than clogging the *Travels* with classical references (he mentions Alexander the Great, but not Megasthenes or Pliny), Polo offered raw observation. He perhaps developed the habit while serving as an envoy of the Great Khan, having witnessed first-hand the perils of disappointing him with insufficiently comprehensive information.[14] Even on matters of religion, Polo rarely sought to judge or compare. He was happy to pass on to his readers Kublai Khan's scepticism about Christianity and Christians: 'ignorant [people who] make nothing of themselves and have no power'. And he suggested of the Buddha, about whose life Polo discovered a little on his travels, that 'if he had been a Christian, he would undoubtedly be a great saint and dwell with our Lord Jesus Christ'.[15]

Travelling along India's south-eastern Coromandel coast, Polo found people diving for 'round and lustrous' pearls, helped by

Brahmins who placed charms on fish so that they did not harm the divers. He was impressed by royal wealth, writing about a king who adorned himself only in gold bracelets, gems and pearls – so fine, claimed Polo, that at any one time he might have about his body wealth exceeding that of a substantial city.[16] Polo was aware that many people considered cows to be sacred, and so would not eat beef. He didn't know why: his informants said only that 'an ox is a very good thing'. He received a more interesting response to a question about why even a king and his courtiers could be found sitting on the floor:

> They replied that it was honourable enough to sit on the ground since we are made of earth and to the earth we must return, from which it follows that no one can honour the earth too highly and no one should scorn it.[17]

Much of Polo's account rings true, if one allows for various layers of embellishment courtesy of Polo's informants, Polo himself, and of course the romance-writer Rustichello. Real south Indian kings can be discerned amidst the names, descriptions and stories.[18] And Polo described customs that would become familiar to travellers of later generations: people chewing betel leaves mixed with spices; eating with their right hand only (reserving the left for 'unpleasant and unclean necessities'); drinking without letting their lips touch the vessel; and using astrological birth charts. Like Megasthenes before him, Polo praised Indian justice and remarked on the lack of theft – a man could sleep in the street with a bag of pearls for his pillow, and expect to find them all still there in the morning. Polo described the cultivation of pepper trees in south-west India, the production of indigo, the drinking of coconut water and palm wine, and the perils of piracy off the Malabar and Gujarati coasts. Some pirates, he claimed, would make captured merchants drink a mixture of tamarind and seawater, inducing them to vomit up any pearls or other precious stones that they might have swallowed in hope of hanging on to them. Less easily concealed, but likewise subject to theft by pirates according to Polo, were horses: known to have been traded, in this era, from the Middle East to coastal India.[19]

Less plausible, but doubtless highly entertaining for readers back home in Europe, was Polo's account of how diamonds were procured from serpent-infested mountains. People would throw hunks of raw meat at the diamonds from a safe distance, wait until eagles picked up the diamond-studded meat, and then grab the meat away from the eagles when they landed on safe terrain. More timid types waited for the eagles to eat the meat, and then salvaged the diamonds from excrement left in nests.

It was perhaps in a similar spirit of openness to being entertained that European readers would have considered another unlikely-sounding claim from Marco Polo:

Cipangu is an island that lies out to the east [of China] in the open sea, 1,500 miles from the mainland. It is an exceptionally large island. The people are white, good-looking and courteous. They are idolaters and are completely independent, having no rulers from any race but their own. Moreover, I can tell you that they are exceedingly rich in gold, because it is found here in inestimable quantities.

You may take my word for it that [the ruler of the island] has a huge palace entirely covered with fine gold. In the same way that we roof our houses and churches with lead, so this palace is roofed with fine gold . . . [All] the chambers, of which there are many, are likewise paved with fine gold to a depth of more than two fingers. And all the other parts of the palace, including the halls and the windows, are likewise adorned with gold. I assure you that this palace is of such incalculable richness that anyone who tried to estimate its value would find it too staggering for words.[20]

Polo goes on to claim that these people possess both black and white pepper, alongside 'pearls in abundance': 'red, very beautiful, round and large'. Less happily, they are given to 'outlandish and diabolical [exploits] . . . wickedness [that] would be too much for Christian ears'. Polo is, of course, going to describe it anyway. When these people capture someone who cannot pay a ransom, they 'call together all their relatives and friends, saying: "I invite you to come and dine with me at my house."' Their captive is the main item on the menu. Cooked in a manner unspecified, their flesh is considered to be 'the finest food in existence'.[21]

Yet more tasty morsels from the mind of Rustichello – or something else? A careful reader of – or listener to – the *Travels* might have noticed that whereas elsewhere in his account Marco Polo was keen to present the 'Great Khan' in the best possible light, when it came to Cipangu he felt bound to relate an embarrassing episode. Upon hearing of that country's great wealth, the Great Khan had resolved to conquer it. 'A huge fleet of ships carrying cavalry and infantry' put to sea under the command of two of his men. But great winds arose, wrecking some of the ships and scattering the rest, leading ultimately to the failure of the mission and the execution of its leaders.[22] Sceptics might dismiss, as yet more fabulation, the claim of a marvellous island protected by powerful winds. But Marco Polo had just widened their world for them, putting Japan on the map.

★

As Mongol power declined in the latter part of the fourteenth century, European merchants found themselves cut off once more from direct access to eastern Asia. With Mediterranean and overland routes alike effectively barred to them by the Ottomans, the Venetians, Genoese and others fell back on deal-making at the nearest still-accessible point for Asian goods: the markets of Alexandria. But their customers resented the high prices, and enthusiasm began to build for a notion that seemed utterly mad to those who believed – as some did – the earth to be a flat disc, with Jerusalem at its centre: that if you sail far enough westwards, you will end up in the east.[23]

This idea was at least as old as Eratosthenes in the third century BCE, and it was given extra credence by the rediscovery, thanks to Islamic scholars, of Ptolemy's *Geography*. Europeans learned, or relearned, how to use longitude, latitude and degrees, while enjoying the false reassurance of Ptolemy's major underestimate of the circumference of the globe.[24] Backed by Isabella I of Castile and Ferdinand II of Aragon, alongside Genoese and Florentine bankers hoping to reap big rewards, the Genoese navigator Christopher Columbus put to sea in 1492. Columbus himself saw his voyage very much in terms of Christian Europe's destiny. He noted in his journal that earlier that year the last remnants of Muslim power had been forced from the Iberian Peninsula. 'The Jews', too, had been 'driven out'. Christendom was on the move.

Having set sail in August of 1492, Columbus hit the jackpot in late October with a sighting of Polo's Cipangu – or so he seems to have believed. In fact, he had arrived off Cuba: part of an enormous region of the world at whose existence no Western map, from the ancient Greeks onwards, had so much as hinted. New maps would have to be made, though not right away. Quite what Columbus had found was still obscure in 1494, when the Treaty of Tordesillas between Spain and Portugal placed a meridian line down the Atlantic, approximately halfway between these new lands and the Cape Verde islands off the west coast of Africa. The Spanish claimed everything to the west of this line – accidentally giving the as-yet-undiscovered Brazil to the Portuguese – and Columbus continued his explorations.

During the course of his first voyage, Columbus changed his mind about Cuba, deciding that it must be mainland China rather than Japan. During his second voyage (1493–6), he made his men swear an oath to that effect. In the wake of his third voyage (1498–1500), Columbus noted in a letter to Ferdinand and Isabella some interesting observations that he had made at a particular point in the ocean: mild air, a deluge of fresh water coming into the sea, compass readings that suggested the sea actually sloped upwards. He had located, he felt sure, the outer reaches of the Garden of Eden.[25]

Right up until he died in 1506, Columbus insisted that he had landed near Cipangu at one point in his explorations, and on mainland China at another.[26] The reality only became clear when in 1513 the Spanish conquistador Vasco Núñez de Balboa traversed the narrow Isthmus of Panama and encountered a brand-new ocean. He immediately claimed it for Spain, wading into its waters with a sword in one hand and an image of the Virgin Mary in the other. A few years later, in 1520, the explorer Ferdinand Magellan entered those same waters after struggling through the straits that would one day bear his name, located at the southern tip of what were by now being called the 'Americas'. The waters seemed preternaturally calm, so he christened them the 'Pacific'.

In March 1521, Magellan became the first known European to reach the island of Guam, going on to claim an island chain to the west of Guam for Spain. He was killed there while seeking Christian conversions, but one of his five ships, the *Victoria*, managed to make it all the way back to Spain in 1522. It earned the accolade of being the first vessel to circumnavigate the globe, and prompted negotiations between Spain and Portugal over the location of an anti-meridian. The Treaty of Zaragoza (1529) handed most of South-East Asia – including the lucrative Moluccas – to Portugal. Spain managed to hold onto the islands where Magellan had died, later naming them the 'Philippines' after King Philip II of Spain. The Spanish also found vast quantities of gold and silver in the New World, which more than made up for losing out in the spice trade.

Having received everything to the east of the Tordesillas meridian line, the Portuguese sent Vasco da Gama on his way to becoming, in 1498, the first known European to reach India by sailing southwards around Africa and up into the Indian Ocean. Reaching the thriving port of Calicut, on the Malabar coast, da Gama quickly became aware of just how profitable the spice trade could be. Pepper briefly retailed in Venice, in 1499, at around 80 ducats per hundredweight, amidst unusual scarcity. The same quantity could be had in Calicut for just 3 ducats.[27]

With profits like this in the offing, the Portuguese set out to establish a military and commercial presence wherever they could. In Calicut, this involved armed confrontation in the opening years of the 1500s, during the course of which the artillery advantage enjoyed by European ships became clear.[28] The Estado da Índia ('State of India') developed from here, via the steady accumulation of modestly sized pieces of land dotted up and down India's coasts, complemented by deals with local rulers. Goa was colonized in 1510, becoming home to a governor-general of Portuguese India (a job title that lasted until 1961). In 1534, a new ecclesiastical province was created: the Diocese of Goa.

Few attempts were made to turn coastal trading stations into major territorial gains. The Portuguese lacked the manpower, and the potential gains were far from obvious. Instead, a highly profitable trading empire was run from bases that came to include Malacca (from 1511), Ormuz (1514), Bombay (1534) and Macau (1557). The Portuguese had achieved end-to-end control of the spice trade, putting middlemen in Venice and Alexandria out of work as cheap Portuguese spices, travelling via the Cape of Good Hope, flooded new markets in Lisbon and Antwerp. In the process, they had created a seaborne taxi service, used by a group of people who sailed out to Asia to preach the gospel but began radically to open up Europe's intellectual and spiritual horizons.

Akbar receiving two black-robed Jesuits.

5.

God's Marines

Europeans departing westwards and eastwards from the Iberian Peninsula in the 1500s were in little doubt as to their right of trade, conquest and Christian conversion. Since as far back as the fifth century, the Catholic Church had asserted its duty to work for a universal Christian commonwealth. This was strengthened in the era of the Crusades by Pope Innocent IV's assertion of crusaders' rights to deprive infidels of their lands if they were violating 'natural law' (as defined in Christendom). The king of Portugal forced a further development in the 1430s, claiming a right to the Canary Islands for the advancement of civilization there and the 'salvation of souls'. He won the argument, and a series of papal bulls followed, ever more strident in their backing of Portuguese power.

By 1500, spurred by the voyages of Christopher Columbus, a 'doctrine of discovery' had been developed, which conferred land and commercial rights on the first European Christian power to 'discover' a new territory. The Treaty of Tordesillas (1494), between Portugal and Spain, was based on a division of potential global spoils that first featured in a papal bull issued the previous year. The terms were clear: the Iberian powers were enjoined to perform 'holy and laudable work' in 'the expansion of the Christian rule'.[1]

Legalism and zeal went hand in hand. When Vasco Núñez de Balboa waded into the Pacific in 1513, sword and image of the Virgin Mary in hand, he wasn't just showboating. He was staking a formal claim. Spanish and Portuguese traders were not always paragons of the religion that they professed, as people in India, China and Japan would soon begin to see. Still, there was real religious enthusiasm present within early Iberian imperialism. Some hoped that the elusive Prester John might yet be found. Others viewed early Christian missions to Asia and the New World in terms of extending the boundaries of Christendom: very much of a piece with the pushing of Islam and Judaism off the Iberian Peninsula in recent years. Church and state would work together, and European ecclesiastical structures would be replicated in the new domains.

Three things helped to change this picture. The first was the brutal treatment of people in some of the newly reached regions, by conquistadors, traders and priests. Some clergy came to sympathize with the Spanish Dominican Bartolomé de Las Casas when he accused his countrymen of 'destroy[ing] infinite numbers of souls' in their rush for gold.[2] 'Christendom' became a more complicated concept, as missionaries relied on their compatriots for transport and security but began, in some cases at least, to regard themselves as protectors or advocates for people being subjected to European violence and exploitation.

The second development was the fracturing of Christendom during the era of religious reformations in Europe: Martin Luther, John Calvin, Catholic renewal and the associated political entanglements, frequently violent, which lasted until the mid-1600s. As a wider world came into focus in the second half of the 1500s and into the 1600s, leaders in the Catholic Church came to appreciate the value of making converts far from home. They would be allies in the fight against Protestantism, and vivid proof of the Church's vaunted universality.

Finally, it was soon clear that Asia was home to societies whose sophistication was at the very least on a par with Europe: philosophical complexity, craftsmanship, knowledge of the natural world, social customs, and forms of economic and political organization. Few in this era regarded Asian religious insights as comparable with Christian revelation. And yet missionaries who chose to focus their efforts on the elites of newly encountered societies found that they would not get far without appreciating the self-understanding of these people. That meant learning Asian languages, and understanding Asian cultures – in a way that went far beyond anything so far achieved by Europeans, and which stood in stark contrast to the exterminator attitude taken in the Americas. By the later decades of the 1500s, trade in spices and other goods was joined by a great gathering-in and hauling homewards of cultural knowledge about Asia: partial and highly imperfect, but revolutionary nonetheless. Setting out to extend its borders, Christendom ended up being changed forever.

By far the most influential early agent of that change was the Society of Jesus. Officially recognized in 1540, the Jesuits were envisaged by their founder, Ignatius of Loyola, as a new kind of religious order. Rather than maintain monasteries as their main loci of operation, 'God's marines' – nicknamed for their loyalty to the Papacy – would be at home on the seas and on the road.

The Jesuits were shaped, in their encounter with Asia, by Loyola's *Spiritual Exercises*. He had grown up in a world where absent, drunk or otherwise unimpressive clergy had compelled people to look after their own souls by reading devotional literature: religious biographies, alongside 'confessor's manuals'. The latter encouraged readers to delve into their consciences and emotions, searching out the motivations that underpinned sin and allowing real remorse to bubble up. The *Spiritual Exercises* emerged from Loyola's immersion in this world, and from his own struggles. During a month-long retreat, an exercitant would be helped – using emotions and imagination – to explore the two greatest mysteries in life: God, and themselves.[3] At home in Europe, spirituality of this sort could be a source of suspicion: amidst all this emphasis on emotions, imagination and spiritual experience, where did ecclesiastical authority come in? But in Asia, it had the potential to foster a particular kind of receptivity amongst missionaries, towards the people amongst whom they worked.

A second influence on the Jesuits was the general European understanding, in this era, that the peoples of the earth were descended from Noah, after the Flood. To this the Jesuits added the theology of Thomas Aquinas: all human beings shared the same powers of reasoning, openness to divine illumination and ability to discern and live a moral life. The missionary task in Asia, especially amongst educated elites, would be to help people develop these capacities, on whose combined basis the truth of the Christian revelation would eventually become clear.

An important boost to missionaries' confidence was the example – compelling to late Renaissance minds – of classical Rome. Its art, virtues and powers of reasoning had rendered it ripe, they believed, for Christianity. Missionaries fully expected to encounter 'false religion' in Asia: the corruption, in some cases by demonic forces, of an innate human sense of the divine. They saw plenty of this in Europe, amongst Protestants and uneducated Catholics. But they were optimistic about the basic human raw material with which they would be working. If they could seek out and engage the elites in countries like India – those who most resembled the best of classical Rome – then the foundations for a Christian Asia might be established.

*

European acquaintance with India was limited, early on in the 1500s, to coastal kingdoms and towns that the Portuguese either controlled or with which they had dealings. Combined with a Portuguese desire to keep details of their lucrative spice trade secret for as long as they could, this left European opinion about the subcontinent patchy and sometimes contradictory. Calicut was claimed by one early writer to be an impressive place: bigger than Lisbon, and blessed with natural abundance and interesting products, including high-quality cloth and brocade, alongside brass- and tin-ware. Another writer disagreed completely, adding that its ruler 'worships the devil'.[4] Most commentators agreed that Indians were 'idolaters', who took many wives, burned their dead and built temples full of animal idols – elephants, monkeys, bulls. But there was very little appetite for exploring Indian religion in any depth. Such an aspiration would have been perverse – why delve into something so corrupted, potentially demonic, and which would soon enough be swept away?

There was much interest, instead, in people's diets, clothes and habits, especially in the wealthy kingdoms of the Malabar Coast and the great south Indian city of Vijayanagar. The latter was depicted, in European accounts, as the warlike and well-defended centre of a loose-knit empire, awash in precious stones. Indian justice and the stratifications of caste were of great interest too, along with medicine, botany and the lives and rituals of the Brahmins. The sense of India as an exotic place was if anything enhanced by early contact, especially after a first haul of 'presents' were brought before Pope Leo X in Rome: a panther and two leopards; parrots and horses; and an elephant, which bowed three times to the Pope before raising its trunk and spraying water over everyone.[5] The mid-1500s witnessed a publishing boom for surveys of Indian life, based on collected letters and travel reports. Portuguese and Spanish authors boasted about their countries' spirit of exploration, while northern European authors and editors encouraged their compatriots to get out there and give the Iberian powers a run for their money.

The major sources of European information about India, along with the rest of Asia, were the Jesuits. They began sending home letters from Asia in the 1540s, and by the end of the 1550s collections were being published in Portuguese, Spanish, Italian, French, German and Latin. Intended to loosen the purse strings of Catholic donors while reminding Protestants of Catholicism's global reach, they came to serve a general interest too. Concerned as they were to counter Indian religion, they paid more attention to it than secular observers. The outlines of Indian mythology started to become clear, and three classes of 'priests' were proposed: Brahmins, gurus and ascetics. Jesuit accounts of the last group slightly resembled those given by Onesicritus and Megasthenes. They told of highly disciplined people who were willing to engage in philosophical conversation.[6]

Amongst these early Jesuit writers was Francis Xavier, who became known as the 'Apostle of the East'. He arrived in Goa in 1542: a place well known by this point to European readers for its rocky cliffs, palm trees, lush vegetation and abundance of natural produce. During the early decades of Portuguese rule there, attempts were made – dubbed the 'rigour of mercy' – to create an outpost of Christendom. They included the destruction of temples, the banning of *sati* and interference with pilgrimage. Orders were issued – repeatedly, suggesting that they were not easily enforced – for Brahmins to be expelled, new churches and schools to be built using public revenues, and preferment in employment to be given to Christian converts. Some of the earliest Indian religious texts to be sent to Europe were obtained during this period of crackdown. In 1558, Goa became an archdiocese, covering a vast region running from East Africa to Japan. Two years later, the Inquisition was established.

Goa also served as a hub for European mission work. It was home to St Paul's College, where generations of boys and young men from across Asia learned Latin, music, maths, theology and local languages, preparing them to teach Christianity to their compatriots. While there, they served as an unofficial translation pool, helping Jesuits to understand the religious texts that the Portuguese collected or confiscated. Christian tracts that were intended, eventually, to replace these texts, were printed at the College in a range of languages, using a moveable-type hand press.

Xavier's early work took him to the Pearl Fishery Coast, where between 1542 and 1544 he ministered to a low-caste pearl-fishing community called the Paravas. Comprising tens of thousands of people, they had converted to Christianity en masse a few years earlier, while seeking Portuguese protection against Arab competitors. With the help of three Tamil-speaking assistants and a short Tamil catechism (which Xavier committed to memory as a means of preaching in a language that he couldn't actually speak), he baptized children, taught the Lord's Prayer, built prayer houses and established the rudiments of a parish.[7]

Xavier's successors on the Pearl Fishery Coast learned Tamil, and the Paravas survived as a Christian community into the modern era. But not all Europeans saw mass conversions as meaningful. Converts remained steeped in their former customs, notably those concerning marriage, the family and participation in 'heathen' festivals.[8] Could they really be called Christians? The question became particularly urgent on the Malabar Coast. The Portuguese had at first been delighted to discover there a Christian community of around 30,000 people, spread across sixty towns, and claiming descent from converts made by the Apostle Thomas himself. It was some way off what the Letter of Prester John had promised, but still: these people were devout, wealthy, active in the all-important pepper trade, and willing to form commercial partnerships with their Western co-religionists.

Problems soon arose. The 'Thomas Christians' appeared to practise an unnervingly corrupted Christianity. Their priesthood was hereditary, rather than celibate. They indulged in lavish gift-giving. They took fasting and festivities alike to an extreme, the latter sometimes carrying on for days and featuring strange music alongside a great deal of dancing. Of the seven Catholic sacraments, whose importance were restated by the post-Reformation Council of Trent, three were missing entirely: Confirmation, Confession and the Anointing of the Sick. The other four – Baptism, Holy Communion, Marriage and Holy Orders – were practised only in odd forms, including the making of circles of rice on the floor around newlyweds. Heathen influences were suspected, as was the malign role of the Church of the East: heretics, in Portuguese eyes, whose sending of bishops to India to look after the Thomas Christian community was a religious and potentially a political threat.[9]

But the Malabar Coast was not controlled by the Portuguese. So a degree of persuasion was required, and the Jesuits were asked to help. The response at first was a combination of exploring the St Thomas tradition, putting up with customs that were either harmless or too entrenched to change, and reforming the rest. Excavations carried out around the place in Mylapore where St Thomas was believed to have been buried yielded objects including a 'bleeding cross' which was reported to sweat blood. Local legends were collected about Thomas and his sayings, amongst which was the rather helpful prediction that 'white people' would one day arrive to carry on his ministry. Much effort was put into educating the next generation of Indian Christians, with some trained to serve as catechists to their own communities.[10]

Reform of the Thomas Christian liturgy included the use of a

European-style host for communion, replacing a more cake-like predecessor. Caste distinctions were permitted: no low-caste Christians would be allowed in Thomas Christian churches. A brand-new form of festivity was invented, combining a Syriac Mass, a Latin Mass sung by Jesuits, other music besides and a volley of gun salutes. Exorcisms were performed, satisfying a shared sense amongst the Thomas Christians and the Portuguese of the reality of malevolent forces. In south Indian culture, these forces might originate in snakes, trees, or the ghosts of people who had died violent deaths. The Jesuits saw the devil at work in Martin Luther.[11]

A broader question was being forced on the Jesuits here: where does the gospel end, and social custom begin? And how far can 'accommodation' of the latter legitimately go, before evangelization turns into the forging of a hybrid heathenism? Pioneering, highly controversial answers would be offered elsewhere in India, and in China, from the 1600s onwards. For now, the Jesuits' efforts on the Malabar Coast – one of the first sustained attempts at intercultural contact between Europe and Asia – ended largely in failure, from the point of view of both sides. The Portuguese authorities continued to regard the Thomas Christians as heretics, and in 1599 a new and zealous Archbishop of Goa travelled down to Malabar and enforced an ecclesiastical solution to the problem. The Synod of Diamper brought the Thomas Christians formally under the auspices of the Pope, and of the Portuguese as their protectors. A lengthy list was issued, of 'bad' or 'erroneous' customs that were said to derive from a combination of Nestorianism and Indian heathenism. The list excluded caste, which the archbishop was forced to accept. But there was enough here to fuel decades of bad blood between the Portuguese and a divided Thomas Christian community.[12]

The Jesuits' biggest hope for India lay further north. While the Portuguese had been building their coastal presence, power had been changing hands on the Gangetic plain. In 1526, Zahiruddin Babur, the ruler of Kabul, launched a raid into India and engaged Sultan Ibrahim Lodi at the Battle of Panipat. Babur's cavalry and cannon won out against the sultan's elephants and infantry, and by the time of Babur's death in 1530 a series of further campaigns had brought most of north India under the control of what became known as the Mughal dynasty (derived from 'Mongol': Babur was descended, on his mother's side, from Genghis Khan).

Babur's grandson, Akbar, extended the Mughal Empire's reach: into Gujarat in the west, and Bengal in the east. He married Jodhabai, an Indian princess, thereby bringing her father and other Indian elites into an Indo-Islamic administration whose carefully ranked and generally well-remunerated members were known as *mansabdars*. Akbar went further still in laying the foundations for a multicultural empire: abolishing the *jizya* (a tax placed by some Islamic rulers on non-Muslims within their domains) and giving up the practice of forcibly converting enemies to Islam.

With the Portuguese, Akbar reached a wary diplomatic accord. But it was clear to both sides that their maritime interests on the coasts of Gujarat and Bengal would always be in potential conflict. So it was out of a mix of religious and political self-interest that in 1579 Akbar sent an invitation to Goa for 'two learned priests' to join him at court and engage in philosophical debate. He hoped to size up the Portuguese as a potential threat, and he thought that Christians might make for an interesting addition to his regular discussions with Muslims, Brahmins, Jews, Jains and Zoroastrians.[13]

There was great excitement in Goa when the invitation came in. The Jesuits did not focus exclusively on the elites of the places where they worked. But part of their interest in understanding and, where possible, accommodating the cultures with which they came into contact was the hope that from the conversion of influential people at the top of society the rest might follow. Evangelistic opportunities did not, therefore, come much bigger than Akbar. Might he do for Christianity in India what Emperor Constantine had done for it in the West? Might Akbar even be recruited to Europe's wars of religion, helping to smite the Protestants back home? Optimistic rumours began to circulate that Akbar had developed a devotion to the Virgin Mary, and might now be on the cusp of conversion.[14]

Three Jesuits, led by an Italian aristocrat, Rodolfo Aquaviva, arrived at Akbar's court in Fatehpur Sikri in 1580. Early audiences were encouraging. Akbar, the missionaries reported, was doing his best to understand the concept of the Trinity, and how it was that God could have a son who became a man. He seemed to want Christians and churches in his lands, as a means of equalling his Ottoman rivals in their cosmopolitanism. And it was clear from debates at his court that there were tensions between the emperor and orthodox mullahs in his orbit. Over time, however, Akbar's desire to pursue these questions entirely by means of logic alone became a sticking point. Wanting to see miracles for himself, he suggested at one point that the Jesuits walk through fire carrying a Bible, while a mullah at his court (for whom Akbar apparently had little affection) did the same with the Qur'an. He also appeared resistant to the Christian ideal of monogamy.[15]

The Jesuits – or *siyāhposh* ('black-robes'), as they were known at Akbar's Persian-speaking court – stuck with their task nevertheless, teaching Akbar's son Portuguese while picking up Persian themselves. They argued late into the night with Sunnis, Shiites, Brahmins and Jains.[16] They gave Akbar exotic presents including European paintings and engravings, making the most of the shared symbolism in Christianity and Islam. They read to him when requested: Akbar was illiterate. And they joined him on one of his military campaigns, as a means – if nothing else – of gathering useful intelligence on a major world power.[17]

Still, the mission petered out in 1583, and subsequent ones sent in 1591 and 1595 reached the conclusion that although Akbar's commitment to Islam was indeed weakening, the beneficiary was not to be Christianity. Akbar was busy weaving a broad syncretic faith, largely around his own person, from favoured mystical and ethical strands of different traditions. This religious movement, with a select membership of fewer than twenty people, was known as 'Divine Faith' (Din-e-Ilahi). It was a clever bit of myth-making, enhancing Akbar's status amongst his subjects. To the Jesuits, it looked like a personality cult. One missionary claimed that Akbar was touting himself as a new prophet, and was being worshipped as a saint – even some-times addressed in public as 'God'. (Akbar was making enterprising use, here, of the Islamic proclamation *Allahu Akbar*. Meaning 'God is great', it might also be taken as 'God is Akbar'.)

Dashing Jesuit hopes of what would have been the conversion of the century, Akbar instead drew them into the kind of cultural exchange for which his empire would be remembered. Fatehpur Sikri's architecture combined classical Islamic with Rajput styles. Mughal court painters, celebrated for their miniatures and illumin-ated Persian manuscripts, also produced art in the style of late Renaissance Europe. Mughal palaces, tombs and gardens, too, became markers of a great multicultural legacy.

Many of the Jesuit missionaries had a strong visual sense. They were known for the spiritual practice of 'imaginative contempla-tion', in which a person would situate themselves in a biblical scene and then allow it to play out from there. Ignatius of Loyola had meditated daily in front of images, while Francis Xavier carried a suit-case packed with icons and illustrated books around Asia. Working with a Mughal court historian, one of the Jesuits produced the first Catholic literature in Persian, expressing key ideas using allegorical imagery drawn from Sufism, of mirrors and hearts. These became contributions to a large Mughal library of European works, which soon included everything from Aquinas' *Summa Theologiae* to Loy-ola's *Spiritual Exercises*.[18]

Art, architecture, robes, ritual, music, incense: these things offered an immediacy of communication that early, stumbling attempts in foreign languages could not match. Aquinas himself had said that wonderment could be a way to God. As the 1500s drew to a close, India had yet to become the roaring missionary success for which Xavier and his colleagues might have hoped. But there were hints, here, of new things that could be tried in fulfilling the promise of the subcontinent. Further to the east, in China and Japan, experiments with some of them were already underway.

Arrival of the Europeans. Section from a seventeenth-century folding screen.

6.

The Challenge of China and the
Promise of Japan

Europeans at the dawn of the 1500s drew most of what little they knew about China and Japan from their reading of Marco Polo. Where China was concerned, they also had an account from the Franciscan friar William of Rubruck, who had learned about the country while at the court of Kublai Khan at Karakorum in the mid-1200s.[1] China was vast, urbanized and well-governed; technologically and commercially advanced; a place of enormous wealth in precious metals, stones and silks, where the women were modest and some of the money was made of paper. These impressions were generally confirmed when Portuguese seafarers and merchants encountered Chinese goods in south-western Indian markets. They included porcelain: remarkable to look at, but of uncertain retail potential back in Europe.[2]

After the Portuguese captain Jorge Alvarez reached southern China in 1514, and the Portuguese began trading unofficially up and down the coastline, the first piece of information added to this store of knowledge about China was that Europeans were not especially welcome. Herodotus had once imagined the Greek city states to be the civilized centre of the world, with familiar and more-or-less acceptable people for neighbours but with strangeness and savagery increasing with every pace one took outwards from there. In a similar way, China had for millennia seen itself as the 'Middle Kingdom': the centre of the physical and moral universe. Its immediate neighbours – Korea, Japan, Vietnam, the Ryukyu Islands – were heavily influenced by Chinese culture, and enjoyed close tributary relationships. An inner Asian zone followed next, then came the 'outer barbarians'. These included the newly arrived Europeans, amongst whom the more classically inclined soon realized they were on the wrong end of a Herodotean worldview.[3]

The Portuguese appeared to the Chinese simply not to understand the rules of a tributary relationship. Embassies were permitted to enter China now and again, to pay respects and bring gifts to the Ming emperor (whose dynasty ruled China from 1368 to 1644). They would be allowed to engage in a little private business during their journey. Travel and trade were otherwise tightly controlled. Between 1405 and 1433, the Ming had sent out treasure ships on a series of tribute-gathering voyages around the Indian Ocean, visiting more than thirty countries as far away as East Africa.[4] But officially sanctioned Chinese travel beyond its borders was limited in this era, and ordinary Chinese were forbidden from engaging in unsanctioned trade with foreigners. They could not even decide to leave the country without permission, such were historic fears both of invasion (primarily from the north) and of the corruption of the country's culture by outside influence.

Coastal smuggling and piracy had, of late, become a serious threat to these arrangements. And early reports about the Portuguese placed them squarely in this category: they had seized Malacca, a long-time tributary of China, and a captain by the name of Simão de Andrade had insulted and attacked Chinese coastal officials.[5] So it was that some of the earliest Portuguese writings about China were produced from a prison in Canton (Guangzhou), to which members of a first embassy to Peking, in 1517, were confined after failing to win an audience with the emperor.[6]

The difficulty of meeting the emperor understandably loomed large both in these and subsequent writings, as did the dramatic obeisances required in his presence (a series of genuflections and touching of the head to the ground, known as the kowtow). His country was divided into provinces, all well-watered by riverways and administered by a highly stratified bureaucracy of 'mandarins' drawn from a class of literati. The reputation of these men amongst early Portuguese commentators was mixed. Some lauded the administration of Chinese justice as careful and fair, arising out of a society that looked after its vulnerable. Others claimed that Chinese officials were idle and dishonest, cruel in the punishments that they oversaw – from wooden cages to bamboo whips enthusiastically applied to prisoners' thighs – and widely disliked by ordinary Chinese. Witnessing what appeared to be the underdevelopment of Chinese weaponry compared with European artillery, one of the imprisoned Europeans was moved to claim that a 'taste of the Portuguese sword' would be enough to start a revolt, leaving him and his compatriots not just free but in charge of Canton.[7]

The Portuguese sword stayed in its scabbard. Instead, it was with tacit official permission that in 1555 they began to develop a harbour settlement on the sparsely populated Macau Peninsula, located on China's southern coast at the mouth of the Pearl River.[8] By the early 1580s, there was enough information on the Chinese – and sufficient interest about them, in Europe – for the Pope to ask an Augustinian monk named Juan Gonzàlez de Mendoza to put it all together for publication. *Historia de las cosas más notables, ritos y costumbres del gran reyno de la China* (*History of the Most Notable Aspects, Rites and Customs of the Great Kingdom of China*, 1585) was translated into six other European languages and reprinted multiple times.[9]

The *Historia* marked the beginning of widely held positive views of China in Europe. Astonishingly, in this 'mightie kingdom . . . there [was] neither prince, duke, marquesse, earle nor lord'.[10] Power lay instead in the hands of mandarins who gained their positions after taking highly competitive examinations. Salaries and expenses paid by the emperor, they wielded extraordinary power in administering the country's fifteen provinces – each of which was bigger than any European kingdom. Households were organized in groups, their members required to report 'any trespasse or fault' to local officials, on pain of punishment themselves. That punishment could be severe, from imprisonment and whipping through to execution. This last fate was claimed by Mendoza – his figures most likely made up to support a general point about harsh Chinese penalties – to befall 6,000 people in each province every year.[11]

This was a learned place, from medicine to astronomy. It was peaceable, and well-fed: pork, chicken and duck; vegetables, fruit, fish, eggs; and the southern staple of rice. The country's architecture was impressive, from temples and mandarin compounds to roads, bridges and of course the Great Wall in the north. Arts and crafts were noted for their sophistication, as was the Chinese language, the ritual drinking of *cia* (tea) and the practice of foot binding – attributed to an aesthetic preference in China for smaller feet. The people themselves were said to be courteous, though in matters of religion they were of course hopeless idolaters: they worshipped the heavens, cast lots and prayed at wayside shrines, occasionally laughing as did they did so – a sure sign of religious corruption.[12]

Mendoza reported that the Apostle Thomas had travelled to China, only to return to India having given up on the place.[13] Early Jesuits no doubt sympathized. The Chinese authorities proved resistant to having missionaries in their midst, leaving them confined mostly to Macau and ministering to the Portuguese who were living there. Beginning in 1579, Alessandro Valignano made it a mission priority to learn the Nanjing dialect of spoken Chinese, which was used by the literati elite of Guangdong province. Still a daunting proposition centuries later, when dictionaries and grammars and tutors were available, the best that the Italian Michele Ruggieri could be offered when he embarked on the task was a room a little way away from the other Jesuits in Macau where he might at least struggle in peace.[14]

After three years, Ruggieri's Chinese was good enough that when he joined Portuguese merchants sailing up the Pearl River to Canton, he managed to talk one of the local literati into giving him the use of a house in the city. The merchants who accompanied him were meanwhile required, as usual, to sleep aboard their ships.[15] Over the years that followed, both Ruggieri and his fellow Jesuit Matteo Ricci found China's literati to be congenial company. These two late-Renaissance Italians had come halfway across the world, and found kindred spirits. Both parties put a premium on education, on continuous learning from virtuous ancient forebears – Greeks,

Romans or Kongzi ('Confucius', *c.* 551–479 BCE) – and on the practical utility of mathematics and technology.

Reading the Confucian classics against the backdrop of ancient Chinese history, Ruggieri and Ricci were struck by the use of the terms *tian* and *Shang Di*. The first was translatable as 'heaven' or 'God', depending on whether you understood it as a law or a being; the second meant 'Lord on High'. This suggested that Confucius, in his day, had combined high moral teachings with a form of monotheism.[16] Ruggieri left China for Rome in 1588, never to return. But Ricci remained, discovering familiar Stoic threads in Confucianism, including an interest in friendship. He published a widely circulated book called *Jiaoyou Iun* (*Essay on Friendship*, 1595), featuring aphorisms from 'Western sages' such as Seneca.[17]

Official hostility towards missionary activity in China had not changed, and there was concern amongst the Jesuits about whether they would achieve anything there. But Ricci had made an important start, gaining friends amongst the literati and steadily working his way northwards towards Peking. At the turn of the seventeenth century, his great aim would be fulfilled: an invitation from the Wanli emperor to enter the Forbidden City.

★

Where Columbus had failed to get to Japan in 1492, a small band of Portuguese traders succeeded by accident fifty years later. Blown wildly off course in a storm, in 1542 or 1543, they ended up at Tanegashima: a small island off the southernmost tip of Kyushu, which was in turn the southernmost of Japan's four main islands.

First to make landfall in China, Jorge Alvarez soon became one of the first Europeans to spend time on the Japanese coast too. He and others reported back on a land that was short on the gold promised by Marco Polo but had much to recommend it nonetheless. There were green, forested hills, through which typhoons and hurricanes sometimes raged; rice paddies, where at home one might find pastureland for cattle or sheep; and low-rise homes fashioned from wood, stone and clay, comprising airy rooms all open to one another. The people were of average height, and fair in complexion. The poor dressed in wool (more likely it was cotton), the rich in silk, and everyone was quietly spoken – to the point, almost, of whispering. Proud, and precise about status, the Japanese nevertheless showed great kindness to strangers. Everyone ate sitting on the floor, using sticks to pick vegetables, fish and rice from black bowls that were red on the inside.[18]

'The best who have yet been discovered.' Such was the verdict of Francis Xavier, who sailed from Malacca to the port of Kagoshima, in Kyushu, aboard a Chinese pirate ship in August 1549. He was joined by two other Jesuits, along with a young Japanese man named Anjirō, who had fled Japan a few years earlier in the company of Alvarez after being accused of a murder.[19] Anjirō had gone on to study Portuguese and theology at St Paul's College in Goa, where he became the first known Japanese convert to Christianity and joined the ranks of the Jesuits' early informants on Asian life.

Anjirō's insights about the way Japan was ruled were generally encouraging. Where India was a patchwork of powers spread across a subcontinent, Japan had at the helm a single divine emperor, on whose behalf a shogun – or 'Goxo', to the early Jesuits – was charged with keeping order amongst the country's well-armed provincial lords. He was having a tough time of it, the Jesuits soon came to see. These lords held real power in Japan, during a period known to posterity as the *sengoku jidai* or 'Warring States era' (1467–1615).

The Jesuits also heard from Anjirō about the particular flavour of heathenism that held sway in Japan: Buddhism. They found some of the details fascinating, chiming as they did with their belief about ancient Christian evangelization conducted in this region by Thomas the Apostle.[20] The Japanese, Anjirō claimed, used altars, bells, rosaries, incense, statues and paintings in their worship. Their main deity had three aspects – reminiscent, for hopeful Jesuits, of the Christian Trinity. They were aware of heaven and hell, and they recognized people who pursued the religious path with particular commitment as *hotoke* ('buddhas') – not unlike saints, thought the

Jesuits, keen to discern the salvific thread in any new religion that they encountered.[21]

There was more. Buddhism, the Jesuits learned, had a monastic component, characterized by communal living, prayer, chanting and fasting.[22] Better still, it had been founded by a holy man who preached a single creator god more than 1,500 years ago. This man had given commandments, including prohibitions on killing and theft, and had lived somewhere to the west beyond China, in a place called Tenjiku. To the Jesuits, as yet unaware that Tenjiku meant 'India', this sounded like a corrupted memory of Jesus Christ. Anjirō also made clear that the Japanese would only become Christians once they had asked lots of questions, tested Xavier's knowledge and observed him for at least half a year to see whether he lived in accordance with what he preached.[23]

Here was a culture that seemed to place a high value on natural reason and personal conduct, and to understand their combined role in helping people towards religious truth. Xavier was so impressed that he adopted the name of what he had been given to understand was the main Buddhist deity – 'Dainichi', the celestial Buddha – when he first preached the Christian God in Japanese, using a script prepared by Anjirō. All did not go to plan. Preaching from the steps of a Buddhist monastery in Kagoshima, Xavier was rewarded with 'jeers and laughter'.[24] Elsewhere, one of his Jesuit companions gave an hour-long sermon before the powerful lord Ōuchi Yoshitaka, only to be abruptly dismissed once he finished speaking.[25]

One of the things that the Jesuits had not yet realized about Japan was that poverty lacked the religious resonance that it possessed in Europe, where in the early days of what became the Society of Jesus, Ignatius, Francis and their companions had gone about in sackcloth.[26] In Japan, someone turning up to meet a lord looking shabby was regarded as offering insult rather than inspiration. Coupled with the very poor Japanese of the Jesuits' first *Summary of Christian Doctrine*, and the emphasis placed in early preaching on the evils of sodomy (homosexual relationships amongst monks and samurai were commonplace and unremarkable in Japan), it is not difficult to see why Xavier was laughed at and his colleague turned away. Matters got worse when Xavier was refused an audience with the emperor in Kyoto. Bearing no official letters and no proper gifts, he was simply not taken seriously. A two-month journey in the depths of the Japanese winter was wasted.[27]

But the Jesuits learned fast. In the spring of 1551, Xavier himself appeared before Ōuchi Yoshitaka, in formal dress and with gifts and official letters in hand from the Portuguese authorities in India. He was rewarded with the use of an empty monastery, to which a number of interested visitors came and eventually converted to Christianity. He discovered, meanwhile, that some Buddhist monks to whom he had earlier preached 'Dainichi' had assumed that Xavier was bringing them a new interpretation of Buddhism, fresh from its homeland – Xavier had mentioned India as his point of embarkation for Japan. Realizing their mistake, Xavier and his fellow missionaries immediately began to use the Latin word 'Deus' instead, while denouncing Dainichi as 'an invention of the devil'. Offended Buddhists took to pronouncing Deus as *dai-uso*: 'Great lie'. Better mutual understanding did not always bring better relations.[28]

Xavier left Japan later in 1551 having made at least 800 converts – possibly many more[29] – and having established relationships with a number of influential lords. The power of Portuguese trade loomed large in this process. China's coastal piracy problem had persuaded the Chinese emperor a few decades before to bring his country's lucrative trading relationship with Japan to an end. The 'southern barbarians' (*nanban*) – as the Japanese called the Portuguese, because they originally approached Japan from a southerly direction – duly stepped in, establishing a trade route running between Macau and various southern Japanese ports.

Raw Chinese silk could be sold in Kyushu for up to ten times its purchase price in China, while silver and various Japanese goods – including swords and lacquerware – were shipped in the other direction. Novel items and ideas from Europe and India made it into Japan, too, via this trade: tobacco, chairs, medicine, surgery, astronomy and art (including oil painting, *chiaroscuro* and perspective). At the same time, Japanese products created increasingly for an export market began to find their way back to Europe. Heat-resistant lacquerware was popular, as were chests and writing desks fashioned from exotic woods and inlaid with silver, mother-of-pearl and tortoiseshell. The China–Japan trade alone is estimated to have been worth around 500,000 silver ducats in annual profit by 1580.[30]

This thriving commercial relationship was captured by painters of the Japanese Kanō school in their *nanban byōbu*: folding screens that depicted – in a combination of strong colours, gold leaf, lacquer and silk – European people, fashions and activities. They painted bales of Chinese silk and imported Persian horses being offloaded from black-hulled Portuguese carracks – sailors swinging high in the rigging – alongside processions that reflected Portugal's global reach in this era: European sailors working alongside Indians, Malays and African slaves. Portuguese clothing and accessories were of particular interest: cloaks, buttoned doublets, baggy breeches and ornamentation designed to be hung about the body, including rosaries, reliquaries, gold chains, crosses and daggers. *Nanban* fashion soon spread amongst Japan's elite.[31]

The Jesuits took part in Portugal's trade, building new churches and colleges back home in Europe from the profits. More important, however, was the warm welcome that the trade earned them amongst rulers of coastal provinces in south-western Japan, who hoped to see the foreign *kurofune* (black ships) use their ports. Kyushu became promising mission territory as a result, and a number of provincial lords converted to Christianity. One of them, Ōmura Sumitada (baptized 'Dom Bartolomé'), gave the Portuguese the use of a natural harbour. Japanese and European planners together turned it into the purpose-built international trading town of Nagasaki. It became a hub for Jesuit activities, including educational and publishing ventures funded by their trading profits.

In Japan, as in China, one of the Jesuits' jobs was to write back to

Europe with news of the culture they had encountered. Where Ricci and others extolled the virtuousness of the Confucian literati in China, Jesuits in Japan were particularly impressed by Zen: a blend of Indian Buddhist teachings with Chinese ideas – notably Taoism – which had become popular amongst the country's warrior aristocracy. Some aspects of Zen were deeply disturbing for the Jesuits. It regarded nothingness, rather than being, as reality's supreme principle. There was no God to be worshipped, and no salvation to be worked for. Instead, 'men of great meditations' spent hours in contemplation and the reading of sutras, inside large and independent monastic complexes. Cynics in Europe suggested that this would be congenial for inveterate sinners: one could meditate to alleviate the anxiety caused by wrongdoing, and no final punishment need be feared. But the Jesuits saw and heard enough about Zen while in Japan – not least its connections with calligraphy, poetry, art and the tea ceremony – to regard it as the apex of Japanese religion.[32]

Popular religion in Japan was meanwhile accorded scarcely more respect than its idolatrous counterparts in India and China. Some of it, the Jesuits discovered, involved praying to particular buddhas or *kami* (the gods of Japan's indigenous religion, Shintō). Devotees of Amida Buddha, who believed they had only to call on his name in order to be saved, appeared strikingly similar to followers of Luther in Europe: deluded into imagining an easy path to God, with a person's good or bad deeds neither here nor there. One aspect of Asia's promise for European Catholics in this era was its provision of exotic and consoling proof of how the devil sows similar seeds of error in all human hearts.[33] Nevertheless, Buddhist priests of all sects appeared to enjoy wealth, social sway, educational influence and broad cultural kudos. For the Jesuits, they were enemy number one.

One of the difficulties of dealing with a civilized people was that they asked a lot of questions. Why had God hidden himself until now from the people of Japan? Were their ancestors really damned, having not heard the gospel during their lifetimes? Alongside seeking to answer such questions, once their linguistic skills were up to it, the Jesuits found that they could more effectively transmit something of the mystery and grandeur of their God through aesthetics and ritual. They requested rich vestments to be shipped out from their base at Goa: gold cloth, brocade, velvet, helping them to compete with the Buddhists in providing magnificent processions and funeral ceremonies. Palanquins and silk banners were employed, alongside torches, candles, holy water, crucifixes and the solemn recitation of prayers in Latin. Japanese elements, including paper lanterns, were easily worked in. So keen were the Jesuits to measure the effectiveness of these efforts that they occasionally made records of which converts cried during services.[34]

Japanese pride and refinement proved to be a challenge, too. One provincial lord informed Alessandro Valignano, after he arrived in 1579 to assess the mission's progress, that missionaries who expected converts to emulate the 'barbaric and vulgar ways' of the Portuguese were regarded by his fellow Japanese as deeply unintelligent.[35] Valignano responded by requiring missionaries to learn Japanese etiquette and eat as the Japanese did: chopsticks, small bites, avoiding meat and the associated filth of keeping live animals indoors. A Japanese twist on the traditional Jesuit cassock and cloak was to be worn, and kept fastidiously clean: Valignano was convinced that the Japanese prized cleanliness extraordinarily highly. This was part of a general sense of decency that persuaded him to compare them favourably to the pagans of ancient Rome – high praise, from a late-Renaissance humanist. Jesuit residences were, in future, to be built in the Japanese style, including a room given over to welcoming visitors with the tea ceremony.[36]

Finally, Valignano required that more Japanese be admitted to the order. 'Japan is not a place', he wrote, 'which can be controlled by foreigners, for the Japanese are neither so weak nor so stupid as to permit this.'[37] Within a few years, of a total of eighty-five Jesuits working in Japan, twenty-nine were Japanese. They were an invaluable source of understanding, and more persuasive as preachers than foreigners could ever hope to be. Japanese catechists were trained and deployed for the same reason. Known as *dōjuku* (named after a similar assistant role at the bottom of the Buddhist priestly hierarchy), they engaged in itinerant teaching, translation and interpreting. When no priest was available, they even led services, baptized people, buried the dead, and heard the confessions of the sick and dying.[38]

Only men enjoyed the formal role of *dōjuku*, but a number of Japanese women served informally as catechists. They included the aristocrat Kiyohara Ito (1565–?), chief lady-in-waiting to Lady Hosokawa Tama. Hosokawa once managed to attend a service at the Jesuit church in Osaka, interrupting the sermon to query it on the basis of her own Zen Buddhist understanding. Thereafter she was intrigued, and since her high status limited her movements outside the family compound, she had Kiyohara attend catechism classes and Mass on her behalf. Kiyohara would relay questions from her mistress, and bring back answers from the Jesuits.

Kiyohara was eventually baptized, taking the name 'Maria'. And when it became clear that Hosokawa would be unable to receive baptism from a priest, Kiyohara was taught the rite herself. She baptized her mistress as 'Gracia' in 1587. Here was a vivid sign of how far accommodation might take the Jesuits: hailing from a culture where the priesthood was dominated by men, they trained one woman to baptize another.[39]

By the early 1580s, the Jesuit mission was on such a high – 150,000 converts, 200 churches and outright control of Nagasaki – that their struggling colleagues in Macau became heartily sick of hearing about it.[40] Thanks to the formidable linguistic skills of the Portuguese Jesuit Luis Fróis, friendly relations had been established with Oda Nobunaga: the greatest warlord of the era, whose territories by this time included Kyoto and its surrounds. He allowed the missionaries a free hand in evangelizing, granted regular audiences to Fróis – once grilling him for three hours about India – and shared their enmity towards Japan's Buddhist establishment, some of whose temples were fortified and defended by warrior-monks. The

Jesuits could do little more than debate with their Buddhist rivals, and emulate their liturgies. Nobunaga's repertoire ran to swords, spears, bows and arrows, starvation and fire, along with arquebuses based on imported Portuguese designs (a cherished feature of samurai armour in this era came to be a certain tell-tale dent: proof that it could stop a bullet).[41]

With Japan now easily the most promising region of Asia, the time appeared ripe, to Valignano, for giving Europe's first generation of Japanophiles something to savour. Enjoying evocations of Japan in missionary letters was one thing. How about actually meeting some Japanese?

Four Christian seminarians in their early teens were chosen to make up an embassy to Europe. Mancio Itō represented the Lord of Bungo, and Miguel Chijiwa represented the lords of Arima and Ōmura. They were joined by two companions: Julião Nakura and Martinho Hara.[42] Besides impressing Europe's aristocracy with the achievements of the Jesuits in Japan, Valignano hoped that the boys would have the chance to witness the 'greatness and wealth of our kingdoms and cities . . . and the prestige which our religion enjoys in all of them'.[43] There was a need to provide reassurance on this point, since Japanese Buddhists sometimes claimed that the missionaries' real motive for coming to Japan was to escape a poor and lowly situation back home.[44] The boys could not be permitted to encounter any Protestants on their journey, or any other evidence of Christendom's travails, lest news get back to Japan. That meant Jesuit chaperones, at all times, and the use where possible of Jesuit houses for accommodation.[45]

The embassy set sail from Nagasaki in February 1582, travelling via Macau and Goa, where Valignano was forced to take his leave of them to continue his work in Asia. They arrived in Lisbon in the summer of 1584, proceeding from there through Toledo and Madrid. They attracted considerable attention along the way, for the European military escort which sometimes accompanied them and for the exotic attire in which they travelled: multi-layered kimono of white silk, adorned with figures of birds; white *tabi* socks and sandals; and a combination of *katana* (Japanese sword) and dagger, both in richly ornate scabbards fashioned from materials that included ground gold and mother-of-pearl. In Madrid, they met King Philip II, who quizzed them for an hour on topics including their clothes and diet – he found it remarkable that they drank 'hot water' (tea) not just in winter but all year round. The king also perused the presents that the boys had brought for him, including a bamboo desk that had originally been given to Valignano by Oda Nobunaga. Passing through Florence and Siena, guarded from beggars at points along the way by soldiers commanded by Raffaelo de' Medici, they arrived in the Papal States in March 1585. On the final stretch to Rome, they were trailed at points by a crowd of up to a thousand people, thanks in part to the welcoming party that was sent out to meet them: papal cavalry and Swiss guard, alongside drums, trumpets and all manner of local dignitaries.[46]

Pope Gregory XIII received the boys in the Sala Regia, attended by a swell of cardinals, archbishops and bishops. They genuflected, prostrated and kissed the Pope's feet, apparently moving him to tears. Next came a speech of welcome, given by a Portuguese Jesuit by the name of Gaspare Gonsalves. The Japanese, he declared, were a 'warlike and cultured people' (both things being desirable), who lacked only 'the light of the Christian faith'. Now they had it. Many centuries ago, Gonsalves pointed out, an embassy had arrived from India to greet the Emperor Augustus in friendship. Here, now, was a group of Asian envoys arriving to make obeisance.[47]

Pope Gregory XIII died while the boys were in Rome, giving them the opportunity of attending the enthronement of Pope Sixtus V. Mancio Itō was one of those chosen to present the new Pope with holy water, and frescoes commemorating the great event became notable for the presence of Japanese faces.[48] The long journey home took in a host of Italian cities, amongst them Venice, where the locals were initially reluctant to extend much of a welcome. They were unimpressed with the boys' diplomatic credentials, and despondent about the chances of getting in on the East Asia trade.[49] Invitations to the courts of France, Savoy and the Holy

Roman Emperor had politely to be declined for the sake of the schedule, and the boys embarked at Lisbon for Goa and then Macau.[50]

What did the Europeans who witnessed this tour make of the Japanese envoys? Some fell in love with their clothes. Catherine of Braganza had a set created for her son Duarte, made him put them on, and then – to merriment all round – bade the boys from Japan come and greet one of their 'countrymen'. Humouring their host, the boys adjusted the clothes for Duarte and showed him how to hold a *katana*.[51] Laughs of a less generous sort were had at the boys' expense by members of the Roman general public, who were so rude about their clothes that Pope Gregory had to supply his visitors with European alternatives, of black velvet with gold braid.[52]

For the most part, however, Europe's elite were impressed with the boys' courtesy and dextrous use of chopsticks; their fresh and innocent piety (not least when encountering relics in Florence's Duomo); their ability to dance and hunt; and their command of European languages and musical instruments, including the lyre and guitar.[53] Translations of the official account of Pope Gregory's reception were amongst almost eighty publications produced in Europe about the embassy after it returned home.[54] One came from a German pamphleteer, wishing that the embassy had visited his country and learned something of that 'dear man of God, Martin Luther'.[55]

Travelling via key points in the Portuguese Empire – Mozambique, Goa, Malacca and Macao – the four boys finally arrived back in Nagasaki in July 1590, to find the prospects for Japanese Christianity much changed. Just a few months after they had left for Europe, back in 1582, Oda Nobunaga had died a fiery death in Kyoto. His successor, Hideyoshi Toyotomi, was a fan of *nanban* fashion and was keen on trade with Portugal. But he had been astonished to discover the power of the Jesuits in Kyushu: their control of Nagasaki, their friendships with Christian lords, and the destruction – according to what Hideyoshi had heard – of shrines and temples. Hideyoshi brought Kyushu under his own control in 1586, and issued an edict the next year giving the Jesuits twenty days to get out of his country. It was not immediately enforced, but the status of the mission in Japan had clearly changed.

Hoping to improve Jesuit fortunes, Valignano took his four envoys to meet Hideyoshi at his new palace in 1591, where they paid him a similar sort of respect to that offered to Pope Gregory in Rome. The boys gave a musical performance that included singing in harmony in the Western style, and in general the audience seems to have been cordial.[56] But the edict of 1587 remained in place, and ten years later Hideyoshi's anger at the missionaries – and Europeans in general – boiled over. Never reconciling himself to the idea that Christianity posed no political threat, Hideyoshi was all too ready to believe the captain of a Spanish galleon that ran aground off the Japanese coast in 1596, when he claimed – in an effort to get Hideyoshi to return seized cargo – that Christianization in Japan was a precursor to colonization. Hideyoshi responded by ordering the execution of every Christian in Kyoto and Osaka.[57] After an intervention by the governor of Kyoto, the number was reduced to twenty-six, including three Japanese Jesuits. They were taken up a hill overlooking Nagasaki in February 1597, and crucified.

Portugal's global network now began to work against Japan and its reputation back in Europe. A procession was held in Macau in December 1597 to honour the dead, accompanied by paintings depicting the grisly events – which were rumoured to have included the stoning of the condemned and the stuffing of weeds into their mouths. Similar images found their way to Spain, Rome and the New World. One of the crucified men, born in Mexico City, became Mexico's first saint. Literary accounts did the rounds, too, and by the time a second Japanese embassy arrived in Europe in 1614 – this one sailing eastwards across the Pacific, traversing Mexico and then crossing the Atlantic – the reception in some quarters was notably less warm.

Hideyoshi's death in 1598 brought a brief reprieve for Japan's Christians. His successor, Tokugawa Ieyasu, succeeded in unifying Japan, and was keen on maintaining links with Europe and the New

World. But the Tokugawa shogunate remained weak in its early years, and Ieyasu's descendants decided that the Portuguese, the Jesuits and Japan's Christians were more trouble than they were worth. Across the 1630s, a series of edicts were issued expelling the Portuguese and Jesuits from Japan, and banning Christianity. Especially bitter for the Jesuits was the sight of old enemies having the last laugh. Buddhist temples and priests were recruited to help stamp out any lingering remnants of Christianity, while international trade out of Nagasaki ended up in the hands of the Protestant Dutch.

Japanese Christianity lived on in covert form, on the island of Kyushu especially. But there would be no return to the 'Christian century', when the country's Christian community had reached between 300,000 and 500,000 people, out of a total population of around 20 million people.[58] Still, the twenty-six martyrs aside, the Jesuits had succeeded in creating a positive image for the Japanese in Europe – no one more so than Luis Fróis in his *Treatise* (1585). He imagined the Japanese as a sort of mirror image of Europeans, pioneering a highly influential 'we do x, they do y' mode of cultural comparison. 'In Europe, baring even one's foot before a fire to get warm would be considered strange; in Japan, anyone standing before the fire to get warm unabashedly bares his entire backside.' 'In Europe, the confinement of daughters and maidens is very intense and rigorous; in Japan, daughters go unaccompanied wherever they please for an entire day, and many do so without informing their parents.' 'In Europe, the love felt between male and female family members is very strong; in Japan it is weak and they treat each other like strangers.' 'With us, it is normal to whip and punish a child; in Japan, this is very rare and they only reprimand them.' 'Our children have little command and excellence in their manners; children in Japan are exceedingly thorough in their manners, so much so that they are amazing.'[59]

The promise of Japan would frequently be expressed in this way, across the centuries to come, while some of the things that had most impressed the Jesuits would find fresh devotees: Zen, food and of course the tea ceremony – whose early modern development, it has been claimed, owed something to the influence of the Catholic Mass.[60] The Jesuit role in Japan was over, for the time being. While they turned their attention elsewhere, across the 1600s and early 1700s, the interpretation of Japan for European audiences passed into new hands. For most of the 1500s, Catholic southern Europe had enjoyed pre-eminence in Japan, and in Asia generally. By the end of that century, things were beginning to change. The Dutch were coming. And the English were lacing their boots.

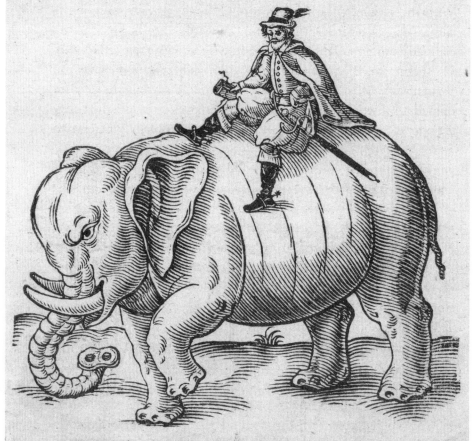

THOMAS CORIATE
Traueller for the English
VVits : Greeting.

From the Court of the Great MOGVL, Resi-
dent at the Towne of ASMERE, in
Eafterne INDIA.

Printed by W. Iaggard, and Henry Fetherfton.
1616.

Thomas Coryate astride an elephant in India, appearing on the title page of
Thomas Coriate: Traveller for the English Wits (1616).

7.

England's Legge-Stretchers

Your praiers doe even stinke before God, and are of no more force
than the cry of thy camell when thou doest lade or unlade him.[1]

With these words, the Englishman Thomas Coryate reached the
climax of his impromptu oration, delivered in 1615 before – he
claimed – an audience of around one hundred people in Multan.
His theme was the pointlessness of Islam generally and its piety in
particular. If Muslims knew the ugly truth of their faith, Coryate
opined, they would trample on the Qur'an, spit on it, and then bury
it under a toilet.[2] 'I my selfe', he added, 'have already written two
better bookes (God be thanked).'

This was the age of early English diplomacy, trade and religious
encounter in India. Fortunately, Coryate was professionally involved
in none of these enterprises. He was a different breed of traveller:
someone who ventured abroad for fun, exploration and the building
of a reputation back home. From unpromising beginnings – crossing
the English Channel, he recalled 'varnish[ing] the exterior parts
of the ship with the excrementall ebullitions of my tumultuous
stomach'[3] – Coryate rose to fame as the 'Legge-Stretcher'.

The English as a whole had been unpromising voyagers until
relatively recently. Perhaps the two men reported in the *Anglo-Saxon
Chronicle* to have been dispatched by King Alfred to the tomb of St
Thomas the Apostle made it all the way to India. Maybe a text exists
somewhere, detailing the adventures of Sighelm and Aethelstan. If
so, Richard Hakluyt would no doubt dearly have loved to see it. An
Elizabethan collector and publisher of travel accounts, his *Princi-
pal Navigations, Voyages, Traffics, and Discoveries of the English Nation*

(1589) was intended to prove to fellow countrymen and sceptical continentals alike that the English were capable of getting out there in the world. Most travel literature in English, up until this point, consisted of the translated deeds of more venturesome Europeans, Marco Polo amongst them. That would not do. The English, Hakluyt insisted, were people 'full of activity, stirrers abroad, and searchers of the remote parts of the world'.[4]

The English had not been entirely idle. Queen Elizabeth's grandfather, King Henry VII, had backed the Venetian citizen and adopted son of Bristol, John Cabot, in his attempt to reach Asia back in 1497. Mindful of papal authority and Iberian sea-power, he had hoped to find a north-westerly route to Asia.[5] Sailing his modest little ship *Matthew* northwards and westwards across the Atlantic, he made landfall at what he believed must be the north-east coast of China. He and his crew spotted tantalizing signs of life: trails leading inland, the remains of a fire, a needle for making nets (the waters were teeming with cod) and snares for catching game.[6] They proceeded to plant some English and Venetian flags, before returning home convinced – like Columbus around the same time – that on the next voyage they would find Cipangu, with its legendary gold. Cabot embarked on that second voyage in 1498, but was never heard from again.[7]

Both John Cabot and Henry VII were succeeded by sons determined to take up their fathers' mantle. Sebastian Cabot made one, perhaps two, sea crossings during the early 1500s, knowing by now that his father's 'newfoundelande' was located not in China but rather North America.[8] In 1520, Henry VIII and Cardinal Wolsey began plotting and scheming a voyage to North America, hoping to enlist Sebastian Cabot to lead it. But potential sponsors amongst the merchants of London were unconvinced that the balance of risk with probable trade rewards ran in their favour. Henry's attention soon returned to conflict on the continent.[9]

A little over thirty years later, Sebastian Cabot became involved in planning a fresh English attempt to seek out a passage to Asia, this time by heading north-east. Three ships departed England in May 1553, their crews charged with discovering and logging the commercial needs of each new group of people they might encounter. They were ordered to do so peacefully, though use of beer or wine to loosen local tongues was permitted. The small fleet made it up around the Scandinavian Peninsula, before running into storms just off the arctic Kola Peninsula. The crew of two of the ships decided to see out the winter off the peninsula's northern coast. They had plenty of food and warm clothes, but it was not enough. Freezing winds, scurvy, trapped fumes from stoves burning below deck – one or more of these perils seems to have overcome them. The men were discovered dead by local fishermen early the next year.[10]

The third ship fared better. Piloted by Richard Chancellor, it sailed on and then southwards into the White Sea, from where some of its crew travelled upriver in their pinnace. From there, with local help, they proceeded on sleds and on horseback all the way to Moscow. First diplomatic contact was thereby made with a hitherto little-known country in December 1553, as Chancellor was granted an audience at the Kremlin with a young – and not yet *too* 'Terrible' – Tsar Ivan IV.[11] They spoke through an interpreter, a gift was made of English cloth (for which the English were hoping to find markets in Asia), and a dinner was hosted by the tsar with impressive ceremony. A doomed passage to Asia became a promising maritime trade route running between western Europe and Russia.[12]

The commercial model used for making the most of that route was novel, and important. Up until now, maritime merchants had occasionally combined resources, while keeping their profits private. In 1555, with the chartering of the Muscovy Company, England's first joint-stock company was born. Cabot's knowledge of how Italian city-states funded their enterprises may have contributed to this new model in England. He was appointed governor, for life, of a trading company that welcomed any and all investors – pooling the risk and pooling the rewards.[13]

With a north-east passage remaining elusive, though stakeholders in the Muscovy Company continued to live in hope, it was by risking – even relishing – the prospect of conflict with Portugal and Spain that the English finally made it to Asia. While Sir Francis

Drake made a name for himself across the 1570s and 1580s – explorer, pirate, slave trader, circumnavigator of the globe – merchants in London put together England's first commercial mission to Asia. It was launched in February 1583, thanks to what Richard Hakluyt described as the 'speciall industrie of . . . worshipfull and worthy Citizens': three merchants by the name of John Newbery, John Eldred and Ralph Fitch, along with a jeweller named William Leeds and a painter, James Story.

Led by Newbery and bearing a letter each for Akbar and the Chinese emperor from Queen Elizabeth, the group made their way to the Levantine coast aboard the *Tiger*.[14] They continued overland via Aleppo and towards Ormuz. Eldred stayed behind en route to do some business, but the other four made it to Ormuz in September. There they were promptly taken prisoner by the Portuguese, after a Venetian merchant decided to deal with potential rivals by accusing them of spying. Newbery suspected that wounded Portuguese feelings might also be in play, given Drake's recent record in attacking their shipping.[15]

The group were taken to Goa and imprisoned there, until two Jesuits agreed to stand surety of 2,000 ducats for them. They were set free, and James Story agreed to become a lay Jesuit brother – rumour had it that the Jesuits wanted him to paint their church. Hearing that they were soon to be arrested again and taken to Portugal, the other three broke the terms of their bond and escaped Goa in April 1584. They journeyed northwards through the Deccan region to Akbar's court at Fatehpur Sikri, casting merchants' eyes along the way over jewel markets, high-quality silver currency, large-scale cotton cloth production and an abundance of pepper, spice, corn, rice and fruit.[16]

Before arriving at Fatehpur Sikri, they passed through the city of Agra, where Akbar's grandfather Babur had built palaces and planted gardens, and where the Mughal nobility enjoyed their riverside homes.[17] It was, Fitch later reported, 'a very great citie and populous, built with stone, having faire and large streetes, with a faire river [and] castle'. Both Agra and Fatehpur were, noted Fitch, much larger than London. And down the full length of the 20-mile road that separated them ran a constant stream of people and traffic: 'fine carts . . . carved and gilded with gold', and merchants from India and beyond, dealing in silk and precious stones. Fitch felt as though he were in a town for the entire journey between the two cities.[18]

At Fatehpur, Newbery was at last able to present his letter to Akbar, whom Fitch recalled was clad in a simple white tunic. The emperor was too preoccupied with domestic affairs to do much more than take receipt of their letter, and the Englishmen's visit to the Mughal court ended up being a brief one. But Fitch made his way home only after a lengthy, information-gathering detour that took in details of trading prospects and the Mughals' extraordinary wealth – their empire was responsible, in this era, for up to a quarter of all the world's manufacturing.[19] The emperor himself was, on Fitch's telling, the proud possessor of 1,000 elephants, 30,000 horses, 1,400 deer and 800 concubines.[20]

Leeds, the jeweller, and Newbery remained in India, the former entering Akbar's employ and the latter heading off for Lahore. Both disappear from history at this point. Fitch meanwhile headed to Bengal via Varanasi, where he painted a sympathetic portrait of people performing ritual ablutions in the Ganges but was confused by their reverence for an Indian holy man. All Fitch saw of him was that he sat on a horse and pretended to sleep: 'They took him for a great man, but sure he was a lazy lubber.'[21]

Fitch returned to England via Burma, Malacca, Sri Lanka, India's Malabar Coast and – this time apparently without incident – Goa and Ormuz. Arriving back in April 1591, he became something of a celebrity as news of his travels spread. He recalled them from memory for Richard Hakluyt, borrowing from a detailed account by the Italian traveller Cesare Federici as he did so.[22] The ship on which the group had first set sail was meanwhile immortalized by William Shakespeare in *Macbeth*: 'Her husband's to Aleppo gone, master o' the Tiger'.

Fitch had not returned with any Asian merchandise. Instead, he brought back bags of confidence in what fellow Englishmen might achieve, together with unprecedented intelligence on Asia's riches, spices and trading routes. This caught the attention of a group of London merchants led by Thomas Smythe, who in 1600 were at last granted a royal charter to trade in the 'East Indies' – understood to run a vast distance, from the Cape of Good Hope eastwards all the way to the Magellan Straits. The terms of the charter included a precious fifteen-year monopoly, alongside extensive rights – useful in the ambiguity of their phrasing – to control territories in which they ended up operating. It was grandiose stuff for a relatively poorly funded enterprise, many times smaller than its Dutch rival, the VOC, at its formation in 1602. England's nobility was in any case more interested, at this point, in the potential of Virginia.[23] Still, the 'East India Company' would, in time, do all right for itself.

*

Of all the pleasures in the world travell is (in my opinion) the sweetest and most delightfull. For what can be more pleasant than to see passing variety of beautifull Cities, Kings and Princes Courts, gorgeous Palaces, impregnable Castles and Fortresses, Towers piercing in a manner up to the cloudes, fertill territories replenished with a very Cornucopia of all manner of commodities as it were with the horn of Amalthea, tending both to pleasure and profit, that the heart of man can wish for.[24]

Here was Thomas Coryate's case for travel, laid out for readers of his first book: *Coryats Crudities: Hastily gobled up in five Moneths travells* (1611). His journey on that occasion had taken him from his home of Odcombe, in Somerset, on a circuit of major European sights in Paris, Turin, Milan, Venice, Zurich, Strasbourg, Frankfurt and Nijmegen. Coryate covered around 2,000 miles, mostly on foot, and in a single pair of apparently very hard-wearing shoes. These he hung, with great solemnity, in his local church after arriving home.[25]

Coryats Crudities won for its author a degree of notoriety, though perhaps not much respect, in his circle of friends at the court of young Prince Henry, son of King James I.[26] Educated at Winchester

School and Oxford University, Coryate's provincial origins and failure to actually earn a degree left him grasping after whatever status he could get. That often meant playing the fool, albeit an erudite one – standing on his head and reciting Greek. As one observer put it, 'sweetmeats and Coryate made up the last course at all court entertainments'. Elsewhere he was described as an anvil for courtiers 'to try their wits upon'.[27]

Famous for walking most of the way on his travels – hence his nickname – Coryate was also happy to do the legwork when it came to self-promotion. He arranged and paid for the licensing and printing of the *Crudities*, and solicited poetical contributions from friends and acquaintances. This backfired magnificently. They offered rude responses, and Prince Henry then demanded that Coryate include them in his book.[28] The gist of John Donne's contribution was that Coryate was a 'great lunatic', who ought once again to leave the country:

> Go, bashful man, lest here thou blush to look
> Upon the progress of thy glorious book,
> To which both Indies sacrifices send.
> The West sent gold, which thou didst freely spend,
> Meaning to see 't no more, upon the press.
> The East sends hither her deliciousness,
> And thy leaves must embrace what comes from thence,
> The myrrh, the pepper, and the frankincense.[29]

The very next year, 1612, Coryate took Donne's advice. He sailed to the Ottoman capital Constantinople, and proceeded from there via Jerusalem, Aleppo and Isfahan all the way into the Mughal Empire. Dressed in 'Oriental' clothes, Coryate had to pause now and again to await the next caravan, in whose relative security he might continue to walk. These, he explained in a letter to his mother, consisted of a large group of merchants and their pack animals – camels, horses, mules, asses. The caravan in which Coryate travelled from Isfahan to India was some 6,000 people strong.[30]

Coryate passed through the Hindu Kush, crossed the Indus – 'as broad againe as our Thames at London' – and arrived in Multan, where he delivered his inflammatory oration on Islam. In Coryate's recollection, it was a riposte to an Indian Muslim who had declared him an infidel. With around a hundred other people supposedly listening in, Coryate's journey to India might have reached a fatal conclusion a mere 40 miles from the Indus. Fortunately, his accuser had addressed him in Italian (having once been taken as a slave by Florentines), and Coryate had replied in kind.[31] In the end, the episode gave rise to one of Coryate's first observations about Mughal India. 'If I had spoken thus much in Turky or Persia', he declared, 'they would have rosted me upon a spit; but in the Mogols dominions a Christian may speake much more freely.'[32]

Coryate continued on to Lahore and then to Agra, passing through some of the best agricultural land he had ever seen. He arrived at the new Mughal capital of Ajmer in July 1615. Akbar had died a decade before, succeeded by his son: the Emperor Jahangir ('Seizer of the World'). August was the emperor's birthday month, so Coryate got to witness an event that spoke eloquently both of Jahangir as a 'verie worthy person' and of the opulence of his empire:

> That daie he weighed himselfe in a paire of golden scales . . . (a custome that he observeth most inviolablie every year) laying so much golde in the other scale as countervaileth the weight of his body, and the same he afterward distributed to the poore.[33]

Coryate seems to have taken to Jahangir immediately. He described him as olive-skinned, well-proportioned, inclined to speak respectfully of Christ as the 'Great Prophet Jesus', and a man who treated Christians well. He also owned a magnificent collection of 'the strangest beasts of the world', gathered from across his vast territories. Where Herodotus had written about the world largely on the basis of hearsay – as Coryate was keen to point out, in his *Crudities* – the Legge-Stretcher saw some of these 'beasts' with his own eyes.

They included two animals that Coryate insisted on calling 'unicornes', but which presumably were rhinoceroses.[34] Twice a week, courtiers enjoyed an elephant fight, in which the contenders were sometimes more than 13 feet tall:

> They seem to justle together like two little mountaines . . . were they not parted in the middest of their fighting by certaine fireworkes, they would exceedingly gore and cruentate one another by their murdering teeth.[35]

What more could a weary traveller ask for, except perhaps to enjoy all this in the company of some friends from back home? In this, too, Coryate was blessed. A man named William Edwards was at court when he arrived, busy keeping alive the so far futile efforts of the East India Company to persuade Jahangir to grant them a trade deal. Coryate was able to lodge with Edwards, free of charge.[36] Then, in the autumn, Coryate received news that 'a deare friend of mine', Sir Thomas Roe, had docked at Surat, in Gujarat.

The East India Company (EIC) had established a factory at Surat in 1612 after battling the Portuguese at sea. But relations with the Mughals were not yet on a firm footing, and the EIC had become fed up with relying on chancers and freelancers to get things done. John Mildenhall was a case in point. He had negotiated with Akbar in Agra on the basis of fake diplomatic credentials, and then petitioned the EIC and King James for the equivalent of a consultancy fee, in opening India to trade. Mildenhall failed to make his fortune in the end, but he did make a name for himself. It was inscribed in Portuguese – 'Joa de Mendenal' – on what is thought to be the oldest English monument in India: a tombstone, placed in Agra's Roman Catholic cemetery sometime in or after 1614: 'Here lies John Mildenhall, Englishman . . . RIP'.[37]

The EIC later sent their own man, in the form of Captain William Hawkins, who was fluent in Turkish (one of the languages spoken in the Mughal Empire). The Portuguese had been worried enough about Hawkins to try to kill him on at least three occasions – so Hawkins later claimed, at any rate. They came at him with rapiers and pistols at a feast in Surat. Thirty or forty men later attacked him at his lodgings. And soon after he began his journey to Agra, he discovered a plot to poison him.[38] Narrowly escaping each time, Hawkins hired himself a bodyguard – fifty Pathan warriors on horseback – and made it to Agra in one piece, in 1609.[39] Jahangir enjoyed his company, and gave him an official rank in the empire alongside an Armenian Christian wife, Mariam Khan, from his *haram* – but not a trade deal. Boredom and alcohol did for Hawkins in the end. He made the mistake of appearing at court slightly the worse for wear, shortly after Jahangir – seeking to break his own habit of opium and wine – had instructed his courtiers not to drink. Hawkins received a public reprimand from Jahangir, and left India with his wife in 1612.[40]

Sir Thomas Roe was an altogether different prospect: aristocrat, Member of Parliament, experienced diplomat and now the royal envoy of King James to the court of Jahangir, charged with obtaining a *firman* (permit) to trade anywhere in India.[41] So pleased was he to see Thomas Coryate after his long journey that it seemed as though 'the fates have sent [him] hither to ease me'.[42] Coryate soon moved into Roe's quarters, continuing his lucky run of free expat accommodation.

Having broken into the court of Prince Henry thanks to his sense of humour and gift with words, Coryate hoped the same might be possible at the court of Jahangir. He set about polishing his Persian, until he was ready one day to appear before the emperor – dressed in Indian clothes – and bid for his attention, as the great man looked down on his court from a window high above. Coryate began by paying respect to Jahangir, as 'Lord Protector of the World', and to England, as 'the queene of all the ilands in the world'. He announced that he had come to India to see Jahangir, elephants and the Ganges, and to gain safe passage from the emperor to visit Samarkand and the sepulchre of Tamerlane. Coryate managed to work into his short oration a mention of the 3,000 miles that he had travelled on foot to be here: 'labour and toile, the like whereof no mortall man in this world did ever performe'. Jahangir humoured Coryate for a while, explained that he could not help him with safe passage (the rulers of Samarkand were no friends of his) and then tossed down some money from his window.[43]

Coryate was not displeased with this outcome. He had been swindled and robbed on his way to India, and was now pretty much penniless. A conversation with a legendary figure in world affairs, plus a hundred pieces of silver, was a good afternoon's work. Roe was less happy. He scolded Coryate for going before Jahangir like a beggar, doing considerable dishonour to his country in the process. Perhaps Roe was feeling a touch dishonoured himself: the shabby supplicant, of little account, as Jahangir stalled in order to weigh his diplomatic options – playing the Portuguese off against the English.

Thomas Coryate left the Mughal court in September 1616. He travelled to Agra, carrying on to Hardwar to witness people bathing in the Ganges. By November 1617, he was ill, out of money and perhaps low in spirits. He headed for the port at Surat, preparing to go home, and encountered there some English company and a great deal of fortified wine. Happy days were had, but they were his last. Thomas Coryate died at Surat in December 1617, probably of dysentery, and was buried there.[44]

Sir Thomas Roe returned to England two years later, sharing some unwanted company on the voyage home. Captain William Hawkins had left India with Mariam Khan, the wife bestowed upon him by Jahangir, back in 1611 or 1612. He had died on the way home, but Mariam Khan made it all the way to London, becoming one of the first women from Mughal India to do so.[45] There she remarried, to the ship's captain, Gabriel Towerson, and the two of them returned to India in 1617. When the Towersons arrived at Surat, they did so together with a newlywed couple called Richard and Frances Steele, the latter heavily pregnant, and a widow named Mrs Hudson, who had brought £100 with her to try her luck as a trader.[46]

None of this sat well with Roe. Neither he nor the East India

Company regarded India as a place for the stretching of female or infant legs. The EIC expressly forbade employees from taking wives out to India with them, on the basis that they were constitutionally unsuited to seafaring, would distract the sailors, and might bring bad luck. Soon, there was the added worry of what the Company might owe to a wife if she were to be widowed. Roe wrote to Surat from Jahangir's court, asking that Mrs Steele, at least, be sent home.[47] But the entire party made it to Agra, where Mariam's status as a noblewoman and former member of Jahangir's *haram* made it difficult for Roe to insist on anything. Coryate had observed of the *haram* that Jahangir 'keepeth a thousand women for his own body' – not, it seems, appreciating their noble status: they owned property, engaged in trade via middlemen and in some cases did private deals with the Portuguese and the English.[48]

Roe was left seething as Mariam and Gabriel Towerson started arriving at court with a small entourage of servants – no less amount of fanfare, noted Roe, than he employed as a royal envoy. Richard and Frances Steele, too, began living the high life. Richard hoped to persuade Jahangir to employ him to design a water system for Agra, and behaved at court as though he were a rival to Roe in status. Frances, by now expecting her second child, acquired her own coach, horses and servants, alongside a high-ranking new friend: Jana Begum, the daughter of a senior courtier. Frances would travel to her home in a chariot drawn by white oxen and attended by eunuchs, to enjoy fine food, conversation and the exchange of gifts.[49]

Exasperated, humiliated, Roe was only too pleased to leave India in 1619 – even if it had to be in the company of the Steele family and Mr Towerson, who had decided to return home. Mariam Towerson remained in Agra with her family, while Mrs Hudson sailed back to London nursing a large payload of goods to sell. The details of Hudson's entrepreneurship in India remain mysterious, but by making a short trip and then banking some cash she was blazing a trail for which young men in EIC employ would shortly become famous – infamous – both in India and in Europe. Jahangir helped lay the ground, giving Roe what so many of his predecessors had departed without: trade permissions. These were limited in scope, but back in England an old proverb was doing the rounds: 'give him an inch, and he'll take an ell' (an 'ell' being 6 handbreadths, or around 45 inches). Jahangir had given an inch. The EIC would be taking many, many ells.

PART TWO

Downward: Fathoming Asia
(1600 to 1910s)

Roberto de Nobili in Brahmin dress.

8.

In Search of Souls

Keen perhaps to reassure his mother that body and soul alike were holding up well on his travels, Tom Coryate roundly denounced, in one of his letters, the 'superstition and impiety most abominable' practised by 'brutish ethnicks . . . aliens from Christ and the common-wealth of Israel'. Tough talk, but his heart wasn't really in it. Such people didn't shock him – they fascinated him. Coryate had looked forward, at Hardwar's famous bathing festival, to the spectacle of hundreds of thousands of people washing in the Ganges. Some, he had heard, would throw 'a world of gold' into the river, in coin and in 'massy great lumpes and wedges'. There would no doubt be 'other strange ceremonies' besides, 'most worthy the observation'.[1]

The actual nature of heathen beliefs, and the fate of heathen souls, was of little interest to Coryate. Nor was it of much concern to the East India Company, as its Indian outposts began to multiply across the 1600s. This was the domain, instead, of that other – and at this point much greater – transnational organization: the Society of Jesus. Japan was off-limits to the Jesuits from the 1630s on, though a number of them managed to get in and minister covertly to their congregations. In India and China, risks of a different kind were taken. Delving into the thought-worlds of Brahmin and literati elites, in search of purchase, Roberto de Nobili (1577–1656) and Matteo Ricci (1552–1610) went beyond learning the necessary languages. They and their successors lived with – and *as* – the people they hoped to convert.

Indian and Chinese critics dismissed this as dishonesty, even play-acting. Sceptical Europeans predicted the rise of new 'Christian' communities, which would be full of people living immoral lives and indulging in the sort of strange ceremonial found amongst the Thomas Christians of the Malabar Coast. The arguments went back and forth in Europe for decades, all the way up to the Pope.

Europeans' appetite for travel literature meanwhile grew, as interest in Jewish and Islamic ideas, alongside ancient Greek, Roman and Egyptian gods, expanded to encompass cults and customs across Asia and the New World. Few readers at the start of the century would have countenanced comparing any of this with Christianity. It was deeply impious but also nonsensical to set God's self-revelation in Jesus Christ alongside beliefs and practices whose origins lay in some combination of human error and demonic inspiration. Nor had the mindset yet developed whereby something called 'religion' could be abstracted from a broader culture and offered up for comparison. Christianity was the stuff of everyday life in Europe: the God-givenness of nature, birth and death, right and wrong, good and evil. It was a landscape in which people lived, not a painting hanging on a gallery wall, open to appraisal from passers-by.

Still, an important dimension of the Christian outlook was understanding history in terms of the working out of God's purposes. Newly encountered parts of the world had somehow to be fitted into those purposes, and part of that task involved explaining how people living in them had come by their ideas about the divine. An influential early effort was made by an Anglican clergyman, Samuel Purchas. Drawing on travel accounts such as those of Ralph Fitch, *Purchas His Pilgrimage* (c. 1614) offered an account of the development over time of 'Heathenish, Jewish and Saracenicall' religions.

There was a polemical element to Purchas' project: he sought to demonstrate that 'Popish rites' were pagan in origin. Ten years later, Edward Herbert set himself the task, in *De Veritate* (*On Truth*, 1624), of exploring the 'Common Notions' to be found in 'every religion'. He suggested five: belief in a single Supreme Being, the obligation to worship that Being, the importance of living a pious and virtuous life, the requirement for repentance, and the reality of rewards and punishments in a life to come. Religious revelation of some kind was widely claimed, Herbert reported, but might be suspect on a range of bases: sheer implausibility, the risk that hallucination or the activity of evil spirits might be involved, or the potentially untrustworthy nature of self-interested priests claiming to be recipients of revelation. False revelation might cloud or confuse a person's pure and God-given capacity to apprehend the divine.[2]

Neither de Nobili nor Ricci sought a role in this comparative project. But their unprecedented attempt to fathom two advanced Asian cultures provided much fuel for it. It was thanks to Ricci and his successors that the teachings of Confucius and the lives of the literati came to be regarded in Europe as exemplary of the sort of universal human virtue that Herbert had in mind. De Nobili was often harsh about Brahminical religion, but he revealed its impressive depth and complexity to his readers. And by living as a Christian *sannyasin* – one of the 'naked philosophers' of old – he contributed to a deepening European questioning of Christendom. What was indispensable in religion, and what was a matter of mere trappings – clothes, rituals, beliefs, priests? What might a future religion look like, free from such things?

★

Arriving in Goa in 1605, de Nobili spent the early months of his time in India learning to speak Tamil in some of the Christian villages developed by Francis Xavier. When his superiors later moved him to the ancient city of Madurai, known to – and perhaps visited by – Megasthenes in the fourth and early third century BCE, he quickly saw why it was that a fellow priest, Gonsalvo Fernandes, had not made a single convert there in ten years of trying. Local people referred to Europeans as *farangi*: a Persian term derived from 'Franks', with unhelpful connotations of foreignness and barbarism. These Europeans ate beef, they drank alcohol, and they either had no concept of maintaining ritual purity or they simply didn't care.[3]

Thanks to some early conversations with Brahmin informants, de Nobili identified three groups of people in south Indian society. There were 'atheists', by which he appears to have meant Buddhists, such was the hostility felt by Brahmins towards this breakaway tradition – by now in steep decline. There was a mass of 'idolaters': people devoted to one or more lesser deities, whose beliefs were of little more interest to de Nobili than they were to Coryate. Finally, there were the Brahmins themselves. They were heirs, de Nobili came to realize, to an ancient and philosophically sophisticated system of thought and action: learned people seeking wisdom, of the sort whom the apostle Paul had encountered on his tour of the Graeco-Roman Mediterranean. Given the respect in which some of these Brahmins were held, their conversion to Christianity might lead to many more from lower down the social ladder.

De Nobili was convinced that if Brahmins could be shown how to inquire more rigorously into their own worldview, to which de Nobili believed his own philosophical education gave him superior access, they would in time discover its shortcomings.[4] The chances were slim, however, of Brahmins being willing to engage at this level with mere *farangi*. So de Nobili exchanged the Jesuit residence in Madurai for a modest mud house in the Brahmin area of the city. He swapped his black soutane for the ochre robes of a *sannyasin*. He began bathing in accordance with local custom and eating only once per day, cross-legged on the floor, with a banana-leaf for his plate. To prepare his exclusively vegetarian diet and do his laundry, he employed Brahminic helpers, thus maintaining the expected ritual purity. He also shaved his head, pierced his ears, carried a *sannyasin's* staff and applied the *tilaka*: a figure drawn on the forehead in sandalwood powder.[5]

With the help of a young Brahmin called Śivadharma, who advised him on the details and who later became a Christian, Roberto de Nobili thus completed his transformation into Tattuwa-Bhodacharia Swami: teacher of the true veda (knowledge), and the true dharma (righteousness in how one lives).[6] This was no temporary evangelistic disguise. De Nobili maintained his new identity even when travelling to meet fellow Europeans, and he refused any longer to associate with low-caste Christians amongst the Paravas.[7] When Brahmins came calling, de Nobili acted in what he saw as the manner of a true *sannyasin*, and refused to meet them on their first attempt. When he did finally grant them an audience, he insisted that he was not *farangi* (true, if one defined the term narrowly as 'Portuguese'), and that he was not preaching the *farangi* faith. He was *kshatriya* (warrior-aristocracy): second below Brahmin priests in India's four-tier system of caste.

With the help of his early converts, around fifty in six months, de Nobili learned Sanskrit, becoming perhaps the first European to do so.[8] This gave him access to the Vedas, parts of which he committed to memory, allowing him – in the Indian style – to illustrate his arguments in debate. He also adapted his teaching to match local variation where he could. Encountering worshippers of Shiva as the supreme deity, who believed that God sometimes takes on the bodily form of a guru, de Nobili presented himself as a man sent by the 'divine guru', Jesus Christ. Christ, he said, had come to earth both to impart knowledge and to live an exemplary life, not unlike a *sannyasin*: rejecting worldly wealth, and prepared to die an ignominious death.[9]

Called upon by colleagues to explain his evangelistic style and his allowing of Brahmin converts to retain aspects of their tradition, including the wearing of the sacred thread, de Nobili distinguished the fundamentals of faith from mere 'social customs' (*mores civiles*). In their original pagan settings, he pointed out, the exchange of wedding rings, the wearing of a veil by women and the crowning of conquerors with laurel leaves had all been freighted with superstition. And yet European Christians now practised them as customs nonetheless. The same, de Nobili argued, ought to apply in India. If a custom is not inherently sinful, then it need not be dropped. This could include wearing the sacred thread and *tilaka*, and growing a lock of hair on the top of the head.[10]

In his *Report on Certain Customs of the Indian Nation* (1613), written with the help of Śivadharma, de Nobili claimed that Indian texts such as the *Laws of Manu* were in fact mainly concerned with rules and behaviour. He went further: the Brahmins of Madurai were not priests at all, as Francis Xavier had imagined. They were – as Megasthenes had seen – philosophers, the elite scholars ('*doctores*') of their society. De Nobili included more than one hundred Brahmin affidavits to support his case.[11]

Whether out of conviction, or a desire to avoid the clutches of the Inquisition, de Nobili showed little sign of sympathy for what he did regard as the religious elements of Brahmins' lives. He rejected popular Indian imagery of multiple paths heading towards the same destination, or rivers meeting in a single great ocean. And he argued forcefully against the idea that the incarnation of God in Jesus Christ was comparable to accounts of 'divine descent' by Indian deities. The idea of Krishna being an avatar of Vishnu, for example, was simply an idolatrous mistake. Such things had their origins, argued de Nobili, in human frailties and failings. A mighty ruler demanding devotion might end up being recalled and worshipped as a god. The broken-hearted parents of a dead child might become the first devotees of an eventual cult.

Missionaries, thought de Nobili, should resist superstitions like these, while at the same time remembering that in Jesus Christ, God had decided to reveal himself in a way that Jews of 1,600 years ago would be able to understand. At the very core of Christianity, then, was the idea that the divine accommodates itself to local circumstances. The role of missionaries was to help things along, by discerning the difference between cultural accommodation and harmful error.[12]

Not all Jesuits were convinced. Living in Asia, and possessing linguistic skills that few could match, de Nobili, they concluded, wielded more power than was healthy. For him to adapt the new-year *poṅkal* feast so that the rice was cooked in front of a crucifix rather than an idol might be harmless enough, as a one-off concession. But make enough changes like that, including the writing of

Tamil hymns in classical Indian metre, and sooner or later you would be creating whole new liturgies. Purely linguistic concessions, too, came with serious potential problems. Some were obvious: one should not use a Portuguese-derived word like *Mīsai* for Mass in south India, because it sounded like the Tamil word for 'moustache'. In other cases, the dangers could be more subtle. For de Nobili to use the word *pūjā* ('sacrifice') for Mass risked allowing converts to remain caught in their old religious web.[13]

There was wisdom, argued some of de Nobili's detractors, in encouraging converts to wear European clothes – as was done during the early years of Christian mission in India. The aim was not to try to turn them into Europeans, but to make the point that true conversion was a radical act, and that some old customs had to go.[14] For many European missionaries that included caste: it was contrary to gospel teachings about radical human equality before God, and it left missionaries having to minister separately to different groups of converts – assuming that higher castes would agree to become Christians at all once they learned that Christianity was open to everyone.

Controversies over Jesuit attempts to accommodate Catholicism to Indian culture – especially the work of de Nobili – made it all the way to the Jesuit-educated Pope Gregory XV, who in 1623 gave provisional support to de Nobili's approach in an Apostolic Letter.[15] This was, however, far from the end of the matter. The question of how culture and religious truth relate to one another remained a bone of contention – and a source of great fascination – in the meeting of 'West' and 'East' for many centuries after De Nobili's death, at Mylapore in 1656.

★

In 1601, Matteo Ricci gave the Jesuits in China a first foot in the door at the Forbidden City. He owed the privilege largely to the reputation earned for him by his Chinese *Essay on Friendship* (*Jiaoyou lun*, 1595), which featured sayings on the subject from a selection of 'Western sages' including Herodotus, Aristotle, Cicero and Seneca.[16]

Where Roberto de Nobili worked, amongst south India's Brahmins, to piece apart acceptable customs and respectable philosophy from superstition and idolatry, Ricci's task in China was somewhat simpler. Idolatry and superstition were, in his understanding of China, primarily confined to Buddhism and Taoism, which held the bulk of the population in thrall. His target audience, on the other hand, was the literati.

The Confucian canon, in Ricci's day, consisted of the 'Four Books': the *Analects*, the *Mencius*, the *Great Learning* and the *Doctrine of the Mean*. The *Analects* was a collection of fragments concerning Confucius' life and thought, including his teachings on *ren* ('humaneness', or 'benevolence') and *shu* ('reciprocity'): 'What you do not want done to you, do not do to others'.[17] The *Mencius* was a compilation of the teachings of the 'second sage' of the Confucian tradition, Mengzi (372–289 BCE) – the name 'Mencius' was, like 'Confucius', a Jesuit Latinization.

Key themes for Confucius, further developed in the centuries after his death, included proper conduct in relationships with others, such as reverence for one's parents. One of the most impressive aspects of Confucian virtue, for Ricci, was that it was practised as an end in itself, and not with eternal reward or punishment in view.[18] Ricci came to regard Confucius as 'the equal of the pagan philosophers and superior to most of them', his excellent morality rooted in universal natural reason.[19] The literati's generally low view of Buddhism and Taoism meanwhile reflected well on them, though they made use of Buddhist rites for funerals, and some were inclined towards blending ideas from the two religions.[20]

By the time he arrived at court in Peking, Ricci had long since adopted literati dress. He wore robes of dark purple silk with a blue trim, and his hair and beard were cut in the appropriate fashion.[21] Ricci benefited, too, from literati interest in practical pursuits. The Ming Empire was felt to be entering a period of decline, and in response there had been a surge of interest, of late, in *shixue*: 'solid [i.e. practical] learning'.[22] Ricci's possession and understanding of recent European manufactures such as mechanical clocks, along-side his grasp of subjects from perspective and *chiaroscuro* in art to Euclidean geometry, helped to win him his audiences amongst the literati (the Chinese had possessed mechanical clocks for centuries, but they used water or sand rather than weights and pendula, as European ones did). It was to a pair of chiming mechanical clocks, which he brought with him to Peking, alongside a clavichord, that Ricci apparently owed his permission, gained from the emperor, to establish a residence and a church in the city.[23]

Critics of the Jesuits in China liked to point out that courtiers were more interested in their technical know-how than their God. But for Ricci, this was a false distinction. He presented all his learn-ing, spanning religion and natural philosophy, as a single package: *Tianxue*, or 'Celestial Teachings'. Creating a world map for the liter-ati, he challenged China's place in that world both literally and figuratively. According to the dominant Chinese understanding of the time, China was centrally positioned on a flat, square-shaped earth, at whose periphery sat smaller countries along with the Four Seas. The heavens, imagined as circular in shape, hovered above. Ricci left China at the centre of his maps, but he added oceans and other countries, portrayed in more realistic proportions on the sur-face of a spherical earth. He also let a few little lies slip into his revelation of cartographical truth. These included a notation added to the city of Rome, to the effect that 'all European countries revere' the Pope – an assertion likely to have been greeted with bitter laugh-ter back home.[24]

Of critical importance to the Chinese court was the ability of a spherical earth, situated at the centre of the cosmos, to offer an improved understanding of celestial events. Such events, and the correct conduct of the emperor in managing life below, were under-stood to be intimately interlinked. The accurate prediction of eclipses was essential: an unpredicted eclipse could be construed as ominous – not least by the emperor's enemies.

By the time of his death in 1610, never having personally met the Wanli emperor, Ricci's strategy had helped to win some high-ranking converts. These included the 'three pillars' of Chinese Catholicism: Xu Guangqi (baptized in 1601), Li Zhizao (1610) and Yang Tingyun (1611). Ricci's broader importance to the mission, beyond evangelism, involved discoursing on mathematics, cartography, astronomy and mnemonics (the last of especial interest given the requirement for literati to memorize the Confucian classics), while allowing the 'pleasant odour' of his faith to waft around the Forbidden City. By keeping the court happy, and allowing word to spread across China of the Jesuits' acceptance at the highest levels of society, he gave Jesuits elsewhere in the country the security they needed to evangelize and to confront Buddhist and Taoist rivals.

That security proved not always to be watertight. In 1616, six years after Ricci died, a senior mandarin in China's second imperial city, Nanjing, accused the Jesuits of residing in China illegally by passing themselves off as locals. Some of the scholarly ideas that they claimed to be teaching went against Chinese orthodoxy. They were using bribery to achieve conversions (the Jesuits would have described it as 'gift-giving'): paintings, prisms and clocks, for local elites who liked a bit of exotica. They were also, it was said, spying for the Portuguese.[25]

Arrests followed in Nanjing and Peking, and for a time it looked like Jesuits in mainland China might be forced to retreat to Macau. When news came in of renewed Manchu raids into northern China in 1618, some of the missionaries inclined to the view that these barbarous northerners – whose horses were rumoured to feast on Chinese flesh – were being used by God as an unlikely instrument of divine rescue. As Manchu raids were joined by banditry and peasant revolts, growing chaos across China in the 1620s and 1630s gave the Jesuits a chance to regroup and expand. By 1631, twenty-six priests were at work across eight of China's provinces. A few years later, around 4,000 people were being baptized every year.[26]

Much of this success came in rural China, where competition took the form of sorcerers and Taoist masters. Missionaries placed heavy emphasis on miraculous stories of the saints, incense and holy water, healings and exorcisms. And they worked with converts to create Buddhist- and Taoist-style devotional confraternities, led by members of the laity. Male catechists and informally employed women played an important role, the latter encouraged to evangelize by reciting or singing prayers while they worked. Hundreds of Chinese Christian texts were printed, making the most of China's cheap and plentiful printing technology and the absence, in a turbulent era, of effective censorship.[27]

Making converts amongst the literati continued to prove difficult, not least because of the enormous social and psychological barriers involved for them. Doing away with concubines, who might furnish a man with an heir, seemed strangely self-defeating. Removing ancestor tablets from one's home meant losing the means of paying filial respect.[28] The notion of Creation, brought into being and sustained by God, felt foreign for people who understood the universe to be governed by forces like *yin* and *yang*, and by the five elements, all operating within great cycles of time.[29] The idea of an immortal soul residing in a perishable body seemed implausibly dualistic, such was the Confucian view of the oneness of nature. And where de Nobili had had some success in India by suggesting that Jesus Christ's ignominious death was just what you might expect from the 'divine guru', China's literati found the crucifixion not so much moving as shocking. Corporal punishment was reserved for the very lowest in society.[30]

Concessions had to be made, and the major one was allowing converts to hold onto their ancestor tablets, as the focal point for what missionaries insisted were purely civil rites.[31] This seemed deeply unwise to some of the Spanish Franciscans and Dominicans who came to evangelize in China. They were accustomed to working in places like the Philippines and the New World, where force of arms generally obviated the need for accommodation to local practices or sentiment – in the darkest days, cultural interaction began and ended with smashing things up, or setting them on fire.[32] Chinese converts, they claimed, continued to believe that the spirits of deceased family members inhabited their ancestor tablets. Worse, they worshipped these spirits, in hope of protection or rewards. Rumours reached Jesuit ears of friars walking the streets preaching that 'Confucius is in hell'.[33]

The Chinese rites controversy became a counterpart to the Malabar controversy surrounding De Nobili. It, too, would reach all the way to Rome, doing serious damage to Christianity's prospects amongst the literati. For the meantime, the Jesuits were able to cling on to the position in Peking that Ricci had won for them. After Manchu armies took the imperial capital in 1644, they managed to persuade the first two Qing emperors, Shunzhi (reigned 1644–61) and Kangxi (1661–1722), of their value. Together with literati colleagues, they helped to assemble cannons, clocks and watches, advised on agriculture and architecture, and created maps, calendars and works of art – European art was scarcely less popular at the Qing court than it was at the Mughal court.[34]

It was clear by now that the conversion of China was going to be a long haul. Generations of Jesuits got used to the idea that having signed up to win Asia for the Almighty, their day-to-day lives were to be spent fixing clocks. The Kangxi emperor went as far as creating a workshop dedicated to the manufacture of Western-style ornamental clocks, known as the 'Office of Self-Ringing Bells'.[35] They could at least console themselves with the thought that despite its ups and downs, the mission was making progress. By the end of the 1600s, the first Chinese Jesuit priests had been ordained, the country was home to an estimated 200,000 Christians and thanks to an Edict of Toleration issued by Kangxi it was possible for evangelism and the practice of Christianity to carry on in peace.[36]

★

Missionaries in the decades after Ricci wondered about the morality of putting their learning to use in support of heathen beliefs and practices, helping literati at court to determine auspicious and inauspicious times for the conduct of imperial ceremonies.[37] In 1664, they discovered that there could be political risks, too. Enemies of the German Jesuit astronomer Johann Adam Schall accused him of causing the deaths, three years earlier, of the Shunzhi emperor and one of his consorts, by making an observational error that led to their dead child being improperly buried on an inauspicious day. Schall was found guilty of the death of Shunzhi, despite the two having been so close that Shunzhi referred to Schall as *ma-fa*, Manchu for 'Grandpa'. Schall only narrowly avoided execution by dismemberment, five of his Chinese assistants were beheaded, and all but four of China's Jesuits were confined to Canton, initially under house arrest. Schall was vindicated a few years later when Kangxi revisited the case, but by this time he was dead. His Jesuit colleagues had to wait seven years before they were permitted to resume their mission work.[38]

Risks aside, the primacy placed at the Chinese court on the practical value of cartography and natural philosophy, as opposed to its theological implications, at least helped to prevent controversies back home in Europe from damaging the Jesuits' position in China.[39] The authority of the Catholic Church was under challenge not just from Protestant rivals, but – implicitly, at least – from mathematicians and astronomers too. Ever since the apostle Paul had sought a hearing for the gospel amongst audiences brought up on Graeco-Roman thought, Christian writers had been making the case that God's revelation of Himself could be found in two 'books': the Bible, and the book of nature. Generous use was made of Psalm 19:

> The heavens declare the glory of God;
> the skies proclaim the work of his hands.
> Day after day they pour forth speech;
> night after night they reveal knowledge.

The likes of Johannes Kepler and Galileo Galilei agreed. Mathematics and astronomy were valid and successful enterprises because of the harmony that existed between nature and human reason, both of which were gifts from God. The famous controversy over Copernicus' heliocentrism theory, in the early decades of the 1600s, did not change that fact. The controversy was not so much 'science versus religion', as it would later be understood, as Galileo's hubris versus his own best interests. The Jesuit Cardinal Bellarmine, an uncle of Roberto de Nobili, was confident that the Church would accept the theory if it could one day be demonstrated. For now – and Bellarmine had looked through Galileo's telescope himself – he did not think that it had. Nor, for that matter, did Galileo. The Catholic Church condemned the idea in 1616, and after Galileo continued to advocate for it anyway in his writings – crossing an important line into scriptural interpretation and insulting Pope Urban VIII along the way – he was tried, condemned and made to recant.

Obedience to Rome prevented the Jesuits from teaching heliocentrism after 1616. Instead, from the 1630s they taught the system put forward by the Danish astronomer Tycho Brahe. This was a mathematically useful and theologically sound compromise between geocentrism and heliocentrism, in which the planets revolved around the sun, but the sun revolved around the earth. At the same time, they passed on some of the computational improvements resulting from the Copernican theory, and gave due credit for them to Copernicus – but without discussing the actual hypothesis involved.

In the early 1700s, Chinese scholars including Huang Baijia caught wind of heliocentrism nonetheless. One or more Jesuits appears to have spilled the beans. But Chinese astronomers continued to focus on calculating the movement of celestial bodies algebraically, for the purpose of creating accurate calendars. They did not worry overmuch about what any of it might mean for the cosmic importance or otherwise of human beings. The Jesuits' case for Christianity thus remained undamaged, if still apparently rather ineffectual at the highest levels in China. Meanwhile, they were able to keep from

Chinese eyes and ears the ridicule that some back in Europe were levelling at the Catholic Church over its stance on heliocentrism. Far more of a problem would be the Jesuits' inability to control the flow of information back the other way, from China to Europe – and the uses to which it would be put.[40]

Le Jardin Chinois. Engraving by Jacques Gabriel Huquier, after François Boucher (1742).

9.

China in Europe

They gather its leaves in springtime and place them in a shady place
to dry, and from the dried leaves they brew a drink which they use at
meals and which is served to friends when they come to visit.[1]

Matteo Ricci's description of the preparation and taking of tea in
China helped to feed early European fascination with what
seemed, to sceptics, like the drinking of slightly off-colour hot
water. In Japan, Alessandro Valignano had understood the cultural
importance of the tea ceremony, but remained bewildered by
the high value placed by regional lords on rustic-looking caddies
and cups:

> The [Lord] of Bungo once showed me a small earthenware caddy
> for which, in all truth, we would have no other use than to put it in
> a bird's cage as a drinking trough . . . he had paid 9,000 silver taels for
> it, although I would certainly not have given two farthings for it.[2]

Japan's naturalistic *wabi-sabi* aesthetic would not take off in the
West for many years yet. But already in the 1650s, trading ships were
returning to Europe from southern China laden with 'chaa', or
'chaw'. In the homes of English and Dutch elites especially, it
formed part of a stimulating triumvirate alongside Arabian coffee
and Mexican chocolate. Caribbean sugar enhanced the palatability
of all three.[3]

Market demand, especially as the drinking of tea spread down
the social order in places like England, put pressure on European
traders to gain ever better access to Chinese markets. And yet Qing

emperors showed little more interest in foreigners and trade than their Ming predecessors. The Portuguese and Dutch sent embassies to Peking early in the life of the new dynasty, only to be offered the usual tributary status, with its heavily circumscribed trading opportunities. Coastal trade opened up a little from the 1680s, but dealing with China remained more onerous than Europeans would have liked.[4]

Information about China flowed more freely, albeit heavily skewed by Jesuit self-interest. The country, Europeans were given to understand, was well-governed: from the venerated 'Son of Heaven' at the top, with his concubines and eunuchs, down through multiple layers of civil bureaucracy staffed by men of impressive learning. In case that bureaucracy should suffer bad apples or unfortunate episodes, another organization existed – the Censorate – to keep an eye on proceedings and report back to the emperor. Described by one of the Jesuit writers as 'keepers of the public conscience', the Censorate was permitted even to comment on the conduct of the emperor.[5] Little in need of such interventions, in European eyes, was the great Kangxi emperor (reigned 1661–1722). An important ally of the Jesuits, he was written about by them with particular warmth. China was also a peaceful place, so much so that in the late Ming era five times as much gunpowder had been used in firework displays than in any military activity. Its people were remarkable for their humility, chastity, industry, frugality and filial piety, paying great attention to manners, status and ceremony.[6]

The popularity of tea was helped early on by its association with this elevated civilization. The beverage was but one aspect, claimed the clergyman and essayist John Ovington, of the 'Genius of those People', whose national drink Westerners had begun sampling for the sake of 'Curiosity', 'Novelty', 'Pleasure' and its possible 'Medicinal Vertues'.[7] The likes of Ovington were the influencers of their day, writing with commercial kickbacks in mind: Ovington received a perquisite from the East India Company for his positive pamphlet on tea in 1699. Poets, satirists, physicians and painters took over where he left off, steadily working tea into everyday life – although with Asia less in mind: one would be more likely to find poets placing tea on the banqueting tables of Greek gods than in the hands of still only hazily understood Chinese deities or sages. Discussion of the potential health benefits of tea was likewise shaped by European rather than Chinese medical ideas. And far from being the centrepiece of silent ritual, as in Japan, the British were encouraged by taste-makers of the 1700s to take their tea around a table, accompanied by polite conversation – or, as Samuel Johnson put it, 'prattle'.[8]

As tea became ordinary, those left hankering after the exotic could look to porcelain for inspiration ('China-ware'; later, simply, 'china'), with its whimsical willow patterns and calming shades of white and blue. They could place orders for 'China paper' (or 'India hangings'), whose dominant motifs, painted with a lively brush in vivid colours, included people in Chinese dress alongside birds, flowers and bamboo. Much of it was created specifically for the export market on production lines in Canton: Chinese people themselves generally preferred plainer walls. And outlines were often block-printed rather than hand-painted, though few European customers would have realized. For them, China paper was special: rare, fantastically expensive, and clearly from a different world when compared with the fusty old tapestries that might be hanging nearby.[9] Those lucky enough to combine a love of *chinoiserie*, as it became known, with a decent amount of outdoor space could consider installing pagodas or arched bridges. Special occasions might call for silken mandarin robes, adorned with images of flowers and dragons. The Duchess of Dorset went as far as adopting her very own Chinese child: a boy by the name of Wang-y-Tong, upon whom she bestowed a classical education and who served her for a while as a page before returning to China.[10]

The taste of tea, the clink of porcelain, the brush of silk. For most eighteenth-century Europeans, this would have been about the extent of their contact with China. For some, however, the notion that at the other end of the world there existed an ancient, advanced civilization had the effect of focusing the mind. Might it have contributions to make to some of Europe's pressing dilemmas?

Cardinal Bellarmine had reassured a colleague in 1615 that the Catholic Church would accept heliocentrism if it could be proven. But in that same letter, he admitted that if heliocentrism *were* shown to be true then serious enquiries would have to be made into why scripture had been so badly misunderstood up until this point.[11] Though Bellarmine didn't say so, the problem went far beyond this single issue. A method of acquiring knowledge about the world was emerging, involving systematic observation of its measurable aspects, such that a lone astronomer might conceivably challenge a powerful institution like the Catholic Church. Protestants claimed that the Bible was self-authorizing, and the same would increasingly be claimed by natural philosophers about the book of nature: priestly interpretations would be neither here nor there. What was more, nature's secrets, once revealed, would prove less subjective, less elusive than religious knowledge of the kind that the Jesuits were claiming and proclaiming in Asia. 'Show me', Akbar had said, to missionaries preaching at the Mughal court. And they had been stumped. Make the same demand of Robert Boyle, laying down the foundations for modern chemistry in the second half of the 1600s, and he might invite you to a public demonstration.[12]

That demonstration – part experiment, part theatrical event – might well take place at the Royal Society of London for Improving Natural Knowledge, which Boyle had helped to found in 1660. The old institutional centres of Christendom had not gone away. State and church continued to work hand in hand, with political protection passing one way and divine legitimation the other. Europe's universities remained closely tied to established Churches, determining what might be taught there and who might attend (no Catholics or nonconformists at Oxford or Cambridge). Nor were those universities greatly concerned about having their monopoly on useful learning overturned: at the opening of Oxford's Sheldonian Theatre in 1669, the Public Orator to the university, Robert South, dismissed the fellows of the new Royal Society as men who 'can admire nothing except fleas, lice and themselves'. Still, more and more of Europe's intellectual life was happening away from old and venerable institutions, from public events at the Royal Society to conversations in coffee-houses. People referred to the latter as 'penny universities', for such was the cost of entering an establishment and gaining access to its books, newspapers and educated – or, at least, opinionated – clientele. This was the era of the gentleman amateur, too, promoting his discoveries in printed journals – with reasonable hope of being read abroad, thanks to a boom in translation.[13]

The possibilities were multiplying in Europe, for generating and sharing knowledge. But how to sift ideas coming in from elsewhere? Much was made, by universalists, of 'natural religion': an innate, God-given sense of the divine, guaranteed to shine through once cultural accretions were set aside. Ditto 'natural theology': a tradition of purely philosophical reflection on God, without recourse to revelation. Both were compatible with Christianity, but Europeans who were inclined towards scepticism about Christian revelation – some mistrusting, in the wake of the continent's religious wars, its institutional keepers – increasingly found in natural religion and natural theology more solid foundations for their outlooks. Missionary reports from Asia contributed, unwittingly, to this shift, providing example after example of cultures where an innate sense of the divine was obscured or corrupted by false beliefs, faulty understanding and unscrupulous priests. It was difficult to read such critiques without finding something familiar in them from Europe's recent history.

Universalism was one of two general responses in Europe to an intensifying awareness of the sheer range of thought and custom around the world. The other response emphasized difference, deep and fundamental. After reading Juan Gonzalez de Mendoza's account of China, the French essayist Michel de Montaigne (1533–92) scribbled the following about the country, in the margins of one of his own books:

[Here is] a kingdom whose government and arts, without dealings with and knowledge of ours, surpass our examples in many branches of excellence, and whose history teaches me how much ampler and more varied the world is than either the ancients or we ourselves understand.[14]

As with his famous line about cannibalism – 'each man calls barbarism whatever is not his own practice' – Montaigne was offering a slightly mischievous scepticism here, rather than what would one day be called cultural relativism.[15] And yet the implications were stark: if a civilization like China's could survive and thrive on the basis of ideas and social arrangements so distinct from those of Europe, did human beings share anything fundamentally in common? If they did – and here was a more positive way of looking at things – might China ride to the rescue, where European life and thought appeared to stand in need of renewal?

*

Dodgy priests, bloody wars, far-fetched accounts of the miraculous and growing knowledge of advanced civilizations far to the east. Here were four reasons why, for increasing numbers of Europeans across the 1600s, a plausible religious outlook was one that tilted away from revelation and Church authority and towards their own faculties of faith and reason. Problems remained, not least questions about where morality came from – where, indeed, *any* human ideas came from.

The mathematician and philosopher René Descartes (1596–1650) became synonymous with these sorts of questions. Drawing on Montaigne, he used cannibalism and China as two means of making the same point: culture and custom vary so much, across place and time, that we cannot consider them reliable sources of knowledge.[16] Descartes pioneered a rigorously subtractive approach to knowledge instead, doing away with whatever seemed potentially unreliable. He concluded that his own mental world (*res cogitans*) was undeniably real, its freedom and coherence ultimately guaranteed by God. Physical reality (*res extensa*) was qualitatively different. It was mechanistic, and known only imperfectly via the senses. To the extent that other people are part of that physical reality, each of us is alone.

A major advantage of this effective split between mind and matter was that it helped to free natural philosophers – the 'scientists' of the future – from any suspicion of impiety. They were exploring the world of matter, via measurement and observation, rather than presuming to include God or the soul amongst their objects of enquiry. At the same time, Cartesian 'dualism' raised a whole host of problems, in response to which China received its first call-up to perform philosophical service in Europe.

The Catholic priest and philosopher Nicolas Malebranche (1638–1715) set out to answer the question of how mind and matter, as completely different substances, could possibly affect one another. How could minds control bodies? How could the external world lead to images and ideas in the mind? Malebranche put God at the centre of his explanation: when a person decides to lift their arm and it lifts, God is the cause both of their will to lift their arm *and* its physical lifting. The conundrum of how spirit and matter communicate was solved by concluding that they don't: God underpins both.

A serious potential threat existed to this view of things, in the person of Baruch Spinoza (1632–77) – the 'impious Spinoza', as Malebranche called him.[17] Spinoza's response to Descartes was to suggest that the mental and the physical must in fact be two aspects of the same infinite substance, which in turn is identical with God. For this, and for his rejection of the notion of unique religious revelation, whether Jewish or Christian, Spinoza was accused of atheism and a fatalistic determinism.[18] Malebranche took these ideas on, via the unusual device of a *Dialogue between a Christian Philosopher and a Chinese Philosopher on the Existence and Nature of God* (1707).

There was a certain chutzpah to his project. Malebranche had not been to China. He had not met any Chinese philosophers. And he seems not to have read any Chinese philosophy. He had, instead, received a précis from some missionary friends, who hoped that he might supply them with some philosophical ammunition to help win over the literati. That précis included a key concept, *li*, from an eleventh- and twelfth-century revival in Confucian thought, which the Jesuits dubbed 'Neo-Confucianism'. *Li* referred to an order, pattern or unifying principle, which runs through all things. In the ethical sphere, a person can discern the right way to behave by stripping away false ideas or desires, clearly apprehending *li*, and then acting in accordance with it.[19]

Li first became a concern for Europeans during battles over Matteo Ricci's method of ritual and sartorial accommodation to Chinese life. If *li* was reducible ultimately to matter, then despite their much-vaunted ethical sensibilities the literati were, when push came to shove, materialists and atheists. Accommodation to Chinese culture would therefore be a bad idea. If, on the other hand, *li* was closer to divine reason, or God, then accommodation made sense.[20]

Malebranche thought along similar lines to Ricci and Roberto De Nobili. Reason was universal, so the evangelistic task in Asia involved working out Asian equivalents for European words and concepts and then using reason to demonstrate the superiority of European thought in key areas. Malebranche's *Dialogue* is essentially the story of a Christian philosopher managing to do just this. He persuades his Chinese counterpart to modify his understanding of *li*, in steps: from an ordering principle within matter, to a principle of wisdom inherent within nature, to a being that is wise, or intelligent. Finally, '*li*' is exchanged for 'God'.[21]

Critics of Malebranche observed that his 'Chinese philosopher' looked a little like Spinoza in a mandarin robe: this was really a European debate, with scant relation to Chinese ideas.[22] The same could have been said about the way that John Locke (1632–1704) recruited China to his cause, in his famous *Essay Concerning Human Understanding* (1690). Locke regarded claims about 'innate ideas' as false, including what Descartes called his 'clear and distinct idea' of God. Anything in our minds, Locke argued, will ultimately be traceable back to impressions received via the senses, with 'simple' ideas coming together to form 'complex' ones. Agreeing with those who suspected China's literati of being atheists, he offered them up as highly civilized proof that the idea of God was not, in fact, innate.

The only European philosopher of this era to go to any genuine depth with Chinese thought was Gottfried Wilhelm Leibniz (1646–1716). Where thinkers like Descartes seemed to raise the spectre of nature being merely mechanical, and morally neutral, Leibniz thought that he detected in the concept of *li* the coming together of laws of nature with laws of morality. More generally, he counselled Europeans to deal patiently and respectfully with Chinese thought. Chinese ethics, and filial piety in particular, had a great deal going for them – so much so that Leibniz wondered whether China might send missionaries to Europe.

In his grand vision of reality, Leibniz saw no need to choose between universalism and relativism. He argued that the world is made up of an infinite number of simple substances, which he called 'monads': like atoms, except that they are immaterial, and each possesses consciousness of a kind. Each monad has its own perspective on truth, meaning that multiple expressions of the same truth are inevitable – including at the collective, cultural level. The aim of philosophy, he thought, ought to be to gather in as many of these perspectives as possible.[23]

Big questions about reality ought to have broad appeal, but not everyone was equipped to plough through Leibniz or follow the calculations of Isaac Newton. That left an important role for people capable of popularizing, interpreting and connecting the major intellectual currents of their day. One of the greatest was Voltaire (1694–1778): critical, witty, eclectic in his reading and voluminous in his output – and probably the most important Sinophile of his generation.

Voltaire's first love was England, where a short period of exile yielded one of history's most incendiary travel reports: the *Lettres philosophiques* (1734), which contrasted an idealized English 'liberty', 'wise boldness', curbing of monarchical power, and religious tolerance with French 'slavery' and 'foolish superstition'.[24] England's open society, claimed Voltaire, had brought forth men like Locke, who '[did] away with innate ideas', and Newton: 'our Christopher Columbus . . . [leading] us to a New World'.[25] Their work could be disturbing in its implications. But rather than reach for the pitchforks, the English had let them go about it, even seeing fit to bury Newton in Westminster Abbey.

Newton was disturbing, Voltaire realized – as he waded into French controversies on the subject – because he appeared to have killed off the cosmos. For Aquinas and Dante, that cosmos was an intricate whole, animated by the divine Spirit. Newton's *Mathematical Principles of Natural Philosophy* (1687) claimed instead that a single force – gravity – was responsible for planetary movements and the falling of objects on earth. God's role was reduced to 'watchmaker', in the analogy used by Newton, Voltaire and many more in later years. He was the creator of that watch, granted, but thereafter was a little like a Jesuit in Peking: watching it tick, perhaps a little bored and morose, and then poking around if something went wrong. For Voltaire and other 'Deists' of his era, what God lost here in terms of romantic appeal he gained by sloughing off the unpleasant aspects of his biblical character: emotional, wrathful and relentlessly interventionist. The Deists' God, by contrast, was calm, thoughtful and benevolent. He was the sort of person one might find in a learned society.[26]

The English, thought Voltaire, might be on their way to creating a society based on the values that he so loved: education, reasoned argument, experimentation, tolerance, freedom and a rejection of the superstitious perversions of 'priestcraft'. But they were not there yet – Voltaire was well aware of the sometimes violent realities of life across the Channel. Was there anywhere in the world where one might find a society that was already predicated on these things? Where scholars, not priests, had the ear of the monarch? Where a clear-eyed and ethical apprehension of God had been preserved, free from idolatry and superstition? And whose longevity gave the lie to cynics who would try to tell you that no such utopia could survive for long?

There was. 'The people of China', declared the French Jesuit Louis-Daniel Le Comte in 1696, 'have preserved for about two thousand years the knowledge of the True God and honoured Him in such a manner as to serve as an example and model even for Christians.'[27] Le Comte no doubt intended these words as yet another affirmation of the Chinese literati's readiness for Christianity. And yet in the era of Deism, the 'True God' was no longer simply the property of Judaeo-Christian tradition. Important too, for Voltaire, was Le Comte's attribution to the Chinese of a system of government that was 4,000 years old, and as perfect now as it had been at its inception – 'As if God himself had been the legislator', wrote Le Comte.[28]

Voltaire put his pen to work, praising China in his *Essai sur les moeurs et l'esprit des nations (An Essay on Universal History, the Manners, and Spirit of History, 1756)*:

The spirit of order and moderation, the taste for science, the cultivation of all the arts useful for life, a prodigious number of inventions that make these arts easier, composed the wisdom of the Chinese ... If there was ever a state in which life, honour, and property were protected by the laws, it is the empire of China.[29]

Confucius was, Voltaire went on, 'neither medium nor prophet . . . but wise magistrate'.[30] Virtuous and well-educated too, he was Asia's answer to France's *philosophes* – and his intellectual descendants were running the show in their country.

There was more. A Chinese system of government dating back 4,000 years was impressive not just for its longevity. It was impressive because it shouldn't be possible – at least according to a biblical chronology of the world that was widely accepted in Voltaire's day. The Flood, in which all but Noah and his family were supposed to have drowned, was dated at around 2348 BCE. The building of the Tower of Babel, until which time humanity was thought to have been a single people, speaking a single language, was understood as having occurred centuries after this. And yet Jesuit research suggested that seven Chinese emperors had reigned before the Flood. Fresh calculations were hastily made, and the idea was mooted that Noah might have had a hand in founding Chinese civilization.[31]

Alongside helping Europe to break its biblical restraints, records suggesting China's antiquity impressed Voltaire because they included astronomical observations dating back as far as 2513 BCE. The Chinese had been natural philosophers from the get-go, it seemed. While other ancient cultures had spent their time inventing 'fables', wrote Voltaire, '[they] wrote their history with the pen and the astrolabe in their hand'.[32] In his play *L'Orphelin de la Chine* (1755), based on a Jesuit translation of a Chinese play – and performed in glorious *chinoiserie* costumes and set – Voltaire depicted the Mongols as barbarous invaders who were civilized by their contact with the Chinese.[33] There was hope, perhaps, for Europe.

*

Voltaire's passion for China, as a potential source of renewal, carried force because it was part of a more comprehensive vision for France, bringing together the religious, political and scientific concerns of the day. François Quesnay (1694–1774) likewise looked to China for inspiration on a grand scale, but he reached rather different conclusions. Nicknamed the 'Confucius of Europe' by his followers, Quesnay saw in China a country with a constitution grounded in natural law, where the role of the monarch was to preserve the harmony and balance – or *tao* – inherent in nature. An enlightened despotism of this kind, supported by a properly trained elite, in the mould of the mandarins, was just what France needed.[34]

Elevated views of China, such as those of Voltaire and Quesnay, were soon on the wane. A current of satire had always run alongside them, using China as a foil for European self-mockery. In the *Lettres chinoises* (1738–42), by the novelist and courtier Jean-Baptiste de Boyer, mandarins stationed around the world reported on the peoples amongst whom they were living. 'Sioeu-Tcheou' found Paris unimpressive: people were ruled by fashion and novelties,

women wore too much powder and make-up, high society toler-
ated adultery as 'gallantry', and key judicial roles were for sale rather
than being awarded on the basis of examination.[35] In a similar vein,
'Lien Chi Altangi', an invention of the Anglo-Irish author Oliver
Goldsmith, wrote home to China about Europe and London. He
described a continent whose history had been chaotic and too fast-
moving of late, and a city whose love of the exotic was a little
embarrassing. One woman confessed to him a 'violent passion' to
see him eat. 'Pray, Sir,' she said, 'have you got your chopsticks
about you?'[36]

By the time of Voltaire's death in 1778, the tide had turned against
both the Jesuits and the 'China' of their hopeful imaginings. Once a
great friend of the Jesuits, not least for his Edict of Toleration for
Christianity in 1692, the Kangxi emperor's patience was sorely tested
by the controversy in Europe over Chinese rites, most prominently
ancestor worship. In 1715, a papal bull condemned these rites, and in
1721 the emperor – who had backed missionaries in favour of accommodating Chinese culture – issued his response:

> Westerners are petty indeed. It is impossible to reason with them
> because they do not understand larger issues as we understand them
> in China. There is not a single Westerner versed in Chinese works,
> and their remarks are often incredible and ridiculous. To judge from
> this [papal bull], their religion is no different from other small, big-
> oted sects of Buddhism or Taoism. I have never seen a document
> which contains so much nonsense. From now on, Westerners should
> not be allowed to preach in China, to avoid further trouble.[37]

In 1724, Kangxi's son and successor, the Yongzheng emperor,
went on to ban Christianity entirely. A few decades later, a European backlash against the Jesuits also gathered pace. The downside
to being a transnational organization was that, sooner or later,
nation states began to resent your reach. Combined with an anticlerical mood in Europe and impatience with Jesuit interference in
politics, this was enough to see the order steadily expelled from

Portuguese, French and Spanish territories between 1759 and 1767, and then suppressed by the Pope in 1773.

Alternative sources of information about China had always been available, mostly less adulatory than Jesuit writings, and these now came to the fore – prompting Diderot to declare that Europe had been hoodwinked.[38] European travellers and merchants tended to deal not with senior literati but with Chinese traders and officials languishing at the very bottom of the bureaucratic ladder (at least some of whom presumably deserved to be there). They had formed, on that basis, a less-than-appreciative view of the Chinese character: cheats, thieves, dishers-out of prison beatings, gamblers with cards and dice, and idolaters willing to waste good food by setting choice dishes before images of false gods.[39]

Few educated Europeans of this era would have wanted to see their own countries judged on the basis of what the lower orders got up to. But even Matteo Ricci, who found so much to admire in China, was repelled by female infanticide, the castration of young boys so that they might work as imperial eunuchs (or 'semi-men', in Ricci's phrasing), the practice of slavery, and magistrates' sometimes tyrannical abuse of power.[40] Montesquieu had meanwhile wondered why such an honourable society needed to use corporal punishment on the scale that China did. Rousseau pointed out that China's vaunted refinement had offered little defence for the Ming against the Manchus.[41]

Even Europe's admiration of China's antiquity and stability had had its day. Born, in part, of the chaotic and violent nature of Europe's own recent history, that admiration was beginning to give way to an ideal of thrusting progress, for which China was not an obvious poster-boy. A long-serving literati class would soon morph, in the European imagination, into hidebound traditionalists. The philosopher Johann Gottfried Herder, a leading light of German Romanticism, described China in 1787 as 'an embalmed mummy, wrapped in silk, and painted with hieroglyphics'.[42] Two years later, the odds of France developing a strong monarchy along the Chinese lines counselled by Quesnay began to lengthen considerably.

Europeans' appetite for the exotic, and for answers to big questions as yet unresolved, was about to find fresh focus. Voltaire hinted at the new destination just a few years before he died. On classic anticlerical form, almost to the last, he declared:

> The rigorous Brahmins developed an inexpressible horror for our monks when they saw them eat flesh, drink wine and entertain young girls on their knees during confession. If their customs were regarded by us as being ridiculous idolatries, ours seemed to them to be crimes.[43]

If the austere promise of one civilization was now on the wane, another could take its place. India might have its darker side, and not every Brahmin was a saint. But there was life there: ancient, pure and primal. And Voltaire's great friends, the English, were beginning to tap the spring.

A View of Calcutta from Fort William.

10.

Calcutta

Calcutta in the 1760s wasn't every European's first choice as an expat destination. Jemima Kindersley spent time there with her two children and her army officer husband in the latter half of the decade, and found it a deeply frustrating place. Located on the Hughli River, around 80 miles up from the Bay of Bengal, it had its share of impressive sights. East India Company warehouses stretched for 3 miles up and down the waterfront, packed with muslin, silk, saltpetre and indigo. The old Fort William loomed protectively over the river, where cargo ships lay at anchor. And around the fort an attractive European enclave was growing up: bright white residential houses, some boasting verandas and generous gardens running down to the river.[1]

But the magic ended there. It seemed to Kindersley as though Calcutta's population of around 200,000 was 'daily increasing in size'.[2] The result was constant and haphazard construction: people building wherever and in whatever style they liked, with little consideration for 'the beauty or regularity of the town'. Part of the problem, thought Kindersley, was that the European 'white town', home to around a thousand people, had not been properly separated from the Indian 'black town'. The result was that 'the appearance of the best houses' was spoiled by the 'little straw huts' in which servants slept.[3]

One of the 'great inconveniencies' of caste, meanwhile, was that each worker confined themselves to strictly limited forms of labour, meaning Europeans had to employ three times the number of people who would have been required back home. This only added to the cost of living, in a town of high rents where biblical weather patterns – hurricanes, heat, lightning, 'hailstones I dare not tell you how large' – required Kindersley and her family to fork out for palanquins, carriages and horses to get around. Furniture was expensive too – and rare: people tended to pick and mix whatever they could find, or else enlist the help of 'blundering' local carpenters. Some sent orders to Bombay, but these apparently took around three years to fulfil, meaning that 'people who have great good luck generally get their houses tolerably well-equipped by the time they are quitting them to return to England'.[4]

That moment of return could, it seemed, not come soon enough for Kindersley. She decorously avoided including in her letters Calcutta's punch-houses and brothels – pictures and prices hanging off the doors – which were frequented by young Europeans there to make some quick money in private trade.[5] But she wrote of an extravagantly high death rate from diseases like 'pucker fever' (an extraordinary two-thirds of Company men in Calcutta never made it home).[6] And she seemed to sense tension in the air, noting rather darkly, though without delving into the subject, that while the English generally helped one another out, their parties occasionally turned 'violent'.[7]

Much had clearly changed about European, and particularly English, attitudes towards India in the century and a half since Thomas Coryate was there and Emperor Jahangir had granted the EIC its first trading permissions. A new relationship was emerging between the two countries, which appeared in Kindersley's writings as a curious mix of entitlement and responsibility. The success of England's North American colonies, its emergence as a constitutional monarchy in 1688, wars fought with Catholic continental powers and a newfound dynamism in discovery and trade all came together to produce, in Kindersley and others of her generation, a sense that world affairs favoured the English, and that this was nature taking its course.

Such an outlook was evident in Kindersley's account of the Mughal Empire's decline across the eighteenth century, and the rise of English (and later British) influence. Historians of the future would focus on the economic and political problems under whose weight Akbar's great cosmopolitan coalition began, during the reign of his great-grandson Aurangzeb (1658–1707), to collapse, leading to a reversion of some parts of India to smaller and frequently successful kingdoms. They would point to the way that the English East India Company and its French rival became adept at manipulating these kingdoms. Operating out of fortified trading stations – the English at Madras, Bombay and Calcutta; the French at Pondicherry – they supplied a mix of mercenaries, weapons and training in contemporary European warfare, in return for cash or revenue rights. Local rulers were often allies at first, but later became debtors and dependents, some of them dragged into Anglo-French conflicts that ended up being fought around the world: the War of the Austrian Succession (1740–48), and the Seven Years' War (1756–63).[8]

All this was coming to a head as Kindersley arrived in Calcutta. The city had been the last of the EIC's three main trading stations to take shape, its origins lying in the acquisition of land across three villages (Kalikata, Sutanati and Govindpur) back in the 1690s.[9] The growth and steady fortification of Calcutta led to conflict in 1756–7 with the Nawab of Bengal (the region's semi-autonomous ruler under the Mughals), and then again in 1764 with a broader Indian coalition including the Mughals themselves. British victories on both occasions ended up placing much of eastern India in the hands of the EIC. Where silver bullion had previously been shipped up the Hughli River to pay for the region's sought-after textiles and other goods, these could now be bought using land revenues collected by the EIC. A trading company had effectively become a government. And Calcutta was its capital.

In her own account of these momentous decades for India, Kindersley borrowed – indeed quoted at length – from Montesquieu. She depicted the Mughals as deteriorating, under the influence of India's hot climate, from 'hardy and warlike' invaders to worn-out despots. The people of India ended up doubly afflicted: by climate and by tyranny – 'the second man in a despotical government', noted Kindersley, 'is but the first slave'.[10] The result, at least in north India where Kindersley spent most of her time, was a population lacking justice, property rights and dynamism of any kind. She regarded this last as playing to the EIC's advantage, since the quality of Bengali textiles – cotton (muslin) and silk – owed much to the slow patience of their weavers.[11] But it was a tragedy for the country.

To make matters worse, 'the wise men of the East' had 'disappeared'.[12] While Europe's learned classes were making 'constant improvements and new discoveries in science', India's Brahmins clung to what their forefathers had handed down, while forbidding people from making enquiries of their own. The result was a religion 'overgrown with absurd and ridiculous ceremonies', and the abandonment of a naturally charitable and mild people to superstition, greed and deceit.[13] A Protestant disdain for priests loomed large here. India's 'Hindoos', wrote Kindersley, awaited a Martin Luther figure 'to open their eyes'.[14] Until then, the 'barbarous exertion of vertue' that was *sati*, the self-immolation of women on their husband's funeral pyre, was likely to continue. Though Kindersley conceded that she knew but little of the origins of this practice, she was 'certain' that it had something to do with Brahmin avarice. She pictured them loitering by the pyre, ready to relieve the women of their jewels once their bodies had finished burning.[15]

This high view of their own country – as free, vigorous, manly, inquiring and constitutional – fed into British commentary on India in conflicting ways. For the likes of the EIC's Robert Clive, one of the architects of British power in Bengal, the superiority of British arms was so overwhelming that he regarded his amassing of a personal fortune in India in terms not of out-and-out theft but as entirely natural and justified – accomplished, he thought, with considerable restraint, given that under the circumstances he could have taken a great deal more. For some parliamentarians and members of the public back in Britain, however, Clive's extraordinary wealth – which he pumped into everything from property and politics to Chinese art, becoming in the process one of Britain's first 'Nabobs' (a corruption of 'Nawab') – had been achieved by a thoroughly un-British regime of EIC brutality and corruption. Speaking in the House of Lords, William Pitt aired a widely shared concern of the era: that 'Asiatic principles of government' – by which he meant power rooted in wealth and self-interest, rather than concern for a country's people – might find their way back to Britain from India, and cause contamination.

Efforts were duly made at the reorganization and reform of the East India Company's operations in India. In 1773, the post of governor-general was created in Calcutta, elevated above the administrations in Bombay and Madras. A supreme court was established, on which would sit four judges. This was followed, in 1784, by the creation of a Board of Control in London, to oversee the political dimensions of the Company's affairs.

Aspiring to administer justice meant seeking out and trying to understand the different laws under which Indians lived. This required the kind of immersion in local languages and ideas that the Jesuits had pioneered some 200 years before. England's answer to the Jesuit strategist Alessandro Valignano was India's first governor-general, Warren Hastings. Fluent in Bengali, Urdu and Persian, he advocated language-learning amongst Company men both as an effective means of governance and a way of keeping them out of trouble – infamous as they were for spending their free time indulging in alcohol, gambling, opium, mistresses, prostitutes, tobacco, illicit money-making and violent crime (furnishing, in the process, the Supreme Court with some of its first cases).[16]

Two East India Company employees had already published influential work on Indian religion by this point: John Holwell, who served briefly as governor of Bengal, and Alexander Dow, who abandoned his stalling career with the EIC to become both a fierce critic of its corruption and a widely read communicator of newly emerging knowledge about India.[17] But Hastings found his most powerful ally in Sir William Jones, who arrived in Calcutta with his wife Anna Maria in 1783 to take up a judgeship on the Supreme Court.

A gifted linguist, Jones had picked up Latin, Greek, Hebrew and Arabic while at Harrow, moving on to Persian while studying at University College, Oxford, and making a name for himself with his publication of *A Grammar of the Persian Language* (1771). Jones was familiar, too, with Chinese literature in translation, thanks to the Jesuits' *Confucius Sinarum Philosophus* (1687). When compared with these riches, Europe's neoclassical culture and recent literature struck Jones as jaded and derivative.[18] In his *Essay on the Poetry of Eastern Nations* (1777), Jones urged Europeans to abandon their scepticism about Arabic and Persian (which tended to be regarded as lesser languages than Greek and Latin). Immersion in the beauty and passion of poetry in these and other 'Asiatick' languages could only be of benefit, he thought, to Europe.[19]

Literary pursuits alone did not pay the bills, and Jones had alighted on the law as the least-worst way of making enough money to build a life back in England for himself and his wife. He hoped, one day, to enter politics without need of patronage, being something of a democratic radical – advocating for universal manhood suffrage and producing poems and pamphlets during the American Revolutionary War in favour of at least de facto independence for Britain's colonies. Jones was notably less radical about India. Perhaps he paused to examine his principles when a letter arrived from his friend Benjamin Franklin, congratulating him on his India post: 'May [you] return from that corrupting Country with a great deal of Money honestly acquir'd, and with full as much Virtue as you carry out with you.'[20] But writing to Edmund Burke in 1784, Jones claimed that Indians were so unused to freedom that to impose liberty upon them would be a kind of tyranny. Government by 'absolute power' was the only way – albeit accomplished according to local laws.[21]

Arriving in Calcutta, the Joneses found the noise, smells and ferocious weather much as Jemima Kindersley had left them. But suitable accommodation was quickly found, and tranquil spots located by the river. There was Mughal cuisine, Bengali ragas and conversation with the city's intellectuals. Most important of all, perhaps, there was a like-minded group of people with whose help Jones could fulfil his dream of establishing an 'Asiatic Society'. Borrowing facilities from his day job, he brought together, in January 1784, a group of thirty founding members in the Grand Jury Room of the Calcutta courthouse. Jones laid before them his ambition for the collective study of more or less everything under the Asian sun, from India across to Japan: languages and culture, geography and natural history, mathematics and physics, botany and medicine, painting and poetry, music and architecture.[22]

Hastings declared himself too busy to accept the presidency of the society, leaving Jones to take the role instead, but he agreed with Jones on the benefits of gathering and sharing knowledge about India. Company men would have something productive to do in their spare time. The effectiveness and legitimacy of British rule in India would be enhanced, after the period of severe criticism back at home that Robert Clive had helped to inspire. Europeans would be encouraged, in time, to revise their generally low view of Indian culture. And Indians themselves would gain a clearer sense of their own inheritance.[23]

The business of fathoming India had broadened, across the last century, from dominance by Jesuits to the making of the first major Protestant contributions. In 1651, a Calvinist minister called Abraham Rogerius, working for the Dutch East India Company, had converted ten years' of observations and conversations with south Indian Brahmins into an influential (if unflatteringly titled) guide to their religion. *The Open Door to Hidden Heathenism* dealt with caste, Brahmin rites of passage and daily rituals, customs including *sati*, and what Rogerius understood to be a combination of a basic monotheism with a polytheistic mythology.[24] His book was soon translated from Dutch into German and French.

In the early eighteenth century, Pietist Lutheran missionaries had arrived in the south Indian city of Tranquebar, where the Danish East India Company enjoyed a modest presence.[25] Amongst them was the German theologian Bartholomäus Ziegenbalg, whose writings confirmed the optimistic Dutch view of Brahminical religion. Ziegenbalg was told by an Indian convert to Christianity that Europeans viewed Indians as polytheists only because monotheism was regarded by Brahmins as an elevated truth, not readily to be shared.[26] France's first major contribution to understanding India meanwhile came in the form of its pioneering Indologist A. H.

Anquetil-Duperron. He hoped that his Latin translation of a highly regarded Persian collection of fifty Upanishads, published in 1802 as *Oupnek'hat* (from the Persian for 'Upanishad'), would become a means for European philosophers to engage seriously with Indian thought.[27]

The Asiatic Society was a step on from all of this: in access to Brahmin informants and religious texts, in the range of projects taken on, and in the wide Western readership enjoyed by the society's publication *Asiatic Researches* – to which Indian alongside European scholars contributed, although the first Indian members of the society were not admitted until 1829.[28] When the first issue was published, in 1788, 700 copies were shipped to Europe, including one for King George III, who pronounced himself pleased with progress.[29]

Jones' own contributions began with language, and moved outwards from there. Not entirely trustful of the Brahmin scholars (or 'pandits') who assisted him in matters of local law at the Supreme Court, he took up the study of Sanskrit for himself in 1785. Few Brahmins were willing to teach the 'language of the gods', as it was often called, to just any old foreigner, and it took a while for Jones to find a (non-Brahmin) teacher who was willing to take on the task. Later accounts of Jones' relationship with his teacher Rāmalocana, no doubt heavily romanticized, depict a quick-tempered scholar who insisted on teaching Jones in a marble-floored room – the easier to cleanse it of his polluting presence afterwards, using Ganges water – and who refused to allow him breakfast before lessons began. Jones apparently had to beg to be allowed a cup of tea.[30]

Whatever the real nature of this enduring relationship, the results were profound. The more Jones explored Sanskrit, the more he was struck by close similarities – not least in vocabulary – with Europe's classical languages. He was soon able to declare Sanskrit the beautiful lost sister of Latin and Greek, claiming connections, too, with languages as diverse as Gaelic and Albanian. The implications were stunning. India was not some far-flung place that Westerners were just now getting to know. It was 'family'.[31]

Jones was not the first European to spot connections between

Greek, Latin and Sanskrit: the Jesuits had noted them more than a hundred and fifty years before. Nor was he the first to recognize the existence of language groups, or evolution over time: the comparative study of Latin and European vernaculars was already under way, and a scholar in the Netherlands had suggested that Latin, Greek, Sanskrit and other languages likely shared a common root.[32] But Jones' methodical and evidential approach – in establishing true cognates between languages rather than mere similarities – was new, and lent credibility to his work. His pre-existing reputation as 'Orientalist Jones' helped, too, as did his talent for disseminating his findings, including his theory of what would become known as the 'Indo-European' language family.[33]

Having established common linguistic ancestry, Jones tried to bring India into a universal account of history, drawing on a combination of European classical authors, the Bible and newly emerging Brahminical sources. These last revealed impressive achievements in astronomy and astrology, leading Jones to suggest that the Brahmins and the ancient Greeks had learned about the stars from the same speculative 'older nation'. Whether for personal or political reasons he adhered, in public at least, to the prevailing European assumption that all the nations of mankind were descended from the sons of Noah: Shem, Ham and Japheth.[34]

Working with Indian scriptures, Jones identified Brahma with the Judaeo-Christian God, Manu with Adam as the first created mortal, and a second Manu with Noah. After the Flood, he claimed, Noah's family had most probably settled in northern Persia. Their descendants had fanned out across the world from there, speaking the common ancestor language – since lost – of Latin, Greek and Sanskrit. Borrowing an idea that he encountered amongst Brahmin interlocutors, Jones suggested that the people of China were originally members of the *kshatriya* (warrior) caste in India, who at some point had abandoned life there and gone wandering off eastwards.[35] Taking all this together, Jones felt confident that India's history went back not much further than 2000 BCE – comfortably after the popular date for the biblical Flood, of around 2348 BCE. Any suggestions of an older history for India were, he concluded, most likely mythological.[36]

Jones' attempt to bring India into the same history as Europe included a foray into comparative mythology. Where Megasthenes had suggested that Greek and Indian gods were in some cases one and the same, known by different names, Jones confined himself to pointing out parallels between Graeco-Roman and Indian deities: between, for example, Janus and Ganesha (gods of wisdom) and Jupiter and Indra (gods of sky and thunder).[37] When it came to philosophy, Jones was prepared to go further. The similarities between the Vedānta philosophical school on the one hand and Pythagoras and Plato on the other struck him as too perfect to be mere coincidence. The thought intrigued Jones that Pythagoras might have travelled eastward towards India in his lifetime.[38] At the very least, the ancient Greeks must, he concluded, have derived their wisdom ultimately from the same source as the sages of India.[39]

*

Omniscient Spirit, whose all-ruling pow'r
Bids from each sense bright emanations beam;
Glows in the rainbow, sparkles in the stream,
Smiles in the bud, and glistens in the flow'r
That crowns each vernal bow'r;

Sighs in the gale, and warbles in the throat
Of ev'ry bird, that hails the bloomy spring,
Or tells his love in many a liquid note,
Whilst envious artists touch the rival string,
Till rocks and forests ring.

William Jones, 'A Hymn to Nárávena'[40]

By the end of the eighteenth century, members of the Asiatic Society were engaged in a wide variety of activities: conversations with Brahmins, collecting artworks, taking trips to see great temples, making translations of stories and plays, putting together botanical collections, learning advanced algebra and exploring Ayurvedic medicine.[41] Christianity being a religion of the book, their expectation for highly developed religions was that texts would be central. They were aware of the four Vedas, and they shared the French Indologist Anquetil's high regard for the Upanishads.

Amongst the earliest texts that lay outside the Vedas were the Dharma-shastras. These were books on correct conduct, one of which, the *Manusmriti* (*Laws of Manu*), was translated by Jones for the use of the Supreme Court. Alongside these ran stories of the gods, varying across the subcontinent but often with central roles for what came to be called the *trimurti* ('trinity'): Brahma the creator, Vishnu the preserver and Shiva the destroyer (often appearing as the cosmic dancer). Other popular deities included Vishnu's wife Lakshmi, goddess of wealth and good fortune, and Shiva's son Ganesha, usually depicted with an elephant's head.

Two great Sanskrit epics came together between 300 BCE and 300 CE. The *Rāmāyana* (*Rama's Journey*) told the story of the deity Rama, an avatar of Vishnu, including the kidnapping and rescue of his wife Sita. The *Mahābhārata* (*Great Epic of the Bhārata Dynasty*) centred around five brothers, the Pandavas, waging war against other members of their extended family. The best-known section of the *Mahābhārata*, in Jones' generation and afterwards, was the *Bhagavad Gita* (*Song of the Lord*): an encounter between one of the Pandava brothers, Arjuna, and the deity Krishna, another avatar of Vishnu. It begins with Arjuna's anxieties about an imminent battle, in which much blood will be spilled, and turns into a philosophical discourse on how to live.

Most Indians, not much concerned with Brahminical rites or the intricacies of the law, drew devotional inspiration from the *Rāmāyana* and the *Mahābhārata*, alongside a vast literature called the Puranas, early elements of which had been emerging in the time of Megasthenes. Composed in Sanskrit and regional languages, they featured stories of gods, kings and much else besides, including a cosmology that placed Mount Meru at the centre of the universe, with various worlds ranged around it into which beings may be reborn. It was in this literature that the great gods of popular theism gained their status. A great many Indians were Shaivites or Vaishnavites: worshippers, respectively, of Shiva and Vishnu as the supreme deity. A third major sect was Shaktism, for whose members Mahadevi, the mother goddess, was supreme.

Earlier generations of Europeans in India had heard stories of these gods, and witnessed their worship. They had seen little point, however, in probing the inner logic of what they regarded as heathenism. Jones and his generation were different. He made use of the Puranas in working out his world chronology, and he brought to bear a talent for poetry in composing hymns to gods like Náráyena (or 'Narayana': one of the forms of Vishnu, variously imagined as floating on or under primeval or celestial waters). These he would read before the Asiatic Society in Calcutta and then commit to print, in which form they circulated around Europe and the United States, inspiring, amongst others, Lord Byron and Ralph Waldo Emerson.[42] Jones' translation of the play *Abhijnanashakuntala* (*The Recognition of Shakuntala*), by the great poet and playwright Kālidāsa (fifth century CE) – whom Jones regarded as the 'Indian Shakespeare' – had a greater impact still: both in his English original and via the French, German and Italian versions that were soon created.[43]

Here was a pattern set to continue into the nineteenth and twentieth centuries: the attractiveness to Westerners of Indian, Japanese and Chinese ideas often relied heavily on the presentational – including the poetical – talents of contemporary writers, from both Asia and the West. What interested those writers to begin with also made a great difference. Thomas Coryate's dismissal of Islam during his confrontation in Multan owed much to the powerful disdain for rival religious traditions that characterized corners of English Protestantism in his era – he was no kinder about Catholicism during his travels in mainland Europe. And yet Coryate's comments also reflected a lack of interest in Islam amongst most Europeans travelling to Asia. The Portuguese in sixteenth-century

India tried to understand, as a matter of pure pragmatism, what differentiated Sunni from Shia. But they otherwise showed little interest in Islam as it was practised on the subcontinent.[44] Nor did many of their English counterparts in William Jones' era, though Jones had a deep love of Persian poetry and (Sufi) mysticism.

The distortions that occurred as a result of Europeans' selectivity were exacerbated by their tinkering with terminology. At the most basic level, for all the talk of 'Hindoos' and 'Hinduism' in Jones' era, there was no such religious tradition in India. The word 'Hindu' came from a Persian form of the Sanskrit word 'Sindhu' (Indus), which had been used – since the time of Herodotus, and from a Persian perspective – to designate the people who lived beyond the Indus River.[45] Europeans came to use 'Hindoo' (alongside 'heathen' and 'Gentoo') to refer to people living in that part of the world who did not belong to clearly defined and well-understood traditions like Christianity, Judaism and Islam. It basically meant 'none of the above', though it came to be associated in particular with the texts and practices of Brahmins – amongst the most respectable of religious interlocutors, as far as Westerners stretching back to Alexander the Great were concerned – with philosophical schools like Advaita Vedānta, and with myriad popular religious practices across the subcontinent (of which Europeans had, as yet, very little understanding).[46] Jainism and Sikhism were both commonly understood by Europeans, across much of the colonial era, as reformed varieties of Hinduism.

This account of Hinduism became bound up with a highly influential version of India's broader religious history. Long ago, it was claimed, this had been a great civilization, capable of producing the Vedas, the Upanishads, the *Mahābhārata* and the *Rāmāyana*, along with schools of philosophy whose diversity rivalled that of ancient Greece. Those achievements had thankfully survived, but most Indians were now in thrall to superstition – a conjecture based on so-far scant observation of the country's religious practices. The early nineteenth-century Bengali writer and reformer Ram Mohan Roy was amongst those who would challenge this version of events.

He did, however, adopt the term 'Hinduism' to describe his own tradition. Its use became increasingly commonplace thereafter.

Where early missionaries had rarely sought wisdom in India, modern secular Indologists, raised in a more liberal religious climate, could simultaneously be devout Christians and remain open to what India had to offer – at least at the level of poetic or philosophical insight into the divine. Jones' own faith was nourished by the beauty that he found in the natural world and in poetry.[47] Introducing his 'Hymn to Náráyena', Jones claimed that 'many of the wisest among the Ancients and some of the most enlightened among the Moderns' believed that 'the whole Creation [is] rather an *energy* than a *work*'. The world's ultimate reality could not be expressed via some 'vulgar notion of material substances'. It was more 'like a wonderful picture or piece of music', conjured in the minds of creatures by the divine.[48]

European readers would have spotted some familiar themes here. Jones talked about the deity Náráyena in recognizably Christian language: as 'the spirit of God . . . moving on the water'. Meanwhile, his broader evocation of pictures or pieces of music recalled Plato and the Idealist philosopher George Berkeley (1685–1753). The latter was known in his day for opposing John Locke's sensory theory of knowledge, which relied on what Berkeley charged was an untenable distinction between two sorts of 'qualities'. Primary qualities, thought Locke, belong to objects in the world: solidity, for example, or motion. Secondary qualities are relative, because they derive from the effect that these objects have on the human mind: colour, smell, etc. Berkeley argued that both primary and secondary qualities are in fact relative: we infer solidity and motion in objects – they don't actually 'possess' these qualities. If you pursue this thought to its proper conclusion, he argued, even objects themselves turn out to be bundles of ideas, dependent on the minds that perceive them. 'Materialism' and 'matter' end up being incoherent concepts.

Supporters of various strands of Idealism – the claim that the world is fundamentally made up of ideas rather than mind-independent 'stuff' – would, in the generations after Jones, find support in Indian and other Asian philosophies. Jones himself, however, was always a poet rather than a philosopher. His 'Hymn to Náráyena' captured the working of the divine spirit, intuited first in the wonders of nature and then – by the end of the poem – grasping the poet in a more direct, infinitely fulfilling way:

> Delusive Pictures! unsubstantial shows!
> My soul absorb'd One only Being knows,
> Of all perceptions One abundant source,
> Whence ev'ry object ev'ry moment flows:
> Suns hence derive their force,
> Hence planets learn their course;
> But suns and fading worlds I view no more:
> God only I perceive; God only I adore.[49]

Jones was less concerned with the permissibility or otherwise for Christians of imagining God and the human soul to be in some sense identical than with persuading fellow Europeans of the exalted view of the divine that had emerged in parts of Asia. In a talk for the Asiatic Society entitled 'On the Mystical Poetry of the Persians and Hindus' (1791) he praised works of philosophical poetry that he regarded as springing from 'the ardent love of created spirits towards their beneficent Creator'.[50] In this poetry one can find, he said, the idea that 'the souls of men' differ not in kind but only in degree from the 'divine spirit' – 'of which they are particles, and in which they will ultimately be absorbed'. The material world, and our attachments herein, are by comparison illusory. We may become so bound up with the material world that we forget this deeper, original identity. But 'sweet music, gentle breezes, fragrant flowers, perpetually renew the primary idea, refresh our fading memory, and melt us with tender affections', until the day of our 'final union' and 'supreme beatitude'.[51]

The prime example of such ideas in Persian literature, thought Jones, was the work of the fourteenth-century poet Hafez. In Indian literature, one found it most profoundly in the twelfth-century devotional poet Jayadeva, in the Upanishads, and in the *Bhagavad Gita*. This last became, in 1785, the first major Sanskrit work to be published in a European language.[52] It was produced, with Warren Hastings' encouragement, by an EIC officer named Charles Wilkins, who had learned Sanskrit while on health leave in Varanasi.[53] Wilkins' work introduced generations of Europeans to the insights of the Upanishads, on which the Gita draws. Krishna teaches Arjuna that the Self or soul is indestructible: 'As a man throweth away old garments, and putteth on new, even so the soul, having quitted its old mortal frames, entereth into others, which are new'. Each person has their own 'natural duty' in life (*dharma*), whose performance – focusing on action rather than outcomes – is the path to God. By living moderately and 'long[ing] after the Divine and Supreme Being, with his mind intent upon the practice of devotion', a person may at death 'goeth unto him'. Towards the end, Krishna asks: 'Hath what I have been speaking, O Arjoon, been heard with thy mind fixed to one point? Is the distraction of thought, which arose from thy ignorance, removed?'[54] Future generations of Western meditators, grappling with a range of Asian practices, would come to understand Krishna's question – and warning – only too well.[55]

★

'A Hymn to Náráyena' came to be considered one of the first works of Romantic poetry. Ludwig van Beethoven copied some of its verses into his diary, alongside extracts from the *Bhagavad Gita*.[56] Arthur Schopenhauer found both inspiration and solace in Anquetil's translation of the Upanishads. Goethe praised the drama *Shakuntala*. And Samuel Taylor Coleridge lauded the depth of reverie captured in the image of Vishnu floating on an infinite ocean. The contours were coming into view, of the modern West's love affair with Indian philosophy and poetry.

This was, however, an affair born and destined to continue in controversy. In his prefatory letter, published with the *Bhagavad*

Gita, Warren Hastings praised Indian literature as eminently worthy of study in its own right: the *Mahābhārata* was up there, he claimed, with the *Iliad* and parts of Milton. But it also served a purpose: 'it is on the virtue, not the ability of their servants', he wrote, 'that the Company must rely for the permanency of their dominion . . . [which is] founded on the right of conquest'. Immersion in Indian literature would help to cultivate that virtue, and so shore up dominion. 'Every accumulation of knowledge', Hastings added, thinking about the broader picture, 'is useful to the state.'[57]

It would be wrong to paint Hastings as a cynic. Colonial rule and an affection for Indian literature were not mutually exclusive. And yet the transmission of wisdom from India to the West was clearly not without taint. Nor was that all. From the time of William Jones onwards, there was a distinct tendency, in Western translation, editing and commentary on Indian texts, to favour its contemplative, recessive and self-sacrificing aspects. These were worthy threads in Indian thought. And it is not hard to see why late eighteenth- and nineteenth-century Westerners disillusioned with interminable religious debates back home might feel an attraction towards them. But commentators including Jemima Kindersley liked to claim that restoring and protecting the natural gentility of the 'Hindoos', following centuries of abuse at the hands of Mughal despots, had become a special responsibility of the British.[58] Gentle, spiritual Indians, absorbed in their divine; hardy, moral Britons, watching over them. The poetry and philosophy of India had the potential not just to lift Westerners up, but to keep Indians down.

Shakuntalā Removing a Thorn from her Foot, painting by Raja Ravi Varma (1898).

Germany's Oriental Renaissance

William Jones died, exhausted, in 1794, at the age of just forty-seven. He had planned to be in and out of Calcutta within a few short years, wealthier and wiser. Instead, the town's South Park Street burial ground became his final stop in life. The images of India, on the other hand, which he and his fellow orientalists conjured in their writings, travelled far further and were much longer-lived. Together with fresh accounts of India penned by visitors and Christian missionaries, they circulated around a Western world marked by revolutions won and lost, the building of empires, and a search for renewal conducted across poetry, philosophy and religion.

For Jones' countrymen, interest in India was bound up with shifting views on the politics and morality of Britain's presence there. By contrast, German explorers of India's potential riches were shaped by the French Revolution: the idealism that underpinned it, what the philosopher Friedrich Schlegel called the 'gruesome chaos' that ensued, and the notion of unified and purposeful nationhood, which Germany had yet formally to attain.[1]

Philosophy found itself front and centre here, with Immanuel Kant (1724–1804) trying to shore up the Enlightenment project by showing how such a thing as human reason really did exist – and that it was not just the combining and recombining of sense data, within a deterministic universe. What Kant called his 'Copernican Revolution' placed a powerful human mind at the centre of everything. Space, time and causality are not objective features of reality, he argued; they are categories applied by the mind, as part of its profound role in shaping sensory information as it comes in. Thanks to this mind, we know right from wrong, and are free to act accordingly. We discern regularity, even purpose, in nature. And on rare, blessed occasions we experience a sense of the sublime and of 'boundlessness', running far beyond our everyday attempts to compass the world with our thoughts. All of this combined, claimed Kant, gives us reason to suspect the existence of a divine order, which is both moral and beautiful. And yet we can't *know* this to be the case. The mind is powerful, but it is also a prison: we cannot break out and gain direct knowledge of the world beyond.

Much of the poetical and philosophical interest in India that developed in the late 1700s and early 1800s, not just in Germany but also amongst Romantics in Britain, was indebted to Kant's vision of reality. Some took up its hopeful aspects, including the 'sublime'. Others, notably in Germany, sought to wriggle free of the strictures that he seemed to be placing on human knowing. Amongst those who looked to Indian sages, philosophers and dramatists, either for inspiration or for ancient corroboration of their own ideas and intuitions, were some of the giants of German literature and thought: Goethe, Schelling, Hegel and Schopenhauer.

None were out-and-out Indophiles. For all the lofty metaphysics and sensuous, nuanced storytelling that they found on offer in India, drama of other kinds seemed lacking. Where was the prophetic call to live a moral life? Where was the dynamism and sense of purpose with which the Judaeo-Christian tradition invested historical time? It might be that India's sages had tapped an eternal wellspring, on which humanity ought, still now, to try to draw. For those, however, who were committed to the idea of progress across human history, it seemed more likely that those sages had furnished the first chapter of a grand, global story in which the action had long-since moved elsewhere.

*

'An embalmed mummy, wrapped in silk, and painted with hieroglyphics.' Johann Gottfried Herder had delivered his harsh verdict on China in 1787, just as Europe was on the cusp of changing its mind about the country. Unflattering travellers' reports played their part, as the Jesuits' lauding of the literati was revealed to be a decidedly partial take on Chinese life. Continued frustrations in trade loomed large, too, as did diplomatic disappointment, most notably the failure of Lord Macartney's mission to China in 1792–3.

Charged with establishing diplomatic relations and a more favourable commercial relationship, Macartney's audience with the Qianlong emperor went famously awry. He refused to perform the ritual kowtow, and Qianlong sent him back to his king bearing a message that amounted to a masterclass in disdain. China had need neither of George III's trade in trinkets nor the presence in Peking of his representative. Qianlong was prepared to excuse King George for his 'ignorance' of China's affairs and for 'wrong-fully importun[ing] my ear' with his requests, attributing it to 'the lonely remoteness of your island, cut off from the world by inter-vening wastes of sea'. He would not, however, be so understanding in the future: 'Tremblingly obey, and show no negligence!'[2]

John Barrow served as Lord Macartney's private secretary on the ill-fated mission, and later published *Travels in China* (1804), in which he conjured a cruelly unjust society marked by tyranny at the top and poverty and resentment at the bottom. He blamed bad governance – on the part of the Chinese, naturally, not the British, who had for decades been allowing the East India Company to ship Indian opium to southern China in hope of narrowing an enor-mous trade deficit.[3] By the 1820s, enough opium was entering China to sustain a million people's habits, adding the image of a drug-addled citizenry to the debit column of a country once regarded in Europe as a kind of utopia.[4]

Still, Herder's comment about an 'embalmed mummy' was more than simple Sinophobia. China, for Herder, was an example of what happens when a society stops 'growing'. As a Lutheran pastor who had studied under Kant at the University of Königsberg, Herder was in search of a meaningful and intellectually robust account of God and God's action in the world. The old-school interventionist deity did not appeal.[5] Nor did his Enlightenment successors: the watchmaker, or the rather abstract God who was accessible to the human imagination only via adjectives like 'perfect' or 'omnipotent'.

Inspired by recently discovered physical forces, including magnetism and electricity, Herder argued that God can be encountered as the primal 'force' (*Kraft*) coursing through nature. This force gives rise to the material world, and then to a range of other forces within it, from the inner life of each human being to the collective life of every nation.[6] For Herder, deeply influential both in Europe's Romantic movement and in the emergence of a German identity, 'nation' was a matter of *Volksgeist*: the particular spirit of a people, dynamically evolving across time. In China's case, *Kraft* had all but run its course. India, on the other hand, was humanity's wellspring. Herder discerned there a perpetual innocence, in the form of the 'gentle' Hindus, who 'do not with pleasure offend anything that lives':

> They honour that which gives life and nourish themselves with the most innocent of foods, milk, rice, the fruits of the trees, the healthy herbs which their motherland dispenses . . . Moderation and calm, a soft feeling and a silent depth of the soul characterize their work and their pleasure, their morals and mythology.[7]

In his own paraphrase of a Vedāntic poem, Herder linked *Kraft* with Vishnu:

> Vishnu is in you, in me, in all beings;
> It is foolish to ever feel offence.
> See all souls in your own,
> And banish the delusion of being different.[8]

Right at the end of his life, Herder encountered a similar vision of unity in a German translation of William Jones' *Sacontalá, or the Fatal Ring*, based on the original Sanskrit play by Kālidāsa. Inspired by a section of the *Mahābhārata*, the play tells the story of a young girl, Shakuntalā, who is courted by a king. They fall in love and marry, but one day Shakuntalā incurs the wrath of a sage, after failing to pay him homage. The sage removes all memory of Shakuntalā from her royal lover's mind, but is eventually persuaded to modify his curse: the king, he says, will recall her if she shows him the ring that he once gave her. To her horror, Shakuntalā realizes that she has lost the precious item – and the adventure continues from here.

Herder fell in love with the play, moved by the moral behaviour of gods and mortals alike, the rich aesthetics and humour, and a delicate balancing of the natural, devotional, sensual and erotic. For his friend Goethe, the play's characterization put European literature to shame, with its reliance on 'caricatures and stupid priests'.[9] Goethe ended up using *Sacontalā*'s opening scene as the model for his prologue to *Faust*.[10]

Goethe also shared Herder's interest in Vedānta and the eighth-century philosopher Shankara. Through his commentaries on major Indian texts, including the Upanishads and the *Bhagavad Gita*, Shankara developed an Advaita Vedānta ('Non-dual Vedānta') philosophy. At its core was a distinction between two standpoints from which reality can be known. From the standpoint of ignorance, reality comprises an individual self, surrounded by people and objects. From the standpoint of true knowledge, it consists of a single consciousness: Brahman, unconditioned and free, with which a person's true Self (*ātman*) is identical. From this second standpoint, the world of separate selves and objects is seen for what it is: *māyā* (illusion). As Goethe put it: 'external appearances and sensations are illusory, and would vanish into nothing, if the divine energy, which alone sustains them, were suspended but for a moment'.[11]

Alongside Herder and Goethe, the brothers Schlegel – Friedrich and August Wilhelm – played important roles in bringing Indian inspiration to early German Romanticism. Both men were poets and critics, who sought relief from what they regarded as the narrowly utilitarian thinking of their day by immersing themselves in the richness of world literatures past and present – searching for a 'new mythology' for their times.[12] Where Herder had *Kraft*, as a means of getting beyond the confines of knowledge set by Kant, Friedrich Schlegel alighted on allegory as a bridge between the everyday and the infinite. 'Every allegory', he wrote, 'means God . . . [and] one cannot speak of God, save allegorically'.[13] The Schlegel brothers also hoped to find in Indian literature evidence of a society less fragmented and less materialistically inclined than much of contemporary Europe. Both learned Sanskrit, but while August Wilhelm went on to become one of Germany's first professional Indologists, Friedrich's estimation of India was bound up with more personal concerns, and wavered wildly as a result.[14]

Friedrich Schlegel studied Sanskrit in Paris, finding confirmation of the rightness of his project during his journey to the French capital. He moved first through an agrarian Germany whose landscape and castles suggested a medieval unity not yet entirely lost, before arriving in a city that seemed to run on wealth, industry and pretension. He came to regard the French as robotic (*Maschinen-Menschen*), while his partner Dorothea found them pedantic, prizing fashion over beauty.[15] The bigger picture, for Schlegel, was that Europe's rediscovery of the classical world in the Renaissance had clearly now run its course. What the continent needed was an 'Oriental Renaissance'.[16]

For Schlegel, as for others in the German Romantic movement, the promise of India's past was impossible to separate out from the promise of Germany's future. He speculated that the people of Germania, whom the ancient Romans had called 'barbarians', might actually have originated in an already highly civilized India.[17] And where William Jones had suggested (correctly, as it would turn out) that an older language lay behind Sanskrit, Latin and Greek, Schlegel placed Sanskrit at the root of them all and claimed that (old) German had developed directly from it – while the mother tongue of his great rivals the French had developed at an additional remove, via Latin. Schlegel offered a positive case for caste too. Viewed in a negative light by many Europeans with first-hand experience of India, for Schlegel it recalled the well-ordered corporatism of medieval Europe.[18]

And yet by the time Schlegel published these thoughts in 1808 his love affair with India was ending. The very same week that *On the*

Language and Wisdom of the Indians came out, he and Dorothea converted to Catholicism.[19] One of the drawbacks of Indian thought, as Schlegel came to understand it, was its closeness to the pantheism of the much-vilified Spinoza, who continued to be associated with atheism and fatalism in Schlegel's day. Herder had tried to rescue Spinoza by pointing out that he had lived during 'the childhood of natural science', before sophisticated ways were available for describing how God might be present in nature. But for Schlegel, the Vedānta philosophy that so impressed Herder and Goethe was 'an opinion at once so comprehensive and all-annihilating' that it finished in fatalism and a loss or rejection of 'right' vs 'wrong'.[20]

Critics disagreed about the role of personal disillusionment versus professional canniness in Schlegel's shocking about-turn. Soon after his conversion to Catholicism he won himself an elevated post as a diplomat. Perhaps, some concluded, he had not cared to bear the career costs of radicalism in politics or philosophy. One described him, many years later, as turning into a 'fat philistine'.[21] Others were more willing to accept that a deep change must have come about in Schlegel's worldview, its impact felt across his personal, political and professional lives.

★

In the first half of the 1800s India found itself enlisted in attempts to make sense of Immanuel Kant's compelling yet confusing worldview. How can a freely reasoning human mind be compatible with a deterministic reality – assuming that that is indeed what lies beyond our minds? Surely 'space' and 'time' must be actual features of that reality, and not just products of the shaping powers of the mind? Such questions no doubt provided the fuel for many a late-night student conversation across these decades. Few of these, however, developed into philosophical visions as famous as those of two roommates at the University of Tübingen: Friedrich Schelling (1775–1854) and Georg Wilhelm Friedrich Hegel (1770–1831).

Schelling became known for an influential form of Idealism, arguing for an infinite and undifferentiated 'Absolute' as the 'holy abyss from which everything proceeds and into which everything returns'.[22] Much of this activity is opaque to us: human conscious-ness rests on countless 'unconscious' processes in nature (a claim with a big future in psychology and psychiatry). The natural sci-ences, limited as they are by human thought, give us an account of 'nature' that captures eddies in the stream rather than the stream itself.[23] Schelling found compelling support for his ideas in India's Advaita Vedānta philosophy, which seemed to him to be 'nothing but the most exalted Idealism'.[24] 'Brahman' was the name given to ultimate reality or 'the Absolute', from which emerges the finite, variegated world of everyday experience.

Schelling's estimation of India was mixed, however. His philoso-phy was deeply bound up with Christian convictions, in whose light the longing for union with the divine that he found in Indian litera-ture looked like a symptom of alienation from the true God of Christian revelation. Deeply interested in what world mythologies might reveal about the emergence of human self-consciousness over time, Schelling came to regard polytheism as a stage along the way to a mature monotheism: the realization gradually dawns that 'God' is not a person, or persons, somewhere in the universe, but instead encompasses all of reality.[25]

Hegel's view of India was less ambiguous. They might have shared rooms as students, but the mature Hegel had little time for Schelling or for Germany's Romantics more broadly, disliking intensely the nostalgia for the distant past that seemed to inform their work. His brand of Idealism presented history and meaning in terms of the steady unfolding of 'Spirit', becoming ever more con-scious of itself. The past is always taken up and included in what comes next. It was foolish, in Hegel's view, to seek to go backwards, or to think about the passing of time as the tarnishing of something original and pure.

Hegel was a serious student of Indian and Chinese thought, who appreciated the increasing professionalism of Indology – most of all the work of Henry Thomas Colebrooke: a successor of sorts to William Jones, who founded the Royal Asiatic Society in 1823, as a counterpart to Jones' Asiatic Society in Calcutta. But Hegel understood India, and Asia more broadly, as part of the early story of the unfolding of Spirit. The action, as it were, had since moved westwards. Hegel found evidence for this in Indian religious practice, as he understood it from sources including the *Bhagavad Gita*: its aim was to tamp down a person's sense of individuality, fostering absorption into Brahman instead. More broadly, Indian thought appeared to value oneness over particularity and dynamism. Here, for Hegel, was the reason why Indian culture had failed to move forward.[26]

Indian thought was most warmly embraced, in this era, by Arthur Schopenhauer (1788–1860). He regarded Christianity as essentially finished, in Europe at least. Protestant Christianity had degenerated: first into mere shallow 'optimism', then rationalism and finally full-on materialism. Catholicism, meanwhile, was no more than 'disgraceful obscurantism'.[27] India offered fresh hope. It was 'sacred soil', the 'cradle of the human race', and home to 'mankind's sacred and original faith'.[28]

Schopenhauer's mother, Johanna, was a novelist, in whose Weimar home could frequently be found some of the luminaries of the age: Goethe, the two Schlegels and the brothers Grimm. For a time, the young Schopenhauer was simply 'Johanna Schopenhauer's son'. Goethe regarded him as a 'strange and interesting man', having perhaps experienced first-hand Schopenhauer's powerful phobia about contagion from other people, via cups, pipes and cigars. This was part of a more general nervousness, which led Schopenhauer to think the worst whenever the postman called, and to keep loaded pistols by his bed at night.[29]

It was under the influence of Friedrich Majer – orientalist, Romantic and disciple of Herder – and thanks, perhaps, to Goethe too, that Schopenhauer began reading *Das Asiatische Magazin* in late 1813. This was Germany's answer to the Calcutta Asiatic Society's journal, *Asiatic Researches*, and Majer was a major contributor. One edition of the *Magazin* read by Schopenhauer contained Majer's German version of Wilkins' translation of the *Bhagavad Gita*.[30]

A few months later, he borrowed from the library the book that would become the 'consolation of my life and . . . my death': the *Oupnek'hat* (1802), Anquetil-Duperron's version of the Upanishads.[31]

As with earlier generations of German Indophiles, Schopenhauer was encountering Indian ideas at one or more poetic removes. Two-thirds of *Oupnek'hat* consisted not of the Upanishads at all. The original Persian translation, from which Anquetil had worked, was prepared by a group of Indian pandits and mystics working under the supervision of the Mughal crown prince Dara Shikoh (1615–59). Son of Emperor Shah Jahan and Mumtaz Mahal (for whom the Taj Mahal was built, as a mausoleum), Prince Dara seems to have been something of a kindred spirit with his great-grandfather Akbar. He had a deep interest in syncretism and Islamic mysticism, and the lengthy commentaries in the book whose production he oversaw leaned heavily towards Sufism and Shankara. In places, a distinction was barely made between translations of the Upanishads and Shankara's own commentary. Anquetil shared the prince's syncretic inclinations. His own explanatory material, which he added to his translation, was rooted in the conviction that the Upanishads, Plato, Kant and Catholicism all pointed in the same direction.[32]

What Schopenhauer encountered, then, in *Oupnek'hat*, was Indian philosophy presented as perennial wisdom. The appeal of this was enormous for a man who had already worked out the basic ideas that were to make his name but found them either unwelcome or ignored for much of his life. Those ideas were most fully expressed in his great work, *The World as Will and Representation* (first edition: 1818). Schopenhauer began by agreeing with many of the findings of 'that giant mind' Immanuel Kant, but parted company with him on the question of whether the world beyond the mind is entirely unknowable. Each of us, argued Schopenhauer, knows ourselves in two ways. We know ourselves as part of the world of representation: a person moving around a landscape. But we also have immediate experience, within ourselves, of 'will' or 'willing'. Kant had some-how missed this second kind of knowledge, which offered a 'narrow gateway to truth'. This will – or Will – claimed Schopenhauer, is the very same force that gives rise to, and shapes, all of nature. Planets form, plants grow, flowers bud, animals fight and reproduce – all of this is the constant unfolding of the same blind Will: a 'universal craving for life'.[33]

Schopenhauer's philosophical workings were Western, at every step of the way. But he found something closely akin to the notion of the world as representation in the concept of *māyā* (illusion). Likewise, he came to associate Will with Brahman: the true, unified reality. As Schopenhauer put it: 'I myself am an irradiated manifestation of the supreme Brahme.'[34] The two were not quite the same. For Shankara, Brahman was ultimate reality. For Schopenhauer, Will was simply as far as humans can go in conceiving of that reality.[35]

A natural pessimist, Schopenhauer came to be associated with a rather grim outlook on life. The world, in his philosophy, was marked by struggle, strife and suffering. Where most European philosophies up until this point gave pride of place to intellect or reason, Schopenhauer traced both of these back to the brain as part of nature, and from there to the Will. Something rang disturbingly true about the picture of the human mind that resulted: error-prone, capricious, uneven in the attention that it paid. Love, too, was removed from its pedestal. Strip away the romantic window-dressing and you find the Will, driving the species onward by furnishing it with the next generation. Purpose within history was likewise a fiction – Schopenhauer regarded Hegel as a 'crude and disgusting charlatan'.[36]

Still, it is possible to overdo Schopenhauer's pessimism. He enjoyed food, theatre and a bit of witty repartee.[37] He believed in art, as a means of gaining temporary respite from the demands of the Will.[38] And he regarded compassion as real and precious, arising as it did from a correct intuition that our separateness from one another is merely part of the illusory world of representation. We are, in fact, one and the same being. One could make a lengthy sermon or philosophical formulation out of this, he thought. Or one could get there in three words of Sanskrit: *tat tvam asi*: the Upanishadic 'Thou art that'.[39]

Alongside the Upanishads, there was much here that resonated with Buddhist thought, especially that of the second-century Indian philosopher Nagarjuna. Fragments of information about the Buddha and his life had been circulating in Europe for many centuries by this time. Origen's teacher Clement of Alexandria (*c.* 150–215 CE) had made brief mention in his writings of Indian philosophers who 'follow the precepts of Boutta, whom they honour as a god on account of his extraordinary sanctity'. Marco Polo had provided updates of his own which were no less positive. But it was only in the early 1800s that Buddhist texts began to be uncovered and translated from Sanskrit, Pali, Chinese, Mongolian and Tibetan.

Schopenhauer's first encounter with this work came in 1813, with his reading of an article in *Das Asiatische Magazin* that was based on a Chinese Chan (Zen) sutra.[40] His reading continued across the 1820s and beyond, and he came to understand Buddhism as textual, atheistic, highly moral, rooted in the life of a great founder, and teaching both the transmigration of souls and the ultimate ideal of nirvana.[41] The parallels with Schopenhauer's own thought were remarkable. Human beings do not receive reality ready-made: our minds shape it for us. We are not easily able to recognize the truth of this state of affairs, and so we get stuck in what Buddhists call 'attachment' – a concept that impressed Schopenhauer as a description of how the Will works in us, and keeps hold of us. We like to ask questions about ultimate reality, which are, in principle, unanswerable: so said the Buddha, so said Kant, and so, in his own way, thought Schopenhauer. This whole state of affairs gives rise to enormous suffering, and only through radical self-transformation can we become free.

The Buddhist idea of nirvana appealed to Schopenhauer as an expression of what happens when this self-transformation is achieved. He was interested, too, in how mystics of the Christian and Vedānta traditions achieved it, and he wrote of his own 'longing' for such a state – 'which is denoted by the names ecstasy, rapture, illumination, union with God, and so on'. Philosophers, thought Schopenhauer, cannot usefully describe this 'yonder of all cognition'.[42] They can say only that it comes about as a result of a 'denial of the Will'. Western religion, on the other hand, *could* say something about it, but had largely failed to do so. 'Like children who fear darkness', wrote Schopenhauer, European Christians offer stories and invoke saints as a means of escaping their trepidation about where a virtuous life, denying the Will, might ultimately lead. Where Indians understand that destination in a positive light, using terms like 'nirvana' or 'reabsorption into primeval spirit', 'we [Europeans] call that which is left *nothing*, and our nature revolts against [it]'.[43]

★

Towards the end of his life, one of Schopenhauer's most precious possessions was a Burmese statue of the Buddha. He acquired it from Paris, had it overlaid with gold, and kept it on his windowsill. He referred to himself, on occasion, as a Buddhist, and insisted that Christianity 'has Indian blood in its veins' – such were the similarities that he saw between the teachings of Jesus and the wisdom that he found in Buddhism and the Vedānta.

Christianity worked as allegory, thought Schopenhauer. The Fall of Adam and the coming of a saviour suggested the ephemeral nature of life on earth and the reality of 'a better existence, inconceivable to us', to which we can aspire.[44] Jesus himself had taught a combination of compassion, sacrifice, humility, forgiveness and self-abnegation – the 'giving up of one's own will . . . turning away from life and its delusive pleasures'.[45] For all that Christianity had since declined, it had been the means by which Europe was introduced to a priceless range of ideas and values, whose origins Schopenhauer located in Asia.

Schopenhauer always insisted that his philosophy was entirely Western. The role of the Upanishads, Advaita Vedāntā and Buddhism seems to have been to provide profound consolation: Schopenhauer's ideas were radical and disturbing in his day, but here they were, present in the minds of Indian philosophers living many centuries before. Developing these resonances, between an ancient past and a shifting present, was the very essence of an 'Oriental Renaissance'. Schlegel had called for one, but turned his back. With Schopenhauer, things had begun to move.

Triad Figure, Interior of Elephanta. Engraving by William Woolnoth, after Samuel Prout (1860).

12.

Intuiting India: From the Vile to the Vast

'Nine and twenty years, and nothing done as yet! Nine and twenty years, and nothing done as yet!' Friedrich Schlegel led the chant, and others soon joined in. They were gathered in a small Berlin apartment, around a table set with chocolates and cakes. The birthday boy was a humble hospital chaplain, Friedrich Schleiermacher, who had moved to Berlin the year before, in 1796. He had become known, in the salons of the city, for his intelligence and quick wit. How, Schlegel wanted to know, could such a man still, in this day and age, be a Christian? His birthday chant was a demand for Schleiermacher to explain himself – in writing.[1]

The resulting book, *On Religion: Speeches to Its Cultured Despisers* (1799), was rather pointedly addressed to Schlegel and co. But Schleiermacher's main claim, that the core of religion is an experience of the infinite via a person's intuition and feelings, helped to make his name around the world. It turned out to be an idea perfectly suited to the nineteenth century, as doubts about Christian doctrine grew, the natural sciences impinged ever more upon questions of religious truth, and the sacred literature of Asia was revealed as not merely picturesque but posing a serious historical and philosophical challenge. Placing intuition over doctrine made it easier to draw practical lessons from the East, while riding out the storms that were coming Christianity's way in the West.

One of the pioneers of this intuitive approach to Asian religion was the Bengali intellectual and reformer Ram Mohan Roy. A global celebrity in his day, his popularity with British and American Unitarians in particular – reaching from Bengal across to Bristol and Boston – marked a new phase in the Western search for meaning in

Asia: the primacy of texts was beginning to give way to the forging of East–West friendships and alliances.

Western impressions of India remained decidedly mixed, however, across the late 1700s and early 1800s. As an East India Company army almost twice the size of the regular British army added fresh swathes of the subcontinent to an emerging empire, some commentators railed against British rapacity, while others spied Providence at work: bringing a grim, degraded corner of the globe under the tutelage of a civilized society.[2] Heir to competing images of India, the British Romantic poets Robert Southey and Samuel Taylor Coleridge, alongside their American literary cousin, Ralph Waldo Emerson, intuited 'India' and its promise in wildly differing ways – ranging from the vile to a sense of a divine Vast.

*

The mistake made by 'cultured despisers' of religion, declared Friedrich Schleiermacher, is that they imagine it to be about doctrine and morality, when in fact it is – at heart – a 'sensibility and taste for the infinite'. Without this, the pursuit of meaning will remain 'an empty game': an endless series of speculations, where one set of concepts is expressed in terms of another – on and on, with actual meaning always somewhere just over the horizon. Even where people have experienced the infinite, via the intuition or emotions, the temptation has always been strong, thought Schleiermacher, to try to turn it into stories and propositions. In this way, since the time of the ancient Greeks, the 'glowing outpouring' from the 'fire that is contained in all religions' had been allowed to cool and harden into 'dead slag'.[3]

Schleiermacher's critics accused him of downgrading religious truth. A miracle, in Schleiermacher's view, was simply an event – any event – experienced with a religious mindset. Revelation was any 'original and new intuition of the universe'.[4] Jesus Christ was divine only in the sense of possessing 'an absolutely powerful consciousness of God'.[5] And life after death was no more than an irreligious fantasy: not having experienced the infinite for themselves, people imagined 'immortality' in the decidedly pedestrian sense of their present life continuing on indefinitely.[6] Schleiermacher was, in short, engaging in theological bomb-disposal: clearing the landscape of anything that salon sophisticates feared might blow up in their faces.

For all that Schleiermacher's idea of religion appeared philosophically weak, it proved culturally robust. It was able to withstand Ludwig Feuerbach's claim that the 'God' of Christianity is no more than a projection of human nature. Ditto the idea, from the emerging world of biblical criticism, that Jesus had just been a remarkable human being, whose very human deeds were documented by his disciples using mythological themes from the Old Testament.[7] Scientists, meanwhile, aged the earth by millions of years, and discovered the origins of humanity and morality in the cut-and-thrust of nature. All of these things could be true, and still the infinite would remain untouched.[8]

Westerners who were inclined to treat Schleiermacher sympathetically found in Ram Mohan Roy an Indian intellectual who had reached remarkably similar conclusions on the basis of his own religious inheritance. Born around 1772 into an orthodox Brahmin family with a history of service to the Nawab of Bengal, Roy's knowledge of Arabic, Persian and Sanskrit gave him access to north India's centuries-old Indo-Islamic culture. Influential strands, by this time, included Islamic rationalism, Vedānta and a tradition of public debate and recital out of which emerged celebrated poetry, music and philosophy.[9]

By the early 1800s, Roy had come to believe that awareness of a single God was common to all people, but habits of mind and worship obscured it: polytheism, dietary rules and a concern with ritualism and religious purity.[10] Such was the power of culture, he warned, that anyone seeking to rid religion of these obstacles would find family members and religious leaders ranged against them. Roy knew as much from personal experience, breaking with his own family over his unorthodox religious views.

A career with the East India Company, from 1803 until around

1814, helped to provide Roy with sufficient funds and fluency in English and contemporary Western thought to enable him to settle down in Calcutta and embark full-time on religious and social reform.[11] In Roy's mind, the two were intimately connected. A failure to interpret Indian scriptures allegorically rather than literally had given rise, he argued, to idolatry, criminality, immorality – parts of Indian mythology were rather racy – and the burning of women in *sati*.[12] Roy conceded that people who were unable to intuit the divine in nature might benefit, at an early stage of the religious life, from praying to various gods. His hero Shankara, the great philosopher, had taught that religious truth must be adapted according to people's capacities. Still, Roy thought that everyone, not just a religious elite, was capable of apprehending 'the unity of God . . . [and] the pure mode of adoring him in spirit'.[13] The task of reformed religion was to find ways of fostering this capacity.

One practical step, taken by Roy himself, was to publish Bengali and English translations of the Upanishads, alongside commentaries inspired by Shankara. For Roy, the Upanishads were the apex of Indian wisdom in their teachings about God and the soul. His use of familiar Deist terms, in his English translations, helped to make texts like the Mundaka Upanishad intelligible and attractive to Western audiences:

As from a blazing fire thousands of sparks of the same nature proceed, so from the eternal Supreme Being (O beloved pupil) various souls come forth, and again they return into him. He is immortal, and without form or figure, omnipresent, pervading external and internal objects, unborn, without breath or individual mind, pure and superior to eminently exalted nature . . .

A knowledge of God . . . is not acquired from study of the Vedas, nor through retentive memory, nor yet by continual hearing of spiritual instruction; but he who seeks to obtain a knowledge of God [above all other things] is gifted with it, God rendering himself conspicuous to him.[14]

Jemima Kindersley had written, just a few decades before, that Hinduism awaited its Martin Luther. To his supporters, who referred to him as 'the Reformer', Roy was very much that man.[15] Like Luther, he sought his tradition's original purity, detested priestly influence, made scripture available in the vernacular, and made a great many enemies. Some of these were orthodox Brahmins, who objected to Roy's denunciation of polytheism: either because they disagreed with him, or because it threatened their livelihoods as liturgists.[16] Others were Christian missionaries, who were happy to see heathenism deconstructed – and by a Brahmin, no less – but who objected when Roy turned his sights on Christianity. Roy's *Precepts of Jesus* (1820) trod dangerous ground, presenting Jesus as a sage-like figure whose teachings had been 'corrupted' by Greek and Roman polytheism.[17] The Holy Trinity – Father, Son and Holy Spirit – was a case in point, Roy argued: polytheism in plain sight.

Roy was celebrated in Calcutta for setting up newspapers, championing English-language education and campaigning against *sati*. He was consulted on the issue by the governor-general, and a ban was imposed in 1829.[18] Roy also established the Brahmo Samaj: an organization committed to his vision of a refurbished Hinduism, which met weekly for readings from Hindu scripture and the singing of hymns – some of which Roy himself composed, as Luther had once done.[19] The Brahmo Samaj would soon find itself at the centre of what became known as the Bengal Renaissance: the rediscovery of India's cultural wealth, its fashioning into a nationalist narrative, and its export abroad as Eastern wisdom.[20]

Roy referred to India as a 'nation', but he was not amongst the British and Bengali radicals calling for Indian independence in the early 1800s.[21] This made it easier for British and American Unitarians to take him to their bosom. They were attracted by Roy's respect for Jesus as a great teacher, his universal theism, and the prospect that his sympathies might shift far enough in their direction that he would help to win India for Unitarian Christianity. Unitarians duly republished and distributed Roy's work and featured him prominently in their letters and newspapers, bringing him to the notice of readers including Coleridge and Emerson.[22]

These publicity efforts, and the success of the campaign against *sati*, ensured Roy a warm welcome when he sailed into Liverpool in the spring of 1831, as an envoy of the Mughal emperor, Akbar II. With Delhi now under the effective control of the East India Company, Roy – given the title 'Raja' by Akbar – had been sent to request a rise in the emperor's pension.[23] Roy found himself mobbed by well-wishers during his journey south to London, where he met King William IV, Benjamin Disraeli and William Wilberforce. He sat in the House of Commons while the Reform Bill was debated, and Robert Owen was said to have striven valiantly, though in vain, to win him to the cause of utopian socialism.[24] Jeremy Bentham mooted the idea of having Roy stand as a candidate for Parliament.[25]

Brilliant, aristocratic, exotic and accomplished: Raja Ram Mohan Roy was a figure of anxious hope for British reformers – even in death. While on a visit to Bristol in 1833, he showed symptoms of meningitis, to which the application of leeches proved unequal. He passed away on 27 September, and his adopted son, Ram Roy, was forced to dispel rumours that the Raja had prayed to 364 gods on his deathbed.[26] Reassured that he had prayed only to 'the one God', bereaved Britons buried Roy at Bristol's Arnos Vale cemetery, and composed hymns, sermons and sonnets in his honour.[27] A sonnet addressed to Roy by the Unitarian reformer Mary Carpenter revealed the respect and relief felt by people like her at finding their values vindicated in faraway India:

> Thy nation sat in darkness; for the night
> Of pagan gloom was o'er it: Thou wast born
> Midst superstition's ignorance folorn:
> Yet in thy breast there glow'd a heavenly light
> Of purest truth and love . . .
> What ardent zeal did then thy life adorn,
> From deep degrading guilt to lead aright

Thy fallen people; to direct their view
To that bless'd Sun of Righteousness.

Carpenter found space in her poem to laud the 'sea-girt land' in
whose soil Roy now rested. 'Thron'd among the nations', it had sent
'many a holy band' to battle tyranny and superstition. Fitting it was,
then, that:

To our blest Isle thou didst with transport come
Here hast thou found thy last, thy silent home.[28]

*

Quite what the 'blest Isle' of Mary Carpenter's sonnet ought to
stand for was the subject of vigorous debate across the late 1700s
and the early 1800s, not least in the great international city where
Roy passed his final days. Some three hundred years earlier, the
navigator John Cabot had departed from Bristol on his ill-fated
search for a north-westerly route to Asia. Since that time, a global
trade in profitable produce and African slaves had bestowed upon it
wealth, beautiful buildings, and a reputation for radical oratory.[29]
A regular speaker at the coffee-houses and Cornmarket in 1795
was a young Unitarian by the name of Samuel Taylor Coleridge:

The English Nation [are] practical Atheists, professing to believe a
God, yet acting as if there were none . . . from Africa the unnum-
bered Victims of a detestable Slave-trade – in Asia the desolated
plains of Indostan and the Million whom a rice-contracting Governor caused to perish.[30]

Coleridge charged that imperialists like Robert Clive – the 'rice-
contracting Governor' – were immiserating India while contributing
to serious social and spiritual harm back home. In return for the 'foul
and heart-inslaving Guilt' inspired by causing death on a prodigious
scale across Asia, the English 'receive[d] gold, diamonds, silks, muslins
& calicoes . . . Tea to make a pernicious Beverage, Porcelain to drink

it from, and salt-petre for the making of gunpowder with which we may murder the poor Inhabitants who supply all these things.'[31] In a critique that would have been familiar to Pliny, writing about pepper and silk, or medieval clerics condemning Europe's addiction to spice, Coleridge linked Asia and the wider world with the stimulation of 'artificial Wants' in British consumers.[32] Urging Bristolians, in the name of 'the inspired Philanthropist of Galilee', to stop buying sugar and rum, Coleridge laid out the terrible consequences of possessing more than one needs: 'Envy, Rapine, Government & Priesthood'.[33]

These were heady times, with the American and French revolutions still fresh in the air – Coleridge had written an ode, while still at school, celebrating the fall of the Bastille.[34] Slaves were rising up across the Caribbean. And reformers were pressing their case in Britain, soon to welcome overseas allies like Roy to their cause.[35] Coleridge and his friend Robert Southey briefly dreamed of meeting a world gone mad with their own model of a sane society. They abandoned university – Southey left Oxford, Coleridge quit Cambridge – in favour of Southey's hometown of Bristol, hoping to proceed from there to America. They would establish a utopian colony: 'Pantisocracy', meaning equal government, by and for all. 'When Coleridge and I are sawing down a tree,' predicted Southey, 'we shall discuss metaphysics; criticise poetry when hunting a buffalo, and write sonnets whilst following the plough.'[36]

Life did not pan out as planned. By the end of 1795, Southey and Coleridge were still in England, and were married men. Revolutionary dreams were meanwhile beginning to fade in France, and before long the spectre arose of Napoleon Bonaparte invading Britain via Ireland. It became steadily harder to prefer French to British politics, especially in the wake of the Slave Trade Act of 1807: although the practice of slavery remained legal, the prohibition of the trading of slaves across the British Empire was regarded as a major step forward.

Southey soon counted himself amongst those who thought that Britain might do some good in the world, as the 'parent country' in India.[37] Hoping to raise the moral tone both at home and abroad through his poetry, he became an avid reader of Christian missionary reports, whose authors appealed to potential donors by offering lurid accounts of the general degradation of Indian life.[38] His imagination primed by boyhood enthusiasm for world mythologies, Southey especially relished accounts of the annual chariot festival held at the temple of Jagannath. One missionary writer, Claudius Buchanan, recalled, with horror, seeing a 'stupendous car . . . about sixty feet in height', rolling along with priests atop it, sitting alongside an idol: 'a block of wood, having a frightful visage painted black, with a distended mouth of a bloody colour. His arms are of gold, and he is dressed in gorgeous apparel.' Buchanan watched a pilgrim offer himself as a sacrifice, laying himself face-down in the path of the chariot, to be crushed under its wheels.[39]

Ram Mohan Roy was amongst those who blamed misreadings of Hindu scripture for scenes like these, which caused 'Jagannatha' to enter the English language as 'juggernaut' and Westerners to gain an exaggerated sense of Indian self-sacrifice – including the frequency with which people offered themselves up to the wheels of the chariot. For Southey, it proved irresistible as poetic source material. After almost a decade of work, he completed his epic poem, *The Curse of Kehama*, in 1810. The eponymous Kehama is a Brahmin priest, who makes sacrifices to Shiva in order to give himself sway over life and death – even to become a god himself. The poem opens with swaying multitudes caught up, half-conscious, in a diabolical funeral procession:

> Midnight, and yet no eye
> Through all the Imperial City clos'd in sleep!
> Behold her streets a-blaze
> With light that seems to kindle the red sky,
> Her myriads swarming through the crowded ways!
> Master and slave, old age and infancy,
> All, all abroad to gaze;
> House-top and balcony

Clustered with women, who throw back their veils,
With unimpeded and insatiate sight
To view the funeral pomp which passes by . . .

Hark! 'tis the funeral trumpet's breath!
'Tis the dirge of death!
At once ten thousand drums begin,
With one long thunder-peal the ear assailing;
Ten thousand voices then join in,
And with one deep and general din
Pour their wild wailing.
The song of praise is drown'd
Amid that deafening sound . . .

Later comes the chariot festival:

Up rear'd on twenty wheels elate,
Huge as a Ship, the Bridal Car appear'd;
Loud creak its ponderous wheels, as through the gate
A thousand Bramins drag the enormous load . . .

The ponderous Car rolls on, and crushes all.
Through flesh and bones it ploughs its dreadful path.
Groans rise unheard: the dying cry,
And death and agony
Are trodden under foot by yon mad throng,
Who follow close, and thrust the deadly wheels along.[40]

By the time *The Curse of Kehama* was completed, Napoleon had become, for Southey, every bit as egregious an example of despotism as Mughal emperors or Brahmin priests.[41] Britain could claim to have stood up to all three. Meanwhile, British modernizers and Evangelicals were winning arguments about their country's rightful role in India. Making the case, in 1835, for spending a modest official education budget on English- rather than Sanskrit-language tuition, a member of the Supreme Council in Calcutta, Thomas Babington Macaulay, claimed that 'a single shelf of a good European library [is] worth the whole native literature of India and Arabia'.[42] The task of offering scholarly interpretations of Indian culture to Western audiences began to pass from British to German orientalists. Only three university professorships of Indology were established in Britain during the 1800s. In Germany, the figure was twenty-two.[43]

Coleridge found happier inspiration in India than Southey had managed. He befriended William Wordsworth in 1797, and both men exchanged politics for nature, as a reliable source of renewal. They tasted the Kantian 'sublime', with its aura of 'boundlessness' and grandeur, on walks in the Cotswolds and the Lake District. But Coleridge, who must have thought of India often, after two of his brothers died there as enlisted men (John in 1787; Frank in 1792), sought the sublime in Asia, too:

> In Xanadu did Kubla Khan
> A stately pleasure-dome decree:
> Where Alph, the sacred river, ran
> Through caverns measureless to man
> Down to a sunless sea.[44]

The inspiration for 'Xanadu' was Shangdu: Kublai Khan's summer capital, tales of which Coleridge encountered in Samuel Purchas' version of Marco Polo's travel account.[45] The 'pleasure-dome', however, was Mughal rather than Mongol, drawn from descriptions of the domed architecture of northern India.[46] Coleridge was taken, too, by tales of the natural splendour of Kashmir, once described by the Emperor Jahangir as 'paradise on earth'. He combined this with what he saw for himself of rural Somerset, living there while composing 'Kubla Khan', sometime, perhaps, in the mid-1790s:[47]

> And there were gardens bright with sinuous rills,
> Where blossomed many an incense-bearing tree;

And here were forests ancient as the hills,
Enfolding sunny spots of greenery.[48]

Around the time of writing 'Kubla Khan', Coleridge confessed to his friend John Thelwall that he yearned 'to behold and know something *great*, something *one* and *indivisible*'. In this precious contemplative state, he found that 'rocks or waterfalls, mountains or caverns, give me the sense of sublimity or majesty!' '*All things*', he went on, rise to the point where they 'counterfeit infinity', returning him to something like the sense, which had occasionally come upon him in childhood, of 'the Vast'.[49] Such a state of mind faded all too quickly, and like his vision, in 'Kubla Khan', of a 'damsel with a dulcimer', it was not easily recovered:

Could I revive within me
Her symphony and song,
To such a deep delight 'twould win me,
That with music loud and long,
I would build that dome in air.[50]

Coleridge found this contemplative state of mind, close to the creative reverie out of which 'Kubla Khan' had emerged, captured in a well-known image from Indian mythology. 'I should much wish,' he wrote to Thelwall, 'like the Indian Vishnu, to float about along an infinite ocean cradled in the flower of the Lotus, and wake once in a million years for a few minutes just to know that I was going to sleep a million years more.'[51]

Coleridge may have encountered this image in William Jones' 'Hymn to Náráyena' or Charles Wilkins' translation of the *Bhagavad Gita*.[52] For a time, he practised silent prayer of the kind recommended in the *Gita*. But as his dependence on opium grew, his capacity for sensing the Vast withered away, and his marriage came to an end – he separated from his wife in 1808 – neither the 'Absolute' of Indian philosophy nor the God of Unitarian

Christianity seemed to offer Coleridge an adequate intuition of the divine.

Coleridge was convinced that humanity's estrangement from nature was part of the price paid, down the centuries, for honing human rationality. The mind had steadily turned inwards, creating a separation between the self and the world, which philosophy must somehow overcome.[53] But Spinoza and Advaita Vedānta seemed to achieve this only with a fatalistic, all-obliterating unity, leaving no room for 'affectionate seeking after Truth', involving a combination of will and reason.[54] Indian pantheism, Coleridge concluded, was but 'a painted Atheism', in which 'an Oceanic God, Man, Beast and Plant [are] mere & merely wavelets & wrinkles on the surface of the Depth'.[55] His view of meditation ended up echoing sixteenth-century Jesuit criticisms of Zen: it was a way of numbing oneself to passion and so robbing oneself of the possibility of virtuous action.[56]

Unitarianism seemed little better. Its rationalism and optimism were well-suited to the daylight hours. But they could not meet him in his night-time terror and guilt – not least over his love for women other than his wife.[57] Sin, and the need for forgiveness, felt so viscerally real to Coleridge that only a personal God, capable of grasping and loving the sinful, felt powerful or plausible. He returned to the Anglicanism of his childhood in 1814, apparently finding in orthodox Christianity and its doctrine of Incarnation the only way of reconciling life's great polarities: transcendence and immanence, infinity and finitude, the godly and the grubby.[58]

To Coleridge's critics, echoing those of Friedrich Schlegel, his turn to orthodoxy and conservative politics amounted to a reactionary betrayal. But though his own interest in Asia faded, Coleridge offered a critical distinction, between fantasy and true imagination or creativity, which later generations following in his footsteps found indispensable. Fantasy, Coleridge suggested, is the mind's combining of fixed ideas in some new way. True creativity is the poet at work, helping to make present to the human imagination 'the infinite I AM'. Here was a way in which Westerners across the twentieth century not naturally given to meditation or contemplation would find real promise in Asia: in the superior ability of its symbols and myths to stoke the exploratory and receptive powers of the imagination.

*

Where Southey revelled in a Gothic horror version of India, and Coleridge turned away, disappointed, from its 'painted Atheism', Ralph Waldo Emerson steadily warmed to Asia across the course of his life.[59] Like Coleridge, he was a Unitarian as a young man, encountering biblical criticism, Schleiermacher and Romantic poetry during his time at Harvard College. His first impressions of India were shaped by grisly missionary reports and Southey's *Curse of Kehama*, which Emerson studied carefully while preparing a poem for Harvard's College Fair in his graduating year of 1821.[60] 'Indian Superstition' was about as generous to its subject-matter as the title suggests. It was intended as a paean to Emerson's own young country – healthy, rich and free – which he envisaged, Southey-like, playing a role in rescuing India from demons, screaming and a 'grim abyss of misery'.[61]

Emerson's Aunt Mary exercised an enormous influence on his poetic and religious imagination, and it was she who wrote to him enthusiastically about the 'learned Hindu' Ram Mohan Roy.[62] The young Emerson replied rather haughtily, conceding a modicum of interest in 'your Hindoo mythologies', while warning about escapism: 'Every man has a fairy-land just beyond the compass of his horizon.'[63] That same year, when his aunt sent him lines from William Jones' 'Náráyena', lauding its Idealism, Emerson copied some of them into his private journal: 'God only I perceive, God only I adore!'[64]

Jones' poetry, alongside laudatory newspaper accounts of Roy's ideas and activities, helped Emerson to overcome his earlier low view of India.[65] But it was only after his wife Ellen passed away in 1831, at just twenty years of age, that Emerson felt driven to explore new and foreign ideas. Ordained, just two years before, to the Unitarian ministry, he suddenly sensed the inadequacy of doctrine and sacraments, and the vital importance instead of a form of religion that emphasized the fullest possible immersion in the here-and-now. He left his pastorate and travelled, at the end of 1832, to Europe. He met some of his heroes – Wordsworth, an ailing Coleridge, Thomas Carlyle – but the moment that changed him came at the Jardin des Plantes, a celebrated botanical garden in Paris. Emerson later recalled it as an epiphany of sorts: he experienced the extraordinary variety of life on display, in terms not of diversity but a natural unity, of which he, too, was a part.[66]

From 1836, what became known as the 'Transcendental Club' began to meet at Emerson's home in the village of Concord. Its members, including Henry David Thoreau and Margaret Fuller, sought to go beyond established religion and conventional politics, and to explore themes ranging from Idealism and unity in the cosmos through to the power of intuition and the ultimate goodness of humankind. Emerson read widely in pursuit of these aims, including the Upanishads, parts of the *Mahābhārata*, Confucius, the *Laws of Manu* and the *Bhagavad Gita*. Surprised to find that Idealism was much older than German philosophy – running all the way back to ancient India – he gave a highly controversial lecture, in 1838, to a group of Divinity School graduates on what Schleiermacher might have called the perils of mistaking slag for living lava.[67] Into the former category, Emerson placed the ideas of a divine Jesus and a personal God. These were legacies, as Emerson put it, of mere 'historical Christianity'. The divine was altogether beyond such notions, and was no one's cultural property:

The intuition of moral sentiment . . . dwelled always deepest in the minds of men in the devout and contemplative East; not alone in Palestine, where it reached its purest expression, but in Egypt, in Persia, in India, in China. Europe has always owed to oriental genius, its divine impulses. What these holy bards said, all sane men found agreeable and true.[68]

Emerson warned his listeners against confusing living faith with propositions, and against offering people a monarchical, miracle-working religion, with little credibility or power of consolation. 'I look for the hour', he declared, 'when that supreme Beauty, which ravished the souls of those eastern men . . . shall speak in the West also.'[69] For him, as for Coleridge, that 'Beauty' was available to anyone capable of realizing that they were 'enbosomed . . . in nature'.[70] They would find in nature a great 'soul', which 'pervades and contains us'.[71] To intuit this soul and its moral law, and to live accordingly was, thought Emerson, the very essence of true 'self-reliance' – far superior to the conformity of 'badges and names . . . and dead institutions'.[72]

It was a testament to America's relative isolation, in these years, from European Orientalism, that when Emerson encountered Charles Wilkins' translation of the *Bhagavad Gita* in 1845, he referred to it mistakenly as 'the much renowned book of Buddhism'.[73] The Transcendental Club did much to overcome that isolation, publishing excerpts from Asian 'Ethnical Scriptures' – Hindu and Buddhist, alongside the sayings of Confucius – in their journal, *The Dial*.[74] In a period when China was not highly regarded amongst Westerners, Emerson stood out in showing warm appreciation for Confucian teachings: here was an ethical individualism, he thought, which took proper account of other people rather than lapsing into self-centredness or egotism.[75]

Deeper than Confucianism, for Emerson, ran India's Advaita Vedānta philosophy. Everyday turns of phrase like 'I am' and 'This is mine' betrayed the great illusion that the Vedānta helped to expose: of a small, lonely self, wending its way in a chopped-up world of people and things – failing to sense, beyond all that, a single, unified reality. Emerson described that reality using the Vedāntic term *paramatman*, alongside his own word: 'Over-Soul'. The 'Indian scriptures', he came to believe, focused on this 'fundamental Unity' in a way that European philosophies so far had not. Seeking to express this in poetry, he took inspiration from the Katha Upanishad and published 'Brahma', in the first issue of a new Boston magazine called *The Atlantic*, in 1857:

If the red slayer think he slays,
Or if the slain think he is slain,
They know not well the subtle ways
I keep, and pass, and turn again.

Far or forgot to me is near;
Shadow and sunlight are the same;
The vanished gods to me appear;
And one to me are shame and fame.

They reckon ill who leave me out;
When me they fly, I am the wings;
I am the doubter and the doubt,
I am the hymn the Brahmin sings.

The strong gods pine for my abode,
And pine in vain the sacred Seven;
But thou, meek lover of the good!
Find me, and turn thy back on heaven.[76]

★

Not everyone in America was ready for *paramatman*. Emerson's poem attracted puzzlement and parodies, alongside letters of support. But he and fellow Transcendentalists like Henry David Thoreau had begun to establish Asian, and especially Indian, thought in American culture as contemplative, vital and close to nature, where so much in everyday American life felt conventional, commercialized and dead. Much the same sentiments would fuel the warm reception afforded to Swami Vivekānanda at the World's Parliament of Religions in 1893. Less happy intuitions of India, offered up in their varying ways by missionaries, Southey and reformers like Ram Mohan Roy, enjoyed afterlives of their own. One of the reasons for Vivekānanda's popularity in Chicago was that a good many Americans had been led to believe that a 'civilized Indian' would be a contradiction in terms.

Coleridge, too, foreshadowed later intuitions of India, with his tentative, hopeful approach, shaped by the shifting politics of his time alongside deep, even desperate personal need. What Emerson celebrated as the 'raptures of prayer and ecstasy of devotion [that] lose all beings in one Being', Coleridge came to fear as a kind of nothingness. Nature, stillness and solitude, those pillars of Romanticism, were all very well. But unless they pointed a person – or, better still, conveyed them – towards something personal, loving and benevolent beyond, then what, in the end, was the point?

> . . . If the breath
> Be Life itself, and not its task and tent,
> If even a soul like Milton's can know death;
> Oh Man! thou vessel purposeless, unmeant . . .[77]

A Hiogo Buddha, by Isabella Bird (*c.* 1878).

13.

The Light of Asia

. . . then marked he, too,
How lizard fed on ant, and snake on him,
And kite on both . . .
. . . till everywhere
Each slew a slayer and in turn was slain,
Life living upon death. So the fair show
Veiled one vast, savage, grim conspiracy
Of mutual murder, from the worm to man.[1]

Buried close to Isaac Newton at Westminster Abbey, in 1882, Charles Darwin came to share with his pioneering predecessor both a resting place and the dubious honour of having his surname become a byword for disenchantment. A 'Newtonian' universe ran like clockwork, and was about as romantic. 'Darwinian' soon came to suggest struggle, cruelty and blind action. Trying his hand as a poet in 1879, the British journalist Edwin Arnold seemed set on trumping Tennyson's 'nature, red in tooth and claw' (*In Memoriam*, 1850) by deploying some Darwinian detail, and dragging humanity into the mire: once God's special creation, set down lovingly in Eden; now, nature's most efficient killing machine, perched atop a pile of bodies.

Just a few decades before Arnold put pen to paper, Eastern pantheism had been numbered amongst the greatest threats to the old ideal of 'Creation'. The capital 'C' suggested sacredness: here was the handiwork of a loving and intelligible God. Something essential was lost if nature turned out to be either a veil with no face behind it, or a giant conjuring trick – as the Indian concept of *māyā*

189

(illusion) threatened to imply. By the late 1870s, threats to Creation had been accumulating closer to home. Geological and fossil findings backed up evidence gleaned by the Jesuits from Chinese records: the world was indeed much older than the Bible suggested, with species coming and going across vast expanses of time. Newly discovered laws of thermodynamics pictured the universe as a closed system, in which energy and matter could be neither created nor destroyed – how, then, did God intervene in human life? Readers of Darwin's two great works, *On the Origin of Species* (1859) and *The Descent of Man* (1871), could be forgiven for concluding that God had little involvement, or even much interest, in human life at all.

This was not – yet – science driving a stake through the heart of Christianity. Since at least the time of Origen in the third century, Christians had treated the book of Genesis as a blend of poetry and history. The precise nature of that blend was difficult to discern, and in theory, at least, the interpretive help of scientists was warmly to be welcomed. If the underlying point of the poetry was that Creation has fallen from an original state of perfection, then it was natural enough that species would die out from time to time.[2] Miracles, by definition, involved the exceptional breaching of natural laws: merely adding more laws to the picture changed little. One could even find, in evolutionary theory, a certain elegance and laissez-faire to the way that God got things done in the world.

And yet, if the 'Book of Nature' was supposed to rank alongside the Bible, in revealing God to humankind, then who was this God who permitted cruelty and waste of life on the scale implied by natural selection? And who were we, as human beings, if morality and conscience were not an intimate link with a loving and law-giving God, but instead a product of evolution?[3] With God and humanity seeming stranger by the day, there was plenty for an aspiring poet like Edwin Arnold to get his teeth into. Matthew Arnold (no relation) had shown the way, in 'Dover Beach' (1867): 'The sea of faith . . . / Retreating to the breath / Of the night-wind'.

In fact, Edwin Arnold was doing something completely different. Seeing the 'grim conspiracy / Of mutual murder' that surrounds him, the observer at the heart of Arnold's poem proceeds to sit down under a tree:

> To meditate this deep disease of life,
> What its far source and whence its remedy.
> So vast a pity filled him, such wide love
> For living things, such passion to heal pain,
> That by their stress his princely spirit passed
> To ecstasy, and, purged from mortal taint
> Of sense and self, the boy attained thereat
> Dhyāna, first step of 'the path'.[4]

'The boy' is launched, by suffering, on a journey: not into bleak, mid-Victorian pessimism, but instead from darkness into light. An unlikely response, perhaps, to reading Darwin – but the 'princely spirit' of Arnold's poem belongs to another age altogether. This is Siddhartha Gautama: the Buddha. Written in part during precious minutes snatched on trains, station platforms and in restaurants – verses sometimes scribbled on shirt-cuffs, or on the backs of menus – Arnold's epic poem, *The Light of Asia*, was an attempt to bring Buddhism to the British, and to the wider West.[5]

Up until the middle decades of the nineteenth century, Western impressions of Buddhism had been vague and generally negative – the pessimistic tone of Schopenhauer's philosophy was, in part, to blame. Here, people concluded, was a godless creed, for whose adherents the aim of life appeared to be the ending of life, in annihilation. This low view of Buddhism began to change, as texts were discovered across Asia that brought into focus the role of a single, remarkable human being in kick-starting a religious movement whose size and geographical reach rivalled that of Christianity.[6]

A northern 'Mahayana' branch of Buddhism, it was now understood, could be found in Tibet, Mongolia, China and Japan, drawing its inspiration from a set of Sanskrit scriptures.[7] A southern 'Theravada' tradition was dominant in Sri Lanka and much of South-East Asia, and seemed closest to the original teachings of the Buddha.

The Christian missionary Robert Spence Hardy, working in Sri Lanka, was amongst the first Westerners to explore Theravada's Pali scriptures, many of them written on palm leaves and stored in wooden boxes.[8] His *Manual of Budhism* (1853) was the earliest Western account of the Theravada tradition, and one of Edwin Arnold's main sources in composing his poem.[9] The collection and translation of Pali texts later became the preserve of the husband-and-wife team Thomas William (T. W.) and Caroline Rhys Davids, through their Pali Text Society.

Neither Hardy nor the Rhys Davids intended for Western readers of their work to become Buddhists. As a missionary, Hardy was working in a well-established 'know your enemy' tradition. If the British authorities in Sri Lanka could not be persuaded to destroy Buddhism – something for which Hardy and other missionaries argued, on the basis that it was clearly idolatrous – the next best thing was to develop an understanding of its tenets, thereby increasing the effectiveness of Christian evangelization.[10] The Rhys Davids, for their part, were motivated by a desire to rid Buddhism of its old pessimistic associations in the West. This they did by portraying it as rational, scientific and concerned with moral self-cultivation. Rooted in the Buddha's strivings and insights, Buddhism was a 'science of the mind'.[11]

Here was a claim calculated to win approval in the second half of the nineteenth century. A small minority of Victorians, including members of the Secular Society founded in 1866 by Charles Bradlaugh, saw the scientific achievements of their age coalescing into a worldview which was capable of disproving and displacing Christianity. Most regarded science more modestly, but no less respectfully, as a method for acquiring and testing certain kinds of knowledge. The Oxford University philologist Friedrich Max Müller was amongst those who sought to borrow a little of this kudos for the world of philosophy and religion. Enough information was now available about religious traditions around the world, he claimed, for the pursuit of a 'science of religion'. Sacred texts could be subjected to scientific comparison, testing for signs of the 'mental faculty' of faith at work – understood by Müller, echoing Schleiermacher, as the human capacity to 'apprehend the Infinite'.[12]

One didn't have to wade through Hardy's *Manual* or attend one of Müller's lectures in order to discover the latest thinking about Buddhism and comparative religion. These subjects began to feature in widely circulated journals like the *Edinburgh Review* and the *British Quarterly Review*.[13] They were the stuff, too, of dinner-table discussion, much of it no doubt fuelled by popular accounts of the Buddha's life and teachings published in the 1870s and 1880s.[14] Just at the point where lurid missionary accounts of popular Indian superstition were taking some of the shine off Hinduism, here, in the historical Buddha, was Asia's answer to Martin Luther. He had battled the priestly hierarchy of his day, and its associated evils of ritual and caste.[15] And he had set in motion a great reform, essentially the Protestantism of Asia.[16] Some were inclined to draw a still grander parallel. Perhaps the Buddha had been to ancient Brahmanism what Jesus Christ was to first-century Judaism: a radical, reforming figure, who had offered a highly ethical teaching rooted in compassion and love.[17]

Against the backdrop of rising Victorian interest in Buddhism, Edwin Arnold's *Light of Asia* became a phenomenal success: in terms of sales down the decades – up to a million copies had been sold by the early 1950s, putting it on a par with Mark Twain's *Adventures of Huckleberry Finn* (1884) – and in attracting book-length rebuttals from concerned Christian clerics.[18] Though he entertained hopes of succeeding Tennyson in the post of Poet Laureate, Arnold owed this success less to his gifts as a bard than a journalist's instinct for their times and audience. What the latter wanted, judged on the basis of *The Light of Asia*'s success, was heroism, exotic adventure, a Christ-like leading man and the redeeming of a scientific picture of nature by linking it to love – reassuring readers that the world around them was, after all, 'Creation'.

The story of the Buddha's life, as told in Buddhist scriptures themselves, went a long way to giving Arnold's Victorian audience what they wanted. Arnold completed the job by playing down the miraculous material, while highlighting parallels between birth stories from the Buddha's previous incarnations and the Christian nativity:

> . . . from afar came merchant-men,
> Bringing, on tidings of this birth, rich gifts
> In golden trays; goat-shawls, and nard and jade . . .
> Waist-cloths sewn thick with pearls, and sandal-wood.[19]

Drawing on his experience as a features writer for London's *Daily Telegraph*, and time spent living and working in India, Arnold conjured a lively and enticing set of birthday celebrations, ordered by the king:[20]

> . . . the ways were swept,
> Rose-odours sprinkled in the street, the trees
> Were hung with lamps and flags, while merry crowds
> Gaped on the sword-players and posturers,
> The jugglers, charmers, swingers, rope-walkers,
> The nautch-girls in their spangled skirts, and bells
> That chime light laughter round their restless feet;[21]

As the famous story progresses, the king seeks to protect Siddhartha from witnessing the suffering of the world beyond the palace gates. But proper to the 'princely spirit', Arnold shows his readers, are curiosity, courage and compassion. A series of unsanctioned sorties reveals to Siddhartha what life is really like: poverty, pain, suffering, death. Pity moves him, in the end, to take a step which Arnold had to handle with great care: abandoning his wife and child.[22] Reassuring readers of the warmth and goodness of marital life, Arnold offers the sort of scenic snapshots that many of them, weaned on travel literature from around the world, would no doubt have expected: the 'stainless ramps' of the Himalayas; the 'pheasant's call and panther's cry'; the 'clatter of wild sheep on the stones'.[23] He lingers, too, over the moment of Siddhartha's reluctant departure, portraying it as the choosing of duty over love.

Siddhartha now dons his lab coat, experimenting with a range of philosophies and practices until the moment of enlightenment arrives, under the famous Bodhi tree. The interconnectedness of everything in nature can, he realizes, be turned from Darwinian 'mutual murder' into mutual salvation – with humankind leading the way. Better still, this is not redemption of the old, discredited kind, for which a man must beg, scrape, pray or pay some dubious priest. One discovers and achieves it for oneself: 'The Soul of Things is sweet', Siddhartha reassures his early audiences, but 'Ye suffer from yourselves.' He lays out the Four Noble Truths: the reality of suffering and sorrow; its origins in human desire and clinging; the possibility of release, by 'conquer[ing] love of self and lust of life'; and the Noble Eightfold Path, as the road that leads 'to peace and refuge'.[24]

The cosmos, Arnold makes clear, is not subject to tyrannical godly whim. What the Buddha discovered was the workings of dharma. The common translation of this word as 'law' brought to mind, for Victorian readers, three pillars of modern Western culture: the Mosaic law, the laws of nature and the rule of law.[25] Since no one is above the law, the Buddha offered, in the Eightfold Path, a means of abiding by it. The reward, for someone who follows this path to its conclusion, is neither an implausible Christian heaven nor the grim abyss claimed by Buddhism's detractors. Instead:

> Never shall yearnings torture him, nor sins
> Stain him, nor ache of earthly joys and woes
> Invade his safe eternal peace; nor deaths
> And lives recur. He goes
>
> Unto NIRVANA. He is one with Life,
> Yet lives not. He is blest, ceasing to be.

OM, MANI PADME, OM! the dewdrop slips
Into the shining sea![26]

★

The Light of Asia was translated into a range of European and Indian languages, and later became an opera, a Broadway play and a feature film – shot in India, with costumes, props and elephants supplied by the Maharaja of Jaipur.[27] It touched the lives of luminaries including Leo Tolstoy, Mahatma Gandhi, W. B. Yeats and T. S. Eliot. Early reviews were sufficiently enthusiastic to inspire a series of rebuttals from concerned Christian critics. One of the major objections to the poem was that Arnold used heavily freighted Christian concepts such as 'sin' to stand for very different Buddhist ideas. The Rhys Davids did this, too, relying on terms like 'church', 'angels' and even the 'Ten Commandments' in their writing.[28] But they were scholars, doing their best while breaking new ground. Arnold was up to something more 'sinister', claimed the American Baptist preacher and professor of literature William Cleaver Wilkinson. Arnold was deliberately raising a suspicion, amongst the weak-minded, that Jesus and the Buddha might be on a par with one another.[29]

This was not merely the crime of suggesting an equivalence between Christianity and other religions – something from which in this era even Max Müller, with his impeccable comparativist credentials, shied away. Buddhism was older than Christianity – so where were people to conclude that parallels between nativity stories came from? Another of Arnold's Christian critics, G. T. Flanders, charged him with encouraging dubious contemporary claims that Jesus had been influenced by Buddhism, and that the gospel writers had drawn on Indian myth. Flanders argued, instead, that some of the myths surrounding the Buddha's life must be Jewish in origin, while others must have been composed after the time of Christ.[30]

What most annoyed critics like Samuel Kellogg, who had worked as a missionary in India, was that Arnold's portrait of Buddhism varied dramatically from the reality of Asian religions in general, as most people actually practised them. Arnold had focused on the Buddha's 'lofty character', and glossed his teachings as 'faith in final good' and 'the immortality of boundless love'. His readers, Kellogg suggested, would presumably not have been happy to learn that southern Buddhism, at least, was atheistic.[31] Nor were Westerners who balked at the idea of evolutionary kinship with lower animals likely to look kindly on the belief that you could be reborn as one. As yet another critic of Arnold, Archibald Scott, put it: the 'true habitat and breeding place' of such a doctrine could only have been, 'like that of the cholera . . . among the degraded and broken-down populations of the East'.[32]

Kellogg suspected, too, that most Westerners raised on conventional Christian ideas about the soul would be disturbed by the Buddhist parable comparing the self to a chariot. It is made up of parts, none of which in itself is the chariot, yet we call their coalescence by that name. In the same way, what we conventionally imagine to be a unitary 'self' is in fact a collection of disparate forces. This was both disturbing and confusing: if no such thing as a self exists, what is it that travels from one body to the next at rebirth? While the philosophical tools and analogies required to answer questions like this remained unavailable in the West, they appeared to be valid criticisms. Only with the advent of Buddhist commentaries published in English would the nuances of Asian thought become clearer. Helpful imagery would begin to circulate too. The self could be likened to a lighted incense stick, rotated in the darkness: it creates the impression of a circle, where no solid circle exists. Rebirth could be compared with the flame of one candle lighting the wick of the next.[33]

Particularly galling for Christian critics who sought to keep Westerners away from Buddhism by reminding them of its terrifying teaching about annihilation, Arnold appeared to employ outright misdirection when it came to nirvana: 'the dewdrop slips / Into the shining sea!' Wilkinson compared this with the delicate way that 'urbane and polished Orientals' spoke about the Buddha 'reposing'.[34] The implication was clear. Once poetry was put aside, Christ simply could not be compared with the Buddha. One died, and three days later rose again. The other died, and three days later he was still dead.

Wilkinson gave over much of his rebuttal – entitled *Edwin Arnold as Poetizer and as Paganizer* – to eviscerating Arnold's literary pretensions. *The Light of Asia* was, in his view, 'a joke'. His commentary on its religious worth was, in places, equally crude. Wilkinson claimed to have fallen asleep while trying meditation, concluding on that basis that Buddhism had a death-wish at its heart – slipping into sleep being loosely analogous to slipping into unconsciousness and death. He wrote off other elements of Buddhist practice, perhaps once again on the basis of trial and error, as 'an infinitely tedious series of self-manipulations . . . You do not get out of yourself. You only get, as it were, more deeply into yourself.'[35]

Elsewhere, however, Wilkinson made an argument with which many defenders of Christianity would have agreed, both in his day and afterwards. Religion, he wrote, ought to be about truth, regardless of time, place and culture. The danger of mounting indiscriminate raids on an Eastern treasure-house was that Westerners would simply seek out spiritual paths that suited their prejudices, or made them feel better. With this in mind, one of the few positive notes that Wilkinson detected in *The Light of Asia* was Arnold's desire to present the Buddha as a monogamous Christian gentleman.[36] If Arnold was worth his salt as a journalist, then the fact that he had chosen to pander to this value meant that it still held sway.

Kellogg made a similar argument, about religion and culture. Referring to Buddhism as the 'fashionable enthusiasm' of the day, he attributed its popularity to a steadily growing tendency for human beings to make themselves the measure of all things. 'The disposition of the age to glory in man', combined with an 'utter contempt for all authority', had resulted, he argued, in people using Darwinian evolution to dispense with divine encumbrance and pronounce themselves masterless in the universe. 'The boastful, self-confident spirit of our age' has little use, thought Kellogg, for a Christian gospel that preaches God becoming man to save the

human race. Far better a man who, through effort and enlightenment, becomes God-like.[37]

★

For Victorian critics of Buddhism, a sure sign of its inadequacy as a
worldview was that the great civilizations of modern times were all
Christian. Show us, they demanded, the elevated society to which
Buddhism has given rise.[38] To which Arnold's answer was: Japan.
Arriving there on a visit in 1889, he was enchanted both by the place
and its people:

> Plunge into the cheery, chattering, polite, and friendly crowd going
> and coming along [Yokohama's] Benten Dori, and it is as if you were
> living on a large painted and lacquered tea-tray, the figures of which,
> the little gilded houses, the dwarf trees, and the odd landscape, sud-
> denly jumped up from the dead plane into the living perpendicular,
> and started into busy being.[39]

Such sentiments were becoming a common feature of Western
travellers' accounts and magazine articles, backed up by paintings,
photographs and art objects sent from Japan to Europe and the
United States. The British traveller Isabella Bird ventured there in
the late 1870s, and was impressed by the great Buddhist temple of
Sensōji, in Tokyo: its imposing red gateway and stone lanterns;
incense wafting through the crowd of visitors, clattering on clogs
over the paved courtyard; the godly and demonic figures looming
out from the dimly lit interior. Buddhism in Japan was, she concluded, 'morals and metaphysics to the educated and initiated, and
an idolatrous superstition to the masses'. Bird encountered those
masses in the bustle of life around the temple complex: 'numerous
places of entertainment, innocent and vicious . . . restaurants, tea-
houses, minor theatres, and the resorts of dancing and singing girls'.
She commended Japan to her readers as offering 'as much novelty
perhaps as an excursion to another planet'.[40]

Here was the language of fresh discovery: testament to the fact

199

that when compared with European encroachments into Indian and Chinese affairs, relations with Japan had been relatively quiet and distant since the expulsion of the Jesuits by the fledgling Tokugawa shogunate, back in the early 1600s. The Dutch, trading from the artificial island of Dejima in Nagasaki Bay, had served as a modest conduit for information about Japan. But Japanese border control had otherwise remained tight until the mid-1850s, when the United States sent a fleet of ships under Commodore Perry to force Japan to open its doors to Western trade and diplomacy. Britain, France, Russia and others soon followed suit, imposing what the Japanese came to regard and resent as 'unequal treaties'.

These treaties had helped to tip the country into civil war, in 1868–9, from which a cadre of young, middle-ranking samurai emerged victorious. They did away with the shogunate, took a teenaged emperor as their figurehead – plucking him from seclusion in Kyoto and plonking him down in a newly-named 'Tokyo' ('Eastern Capital') – and set about equipping Japan with the industrial heft and advanced weaponry needed to avoid the humiliating fate of China just next door. China's emperors had launched a war on drugs across the middle decades of the 1800s, seeking to end the import of tens of thousands of chests of opium every year.[41] Their reward had been armed conflict with the West, the ceding of Hong Kong to the British, and the imposition of a treaty port system that shaded, over time, into pockets of colonial control.

Japan's political elite, fond of using slogans to communicate with their citizenry, would gladly have borrowed 'the light of Asia' to describe their plans in the region. China had led East Asia for centuries, certainly in cultural terms. But Japan, they claimed, was the first country to integrate Western modernity with Asian values.

Westerners who came to know Japan towards the end of the nineteenth century developed more mixed feelings. There was much to love. One found fine art, 'ukiyo-e' woodblock prints, theatre and fashion – a 'Japonisme' trend saw Hiroshige and Hokusai become household names in parts of the West, influencing the likes of Vincent van Gogh and later Claude Monet. There was verdant and dramatic countryside, including the perfect contours of Mount Fuji, from whose summit Arnold penned a few lines of verse in the spring of 1890.[42] And there were the pleasures of mingling with what the Irish-Greek expat Lafcadio Hearn described as 'forty millions of the most lovable people in the universe', all going about their lives at a relaxed pace, and on a cosy and intimate scale.[43]

And yet, in the eyes of Western Japanophiles like Hearn, the country's political class seemed intent on doing away with much of what made Japan special. Arnold saw it too. He sat in the gallery of Japan's new Western-style Diet when it convened for the first time in 1890, and lauded, in a dispatch for the *Telegraph*, the 'Birth of the First Asiatic Parliament'.[44] But he witnessed attempts to dispense with Japanese techniques in painting in favour of shoddy imitations of European artistic styles. And he watched the production of porcelain being warped to fit Western tastes, as old forms of regional patronage were replaced by the demands of an international export market. The Japanese could undoubtedly benefit from Western technology and institutions, but they surely lacked little or nothing in the fields of art, literature and crafts?

Plenty of Japanese agreed with this analysis. Newspaper columnists laughed at their leaders' Western affectations – tuxedoes, ballroom dancing, cigarettes and cocktails – while lamenting their naivety in imagining that Westerners would respect anything but economic and military power. Religious leaders, too, weighed in. A prominent convert to Christianity, Uchimura Kanzō, infuriated by the overbearing attitude of Western missionaries, declared that it was fine for Japanese to learn from Americans about dentistry or cattle-breeding, but frankly embarrassing to take lessons from them on matters of art or spirituality.[45]

Of greatest consequence, for the appeal of Japan in the West, was the response of Japan's Buddhists to these controversies. Facing competition from Shintō and Christian rivals, and accused, in some quarters, of holding Japan back in recent centuries – peddling cosmological lies, stifling inquiry, hoarding the nation's wealth – a number of younger Buddhists set about repackaging their tradition in the 1880s. *Shin bukkyō* (New Buddhism) was close, in some respects, to the idealized Buddhism presented by the Rhys Davids: self-consciously rational, scientific and socially engaged. They offered meditation training to Japan's stressed-out middle classes, and argued in books and articles that when it came to religion, oldest was not necessarily best: in the case of Buddhism, the application of Japanese genius had turned Indian inspiration into the highest form of philosophy and religion that the world possessed. Claims were made, too, for the power of Buddhist practices to render a person psychologically more robust. Here was a new form of Buddhism, crafted with an aspiring Asian superpower in mind, but soon to be sent westward as a form of spiritual first-aid.[46]

★

It was during his short stay in Japan, dressing in Japanese clothes and sleeping on the floor, that Arnold composed his poetical treatment of the life of Christ: *The Light of the World* (1891).[47] Tennyson's lengthy period as Poet Laureate was coming to an end, and Arnold hoped that this new work, dedicated to Queen Victoria, might set him apart from the competition to succeed him. It was not to be, and instead Arnold soon found himself embarking on a shorter and altogether more painful literary project: composing a telegram of congratulation for Alfred Austin, the new Poet Laureate.[48]

Arnold's passing over for this coveted position was more a matter of the lukewarm reception afforded to his life of Christ than any concerns over the soundness of his religious views. Though he was joined on his return to London by a Japanese wife, Tama Kurokawa, he remained a Christian, albeit of liberal inclinations.[49] He never converted to Buddhism. Nor did many Westerners in the Victorian era. Buddhism in the West lacked teachers or temples. It also remained too foreign, and the taboos against its open embrace too strong.

That did not mean that the anxieties of Arnold's critics were entirely unfounded. He represented a poetic, agnostic drift in Victorian religion, encouraged by a growing Western familiarity and comfort with Asian culture: religious ideas, alongside aesthetics and the general sense of place afforded by travel writers like Bird. Orthodox Christians would look back and blame the likes of Schleiermacher, too, for allowing religion's 'cultured despisers' to set the terms on which Christianity would be permitted a presence in the modern world: as a private, experiential affair, making minimal claims to truth – and with even those to be adjudicated according to a narrowed form of rationality, shaped by a scientific-materialist outlook.

Although Christianity retained its central place in society, the late Victorian period was marked by fresh experiments in truth taking place at the margins. In a world filled with publishing houses and societies dedicated to all sorts of causes and points of view, and where public debate was as rigorous and broad in its reach as ever it had been, the Western search for meaning in Asia entered an unprecedented era of discovery and disputation.

Helena Petrovna Blavatsky, a.k.a. Madame Blavatsky.

14.

Experiments in Truth

One of the things that came to distinguish the Buddha from Confucius, in the minds of modern Westerners, was that Confucius seemed less a man than a collection of sayings. You could respect him, in a rather hazy, abstract way, but probably not fall in love. With the Buddha, as conjured up by Edwin Arnold and others, a rule book gave way to a life story, of a struggling and compassionate soul. His early years were a spiritual odyssey of sorts: a model that increasingly spoke to Western life, amidst a proliferating range of worldviews. The writer and activist Annie Besant (1847–1933) was amongst those who, in the late nineteenth century, made public and influential journeys of this kind. She passed through Christianity, atheism, secularism and socialism, before finding a home in Theosophy: a new religious movement, which incorporated elements of Hinduism, Buddhism and the occult.

A certain amount of scepticism surrounded Theosophists' claims to be guided by a couple of Asian 'Masters' living in the Himalayas. Only a handful of people had ever seen them, and they supposedly possessed special powers, including the ability to communicate via letters that materialized out of nowhere. Some of the scepticism, however, was a product of the high noon of empire. A great deal of bluster and pseudoscience had gone into convincing people that the planting of national flags in Asian and African soil was a matter of superior European civilizations guiding the less fortunate. It was easy, on this basis, to accept a 'golden age' theory of Asia: a period of ancient purity and genius, in countries like India and China, which had given way to deterioration. Less natural, for the majority of Westerners in this era, was the notion of Asian spiritual leadership in the here-and-now.

Theosophy went a long way to changing people's thinking, by placing great value on Asia – and on India, especially – both for the religious insights of the past and for the prospect that the region might renew humanity's fortunes. An important role was played, too, by the World's Parliament of Religions (WPR), convened in Chicago in 1893. It boosted a process whose beginnings could be traced back to Ram Mohan Roy at the start of the century: the shifting of the Western search for meaning in Asia from texts alone to flesh-and-blood teachers. At the head of this new generation were the likes of Swami Vivekānanda from India, and the New Buddhist Shaku Sōen from Japan.

Linked to rising tides of cultural nationalism back in their home countries, Vivekānanda and Sōen offered early versions of what would become a defining dichotomy in the twentieth century: between Western cultures that had mastered the external world through science and technology, and Eastern cultures whose expertise lay in mastery of the inner life. As these widely repeated claims about 'West' versus 'East' began to circulate, they did so with a shared value in common: the discerning of truth through experimentation. From everyday meditation through to the esoterica of Theosophy, the assumption was that Akbar's old challenge to the Jesuits – 'Show me' – could, after all, be met in religion, every bit as reliably as in the sciences.

*

Annie Besant (née Wood) was born in London and raised as an Anglican. Neither suited her. 'Three-quarters of my blood and all my heart are Irish,' she declared, adding that as a young woman her Christianity had been fervent, mystical and imaginative – more in tune with Celtic spirituality and the sensory richness of Catholicism than with the 'colder, cruder Evangelicalism' that surrounded her. In her teens, Besant's passionate religious devotion extended to fasting, self-flagellation and 'ecstatic meditation'. Doubts, however, began to emerge when she realized that the four gospels differed, in places, in their accounts of Jesus' life. Marriage to a rather overbearing young clergyman, Frank Besant, and the serious illness of one of their two children, Mabel, compounded her uncertainties, eventually pushing her all the way into atheism. She recalled it as a deeply painful transition, both socially and psychologically. Suddenly, there was 'No life in the empty sky; no gleam in the blackness of the night'.[1]

Separating from her husband in 1873, Besant found solace and purpose in Charles Bradlaugh's National Secular Society. Impressed by a speech given by Bradlaugh on Krishna and Christ as two mutually disproving 'myths' of incarnation, she embarked on a writing and speaking career of her own. Besant became one of the most effective apologists of her day, extolling the intellectually 'safe ground . . . of [scientific] experiment' and a material universe, in which conscious life was an occasional occurrence rather than an animating force. Against those who claimed that secularism threatened to destabilize society, she argued that, in the moral realm, Christianity was more obstacle than inspiration. People felt moved by the wounds of a man who died long ago on a cross, while all but ignoring 'the wounds of men and women, dying in the England of to-day'. The notion that a person's nature and prospects are God-given seemed to be a way of excusing people their indifference to actual sources of misery, including poverty and a lack of education.[2]

The price of making claims such as these, not least as a young woman who was separated from her husband, was to be sworn at, kicked, and have stones thrown at her. Sexual immorality being widely regarded as a consequence and symptom of atheism, Besant suffered endless innuendo about her friendship with Bradlaugh. Her enemies were only too pleased to see her tried in court, alongside Bradlaugh, under the Obscene Publications Act, after they published a controversial book on birth control by an American doctor named Charles Knowlton. They were convicted in 1877, and though their sentences were reversed, and Bradlaugh later became a Member of Parliament, Besant's husband used the scandal to win custody of their daughter, Mabel.[3]

Besant had abandoned her girlhood Christianity, but the idea – or hope – seems to have stayed with her that values like justice, and right versus wrong, were transcendent rather than human in origin.[4] Bradlaugh's brand of secularism lacked this sort of moral and romantic force, and Besant eventually moved on: to socialism, and then to newly emerging ideas about the mind. Studying science at the University of London – one of the first women to enrol there – Besant was struck by the flimsiness of materialist accounts of consciousness.[5] 'The brain secretes thought,' claimed the German scientist Carl Vogt: 'a neat phrase', in Besant's view – 'but what does it *mean*?' The really interesting work in this field seemed to her to be going on elsewhere: in experiments with clairvoyance, clairaudience, the 'unconscious' and hypnosis.[6]

These experiments had roots in the world of hidden forces – magnetism and electricity amongst them – that had helped to inspire Johann Gottfried Herder's vision of God as *Kraft* (force), back in the late 1700s. The forces themselves might be invisible, but their effects could be spectacular. One could enjoy these at 'electrical soirées', where sparks were made to fly in darkened rooms, accompanied by the sound of crackling and the smell of sulphur. A person of particularly stout heart, or irrepressible curiosity, could submit themselves to mild electrocution. Luigi Galvani made dead frogs' legs twitch; his nephew Giovanni Aldini got corpses to sit up and open their eyes.[7]

Franz Anton Mesmer offered a unifying theory for all these forces: 'animal magnetism'. The idea was dismissed as unscientific, but people continued to be fascinated by his experimental techniques: the use of magnets, stroking, 'mesmeric passes' and hypnotic stares to produce trance-like states. Doctors began to explore the therapeutic potential of these states, giving rise, in time, to psychotherapy. 'Spiritualists', meanwhile, noted and exploited the strange powers that some people appeared to exhibit when placed in trances. These included visions, and the ability to read the thoughts of others. The era of the séance had begun. Guests would sit, in semi-darkness, as mediums levitated or spoke with the dead, furniture moved of its own accord, tables made rapping noises, musical instruments played themselves and messages were scratched out on slates by unseen hands.[8]

Mediums quickly became a magnet for satire. But then, didn't real and impressive powers often inspire imitators and charlatans? In an effort to separate the wheat from the chaff, a Society for Psychical Research (SPR) was established in 1882. One of its first missions was the investigation of strange goings-on in India. Alfred Percy Sinnett, an Anglo-Indian newspaper editor, alongside a retired civil servant named Allan Octavian Hume and a writer of aristocratic Russian descent called Helena Petrovna Blavatsky, claimed to have received esoteric teachings from two Masters – or 'Mahatmas' – who were living in Tibet. The method of communication used by Morya and Koot Hoomi was remarkable. The 'Mahatma Letters', as they came to be known, had been sent and received via 'apport': dematerialization in one place, and rematerialization in another. Random scraps of paper were used. As Koot Hoomi explained, there were no stationers' shops in Tibet.[9]

Interviews in India, and calligraphic analysis of the letters, convinced the SPR's investigator, Richard Hodgson, that the whole thing was a sham. The society's report, published in 1885, denounced Blavatsky as an imposter.[10] It was a blow to her reputation, but far from fatal. On the basis of eclectic reading and what she claimed was wide travel and esoteric learning, Blavatsky turned herself into the philosopher-queen of Spiritualism. Across two books – *Isis Unveiled: A Master Key to the Mysteries of Ancient and Modern Science and Theology* (1877) and *The Secret Doctrine* (1888) – she fashioned a grand vision of cosmic purpose, drawing on a wide variety of sources: Egyptian and Graeco-Roman religion, Hellenistic and Renaissance magic, Jewish Kabbalah, Jesus' teachings about the Holy Spirit, astrology, alchemy, modern science, Hinduism and Buddhism.

Blavatsky revived an old word, 'Theosophy' ('divine wisdom'), to describe this body of knowledge and the associated movement that she set out to establish. The cosmos, Blavatsky proposed, emanates in cycles from an impersonal Absolute. Everything in it – planets, animals, Buddhist deities – is interrelated, has purpose, and is composed not merely of matter but of seven principles working in combination. At death, human beings shed their three 'lower' principles, but the rest carry on, driven by karma into a new incarnation. Each person's pilgrimage continues across multiple lifetimes, until their 'spiritual evolution' culminates in a return to the Absolute. People who are particularly far advanced on this journey are known as 'Masters', amongst whom Blavatsky numbered the Buddha, Pythagoras, Plato and Jesus.[11]

Blavatsky saw herself as a disciple and missionary of the two Masters in Tibet, helping to bring their message to the wider world.[12] She founded a Theosophical Society in New York in 1875, with an American Civil War veteran called Colonel Henry Steel Olcott serving as its president. The two travelled to Madras together, establishing the society's international headquarters at Adyar and placing Indian ideas – in particular Buddhism, the Upanishads, the *Bhagavad Gita*, and Shankara's Advaita Vedānta – at the heart of Theosophy.

Annie Besant read *The Secret Doctrine* in 1889. Impressed with the book, she sought an interview with Blavatsky, who at that time was living in Holland Park, London. Where some regarded Blavatsky as a rather difficult individual, given to self-promotion, Besant found her worldly and charismatic: rolling cigarettes, speaking breezily of her travels in far-off places, and avoiding all talk of the occult. Only when the time came to say goodbye did she suddenly train her 'brilliant, piercing eyes' on Besant, and say: 'My dear Mrs Besant, if you would only come among us!' Besant was overcome: 'I felt a wellnigh uncontrollable desire to bend down and kiss her, under the compulsion of that yearning voice, those compelling eyes.'[13]

A guru–disciple dynamic was entering the Western encounter with Asia, its earliest practitioner a Russian aristocrat. Blavatsky was confident enough of Besant's devotion that she made her read the SPR's exposé of the Mahatma Letters before committing to Theosophy.[14] Besant came to believe that pride had long been getting in the way of her spiritual progress, and that Blavatsky had freed her from it – by helping her to 'renounce everything', and accepting her as a pupil.[15] Upon hearing of Besant's embrace of Theosophy, her friend and fellow socialist George Bernard Shaw sought her out to deliver himself of – in his words – 'an unbounded denunciation of Theosophy' and of 'female inconstancy'. Deeply disappointed in her though he was, he did note from their meeting that Besant 'was no longer in the grip of her pride'.[16]

Condemning a spirit of 'nineteenth-century self-sufficiency', which encouraged people to dismiss anything outside the compass of their understanding as 'deception' or 'charlatanry', Besant claimed to have experienced extraordinary things while 'in the infant class of the Occult School'.[17] The astral figure of Master Morya paid her a night-time visit, attended by pulsating waves in the air around him, along with the smell of sandalwood and other Eastern scents.[18] She came to 'know, by personal experiment, that the Soul exists, and that my Soul, not my body, is myself'. That soul was capable, moreover, of leaving her body and learning from teachers living elsewhere. In Besant's view, such discoveries amounted to an enrichment rather than a repudiation of her previous scientific worldview. Western science dealt with the material plane – a useful but limited assignment. 'Eastern science' opened and trained the mind, to the point where it could discern activity on the deeper 'mental and spiritual planes'.[19]

While Blavatsky helped Besant to wrestle her pride into submission, elsewhere Theosophy contributed to a surge in confidence. One of the first callers to a new 'Blavatsky Lodge' – a corrugated-iron outhouse, set up in Besant's garden – was a young Indian law student who, under the influence of missionary critiques, had grown up with a low view of Hinduism. Mohandas K. Gandhi had already 'crossed the Sahara of atheism', as he put it in his autobiography, *The Story of My Experiments with Truth*. But he had never read the *Bhagavad Gita* until two Theosophist friends in London introduced him to it, in a translation produced by Edwin Arnold (entitled *The Song Celestial*). In addition to meeting Blavatsky and Besant, Gandhi invited Arnold, who lived nearby to him in Bayswater, to serve as vice-president of his new vegetarian club.[20] By the time Gandhi's studies in London came to an end, he had added *The Light of Asia* to his list of literary discoveries, and had been swept up in the comparative religious mood of the era. He began to see parallels in the *Bhagavad Gita*, Buddhism, Islam and Jesus' Sermon on the Mount which, in time, would shape his approach to politics.

Some Theosophists saw the hands of Morya and Koot Hoomi at work in all of this. Allan Octavian Hume, sometime recipient of letters from the two Masters, believed that they had used their highly evolved powers to preserve imperial rule in India at the time of the 1857 Indian Uprising. It was now his task, he thought, to help preserve a balance of power on the subcontinent. In 1885, he became the prime mover in establishing the Indian National Congress: the organization which, under Gandhi's leadership, would one day help India to win its independence. One didn't have to be a Theosophist to understand the potential cultural power, in India, of rising respect – Western and Indian alike – for Asian wisdom. The colonial authorities were sufficiently concerned about this that when Blavatsky and later Besant travelled to India, they were placed under surveillance.[21]

In 1891, Annie Besant lost the two great mentors of her life, as both Charles Bradlaugh and Madame Blavatsky passed away. Blavatsky was cremated at Woking Necropolis, and her ashes were divided between London, New York and Adyar.[22] The one-year anniversary of liberation from her body was celebrated with readings from the *Bhagavad Gita* and Arnold's *Light of Asia*.[23] Bradlaugh's burial at the same necropolis must have felt rather more final, to those who shared his worldview. Gandhi was amongst the mourners who boarded special trains from London to Woking for his funeral, joined, he later recalled, by practically 'every Indian residing in London'.[24] Such had been Bradlaugh's support for Indian causes in Parliament that he had earned himself the nickname 'the Member for India'. Amongst his Indian allies were prominent political leaders including Dadabhai Naoroji, who respected Western learning and political principles but criticized colonial rule for straying from and undermining them. Naoroji famously described political and economic injustices in India as 'un-British'.[25]

Two visions for India's future were thus remembered in Woking, in 1891. Bradlaugh, and Indian allies like Naoroji, favoured self-determination along liberal secular lines. Blavatsky, whose Theosophical Society had by this point grown to more than 250 branches on six continents, placed India at the centre of a cosmic drama.[26] Few in this era, or later ones, painted on quite so large a canvas. But a generation of Asian cultural nationalists was beginning to come through, who made connections of their own between religion and the future of their nations, even of humanity as a whole. In 1893, some of them packed their bags for Chicago, heading for history's first global inter-religious summit: the World's Parliament of Religions.

*

Around two hundred delegates, representing forty-five religious traditions and denominations, descended on the brand-new 'white city' of the World's Columbian Exposition, in the autumn of 1893. Marvelling at its fountains, plazas and promenades, enthusiasts compared the World's Parliament of Religions (WPR) to the court of Emperor Akbar, many centuries before. There, too, albeit on a more modest scale, representatives of different faiths had gathered for debate. Max Müller later declared it one of the regrets of his life not to have made it to Chicago.[27]

The WPR did, however, have its detractors. Some, like Ida Wells and Frederick Douglass, condemned the failure to give space to African Americans. Others detected a Western Christian triumphalism at its core. Still others worried that the parliament's comparative ethos risked devaluing their own traditions. In a rare moment of accord, the Archbishop of Canterbury and the Sultan of the Ottoman Empire both declined to support the WPR on this basis. Islam and Christianity were both represented nonetheless, but the former only by one delegate. Some of the many Christian delegates, meanwhile, suffered the ignominy of rising to speak while hundreds of people made noisily for the exits: the WPR audiences – mostly women, since sessions were held during the working day – were overwhelmingly interested in hearing about new and exotic faiths, and were not inclined to hang around once the Asian delegates had finished speaking.[28]

Japanese and Indian offerings at the WPR had much in common: universalism, toleration and Asia's edge over the West in matters spiritual. The Japanese Buddhist delegation was dominated by the modernizing, nation-building forces of New Buddhism. Four priests arrived to take part, alongside two laymen, one of whom, Noguchi Zenshiro, prepared the way for his colleagues by insisting in his opening speech that Japan had rather more to offer the West than silk, fans and tea-sets. The other layman, Hirai Kinzō, began his speech by extolling Japanese open-mindedness, quoting some lines from the medieval Buddhist monk Ikkyū: 'Though there are many roads at the foot of the mountain, yet, if the top is reached, the same moon is seen.'[29]

As far as the WPR's chairman was concerned, Hirai's oration went downhill from there. He had read the speech ahead of time, and had advised Hirai to give a different one. Realizing that Hirai was sticking to his original text, the chairman tried physically to restrain him.[30] He failed, and a packed Hall of Columbus heard Hirai accuse the West of imposing unreasonable trade treaties, 'trampl[ing] upon the rights . . . of a non-Christian nation'. Japanese migrants to cities like San Francisco were, meanwhile, being treated with unforgivable racism. 'If such be the Christian ethics,' Hirai declared, 'well, we are perfectly satisfied to be heathen.' Echoing liberal Indian criticism of British colonial rule, Hirai claimed to have read America's Declaration of Independence with tears in his eyes. If Americans would but treat Japan according to the spirit of that sublime document, they would find in Hirai 'the warmest admirer of [the] gospels'.[31] On the basis, perhaps, of this late concession to his hosts' feelings, Hirai sat down to sympathetic applause.[32]

For charm and diplomacy, there was no matching the real star of the WPR. A disciple of the Bengali mystic Ramakrishna, Swami Vivekānanda had come to America partly in hope of raising funds for religious and social projects back home. The remarkable reception that he received at the parliament helped to set him on his way. It came down, in part, to the low bar set for Indian life and culture earlier in the nineteenth century, thanks not least to highly critical Christian missionary reports. Newspaper reaction, although shot through with the period's racial preoccupations, was overwhelmingly positive. Here was a man who spoke without notes yet with 'the greatest art', combining a 'fine, intelligent, mobile face' complete with 'white teeth' and 'well-chiselled lips', with a 'fascinating personality'. Like a Jesuit, he was canny and accomplished. 'The little sarcasms thrown into his discourses are as keen as a rapier,' noted one correspondent, '[yet] his courtesy is unfailing, for these thrusts are never pointed so directly at our customs as to be rude.' One commentator, inspired by Vivekānanda's combination of modest stature and forceful presence, compared him with Napoleon.[33]

Vivekānanda's case for Hinduism as the world's first and most tolerant religion came with a sting in its tail for his Western listeners. 'Every other religion' laid down dogmas and then sought to force compliance, he suggested, but Hinduism recognized that 'unity in variety is the plan of nature'. A 'Hindu fanatic' might 'burn himself on the pyre', he said – referencing what had become, by now, Western clichés about India's religious extremes – but 'he never lights the fire of inquisition'.[34]

Vivekānanda ended his main address by combining flattering reflections on America's place in the world with an effort to reclaim the notion of 'the East' for Asia:

Akbar's [inter-religious council] . . . was only a parlour-meeting. It was reserved for America to proclaim to all quarters of the globe that the Lord is in every religion . . . The star arose in the East; it travelled steadily toward the West . . . till it made a circuit of the world, and now it is again rising on the very horizon of the East . . . a thousand-fold more effulgent than it ever was before.[35]

Vivekānanda's religious pitch to the WPR was rooted in Advaita Vedānta. Echoing an argument that Ram Mohan Roy had made several decades before, Vivekānanda declared that what critics of Hinduism imagined to be idolatrous polytheism – Vishnu, Shiva, Kāli and the rest – was in fact the stuff of 'spiritual childhood'. It was not wrong in itself, but it was intended to be cast off when the time was right, in favour of mental prayer and, ultimately, union with God. Where Hinduism did make literal claims about the world, he went on, they were in line with discoveries in the natural sciences: the conservation of energy, the idea – increasingly apparent from experimental psychology – that there is more to a person than everyday self-awareness, and an emerging consensus that materialism was unlikely to offer an adequate account of reality. Scientists in Western laboratories were just now feeling their way towards insights achieved, many centuries before, by ascetics living in Indian forests.[36]

Some of those ancient Indian insights had come courtesy of highly developed spiritual practices, which Swami Vivekānanda was more than willing for Westerners to try. He became the first Asian teacher of yoga in America, during his months on tour after the WPR.[37] On one occasion he sat, turbaned and cross-legged, under a tall pine tree on the banks of the Piscataqua River in Maine, and told his small audience that 'yoga' means a method – of which there are many – for 'yoking' oneself to the divine.

Basing his teaching in the Yoga Sutras of Patanjali, a philosopher and mystic from the early centuries CE, Vivekānanda taught his listeners to 'hold the head and shoulders and the hips in a straight line, keeping the spinal column free; all action is along it, and it must not be impaired.'[38] They were then to focus briefly on each part of their bodies, beginning with the toes and working their way up to their heads, regarding each part, and finally the whole, as perfect: a God-given instrument for obtaining Truth. Vivekānanda taught breathing exercises and meditations, and gave an account of the eight aspects, or 'limbs', of Patanjali's yoga: ethical conduct, habits and observances, yoga postures, breath control, withdrawal of the senses, concentration, meditation and absorption. In a departure from Patanjali, Vivekānanda taught the idea of Kundalini: cosmic energy, visualized as a serpent coiled at the base of the spine, the awakening of which was, he claimed, one of the goals of his 'Raja Yoga' ('Royal Yoga').[39]

Japan's Buddhist delegates to the WPR agreed with much of what Vivekānanda had to say about the genius of 'the East'. But they were compelled to part company with him when it came to ancient intuitions of truth. They made the case, instead, for religious evolution: the honing, across centuries, of the Buddha's insights, courtesy of the 'Japanese spirit'. The result was a religious outlook that fulfilled the ever-popular German Idealist strand in Western philosophy, while being perfectly in line with modern science.

Amongst those to make this case was Shaku Sōen, abbot of Engakuji (Rinzai Zen). He had studied at Keio University, one of Japan's first private universities, and he relied for English translations of his talks on another university graduate: D. T. Suzuki, a lay student at Engakuji. Both men became significant figures in the transmission of Zen to the West, having crafted their presentation of it on the basis of a deep and largely sympathetic understanding of their audiences' intellectual history and contemporary anxieties.

At the WPR, Sōen set out to explain cause and effect by critiquing Thomas Aquinas. Where the great medieval theologian had posited God as the 'prime mover', he said, Buddhists denied that there must be a 'beginning' to the universe at all. Sōen seems to have misunderstood Aquinas on this point: he had been writing about causation in terms of an ultimate source of being, rather than a set of dominoes falling in sequence. Nevertheless, here was an early example of what would become a popular twentieth-century pitch: Asian ideas and practices were able to pick up where Western ones left off, the latter having either proven philosophically inadequate or no longer capable of moving, transforming or consoling people.[40]

Religion, and in particular spiritual experience, lay at the heart of

Asian claims to answer a Western search for meaning, at a time when parts of Western Christianity were in crisis. But these things were bound up with the arts and literature too. A defining statement of this bigger picture was offered at the dawn of the twentieth century, by the Japanese curator and art critic Okakura Kakuzō:

> Asia is one. The Himalayas divide, only to accentuate, two mighty civilisations, the Chinese with its communism of Confucius, and the Indian with its individualism of the Vedas. But not even the snowy barriers can interrupt for one moment that broad expanse of love for the Ultimate and Universal, which is the common thought-inheritance of every Asiatic race, enabling them to produce all the great religions of the world, and distinguishing them from those maritime peoples of the Mediterranean and the Baltic, who love to dwell on the Particular, and to search out the means, not the end, of life.[41]

Widely travelled in Japan, China and India, Okakura put forward, in *The Ideals of the East* (1903), a powerful case for his country's mission in the world. He argued that the spirit of Asia, arising out of Indian religion and Chinese learning and ethics, was best revealed and preserved in the region's artistic traditions. Major developments in these traditions had flowed steadily into Japan across the centuries, and it was now only there that the 'historic wealth of Asiatic culture' could be appreciated in its fullness. Possessed of a 'singular genius', which enabled them to accept the new without losing sight of the old, the Japanese had a responsibility, in the new century, to establish a firm place in the world for 'Asiatic civilization' and the 'Asiatic soul'.[42]

Fittingly for a passionate pan-Asianist, Okakura completed work on his book while living in Calcutta. He stayed at a mansion owned by one of the city's most famous families: the Tagores. Residents almost since the city's foundation by the East India Company in the late 1600s, their contributions to its cultural life included leadership, for a time, of Ram Mohan Roy's Brahmo Samaj and latterly the poetry of Rabindranath Tagore (1861–1941): polymath, nationalist, and the first non-European winner of the Nobel Prize for Literature, in 1913. Tagore later recalled that it was upon meeting Okakura that the concept of an 'Asiatic mind' first made sense to him.

Okakura also met Swami Vivekānanda during his time in India, travelling with him by train and horse-drawn carriage to the major Buddhist sites of Bodh Gaya and Sarnath, the sites, respectively, of the Buddha's enlightenment and his preaching of his first post-enlightenment sermon. Both sites had been excavated in the nineteenth century. Vivekānanda was, by now, in his final months of life. His return to India from the WPR had been delayed by lecture tours in the United States and Great Britain. Turning down the offer of teaching positions at Harvard and Columbia, he left a Vedānta Society as his legacy in the West – established in New York in 1894, with chapters in Boston and London – and returned to India in 1896.[43]

A handful of Western women were integral to the early twentieth-century vision of a united Asia. Josephine MacLeod heard Vivekānanda speak in New York, and in addition to visiting India to spend time with him she also travelled to Japan, to help raise money for his newly founded Ramakrishna Mission. She encountered Okakura there, and put the two men in touch. A Northern Irish teacher named Margaret Elizabeth Noble joined Vivekānanda when he returned to India. She became part of his Ramakrishna Order, took the name 'Sister Nivedita', and duly began to have her post opened by worried colonial police. Nivedita helped to edit Okakura's book manuscript and provided its introduction, comparing the role of Indian spirituality in inspiring Asian art with that of Italy and the Catholic Church in the history of European aesthetics. Looking ahead to the new century, she suggested that it might be 'the destiny of imperial peoples to be conquered in turn by the religious ideas of their subjects'.[44]

Annie Besant, too, was by now living in India, having relocated there shortly after representing Theosophy at the WPR. Living first in Varanasi and then later in Adyar, Besant decorated her homes in Indian styles, wore saris, observed high-caste purity rules for a time, studied Sanskrit and campaigned for children's education. Sister

Nivedita did not take to her, nor to what she saw as Theosophy's extravagant claims. She commented to a friend that Besant seemed ready to believe anything 'if only SHE RULES'. Nivedita reported, too, that the apparent preference of the elusive Masters, Morya and Koot Hoomi, for communicating with non-Indians and Anglo-Indians, had begun to strike some in India's nationalist circles as rather out of date. One critic, confided Nivedita to her friend, had suggested that the Masters must be 'the ghosts of [Robert] Clive and Warren Hastings!'[45]

Here was but a hint of how respect for Asian wisdom did not translate into easily agreed political programmes. For Besant, and for Gandhi too, the question of what a free India ought to look like was bound up with their views on the spiritual cul-de-sac in which much of the Western world now found itself. In *Hind Swaraj* (1909), Gandhi used the term *swaraj*, 'self-rule', to express his ideal for his country: the moral and spiritual transformation of each individual, out of which real civilization – as opposed to what he saw as the warped, British kind – could then emerge. Gandhi was writing largely for the benefit of young nationalists who, outraged by the splitting of the powerful Bengal Presidency into two by the British, in 1905, had taken to political violence as a way of fighting their cause.

Similar tensions existed in Japan. Shaku Sōen had followed up his address to the WPR with his own lecture tour of America, teaching his audiences how to meditate.[46] Both Vedānta and Zen were beginning to take off in the West, answering that hunger for direct, intuitive religious knowledge about which Schleiermacher had written, and which was reflected now in the American philosopher William James' book *The Varieties of Religious Experience* (1902). For the Japanese, however, while they welcomed news of Zen's popularity abroad, there was less warmth for the idea that their country ought to preserve itself as some combination of art museum and bucolic paradise for the spiritual edification of foreigners.

Japan had been on the up and up since the WPR: revision of the unequal treaties, about which Hirai Kinzō had complained, and

victory in a war with China, in 1894–5. The country's most spectacular achievement was the vanquishing of Russia, in the Russo-Japanese
War of 1904–5: the first 'win' for an Eastern over a Western power in
many centuries. And yet, although Rabindranath Tagore had composed a celebratory poem in the haiku style, when he visited Japan
just over a decade later, in 1916, he had sought to claim it for a larger
and notably less martial 'East': a 'culture that enjoins man to look for
his true wealth and power in his inner soul'.[47] Japanese critics were
quick to point out that their country had been rather successful, of
late, at finding wealth and power in industry, trade and modern weaponry. Tagore's warnings about succumbing to the temptations of
European-style nationalism went down badly – dismissed by a prominent Japanese philosopher as 'the song of a ruined country'.[48]

★

Tagore could hardly be accused of naivety in the talks that he gave
in Japan, at least not in his concern over European nationalism. His
visit came in the midst of a world war which eloquently exposed
what people like he and Besant regarded as the corruptions of
modern Western life. Besant speculated that the war might have
been orchestrated by the Masters, seeking to move humanity into a
new phase.[49] This was a niche view, but the sight of Christian nations
turning on one another, using weapons of ferocious destructive
power, persuaded a great many reflective souls, in Asia and the West
alike, to rethink the old idea of steady human progress from barbarism towards civilization. Some of them began to wonder whether
'East' and 'West' might come together and reform humanity's collective outlook, and whether they might pursue this task in their
own lives: by exploring, sifting and testing new ideas, in hope of
radically reimagining reality. The era of the spiritual odyssey had
arrived.

PART THREE

Inward: Dwellers on the Threshold
(1910s to 2000)

Hotei Yawning, by Sengai.

15.

Two Worlds

Born on 6 January 1915, Alan Watts grew up in two different worlds. The first was the world of the unheated upper floor at Rowan Tree Cottage, the Watts family home in the village of Chislehurst, Kent. In the chill of its bathroom, he received his introduction to the cosmos, as a grimly inquisitorial and confusing place. His parents pored over what he produced in the toilet, and his mother Emily, raised in a devoutly Evangelical family, taught him prayers while bathing him:

> Let my sins be all forgiven;
> Bless the friend I love so well
> Take me, when I die, to heaven,
> Happy there with thee to dwell.[1]

Verses like these left Watts lying awake at night in his lonely bedroom, resisting the pull of sleep in case he didn't wake up again. Terrified of going to hell, he found images of heaven baffling rather than consoling:

> How sweet to rest
> For ever on my Saviour's breast.
>
> Prostrate before Thy throne to lie,
> And gaze and gaze on Thee.[2]

The upper floor of Rowan Tree Cottage soon merged with the boarding schools to which Watts' ambitious parents sent their only surviving child. Saint Hugh's, near Chislehurst, was his first stop, at the age of seven, followed by the King's School in Canterbury from the age of thirteen. English Christianity was a heavy presence in both. The adult Watts recalled 'bombastic' and 'infantile' hymnody running alongside a much-vaunted deeper induction into the faith, whose most memorable element was a list of the physical torments likely to be brought on by masturbation: from epilepsy to the 'Great Siberian Itch'.[3]

For Watts, this brand of Christianity was bound up with a broader Englishness, which he both feared and detested: the funereal black suit that his father wore for work; residential streets full of 'boxy, red-brick quiet-desperation homes'. Much of what went on behind those buildings' walls seemed equally dowdy and narrow, from furnishings and food to everyday conversation. Writing later in life, and with readers in his adopted homeland of the United States primarily in mind – 'quiet desperation' was an oft-quoted line from the transcendentalist Henry David Thoreau – Watts speculated that the only thing his native country's climate and cuisine had managed to inspire was imperialism, propelling its people across the world in a desperate search for more compelling alternatives.[4]

The second, contrasting world of Watts' early life was his home's warm ground floor. His mother was a school teacher, and amongst her pupils were the children of missionaries working in Asia. Grateful parents, returning home on furlough bearing gifts, bestowed upon Rowan Tree Cottage a coffee table from India, crafted in the shape of a mandala. There were Chinese embroideries and vases too, decorated with images of mandarins at court and warriors taking to the battlefield. A Japanese tapestry depicted the quiet calm of a lakeside teahouse. Watts used to sit amidst this splendour, and listen to his father read from the *Arabian Nights* and Rudyard Kipling. He became a fan of Sax Rohmer's Fu Manchu, preferring his artful skulduggery to the 'suet-pudding heroism' on offer in English works of the era.[5]

This rich, sensory environment extended out into the family garden. It was a place of 'magic' whose lawn, rose trees and 'bouncy little robins' could readily be imagined as the playground and play-mates of fine-featured fairies. There was wild beauty, too, in regions where green fingers didn't reach: mushroom patches and pools of water; bracken and gorse bushes running riot. Encountered at eye level, tomatoes and raspberries appeared to the young Watts as 'glowing, luscious jewels'. Around this mini-paradise, Watts would chase moths, and fire his bow and arrow with his father, Laurence.[6]

Early hints as to how these two worlds might be reconciled – a fearful, wrong-seeming account of life versus the evident goodness of life itself – emerged on the rare occasions when Watts was taken to High Mass. The rituals, singing and silences enchanted him, as did a liturgy so marvellously unintelligible that 'Elizabethan English might just as well be Sanskrit'. The enthronement of Cosmo Gordon Lang as Archbishop of Canterbury in 1928 cast a similar spell: Watts was amongst a handful of boys chosen to carry the archbishop's train, donning knee breeches and silk stockings for the occasion.[7]

The road to reconciliation ran through France. In 1929, Watts was invited to join his school friend, Ivan Croshaw, on a family summer holiday to Saint-Malo and Mont Saint-Michel. Ivan's father, Francis, exuded just the sort of Englishness of which Watts could approve. Wealthy enough not to have to work, he wandered around in a 'decrepit Moorish dressing gown' carrying a dog whip (though he owned no dog) and smoking black Burmese cigars. Watts always looked back on his French adventure with enormous warmth. There was sun, sophisticated food, horse-races, bull-fights and his first alcoholic drink. Returning to England ever more inclined to regard school as beneath him, he was primed for his next discovery: the Irish-Greek writer Lafcadio Hearn – and Japan.[8]

Watts stumbled across Hearn's *Glimpses of Unfamiliar Japan* in a bookshop in Camden Town.[9] From its pages, and from those of *Gleanings in Buddha-Fields* by the same author, sprang a marvellous and exotic place where, in Hearn's words, 'land, life, and sky are unlike all that one has known elsewhere . . . surely the realization, for imaginations nourished with English folklore, of the old dream of a World of Elves.'[10] Inspired by Hearn's enthusiasm for Chinese and Japanese art, Watts began to see how religion, beauty and nature sometimes came together. East Asian painting was often remarkably spacious, giving room to – and affirming – the 'pregnant emptiness' at the heart of Taoism and Mahayana Buddhism. When European and East Asian art were set alongside one another, the first seemed, to Watts, to treat the natural world as a means to an end – the backdrop for making a social or moral point. The latter, by contrast, discerned something in nature itself that was of inestimable value.[11] Hearn's writing about Buddhism and nirvana moved Watts too. For an anxious young man, whose religious upbringing was rooted in reprimand – actual or threatened – the Buddha offered blessed release.[12]

Croshaw began to lend Watts some of his own books on Buddhism, inside one of which Watts found a yellow pamphlet bearing the stamp of the Buddhist Society. It had been established just a few years earlier by a London barrister called Christmas Humphreys. Following his brother's death in the Great War, Humphreys had abandoned Christianity and the Jesus of his childhood – 'a sort of super Boy Scout Chief', as he put it – in favour of Theosophy. He was deeply impressed by Annie Besant when he heard her speak in London, but eventually he became disillusioned with the Theosophical Society's infighting. With his wife Aileen, a veteran of the Great War and one of just sixteen women to receive the Military Medal, Humphreys established the Buddhist Society, and they ran it together from their flat in Pimlico. Watts was delighted to find that such a society existed, and immediately wrote them a letter – in a tone so confident that the Humphreys imagined one of the senior masters at the King's School had developed an interest in the East. They were amazed to find a boy of around seventeen turn up to one of their meetings instead.[13]

Watts himself was scarcely less impressed, upon stepping into the Humphreys' home. He had enjoyed spending time, of late, discussing Buddhism with the breezy and bohemian Croshaw over red wine and cigars.[14] But Christmas and Aileen – 'Toby' and 'Puck' – were in another league. Their flat was a wonderland of artworks, golden buddhas, Persian rugs, swirls of sandalwood incense and a rich library, over whose mantelpiece hung a portrait of Edwin Arnold. The society had even been given the very armchair in which Arnold was said to have written *The Light of Asia* – those parts, at least, which had not been jotted down, piecemeal, on the go, and using whatever writing surfaces were closest to hand.[15]

Here was 'an education', Watts later reflected, 'which no money could possibly buy'. He awarded Madame Blavatsky much of the credit. Her ideas were little more than 'occult science fiction' as far as he was concerned, but she had brought Hinduism and Buddhism to prominence in Britain, and in the process encouraged like-minded people to come together. This last mattered enormously to Watts, as a budding bon-vivant: he was a man who liked his philosophical conversation to have a cosmopolitan edge. Through Toby and Puck – intelligent and worldly-wise figures themselves – Watts met a range of fascinating individuals, including psychiatrists, explorers, Russian exiles and eventually Shaku Sōen's protégé D. T. Suzuki.[16]

School was of interest, now, mostly as a place of Buddhist evangelism and disputation. Watts sparred with his Calvinist housemaster, gave talks to the debating society, and passed around his 'Eastern' reading materials like literary contraband. He discovered an early critic in his own Evangelical Aunt Gertrude. She dismissed Buddhism as selfish, with little time for women and no concept of the importance of suffering as a test. Watts did his best to fight his corner in written replies, revelling in the discovery that enormous numbers of people around the world were as free as he sought to be from the 'bombastic bore' that was the Christian God of his acquaintance.[17]

Alongside reading, conversation and debate ran tentative attempts at spiritual practice. Finding a second-hand copy of Swami Vivekānanda's *Raja Yoga* (1896) in Camden Market, Watts took to practising yoga in his dormitory room while looking out over Canterbury Cathedral. He tried various forms of Buddhist meditation, too, not being able to decide what sort of practice was best. One day in the autumn of 1932, the competing ideas and admonitions jostling for space in his head suddenly became too much. In desperation, he shouted at them to go away – and they did: 'My weight vanished. I owned nothing. All hang-ups disappeared. I walked on air.'

What else was a precocious young man, deeply enamoured with Asian ideas and aesthetics, to do at this point, but compose a haiku?

> All forgotten and set aside –
> Wind scattering leaves
> Over the fields.[18]

*

To his moment of bliss in his boarding-school dormitory, Watts added a moment of blunder that same year. He attempted, for some unknown reason, to answer the questions on an entrance examination for Oxford University in the style of Friedrich Nietzsche.[19] His application was duly turned down, and a lifetime of mutual hostility opened up: between Watts, as a freewheeling amateur philosopher, and university academics who took a self-consciously serious and scholarly approach to Asia. Watts would always remain wary of academics, hurt by their criticism and exasperated by what he saw as a tendency to confuse professional detachment with cold pedantry.

Watts found kindred spirits in Jiddu Krishnamurti, once hailed as Theosophy's 'messiah' and now a popular spiritual teacher, and in D. T. Suzuki, whose writings Watts distilled in *The Spirit of Zen* (1935). When he met Suzuki in person the following year, he found him to be the very ideal of a Zen teacher: 'wisely foolish, gently disciplined, and simply profound'. Suzuki seemed to revel in his reputation as a renegade from Japan's Zen establishment, once declaring that it would be better if all the Zen monasteries in Japan were burned down, so profoundly were they missing the point of Zen.[20]

1936 was also the year that Watts first encountered Carl Jung when he lectured in London. Like Suzuki, Jung was not short of enemies. His predicament was summed up by Watts as having scientists accuse him of 'turning psychology into mysticism', while advocates of religion claimed that he was reducing their beliefs to 'phantasies of the unconscious mind'.[21] Jung was not afraid to go on the offensive against his scientific colleagues, denouncing 'the *misérable vanité des savants*, which fears and rejects with horror any sign of living sympathy', and warning that 'scientific method must serve; it errs when it usurps a throne'.[22]

Ever the upstart, Watts wrote to Jung the day after his London lecture in order to put him straight on a few matters of Asian philosophy. There is no record of Jung replying, but Watts entered into a conversation with him nonetheless: reading everything he could get his hands on, and taking Jung as his primary inspiration in seeking to reconcile Asian religions, Christianity and human psychology. Here, hoped Watts, was a means of tackling anxiety and unhappiness: his own and, in time, that of others too.[23]

As a relatively new and nebulous discipline, psychoanalysis was full of opportunity for people, like Jung, who were given to eclecticism in their thinking. Close to its founder, Sigmund Freud, early on, and then breaking with him over the roles of sex and religion in human life, Jung's great project was to bring together psychiatry, psychology, Spiritualism, world religions and his favourite parts of German philosophy.[24] Like Freud, he used the term 'ego' to describe the centre of a person's conscious awareness. Unlike Freud, he did not believe that the purpose of psychotherapy ought to be the strengthening of that ego against the competing demands of society's standards and an individual's hidden urges and desires. The ego, for Jung, was secondary in importance to a broader and more fundamental 'Self', which encompassed both the conscious and unconscious aspects of a person. The purpose of psychotherapy, and indeed the goal of life, was the balancing and integration of everything which that Self contained. In Jungian language, this was the process of 'individuation'.

Watts' first attempt at combining Asian ideas with Western psychology appeared soon after he read Jung's *Modern Man in Search of a Soul* (1933). The degree to which *The Legacy of Asia and Western*

Man (1937) reflected Jung's thinking was clear in the approving letter which Watts received from the man himself.[25] Watts took as his starting point Jung's idea of treating religion as a system of symbols. That did not mean reducing religion to a mere function of the mind; Jung simply believed, like Immanuel Kant, that human beings can never gain certain knowledge about the world beyond their minds. There was no way of telling, thought Jung, whether the ultimate 'principle of existence' was God, matter, energy or something else entirely.[26]

What one could do, in Jung's view, was ask whether a particular religious system was conducive to flourishing – to 'individuation'. He claimed that the 'Self' contained within it everything needed for this process to succeed. The ego had simply to be persuaded to play along – or to get out of the way, such were its counter-productive tendencies towards grasping and narcissism. When religion helped this process, it could be said to be 'true': in tune with the deepest patterns of the mind, and – on that basis, and on the balance of probabilities – in tune too, perhaps, with reality beyond.

Critics of Jung and Freud often questioned the experimental basis for the claims they made. Case notes and copious jargon seemed designed to give a veneer of scientific respectability to ideas that failed to rise beyond the level of anecdote and speculation. When Rabindranath Tagore met Freud for tea in Vienna, in 1926, the famous poet's long hair, beard and flowing robes reminded Freud of traditional images of God – except 'about 10,000 years older than the way Michelangelo painted him in the Sistine'.[27] Tagore, for his part, came away with his suspicions about psychoanalysis unallayed. It offered, he thought, 'the best opportunity to say anything one wishes to . . . term[ing] the bitterness of one's own mind a science and circulat[ing] it in the form of slander'.[28]

Jung could at least claim to be drawing on a wider evidence base than Freud, who relied on his own small therapeutic clientele, plus congenial findings from close colleagues. Here was the source of Jung's fascination for people, like Watts, who sought practical ways in which Asian wisdom might help to heal Western souls. Jung's reading on the occult for his PhD, and his attendance at séances as part of his research, had led him to discern the presence of similar symbols and themes recurring in the dreams, myths and occult ideas of cultures across the globe, and across time. Jung was not the first to spot this, but it was usually attributed to the movement of people and ideas from place to place – hence Christian concerns, in Edwin Arnold's day, over apparent parallels between the Christian and Buddhist nativity stories. Jung made a different argument. He used the term 'collective unconscious' to describe what he claimed were universally shared patterns in the structure of the mind, out of which emerged similar myths and symbols around the world.

The function of these myths appeared to be to guide the process of individuation. In order to succeed, however – and here was the key point, for Jung and for Watts – they could not be treated merely as stories to be recounted or analysed, comparable to a scenic painting that one might consider from a slight distance. One had to find a way of entering the scene, inhabiting it, living out the story. At the core of Jung's, and now Watts', critique of modern Western life was that Westerners had become accustomed to relating to the world by taking a certain distance from it. This was true of the natural world, where the scientific project of labelling it with Latin had rubbed off on the general population. To know the name that some bird or bush had been given might bring a sense of satisfaction, but for Watts it was a poor substitute for real, participatory knowledge – he liked to compare it to the difference between perusing the map and treading the terrain. There was a similar problem with how people related to themselves, encouraged by a culture of ambition and achievement to imagine themselves as though from outside, as objects or lifelong projects.[29]

The effect on religion of this temperamental shift, by now centuries in the making, was devastating. The idea had gained traction that since other sorts of knowledge could be tested via pure intellectual speculation, the same must hold for religion. For Jung and Watts, this very idea was a symptom of the problem: a culture in which the intellect crowded out other aspects of the personality, leading alternative routes to understanding the world – emotion, imagination, participation – to atrophy, and to feel much less plausible as sources of knowledge.

Religious myths and symbols were, in Jung's view, the primary way in which imbalances like these could be made good in a person's life. But in the West, the imbalance had become so bad that even the ability to relate, as intended, to myth and symbol had been destroyed. Westerners were left standing in front of the painting, unable to go any further. They seemed condemned, in a phrase that Watts applied ruefully to himself, to remain 'dwellers on the threshold'.

As a reading of his own childhood, Watts found that Jung's diagnosis of Western life made a great deal of sense. The Asian aesthetics downstairs at Rowan Tree Cottage, the stories that his father had read to him, his immersion in nature: the richness that he sensed, in all this, was the outcome of myth working as it should. The cold Christianity of his childhood, by contrast, was evidence of its dramatic decline as an effective set of symbols. Watts had not been shown how to engage with a phrase like 'to rest / For ever on my Savior's breast' in anything but a rather literal way, resulting in fear and bewilderment.

Heeding Jung's warnings against Westerners pilfering Asian ideas and becoming 'pitiable imitator[s]' – Jung regarded Theosophy as an embarrassing case in point – Watts concluded, in *The Legacy of Asia*, that the only way forward was a 'Christian renaissance' inspired by Asian wisdom. A major part of that inspiration, he expected, would come from the sense, in places like India and Japan, that religions were primarily 'ways of living rather than ways of belief'. With help, and with luck, Westerners would be able to 'live the Christian story' once again, rather than just pontificating about it, or recalling its key events on the prescribed festive days.[30]

Zen was foremost in Watts' mind, here, thanks to the influence of Hearn, the Buddhist Society and D. T. Suzuki. But through Jung, he started to appreciate Taoism too. Early modern Jesuits in China had generally taken a low view of Taoist religion and its foundational work the *Tao Te Ching*, traditionally credited to Lao Tzu (*c.* sixth century BCE). Europeans of later generations, Hegel amongst them, had followed suit. It was only in the twentieth century that Taoism began to gain recognition and respect in the West, thanks to the German missionary and Orientalist Richard Wilhelm, the Jewish philosopher Martin Buber, and the English Orientalist Arthur Waley, whose translations of Chinese poetry and the *Tao Te Ching* inspired Ezra Pound and W. B. Yeats.[31]

Most significant for Watts was the lengthy commentary that Jung produced for Wilhelm's translation of a Taoist alchemical text called *The Secret Flower*. Jung found in Taoism a recognition of the 'central psychic facts' of life, of which modern Westerners were clearly not the first to lose sight.[32] People in ancient China, too, had suffered with a sense of alienation from nature, and from themselves. They had needed to be reminded that they were intimately part of an ever-moving cosmos: the Tao, or 'Way'. This was best imagined as a river-like flow, in which each person's complete immersion is a simple and glorious given. They needed only to realize this, in order to enjoy it. Immediate realization, over and above moral striving and endless austerities, would become the keynote of Watts' religious vision in the decades ahead.

Watts found Asian inspiration, too, in the writing and teaching styles of great figures like Swami Vivekānanda and D. T. Suzuki. Their general method, found in Shankara's Advaita Vedānta and in the Buddhist concept of 'skilful means' (or 'skill in means'), involved adapting the style and content of one's teaching to fit the capacities of particular audiences or individuals. It could easily be misunderstood as a sleight of hand, dodging difficult questions of doctrine. And it was always at risk of shading into religious elitism, as Watts himself often was – remarking to his publisher, only half in jest, that Asian teachers knew how to 'put the pearls in a place where the swine can't reach them'.[33] From a Jungian point of view, which Watts readily adopted, Vivekānanda and Suzuki were in fact appealing to each person's unconscious, in ways that to the conscious ego often seemed insulting or frustratingly paradoxical. That feeling of insult or confusion was often a good sign. The intellect's domination was being challenged, opening up space for other parts of the personality to mount a long-overdue comeback.[34]

Watts saw a parallel between this teaching style and the work of Chinese and Japanese painters influenced by Taoism and Zen. Rather than representing an object, leaving viewers with little to do but nod their heads, they 'start a movement which is to be continued in the beholder's mind'.[35] Hence the supportive, suggestive use of empty spaces. The 'artist gives enough to excite and too little to satisfy', thereby eliciting from viewers an imaginative response. Here was hope, thought Watts, for dwellers on the threshold everywhere. The religion that most of them knew functioned like an artist who seeks to 'capture a bird on his silk' – 'capture' to be understood, here, in the sense of domestication and confinement. A future alternative, forged with the help of Asian masters and practised as religion ought to be, would at last make that bird fly.[36]

*

Alan Watts was still in his early twenties when he wrote *The Legacy of Asia*, and was spending much of his time with a 'highly satisfactory American girl' by the name of Eleanor Everett. She had walked into the Buddhist Lodge one day in the summer of 1936, with her mother, Ruth. Both had discovered Buddhism several years earlier at the Clarkstown Country Club in Nyack, New York. Its owner was Pierre Arnold Bernard, a.k.a. 'Oom the Omniscient': a talented teacher, and an object lesson in how the intimacy and trust that came to be associated with teaching Asian wisdom in the West was open to abuse.

Yoga had become steadily more popular in America since Vivekānanda's visits, in 1893–6 and 1899–1900. Raja Yoga had been joined by the more physical Hatha Yoga, and Bernard was one of a number of American entrepreneurs to establish themselves as teachers – gurus, even. One of the earliest Westerners who could claim a good knowledge both of yoga and parts of India's esoteric Tantra tradition, Bernard also had the dubious honour of being amongst the first to damage their reputation by associating them with money and sex. In 1910, police raided Bernard's Manhattan home, finding him dressed in turban and gown, and carted him off to jail. The newspapers were soon full of shocking talk of his 'Hindu den' and 'Oriental séances', and of his alleged use of hypnotic power, death threats and morphine to imprison two women against their will.[37]

'The East' already had form, by this point. A popular feature at the 1893 World's Columbian Exposition had been a dancer called 'Little Egypt', who performed a 'hootchy kootchy' dance in the Persian Palace of Eros. She was alleged to have done 'shockingly disgusting' things using her abdominal muscles, drawing somewhat feigned outrage from newspaper reporters and close attention from large crowds of men.[38] Some of the latter, it became clear, were prepared to pay for more of the same. By the time Bernard received his surprise visit from the New York police, a theatrical trend for risqué 'Oriental' dancing was gathering pace. Asia and the Near East were brought together in a blur of incense, sequins and exposed midriffs.

A number of women's rights activists, including Ida Craddock, sought to link yoga and 'Oriental dance' to greater spiritual and sexual autonomy for women.[39] But this only added to worries of the time that American girls were going off the rails in a misguided search for independence. One female critic warned about the tyranny of 'swarthy priests of the Far East', who were more interested in naked women than in God, and who were liable to lead innocent girls astray. The most powerful caricature of Indian men as being obsessed with sex was Katherine Mayo's highly controversial *Mother India* (1927), against which luminaries like Rabindranath Tagore and Mahatma Gandhi felt moved to write rebuttals.

The Bernard scandal, linking Eastern exotica with sexual misadventure, turned out to be too good to be entirely true. He had been in relationships with both of his alleged abductees for a while, and charges of abduction were never proved.[40] One of the women was ruled out as a witness, while the other dropped her complaint and moved out of the area.[41] Bernard and his 'Tantrik Order', meanwhile, went on to establish a 'New York Sanskrit College', whose neighbours complained of 'wild Oriental music and women's cries, but not those of distress'.[42] In 1918, he married Blanche DeVries, a former vaudeville dancer, and under her smart and restraining influence set up a string of new studios whose approach to yoga was less likely to draw police or newspaper attention. DeVries replaced the wine, cigars and dubious intimacies with clean studios, healthy food and yoga mats. It was largely thanks to her efforts, and the backing that she managed to attract from the Vanderbilt family, that Bernard was able to establish his Nyack country club. There, he began to make a great deal of money by catering to the spiritual needs of high-society women who no longer found what they were looking for in run-of-the-mill Christianity.[43]

Ruth Fuller Everett had been one of those women, discovering Zen while at Nyack and going on to study Indian philosophy and Sanskrit at the University of Chicago. In the summer of 1930, she had journeyed through Japan, Korea, China and Manchuria, with her husband, her daughter and a governess in tow. Now seventeen years of age, Eleanor was a pianist, a dancer of the Hawaiian hula, better-travelled than Watts, and infinitely better dressed. Watts was often to be found, in these years, in striped trousers, chamois gloves, rolled umbrella and a Homburg hat. Eleanor introduced colour and informality into his wardrobe, including a felt hat with a brilliantly coloured feather in its band. She also offered a counterweight to Watts' heavy intellectualizing. A practising Buddhist, she was able more naturally than he to let go of her train of thought, and to allow the sort of spaciousness to open up about which Watts often wrote with a degree of wonder, and a twinge of envy.[44]

Eleanor and Alan became a couple, enjoying fine seats at the opera and ballet, practising the hula hip-swing, and spending nights together at Eleanor's apartment in London. Celibacy never featured in Watts' ideal of the religious life. He had been relieved to find that although 'the Buddha had taken a dim view of boozing and wenching . . . he never called it *sin*'. In 1937, Watts proposed to Eleanor, and an engagement party was held at the family home in

Chislehurst that December, before the two of them sailed off to spend Christmas in America. Eleanor became pregnant early in the new year, and the couple married in the spring, at a church in London.[45]

Watts' new mother-in-law set them up with a comfortable home in London, but by this time it seemed certain that Britain would not manage to steer clear of war in Europe. 'To stay and fight seemed valorous,' Watts later recalled, 'but entirely futile.' He might, he reflected, have made a decent intelligence officer, had he the requisite university degree and command of German. Lacking either, and recalling the splendours of America on his recent visit, he decided to relocate to New York with Eleanor. 'When you are standing on top of a collapsing skyscraper,' he concluded, 'there is nothing for it but to take wings, if you can find them.'[46]

Mr and Mrs Watts boarded the *Queen Mary* in the autumn of 1938, and were soon settling into an apartment on Manhattan's Upper West Side. Courtesy of an influx of German Jews escaping Hitler, Watts found his new neighbourhood blessed with lox and gefilte fish, 'leggy olive-skinned girls' and shopkeepers who spelled his name 'Watz'. The city also boasted, noted Watts, in a letter home to his parents, something called a 'hot dog'.[47]

Busy months followed, as baby Joan arrived, Ruth arranged meetings for Watts with literary agents, and he talked his way into library access at Columbia University.[48] He began to study with a Japanese Zen master called Sōkei-an Sasaki, who had served in the Imperial Japanese Army during the Russo-Japanese War, transporting dynamite to the front, before moving to the United States and establishing the Buddhist Society of America in New York.[49] It was at this point that Watts realized how little he really understood about Zen, and he came to appreciate both Sōkei-an's erudition and his earthy style. On one occasion, Watts saw him give a lecture on the Sutra of Perfect Awakening, sitting solemnly in front of the gathered faithful in robes of brown with gold brocade, flanked by candles and an incense brazier. 'In Buddhism, purposelessness is fundamental',

Watts recalled him intoning, in heavily accented English. 'When you drop [a] fart, you do not say "At nine o'clock I drop [a] fart". It just happen[s].' Watts looked on, delighted, as stunned audience members stuffed their handkerchiefs into their mouths.[50]

Having written rather loftily, in *The Spirit of Zen*, about the necessary frustrations of *kōan* study, Watts found the reality distinctly unromantic. He gave up training with Sōkei-an after a few months, and concentrated instead on bringing his blend of Asian philosophy and Jungian thought to small groups of interested people who began gathering for informal seminars at his apartment.[51] Amongst those who attended, paying a voluntary contribution, were 'well-educated old ladies', Jungian analysts, a couple of schoolteachers and businessmen, and an editor at Harper, with whom Watts hoped to publish a book about happiness.[52]

Happiness, for Watts, meant freedom from what had frightened him as a child: a feeling of separation from the world. What we experience as 'selfhood', he wrote, in one of the early newsletters that he posted out to his modest mailing list, is the result of nature 'playing at being lots of different, separate, and self-ruling beings'. To recognize this real state of affairs – to feel it 'in the very depths of one's being' – is what 'Oriental philosophy calls the realization of unity with Tao or Brahman'.[53]

Harper published *The Meaning of Happiness* in 1940, and commissioned Watts to follow up with a children's book on world religions. He was also invited to try out his gravelly, patrician English in radio talks. But something was missing. Watts seems, already, to have been getting bored, repeating the same old ideas and answering the same old questions from guests in his apartment. Watts was also worried about his own spiritual progress. He saw few signs of moral improvement in himself, enjoying the high life as he did, and developing a fondness for his own voice.[54] Was this sense of lack just a hangover from his upbringing? Or was it hinting at something fundamental in life, for which he had yet to find space in his religious outlook?

Watts was unsure. But when he imagined carrying on as he was, he could see himself ending his days attempting to part old ladies from their money by pretending to be a reincarnation of Koot Hoomi, the Theosophical Master from Tibet.[55] He considered a university career, but that would require writing a PhD and spending time around academics. More appealing company, he thought, might be found in churchgoers who were 'ripe' for renaissance.[56] Watts began to float a novel idea with some of his friends in New York. Most were vehemently opposed – but he ignored them. In the spring of 1941, a piece of unexpected news arrived by post at the Watts family home in Chislehurst. Their son was about to start training for the priesthood. 'Everyone here', Watts reassured his parents, 'thinks it a magnificent idea.'[57]

Alan Watts.

16.

God? Brahman? Nirvana?

We fail to see through the window because we are painting
pictures on the glass.

Alan Watts, *Behold the Spirit* (1947)

In September 1941, the Watts family packed up their belongings and
headed out west to Evanston, Illinois, exchanging their small New
York apartment for a five-bedroom house just a short walk from the
shore of Lake Michigan. Home to Seabury-Western Theological
Seminary, linked to the Episcopal Church, Evanston reminded
Watts a little of the village where he had grown up. In letters home
to his parents, he professed himself pleased to have left behind his
city soirées. Some of his guests had brought their 'neurotic tangles'
with them. Others had overstayed their welcome, ending the evening in a 'drunken stupor'. Most of them annoyed him for a reason
that Friedrich Schleiermacher would have understood: their pursuit
of meaning had yet to move beyond a search for new and slightly
more refined religious concepts. Faced with the most famous insight
in the Upanishads – *Tat tvam asi*: 'You *are* that!' – few seemed to
experience and revel in their identity with the Absolute. They preferred to hem and haw, and to pile question upon question.[1]

All in all, Watts preferred the company of the hummingbirds and
butterflies in his new, suburban garden. The local clergy seemed
congenial enough, too – future colleagues, if his two or three years
of study at Seabury-Western went well. Accustomed as they were
to their son's style of letter-writing – jocular, reflective, preachy,

sometimes economical with the truth – Watts' parents perhaps sensed that he was already feeling nervous, and that these were going to be difficult years. His daughter Joan later recalled hearing talk, around the house, of Watts choosing the priesthood in order to avoid the military draft.[2] By the summer of 1941, fears were growing that America might be drawn into the very war that Watts had left Europe to avoid.

A few months later, Japan attacked Pearl Harbor, and Japanese people and culture alike came under heightened suspicion. Sōkei-an and Watts' mother-in-law, Ruth, who by now had become a couple, were questioned by the FBI. Sōkei-an was later taken away to an internment camp, where his health began to deteriorate. A lawyer hired by Ruth managed, eventually, to get him released, and they married in 1944. But Sōkei-an died the following year.[3]

War, decolonization and the raising up of new international institutions all helped to persuade people who were interested in Asia that the long-expected moment of East–West co-operation had at last arrived. Watts was not amongst them. For him, Asia's glories were to be found primarily in the past, and in the pages of English translations of the Upanishads, the *Tao Te Ching*, and the sayings of Japanese Zen masters. A modest exception to Watts' scepticism about the dawning of some great East–West moment was his interest in Aldous Huxley's attempt to promote mystical religion as a basis for humanity's collective renewal. Huxley was living in Beverly Hills, trying his hand at screenwriting for Hollywood while immersing himself in the activities of the local Vedānta Society. *The Perennial Philosophy* (1945) presented passages from mystical writings, East and West, grouping them into themes including 'Silence' and 'Faith', in an effort to show that at the heart of all religious traditions lies the same shared truth.

The intellectual and political attractions of this idea were obvious. For those who saw colonialism as having run its historical course, it seemed natural and desirable that centuries of Western exploration and exploitation of Asia should end in the discovery of common ground. Critics, however, wondered whether a passing political mood made for a reliable guide to eternal truth. Christianity, Hinduism, Buddhism and Taoism, they argued, offered such distinct understandings of the world that one could reconcile them only in a mystical mush, in which religion was left scarcely distinguishable from poetry.

One of the challenges facing anyone hoping for a Christian renaissance was that in the age of quantum physics and the Holocaust, the old Western outlook, centred on the cosmic value of humanity, risked appearing naïve and out of date. It was meanwhile very easy, in a culture saturated with Freud and Jung, to dismiss intuitions of a personal God as a quirk of psychology: the painting of a great cosmic parent onto a reality that was more mysterious, or possibly more banal. An alternative way of reading the times was that two world wars had left people so exhausted and disillusioned that they lacked – for now – the energy and optimism to see that this was, after all, a meaningful cosmos, crafted by a personal and loving creator.

Here, for Watts, was where the historical big picture became interesting: what is it that makes this or that view of the world feel plausible to people, in any given time or place? No single approach to knowledge – religious, aesthetic, scientific – could be relied on, he thought, because to choose one is to beg the question. His commitment to Jungian psychology, at the turn of the 1940s, led him to suspect that much, in the end, depended on a person's own traits and needs, and the events of their lives. The decade ahead was about to make that amply, bitterly clear to him.

*

Watts approached the task of kickstarting a Christian renaissance armed with Zen, Taoism, Vedānta and a raft of new Western writing on Thomas Aquinas and the Christian mystics.[4] Pseudo-Dionysius the Areopagite (late fifth and early sixth century) and Meister Eckhart (1260–1328) had featured in his New York seminars. He hoped, now, to offer them up to midwestern Christians as a counterpoint to what he regarded as the infuriating folksiness of 'What a Friend I

Have in Jesus'.[5] It was a question, thought Watts, of balance. 'We have bodies as well as souls,' he observed: without the support of a tradition – institution, rites, symbols – mysticism could cause 'spiritual flatulence', of a kind that he occasionally found wafting around Aldous Huxley and the perennial philosophy.[6]

In his own life, Watts had begun to find the combination of Jung with Asian thought a little too abstract to be satisfying. In *The Meaning of Happiness*, published while he was still in New York, he had argued that each person's deepest 'Self' is identical with the Absolute, or ultimate reality. Happiness – a mixture of relief and joy – came from having a real experience of that identity. And yet, as Watts put it in a letter to a friend:

> It was possible for anyone having finished [that] book to lay it down with the question 'So what?' Yes, we are united with Reality, and cannot get away from it, but unless that Reality is in some profound sense absolutely good and beautiful, what is the use of bothering to think about it?[7]

Chinese art began to prompt new questions. How could an impersonal Absolute – which Watts sometimes envisioned as an electric current – give rise to a form of consciousness nuanced enough to appreciate, and capture on canvas, 'the eternal significance of momentary details, such as the turn of a bird's wing or the kiss of the wind on a particular blade of grass'?[8] Either consciousness was somehow characteristic of reality itself, or it was the outcome, in human beings, of unconscious laws playing out over time. In the latter case, Watts told his parents, 'my ideas are as meaningless as any other mechanical process'.[9]

Watts gradually found his way to two conclusions on which he hoped to build a ministry. First, reality – 'God' – was personal, in the sense of being 'immeasurably alive'.[10] Second, Western Christianity had gained and then magnificently squandered this insight by trying to squeeze that life into concepts and images. The problems, Watts suggested in *Behold the Spirit* (1947), were obvious the moment you walked into a Protestant church. The 'courthouse furniture of stalls, pews, pulpits [and] lecterns' suggested the kind of God to whom people were forced to relate by 'apologizing . . . asking him not to spank you, and telling him how great and glorious he is'. This was jurisprudence, not religion, and it ran alongside an unhealthily monarchical emphasis on thrones, laws and the smiting of enemies.[11]

Western Christianity, Watts concluded, had developed into a kind of institutionalized pride. Talk of 'grace', and God's free gift of love and acceptance, were vestiges of Christianity's original genius: an appreciation of human closeness to – even union with – the divine. But while this truth remained fresh and vital in Zen, Advaita Vedānta and Taoism, 'the religion *of* Jesus' had become 'the religion *about* Jesus': people had taken to worshipping him, rather than following in his footsteps.[12] That left union with the divine as something that had to be earned, and was largely confined to saints, mystics and the afterlife. For Watts, this was pride masquerading as humility. People paid lip service to the idea of grace, while rejecting it in their hearts on the basis that nothing that was given to all, regardless of status or graft, could possibly be real or valuable. They ought, he thought, to read the *Tao Te Ching*: 'Tao is like water', wrote Watts – paraphrasing Lao Tzu – 'in that it seeks the lowly level which men abhor.'[13]

Alongside pride ran an incorrigible literalism, one of whose most damaging side-effects was an understanding of Creation as the product of 'work' done by God, according to a plan or purpose that would be fulfilled in time. This trapped Christians, Watts argued, into equating meaning with purpose: everything had to be 'about' something, or 'for' something. Then along came the modern sciences, and revealed the universe to be a place where lonely 'lumps of burning gas and mud' expended vast amounts of energy, to no apparent end; and where 'weeds, insects, fish, birds [and] micro-organisms swarm in senseless profusion'.[14] Small wonder that people fled to the comfort of séances, Tibetan Masters, or the stoical, DIY spirituality of Edwin Arnold's Buddha.[15]

None of these alternatives would work, in Watts' view, because they failed to address the problems of pride and purpose. A radical reimagining of 'meaning' was required, alongside fresh images of the divine. India offered limitless inspiration. Where the Christian God schemed and judged, Shiva danced and Krishna played the flute. To most Westerners, play was good when a child did it, when adults were replenishing themselves before getting back to work, or when someone like Bach was writing music – no one enjoyed a prelude or fugue on the basis that it was about something, or moving efficiently towards a destination. The idea of *God* playing, on the other hand, seemed nonsensical and possibly blasphemous. To Watts, this was a sure sign that most Christians did not really believe in a God who was 'immeasurably alive'. If they did, Christian worship would feature a lot less mumbling in 'cattle-pen' pews, and a lot more dancing in the aisles.[16]

Watts' excitement about infusing Christianity with the mystery and joy that he found in Asian religion began to ebb as his studies for the priesthood progressed. The seminary faculty were 'stuffy', their intellectual standards were low, and they were still 'preparing men to go out and bang Bibles in the back woods among lumberjacks and hillbillies . . . [when] the menace to everything sacred is from the intellectuals, the universities, the clever-clevers, both here and abroad.' Out in the parishes, meanwhile, he encountered a 'superficial effervescence of heartiness': fake joy, drummed up by people with no experience of a God who dances.[17]

If joy was a tall order for now, then perhaps mystery would be the place to start. Watts became an enthusiast for Anglo-Catholic ritual, packing his letters to friends and family with talk of vestments, church organs, incense, artwork and altar designs – sometimes including illustrative sketches. Watts begged his Protestant parents not to worry that he had begun to 'traffic in superstition and popery'.[18] Ritual was a practical way for people to fulfil the task set by Jung: of inhabiting the Christian story.

To this end, Watts thought, ministers ought to carry out the prescribed movements at the altar as though they were engaged in a 'sacred dance'; a reminder of the 'great cosmic dance of the stars and all nature which, as Dante says, is moved by love'.[19] Likewise, the receiving of Holy Communion should not be the time to debate, in one's head, whether the bread and wine 'really' became the body and blood of Christ. It was a moment of direct appeal to the unconscious: a call to become 'primitive and childlike', opening oneself up to the mystery of the infinite and the finite coming together. Symbols, after all, were supposed to be exploratory rather than explanatory.

All through his time at the seminary, Watts later recalled, his colleagues suspected him of being a pantheist with a gift for semantics. He struggled to disagree: after he discovered Vedānta and Zen at school, nothing was ever able to beat the consolation of the idea – and the vivid sense – of being one with the Absolute. He was reassured to find a record of this sort of experience in the poetry of Alfred, Lord Tennyson. After repeating his own name several times, Tennyson found that his 'consciousness of individuality . . . seemed to dissolve and fade away into boundless being . . . where death was an almost laughable impossibility'.[20] Here, in Watts' view, was the former Poet Laureate endorsing *Tat tvam asi* ('You *are* that!').

Watts understood, however, the attractions of what the Jewish philosopher Martin Buber called an 'I-Thou' sense of the divine. Watts himself was struck, now and again, by a desire to respond to the joys of life by saying 'thank you' – as if he were in a relationship with the divine, rather than identical with it. The Christian mystics seemed to affirm this: their talk of 'union' with God implied two becoming one. How, then, to 'relate' to God, Watts wondered, 'without trying to kiss my own lips'?[21]

Though he had now abandoned what he regarded as his earlier infatuation with Jung – 'pure psychologism', as he put it – Watts found that the old combination of Jungian psychology with Asian ideas remained the best way to think through practical religious problems. Anyone who is prepared to sit quietly for a short time, he suggested, will see from the swirl of thoughts and emotions that the ego is a bit-part player in a much grander inner drama. The wider field of awareness in which it all plays out cannot adequately be described, because it 'transcends and illumines reason'.[22] But we know, immediately and intuitively, that it exists, because by its light we think, feel and sense the world around us. This, thought Watts, is first-hand experience of the Jungian 'Self', or what the Upanishads call *ātman*: soul, or essential self. The *ātman*, in turn, is identical, at its most fundamental level, with Brahman: the Absolute. Watts found this clearly expressed in the Katha Upanishad:

> The *atman*, the Self, is never born and never dies. It is without a cause and is eternally changeless . . . It does not die when the body dies.[23]

To claim, as a Christian, that 'I am God' might be thought heretical or a sign of madness, Watts pointed out. But to assert that my *Self* is God – that God is the ultimate ground of my identity – would be perfectly in line with Meister Eckhart: 'the Ground of God and the Ground of the Soul are one and the same'.[24]

The West's horror of pantheism, then, came down in part to an inadequate psychology, failing to distinguish until recently between ego and Self. It also had to do, thought Watts, with the warping effect of ancient Greek rationality, a dualistic – 'either/or' – form of thought, which had long been common sense to most people but which placed gross limitations on the imagination. Advaita Vedānta, and some forms of Buddhism, offered an alternative: non-dual – 'both/and' – thinking. From this point of view, Watts argued, it made sense that a truly all-powerful and 'all-inclusive' God would accommodate the most profound, even mind-boggling, sorts of difference – up to and including each person being both identical with God and distinct enough to meaningfully be 'in relationship' with God.[25]

Watts thought it unrealistic to ask ordinary churchgoers to put aside the 'bun-fights, bazaars [and] whist drives' that made up most of parish life in favour of a crash course in Eastern philosophy or a 'long course of spiritual gymnastics'.[26] But here was the beauty of

Asian wisdom, as teachers like Vivekānanda and Suzuki presented it: spiritual progress was more about giving things up – *un*learning. In Christian language, this meant dropping one's pride and accepting the gift of grace. Vedāntins talked about clearing away barriers to the seeing of what was already true: the 'supreme identity of *atman* and *Brahman*'.[27]

Neither Buddhism nor Vedānta, at their deepest, set much store by 'progress', because that notion encouraged a rather limited sense of reality: bound up with chronological time, and finite space. Buddhism expressed this best. Edwin Arnold's *Light of Asia* had presented the spiritual path in terms of striving towards an eventual goal, gesturing poetically towards a cycle of rebirths that culminates in nirvana, or blessed annihilation. But that, for Watts, was the version designed for simpletons. The pearl – if only the swine could reach it – was this: from the point of view of enlightenment, where the infinite and the finite come together, nirvana and the cycle of rebirth are one and the same.

*

The practical dimension of Alan Watts' attempt at a Christian renaissance began in earnest in 1944 when he was ordained a priest. Imagining himself as a missionary to educated sceptics, he was delighted to be given the role of Episcopal chaplain at Northwestern University.[28] The Watts family – Alan and Eleanor, now with two daughters in tow: Joan (six) and Anne (two) – moved into Canterbury House, on campus, and Watts set about refurbishing the small chapel that was located in one of its rooms. There he experimented with putting a Christian twist on his old New York soirées: the same guru personality; the same unlikely marriage of patrician English with earthy turn of phrase; and the same blend of mysticism and spirit of mischief.

Watts' audience consisted mainly of university students, alongside service personnel returning from the war. Together, they enjoyed a mixture of conversation, jokes, Gregorian chant, piano improvisations, smoking and drinking. 'Corny hymns' were banned, and the maximum length for a sermon was set at fifteen minutes. Watts offered lectures, on subjects ranging from psychoanalysis to religious art, alongside private religious instruction and counselling. There were also what his daughter Joan recalled as 'high jinks'. This included Watts driving around town late at night with friends, while – on at least one occasion – a passenger leaned out from the window and shot out the lights in tunnels. Watts sometimes took Joan along for the ride.[29]

Eleanor was involved with some of the hosting and the music. But as Watts spent less and less time with his family, loneliness and stress, combined with a difficult relationship with her mother, left her prone to bouts of depression. These were made worse when she discovered that her husband was having an affair with a graduate student in mathematics, Dorothy DeWitt.[30] As their marriage fell apart, she too began to see someone else: a music student at Northwestern called Carlton Gamer, with whom Eleanor had begun taking piano lessons.[31] When Eleanor told Watts about her affair, his response was to suggest that DeWitt and Gamer both move in with them. This they did, and in the summer of 1949, Eleanor and Gamer had a son together, Michael. It was not, however, the life that Eleanor had envisaged. She applied, successfully, for their marriage to be annulled. Watts recalled, in his autobiography, that Eleanor secured the annulment on the grounds that he was a believer in 'free love'. The phrase that she used in her application was 'sexual pervert'.[32]

Watts realized that he would shortly be at the centre of a scandal, and that his Episcopal ministry would not survive it. He duly resigned his position in the summer of 1950, writing a series of letters of explanation that contained a few last warnings about how a Christian renaissance might go awry. One should be careful, he suggested, about motivation. In an age of great turbulence, it was tempting to embrace Christianity out of nostalgia.[33] The Church risked becoming, as a result, a collective 'clinging': to discipline, belief, prayer and authority. It would be better, he thought, for a person to explore their insecurity rather than run from it.[34] Here, in talk of 'clinging' and security, was a broad hint about Watts' future direction of travel: back to Buddhism, and forward into the world of psychotherapy. Christianity was more deeply mired than Watts had appreciated in pride, purpose and worn-out symbols. Psychotherapy, he thought, was better suited as a Western conduit for the major insight of Asian religion: drop everything, and see who you are.

Responding to one of Watts' missives, announcing the end of his experiment with the priesthood, a Christian friend replied to say that Watts' mini-apologia was 'weak', and read 'painfully like rationalization'. He perhaps had in mind passages where Watts criticized the institution of marriage, along with Western society's repressive attitude towards sex.[35] And certainly, there had always been a strong element of convenience in Watts' image of the Christian God: personal enough to be lively, interesting and joyous, but not so personal as to seek a committed relationship with him, make demands of him or censure his behaviour.

And yet, to an extent that Watts' later celebrity on the West Coast tended to overshadow, he had tried hard during these years to overcome his earlier, rather slavish reliance on Carl Jung and to combine the most compelling aspects of Asian thought, as he understood them, with the Western Christian tradition. Why, he wondered, was Christianity so dominated by the first two 'Persons' of the Trinity, Father and Son? The more abstract and Tao-like Holy Spirit seemed to get short shrift: often depicted as a dove, which was nice but not very compelling, while other biblical symbols for the Spirit – water, breath, flame – were underused. Why did Christians focus so heavily on *what* they believed and worshipped, as though their minds would ever be able to compass it? The *how* surely mattered just as much: emotions, the spiritual life, the sort of leadership and support offered by churches. Watts had also tried to tackle one of the thorniest problems in what later became known as inter-religious dialogue: the question of how a person might simultaneously be one with the Absolute and in relationship with it. In working through these questions, Watts helped to persuade generations of Christians that their tradition possessed more depth and potential than critics allowed. A testament to his influence was the frequency with which his name cropped up in the writings of Christian reformers, across the rest of the twentieth century and into the twenty-first.

In 1950, Watts once again packed his bags, this time for a farmhouse in New York state. It had been arranged for him, along with some modest grant money from the Bollingen Foundation, by his friend Joseph Campbell, the comparative mythologist and great popularizer of Jung's work. The next year, Watts relocated to southern California with his daughter Anne, Dorothy DeWitt – to whom he was now married – the family hamster and Boots the cat. He had been contacted by an old acquaintance named Frederic Spiegelberg, a scholar of Asian religious traditions with whose 'religion of no religion', rooted in a form of nature mysticism, Watts had great sympathy. Spiegelberg was establishing an American Academy of Asian Studies, in San Francisco, and wanted Watts to join the staff. Ahead lay the Beats, the counter-culture and a constellation of brilliant friends and acquaintances.

There would be loneliness too. As those closest to him knew only too well, loving Alan Watts could be a complicated business. And for all his natural bonhomie and relish of intelligent company – especially if he was at the centre of the conversation – Watts' spirituality had an intensely private side. The mysteries of ego, Self, *ātman* and Brahman which so fascinated him were essentially about the individual's relationship to reality. Rather more of a struggle, for Watts, was to understand what Asian culture might have to say on another major modern dilemma: how best to live and work with others – how best to balance odyssey with community.

Mountain peaks around Kurisumala, Kerala, South India.

17.

The Hill of the Cross

Spring, 1958. Atop a remote mountain in Kerala, the English Benedictine Bede Griffiths and his fellow monks were adapting to life in
the clouds. Their ashram, Kurisumala – 'Hill of the Cross' – consisted
of a hut made of bamboo and plaited palm leaves, with an insect-
repelling cow-dung floor. In his early fifties, Griffiths was getting
used to sitting and sleeping on a straw mat, and eating a simple diet
of curry, rice, vegetables and fruit with his hands.[1] A buffalo provided milk, but no meat, fish, eggs or cheese were allowed.

Outside, the air was cool, there was lark song to remind him of
England, and when cloud, mist and rain allowed, a spectacular pan-
orama opened up of peaks and hilly tea plantations. Ana Mudi
stood to the north: the highest mountain south of the Himalayas.
To the far west, the Arabian Sea was 'a faint rim on the horizon'.[2]

Across that sea, many centuries before, had come Roman ships in
search of spice. They carried aboard some of the first Christians to
reach India, giving the gospel a home on the subcontinent long
before it found one in western Europe. Marco Polo had explored
parts of Kerala, too, returning to Europe with tales of pepper trees
and piracy off the Malabar Coast. Of greatest interest to Griffiths
were the Portuguese and their largely unhappy legacy in this hot,
highly fertile corner of Asia. Merchants and missionaries had been
unable to imagine any form of Christianity other than Latin Catholicism: alien to India, and now to growing numbers of modern
Westerners.

Griffiths' mountain-top experiment was intended as a way of
learning, from Kerala's Thomas Christians and India's broader
contemplative genius, how Indian Catholicism might be freed of

European hymnody and heavy Victorian pews, and how Westerners might reconnect with the divine. Like Alan Watts, Bede Griffiths
had fallen in love with the religious literature of Asia, from the
Upanishads to the *Tao Te Ching*. But where Watts found little that
interested him in contemporary Asia, Griffiths hoped to find, still
thriving in India, a sense of the sacred. This feeling of the divine as
a living reality had declined in the West, he believed, since the era of
Dante, Giotto and the glories of Gothic architecture.[3] One way of
restoring it might be to witness the people of India, free since 1947
from British rule, succeed where Britain and other Western countries had failed: modernizing their country in a way that made use
of, rather than steadily sidelined, precious spiritual resources.

*

Before Kerala came the Cotswolds. Alan Griffiths, as he then was,
conducted his first experiment in ascetic living in 1930, shortly after
graduating from Magdalen College, Oxford. Fresh from achieving a
disappointing Second in English Literature – rumour had it that he
threw his degree scroll into the Thames in disgust[4] – he moved into
a small cottage in the village of Eastington with his two closest
friends, Hugh Waterman and Martyn Skinner. Their mission: to see
how a life unsullied by the modern world might be lived.

A devotee of Coleridge, Griffiths may have drawn inspiration
from the abandoned scheme for 'Pantisocracy'. More than a century before, Southey had dreamed of sawing down trees and
hunting buffalo with Coleridge, discussing philosophy and creating
poetry as they went. Now, Griffiths and co. sat amidst the flicker of
candlelight off whitewashed stone, reading books and singing old
English rounds. They slept on wooden beds with straw-filled mat-
tresses, did without drainage or running water, and awoke at six
a.m. each morning to milk their Friesian cow and walk their four
Khaki Campbell ducks down to a nearby stream.[5]

No newspapers, record players or radios were permitted on the
premises. The same went for any literature produced after the seventeenth century. Tea, coffee, sugar and tobacco were banned, since

their consumption would amount to condoning modern methods of transportation. Journeys were made on foot, or perched atop 'Kit': a horse whom the three men learned to ride by jumping on its back and hoping for the best. Cottage conversations about permissible compromise with the modern world included debating whether, if the village blacksmith were able to make an X-ray machine, it would be acceptable to use it.[6]

The Eastington experiment had its origins in a life-changing experience during Griffiths' final year at Christ's Hospital School (best-known alumnus: Samuel Taylor Coleridge). It happened during an evening walk across the school playing fields. He noticed the birdsong of the dusk chorus, as though hearing it for the first time, then found himself overcome by the beauty and 'sweetness' of hawthorn bushes in full bloom:

> A lark rose suddenly from the ground beside the tree where I was standing and poured out its song above my head, and then sank, still singing, to rest. Everything then grew still as the sunset faded and the veil of dusk began to cover the earth. I remember now the feeling of awe which came over me. I felt inclined to kneel on the ground, as though I had been standing in the presence of an angel.[7]

Griffiths found that only the Romantic poets came close to describing this experience. Under their tutelage, he began to infuse his pacifism and socialism – common commitments at Christ's Hospital in the wake of the Great War – with a sense that the modern world was out of touch with the real source of life. Quite what that source might be, Griffiths did not know and university did not help him to discover. The sight of wealthy students lounging around at Oxford confirmed him in his socialism, and in his belief that Western culture appeared poised to join every other civilization in history by ending in fragmentation and failure. T. S. Eliot's *The Waste Land*, James Joyce's *Ulysses* and Oxford's rolling urban sprawl all spoke of that same fate. Large areas of unlovely new housing, from Cowley in the south-east to the expanding suburbs of North Oxford, suggested a tragic loss of contact with nature, and with any compelling notion of beauty.[8]

Judged purely as an experiment in living, Eastington was a failure. It lasted less than a year, and ended in acrimony: 'a foretaste of what hell may be' was Griffiths' assessment, writing to Martyn Skinner many years later.[9] As a chance to read and reflect, however, away from the world that Griffiths had so far known, it was invaluable. One of his tutors at Oxford, a young C. S. Lewis, had been frustrated by Griffiths' obsession with the Romantics, to the exclusion of most other literature and all of philosophy. Once Griffiths had finished his degree, Lewis managed to persuade him to give philosophy and religion a chance. He dutifully made his way through Aristotle, the Bible, Marcus Aurelius, Augustine, Aquinas and Bishop Berkeley. Via a Theosophist friend of his mother, Griffiths also read the *Bhagavad Gita*, *The Buddha's Way of Virtue* (a translation of the Buddha's sayings) and the *Tao Te Ching*.

Griffiths' regard for religion was low. He shared William Blake's estimation of the clerical class: nosy, ignorant priests, 'binding with briars my joys & desires'. Reading the Bible in the Cotswolds, however, Griffiths found that he could immerse himself more fully in its pastoral setting. The Hebrew prophets came across as real and compelling figures, thundering about offences against God, where social critics of Griffiths' day seemed mired in theory and jargon. Jesus went from being the berobed humanitarian of old paintings and recent biblical scholarship to a raw and passionate human being, prone to saying and doing unpredictable things. Second-class degree notwithstanding, Griffiths trusted himself enough as a student of literature to be confident of recognizing authentic voices when he encountered them. Here they were, in scripture.[10]

Reading Tolstoy at school had taught Griffiths to respect the Sermon on the Mount as an ethical ideal. Now, he wondered whether it might be a route back to the consoling reality which he had sensed so vividly on the school playing fields. 'Blessed are the poor in spirit, for theirs is the Kingdom of Heaven' could be read not as a command but as wise counsel: overcome your pride, and be grasped by the true order of things. Griffiths finally tested this proposition at the end of 1931, and it was terrifying.

He was staying with an Anglican mission in the slums of Bethnal Green, to see whether he might have a vocation to the priesthood. One evening, he knelt down beside his bed to pray, resolving to remain there until something happened. At some point during the night, he began to feel his sanity slipping. Part of him wanted it to go: his precious intellectual 'discoveries' of recent months suddenly appeared meaningless, and he was appalled at how highly he had regarded them. Another part of him resisted what felt like the approach of darkness and un-reason – an 'abyss', Griffiths later recalled, 'where all known landmarks fail'.[11] Something then happened, which Griffiths was never able to describe. But when he got off his knees in the morning, London was utterly changed:

> The hard casing of exterior reality seemed to have been broken through, and everything disclosed its inner being. The buses in the street seemed to have lost their solidity and to be glowing with light.[12]

God, he concluded, had 'brought me to my knees, and made me acknowledge my own nothingness . . . out of that knowledge I had been reborn. I was no longer the centre of my life, and therefore I could see God in everything.'[13]

Griffiths found himself steadily drawn to Catholicism, and by the time he was received into the Church, on Christmas Eve 1932, the lesson of Eastington had become clear to him. The steady debasing of life in the West was not really about factories, technology or underwhelming residential architecture. These were all signs of a deeper Western problem with pride, and a closely related failure of the imagination. Creativity seemed to have been reduced to what Coleridge had called 'fantasy': throwing words together, to describe a made-up scene, rather than making art in a way that resembled God's own creative process. Humans were capable, Coleridge had believed, of this latter, far higher kind of creativity. It yielded symbols – in the form of words and images – that could reconnect people with reality.[14] For Griffiths, deeply influenced by Coleridge, the steady loss of the ability to create and appreciate symbols in this way was nothing short of a tragedy.

Griffiths was not alone in sensing this problem. Graham Greene thought that characters created by Virginia Woolf and E. M. Forster seemed to 'wander . . . like cardboard symbols through a world that was paper-thin'.[15] C. S. Lewis felt similarly about George Bernard Shaw and H. G. Wells.[16] G. K. Chesterton, Evelyn Waugh and T. S. Eliot offered similar critiques. All detected in contemporary English literature an impoverishment of modern ways of being in the world. All converted to Christianity in the early decades of the 1900s.

Griffiths was unusual in his sympathy for Asia. Chesterton was scornful of 'Eastern pessimism', and the 'nullity' at which he thought its practices aimed. C. S. Lewis wrote to Griffiths of his irritation at a vogue for Hinduism amongst his students, one of whom had been lending him books on the subject in an attempt to win him round.[17] The literary converts of Griffiths' generation nonetheless shared with Carl Jung a sense that the intellect had become overrated and overworked. 'Reason', wrote Chesterton, 'seeks to cross the infinite sea, and so make it finite. The result is mental exhaustion.' He preferred a simple man's mysticism: 'The morbid logician seeks to make everything lucid, and succeeds in making everything mysterious. The mystic allows one thing to be mysterious, and everything else becomes lucid.'[18]

Lewis always remained suspicious of mysticism, but he gave some of the credit for his Christian conversion to his friend and fellow Inkling J. R. R. Tolkien, for showing him the power of myth. On an evening walk along the River Cherwell one day in September 1931, Tolkien – 'Tollers', to Lewis – had suggested that he try approaching the New Testament not as philosophy or history, but as myth.[19] Lewis should give his imagination free rein, and see what happened. Lewis tried it, and found himself caught in the 'imaginative embrace' of Christianity. Here was a formidable set of symbols, capable of answering fundamental yearnings that had haunted Lewis for years, not least a yearning for unattainable joy.[20]

Freud's influential view of such yearnings was that they could be traced back, via human biology, to the physical constituents of a material universe. Such meaning as they possessed was tied up with the drama and pathos of individual lives and relationships. It was the stuff of psychotherapy and modernist fiction, not religion. Coleridge, Tolkien, Jung, Lewis, Watts and Griffiths believed – in their various ways – something very different. Human yearnings played out in bodies and relationships, but they were rooted in a reality more fundamental than space, time or matter.

Griffiths joined the Benedictines soon after his conversion to Catholicism, and spent more than twenty years as a monk in England, mostly at Prinknash Priory in Gloucestershire. When he left for India in the spring of 1955, the official reason for his visit was to help bring the contemplative life to Indian Catholicism, ideally by incorporating elements of what he knew was a rich Indian tradition of silence and meditation. Unofficially, Griffiths had become convinced that whereas in the West, real faith – understood by him as 'utter receptivity to God' – was ever more the preserve of poets, mystics and monastics, in India it was everywhere. Arriving by boat into Bombay, he saw – or thought he saw – evidence of this:

> We went to the top of Malabar Hill last evening and walked in the gardens. All the world was out there, boys and girls, young men and women . . . all in an atmosphere of radiant beauty. It filled one with a sense of worship for all the beauty in life which we [in the West] have driven out of it. To think of these lovely people, with all the grace of their naked bodies and their exquisite saris, who sit on the ground everywhere, being forced into Victorian pews![21]

Writing to his old friend Martyn Skinner a few months later, from Bangalore, where he was studying and making plans, he saw hopeful signs of India absorbing Western modernity without losing this precious intimacy with reality:

> You find here all that the west has to give – railways, factories, cine-
> mas, banks, buses, blocks of flats, the latest cars and radios blaring in
> the streets. And yet along with this goes on undisturbed all the
> ancient, colourful life of the east. People . . . squat and lie on the
> ground, eat with the hand and wear the simplest clothes . . . The life
> of Christ at Nazareth would have been much the same, and Socrates
> in Athens would have had little difference.[22]

Women in saris working alongside bulldozers; people walking bare-foot in airports; a burgeoning film industry where the dances were demure and restrained, and no kissing was allowed: Griffiths was not blind to the enormous challenges facing India's new leaders – poverty, hunger, low life-expectancy, poor housing – but these vivid early impressions of the country struck him as hopeful signs of modernity being integrated with healthy human life, in a way that the West had largely failed to achieve.[23]

What did failure look like? For Griffiths, the answer was simple: Japan. The far-eastern Eden with which Edwin Arnold and Lafcadio Hearn had fallen in love was, in his view, now long gone. Driven to desperate, notorious wartime cruelty by decades of economic and industrial competition, the Japanese had picked themselves up again only to opt for more of the same. They were now so spiritually reduced that they could find meaning only as salarymen, house-wives and devotees of a rising GDP. Griffiths didn't expect the Japanese to squat in the rubble of their ruined cities, cheerfully reciting haiku. But he was depressed to find that efforts at rebuilding had involved precious little attention being paid to what Japanese art made clear had once been an enviable sense of closeness to nature, and grasp of beauty. The 'great steamroller of modern industrial society' had flattened people out, leaving Japan 'a nation of "artists" [only] in the rather narrow sense'.[24]

Japan was gone, and China was going: lost, it seemed, to the bleak creed of Communism.[25] Of the great Asian civilizations, it seemed to Griffiths that only India remained – and its fate was very much in the balance. Independence from the British had been won with the help of Mahatma Gandhi but in defiance of his vision. In place of the autonomous village republics for which he had argued and laboured, close to nature and the divine, was a centralized industrial economy in the making. India's first prime minister, Jawaharlal Nehru, was neither as anti-religious nor as far to the left as Mao Zedong. There was room in his 'socialistic society' for private enterprise, and for India's religious culture. But following long centuries during which Western interests had held Asian ones back, neither Mao nor Nehru had time to waste on pastoral romance.

India's advantage, as Griffiths saw it, was that Nehru's vision of modernization would take time to achieve, leaving open the opportunity for trying other things. Gandhi was gone, assassinated in 1948 – one of the great regrets of Griffiths' life was turning down an opportunity to meet him in London, back in 1931. But one of Gandhi's disciples, Vinoba Bhave, was carrying on his work. He was walking immense distances around south India, persuading wealthy landowners to donate millions of acres of land to the poor.[26] Bhave's attempts to promote village self-sufficiency and self-governance faced serious obstacles, Griffiths realized, with homespun cloth now requiring a subsidy in order to compete with industrial production.[27] But Bhave clearly believed, as Griffiths did, that the communities of the future had to be founded not just on high religious principles but on reform of life's most basic social and economic relationships. Capitalism pushed the principles of individuality and competition too far; Communism did the reverse. Gandhi and Bhave sought a middle way, based on the voluntary relinquishing of self-interest 'for the common good'.[28]

Griffiths had spent much of the Second World War in his monastery mulling over just such a middle way. For all that Nazism had 'let loose a flood of evil', Hitler's emphasis on family, community and nature in *Mein Kampf* (1925) had in itself, he thought, been laudable. Here, for Griffiths, was a pagan Germanic soul rebelling against 'the order of Christendom'.[29] Under other circumstances, Hitler might have become the 'German Rousseau'.[30] As things were, Griffiths hoped that the war would help to do away with the decaying fabric of Christianity so that 'new life' might emerge. He speculated about the city of Rome being destroyed, and the Holy See, currently 'clogged and bound by the chains of tradition', relocated to England or America, and renewing itself there.[31]

In search of a practical principle for renewal, Griffiths found it in his reading of Buddhist scripture, the Upanishads and the *Tao Te Ching*.[32] It could be expressed in a single word: dependence. In English, 'dependence' carried the sense of living at someone's whim, by dint either of unfortunate circumstances or a weak character. In Asian thought, it meant nothing of the kind. It was a way of describing the fact that beyond a person's everyday sense of individual autonomy lies the deeper truth of their connection to the rest of reality.[33]

Gandhian social work revealed the liberating potential of dependence: real freedom, claimed Griffiths, was 'freedom from self-interest'.[34] He wondered how a taste of this freedom might be brought to the West. The last time that the Western world had enjoyed a renaissance it had been brought about with the help of monasteries: their learning and creativity; their model of community. Full of hope that something similar might happen again, Griffiths headed south from Bangalore to embark on a new venture. It was time for an Indian Eastington.

*

Bede Griffiths trekked up to his new mountain home, in the spring of 1958, in the company of Father Francis Mahieu, a Belgian priest who, after three failed attempts to obtain a visa for India, had been granted one by Prime Minister Nehru himself. Mahieu hoped to bring Christianity and Hinduism into conversation, and Nehru very much approved. The name of their ashram, Kurisumala, was borrowed from the mountain opposite theirs. A little higher than their own, and popular as a Christian pilgrimage destination, it put Griffiths in mind of Helvellyn, in the Lake District.[35]

Mahieu was to be in charge at Kurisumala, with Griffiths as his deputy. Settling into their bamboo hut, both donned the saffron robes (*kavi*) of an Indian holy man. Incorporating a long tunic made from homespun cotton, with a shawl thrown over the shoulder, they were a gift from their local bishop, Mar Athanasios. Griffiths was delighted to be following in the footsteps of his great hero Roberto de Nobili, who long ago had deported himself in much the same way.[36]

The romance of the hut faded quickly, amidst high winds, torrential rain, the subtropical sun and damp so pervasive that Griffiths was forever moving his precious books around to stop them going mouldy.[37] Mahieu arranged for some of the local blue-, green- and red-hued granite to be carried up the mountain to them for the building of a more permanent structure, complete with damp-proof course and a corrugated-iron roof.[38] Kurisumala soon boasted an oratory, community quarters, a library and two small guest rooms. Thanks to the pineapples that grew 'like cabbages' all around them, alongside milk sales from a small number of dairy cattle, Kurisumala managed to survive and expand. Local villagers began to visit for *satsang* in the evenings: an Indian practice (the Sanskrit means 'company of good people'), in which a group would gather together for worship of some kind. Some made use of the ashram's dispensary, which distributed medicine, wheat and powdered milk.[39]

According to Griffiths' ideal, a monastery ought to be at the heart of its community. He tried to put this into practice with a project near Madurai inspired by Vinoba Bhave's *sarvodaya* ('service of the people'), comprising a small ashram and poultry farm. He even met with the man himself to discuss practicalities.[40] It took a while, however, for Griffiths to appreciate his neighbours in rural Kerala. In his mind, they lived simply, close to God. In reality, they seemed to lack any 'creative impulse', and to live at the mercy of superstition. Some would visit the ashram in search of holy water, to rid their cow of an evil spirit. Children showed greater promise. 'Brilliant and intelligent and humane', they walked miles each day to school. Too many, however, moved away to the towns when they grew up.[41]

Griffiths found, after a while, that love, sympathy and a better understanding of India's history and culture helped to improve his estimation of the people around him. He was especially moved by the imagery, music and ritual amidst which the Thomas Christians lived and worshipped. All but untouched by Greek philosophy and Latin tradition, their liturgy was rooted, instead, in ancient Syriac: a poetical language, similar to the Aramaic spoken by Jesus. Much of it was translated into Malayalam, including the services that punctuated the long monastic day at Kurisumala, beginning shortly after 3 a.m. The liturgy, wrote Mahieu, 'takes us back to heaven every three hours'.[42]

Here, perhaps, was the kind of Christianity of which Watts might have approved, far enough removed from everyday Western life and language to have some chance of working its long-lost symbolic magic. Griffiths wondered about this, as the months went by and new brothers began to join the ashram – sixteen within the first year and a half.[43] He shared with Watts a sense that Greek philosophy was partly to blame for Western culture becoming overly centred on humankind, and so narrowly rationalistic in the way that it apprehended the world. George Orwell's description of heaven, as 'choir practice in a jeweller's shop', said it all: Westerners struggled to imagine reality in terms other than the step-by-step passage of time, making the afterlife appear interminable. No wonder the number of what Alan Watts called 'dwellers on the threshold' was growing by the day.

For Griffiths, the best way of testing an idea was fully to immerse himself in it. Life in India, and at Kurisumala, helped him to do that. He was now able to read the *Bhagavad Gita* in Sanskrit, albeit slowly.[44] And alongside literature, he had come face to face with some of India's monumental architecture. The eighth- and ninth-century cave temples of Elephanta Island, in Bombay Harbour, were a revelation: a 'forest of pillars . . . creat[ing] an atmosphere of mystery and immensity', wrote Griffiths, from out of which loomed, in the semi-darkness, a three-headed figure of Shiva, showing God's 'benign and terrible and contemplative aspects'.[45] For Roberto de

Nobili, Shiva had been someone else's god: an impostor, born of distorted thought and belief. For Griffiths, this was God – striking him with fresh force and salutary strangeness.

After an experience like this, Griffiths did not need theories to convince him of the argument, made in differing ways by Coleridge, Jung and C. S. Lewis, that symbols possessed revelatory power. But still, Griffiths loved to read, and so when the monastic regime at Kurisumala allowed it, he dipped into one of his new favourite writers: the Sri Lankan philosopher and art historian Ananda Coomaraswamy. From him, Griffiths drew the idea that real art must be rooted in a particular cultural tradition running back into the deep past: beyond the dawn of discursive thought, and into a world where symbols were the primary means of making the divine present to people's minds.

Griffiths found broad support for ideas like these in the philosophers Owen Barfield and Jacques Maritain, the Catholic theologian Karl Rahner, and of course Carl Jung. One of his regular correspondents was an English Jungian analyst by the name of Mary Allen, for whom he had long been acting as a spiritual director of sorts, and who was helping to fund his work in India. He would share with her his speculations about India and the unconscious, and she would rein in the wilder ones.[46]

There was still much about Indian thought that Griffiths could not accept. He was prepared to allow that the Absolute described by Advaita Vedānta was identical with the Christian God, and that stories of Krishna and Rama represented mythology of the most profound kind.[47] Christianity remained, however, the 'perfect way'. It was what C. S. Lewis called a 'true myth': a myth, because it answered deep human yearnings; true because the balance of evidence suggested that the gospels depicted actual historical events. This did not drive a wedge between Griffiths and Hinduism. His respect for Indian culture, heightened during months and years at Kurisumala, convinced him that an idea like karma, though allegorical, must be getting at something profound. This, in turn, persuaded him with ever more force that all religious concepts 'point to a reality [that] *infinitely* transcends them'.[48]

Always intending to go back to England after a few years in India, Griffiths dreamed of overhauling church services so that people could experience Mass as originally intended: a recreation of the drama of 'the life and death and resurrection of Christ', in which people were invited to 'share mystically'.[49] Where Watts had largely given up on Christianity by the early 1950s, Kurisumala's Syriac- and Malayalam-language liturgy reassured Griffiths of the potential for Westerners to experience old forms of worship in radically refreshing ways. He was especially taken by the way that Syriac services seemed designed to encourage 'repentance (with tears) . . . [as] the way to break down the barrier' that prevented grace from entering a person's life – leaving them dwelling on the threshold.[50] The parallel with modern psychotherapy struck Griffiths as uncanny: capable of inducing – or releasing – creative humiliation, as the first step towards *metanoia*, or 'turning around'. Perhaps, he wondered, religion and therapy might one day work closely together.

Like Watts, Griffiths enjoyed mulling ideas in writing, from personal letters to pieces for magazines and newspapers. During the early 1960s, these writings, and in particular his autobiography, *The Golden String* (1954), garnered him a modest international celebrity. When Queen Elizabeth and the Duke of Edinburgh visited India in 1961, he was invited to meet them. He refused, thinking it too grand an occasion. But he travelled to America in 1963, receiving an award for his ecumenical work and broadcasting a number of talks on NBC radio.[51]

At the same time, Griffiths' gifts as a mentor were winning him the admiration of some of the younger monks at Kurisumala, to the point where Father Mahieu began to feel his authority being undermined. In 1967, the situation became so tense that Mahieu announced that he was taking a year's sabbatical – and that when he got back, either he or Griffiths must leave the ashram.[52] Griffiths was poised to return to England and to Prinknash when news came in that another Christian ashram was in need of leadership: Shantivanam – 'Forest of Peace' – 200 miles to the east in Tamil

Nadu. It was to become Griffiths' home for the next quarter of a century. There, often in the company of a strange new breed of 'hippies' – refugees from the Western world which Griffiths himself had fled when he was their parents' age, first to a monastery and later to India – his international renown would grow, his 'marriage of East and West' would be effected, and the New Age would be born.

Erna Hoch at Nur Manzil.

18.

The Palace of Light

The Swiss psychiatrist Erna Hoch flew into Bombay in April 1956, almost a year to the day after Bede Griffiths arrived. He had travelled the old-fashioned way, by sea. Hoch's first impressions of India came from the air: the 'yellow broth' of the ocean below, giving way to the 'scorched yellow-brown' of the land.[1] No less than her mode of transport, her profession was regarded as the future. A figure like Griffiths might attract respect for his monastic commitment, and no doubt for some he cut a romantic dash, praying away on a mountain-top in his ochre-coloured robes. But as the mind sciences steadily came into their own after the Second World War – psychiatry, psychology and psychotherapy – hopes were high of shining fresh light into the still inchoate world of the inner life.

Practitioners would be the first to admit that it had taken a while to get the mind sciences off the ground. There were essentially two ways of gathering the necessary experimental information. Focusing on the body, as an object or mechanism, one could perform psychological tests, take and compare case notes on the course of illnesses, and investigate the anatomy of the brain and nervous system, to the extent that technology allowed. Alternatively, one could collaborate with patients and clients, and seek to understand mental health and illness from within. Asylum doctors had long been doing this, one claiming that a knowledge of Shakespeare and the ability of discernment mattered more in his line of work than medical qualifications. More recently, Freud and Jung were amongst those seeking to map human beings' mental world, or 'psyche', and to develop theories and therapies on that basis.

By the time that Hoch began her career as a psychiatrist and psychotherapist, the distinctions were becoming clearer between diseases of the brain that were regarded as incurable, such as dementia, and 'functional' disorders, which could, in theory at least, be treated. Still, it remained the case for serious mental illness that, as a German asylum doctor put it at the start of the twentieth century, 'we know a lot, and can do little'.[2] For all their original good intentions, asylums had by this time earned a reputation, in the popular Western imagination, as grim places for the long-term warehousing of the mad, the criminal, the inconvenient and the unloved.

The 1950s brought glimmerings of hope, from the first truly effective antipsychotic medication, chlorpromazine, to an experimental new drug of which Hoch had 200 tablets and 50 vials stashed in her luggage: lysergic acid diethylamide – LSD.[3] Its mental health benefits were, as yet, unclear. But one of her Indian colleagues, Dr Kannu Rajan, hoped that ingesting it might allow him to better understand his schizophrenic patients at the clinic where he worked and where Hoch was due to start as clinical director: Nur Manzil – the 'Palace of Light' – in Lucknow, north India.

Countries like India and Japan were becoming attractive research prospects for the mind sciences. Work with soldiers and refugees, during and after the war, had persuaded psychiatrists to pay close attention not just to a person's patterns of thought and life history – as Freudian and Jungian therapy tended to encourage – but to their wider environment too. A picture of mental health and illness was starting to build in which society's conventions and pressures were given more of a role than ever before. Postwar gloom in countries like Britain and America naturally lent itself to the asking of hard social questions. Meanwhile, the advent of commercial air travel made it possible for enterprising psychiatrists and psychotherapists to travel to Asia, to explore afresh the ways in which people are shaped by their societies: how they are brought up, what their schools demand of them, how the workplace shapes them, and the fundamental assumptions about meaning and value on which all these things rest.

Erna Hoch was one of the pioneering figures in developing this new dimension to mental healthcare. Professionally, she was amongst the first to engage in 'transcultural psychiatry', comparing mental health and illness across cultures. Personally, she was motivated, in moving to India, by the hope that she might find something there to help her overcome her loneliness and sense of separation from the world. Despite their very different vocations, she shared with Bede Griffiths the feeling that reading Indian literature – poetry, scriptures, philosophy – was not enough. She wanted to see what life looked like when it sprung from that soil.

Erna Hoch was born in 1919, in the town of Bülach, near Zurich. India was a presence in her life from the very beginning, thanks to her family's service – for three generations and counting – with the Basel Mission in Mangalore. Dotted around the Hoch home were bowls of cashew nuts, brilliantly coloured glass bangles, and toys including a bull carved from sandalwood. This last exercised a 'strange attraction' for Hoch, as a child: 'forbidden, dangerous, awe-inspiring'. A cherished photograph showed her father Fritz as a little boy, standing alongside his siblings and an Indian *ayah* wearing a sari.[4]

Stories brought the curios to life. Former or furloughed missionaries – 'humble' and 'virtuous', in Hoch's estimation, but with little 'sense of fun and joy' – told tales of a harsh climate spawning terrible diseases, jungles stalked by wild animals, and people whose resistance to Christianity could at turns be dogged and cruel. Children's plays were occasionally staged in Bülach, respectfully recreating a form of toil so hard and thankless that it was regarded as a form of martyrdom. Hoch herself featured in one, playing the friend of an orphaned Hindu girl who wails a plaintive begging song before being brought at last to Christ.[5]

Hoch's life was so happy, as a child, that moving on to high school felt like being 'thrown out of paradise'. She encountered hell-fire preaching, along with hushed and confusing talk of sex. Her father's wholesome world, as a small-town Protestant clergyman, began to seem naïve, and some of the adults around her were revealed as hypocritical – turning up to church, yet living their lives as though none of it were true. Christianity made less and less sense. How could love and eternal damnation be part of the same picture? Why did her father say that death meant going home to God, and then turn so serious and solemn when someone passed away? What was she to make of her good fortune in growing up in a Christian country, while people elsewhere in the world depended for their salvation on the coins dropped into mission boxes at church? One of these was decorated to look like a hillock, featuring a small child on top: the 'Little Negro', kneeling in prayer, his head nodding whenever a coin went into the box.[6]

Entering her teenage years in the early 1930s, Hoch remained convinced of a 'spiritual dimension' to life: an 'eternal source', to which human beings were bound to find their way home. Alan Watts understood this return home in terms of more or less effortless realization. Griffiths was interested in how society as a whole might find its way back. For Hoch, who struck her parents as restrained and self-sufficient to the point of hard-heartedness, it was a 'personal venture'. She resolved to equip herself for a lone spiritual quest by becoming 'strong, tough, independent'. This included trying harder in sports at school, and persuading her parents to let her join the Girl Guides. She began to produce 'complicated pieces of knitting' by herself – a modest response, perhaps, to an existential crisis, but it appears to have been a daughterly declaration of independence aimed at her mother, and a successful one at that.[7]

Hoch's reading, during these years, took her all over the world. She was struck by the richness of Indian literature and its parallels with Christianity, not least between the birth stories of Krishna and Jesus. She read the Christian mystics, though she later recalled them having little to say to teenaged girls. Closest to her heart were the Stoics. 'Pagans' they might have been, but they had prized courage and conscience. Hoch was delighted to find Epictetus on Fritz's bookshelf, alongside a well-thumbed copy of Marcus Aurelius' *Meditations*: a hint, in lieu of a conversation, that her father might know how she was feeling.[8]

Hoch's life began to mirror that of Carl Jung: the child of a rural

Swiss clergyman, doubting what her father preached, going on to study medicine at the University of Basel – Hoch enrolled in 1940 – and then specializing in psychiatry. By her own admission, Hoch was not a natural at the bedside. Her crediting of the Stoics with helping her to develop a 'patient tolerance of other people's short-comings' suggests an ongoing struggle to suffer fools with any degree of gladness. But delusions and strange moods fascinated her, and she was inspired, too, by a short period working for the Red Cross in military hospitals and refugee camps during the early months of the Second World War. She meanwhile kept up her search for meaning, spending spare moments at university sitting beside a pond on campus, reading the *Bhagavad Gita* and Buddhist scriptures.[9]

Working part-time during her studies, in a psychiatric nursing home where her father offered pastoral care, the limited therapeutic repertoire of Hoch's chosen discipline became painfully clear to her: insulin, opium, electric shock, compassion – and God.[10] Invoking the deity was unremarkable in this era, in almost any area of life, but as a religious sceptic and budding Indophile, Hoch was intrigued. How were religion and mental illness related? How might the former cause or help to cure the latter?

Hoch thought that she saw a connection between rigidity in religious belief and certain forms of mental illness. She found, too, that talk of a higher power could sometimes be therapeutic. More personally, there were surprising spiritual benefits to caring for others. Working for a time as a private nurse, she found that when she put aside her own 'selfish concerns', and devoted herself to a task of love in caring for a patient, 'forces . . . not one's own' worked through her. She became 'more transparent [to] an inner light'.[11] Finally, in 1946, she came to appreciate, from a patient's point of view, the healing potential of religious community. Recovering at an alpine sanitorium in Leysin after becoming critically ill with tuberculosis, Hoch dreaded the inevitable clerical visit: someone coming to 'kneel on my soul', as she put it. Instead, she was struck by the therapeutic power of the ecumenical religious services in which she was invited to take part. People from Protestant, Catholic and Greek Orthodox traditions prayed as a single group, united by a sense of 'belonging together'.[12]

Like Bede Griffiths around the same time, Hoch began to feel that her reading – Ramakrishna, Vivekānanda, Aldous Huxley's writings on the perennial philosophy and Vedānta – was urging her eastwards. She was pessimistic about her chances of finding work there. A newly independent India had presumably had its fill of Europeans for the time being, and it seemed unlikely that a nation with ambitious plans for development would regard psychiatry as a priority. But in 1955, Hoch came across an advert in the Swiss *Medical Bulletin*. A psychiatric clinic in Lucknow, established a few years before by the American Methodist missionary Dr E. Stanley Jones, was looking for someone to serve as clinical director while the incumbent took a couple of years of leave.[13] The salary on offer was 'pitifully low'. Still, here was a chance to go to India, not as a tourist but as someone with a place to be and a purpose to fulfil. Hoch cleared out her flat, packed her bags, and headed to the airport.

Hoch was pleased to find the rather dreary look of the subcontinent from the air replaced by a riot of colour on the ground, much of it worn on the bodies of the people around her as she made her way through Bombay Airport to catch a connecting flight to Delhi. An overnight train journey followed, getting her to Lucknow and finally to Nur Manzil: a modestly sized clinic built in Islamic style, complete with cupola. Inside, her much-prized privacy was preserved: she shared her room and bathroom only with a handful of lizards, who caught mosquitoes for her but occasionally woke her up when they fell with a thud from the ceiling at night.[14]

Out in the garden, there was birdsong, striped squirrels who put Hoch in mind of Disney films, and monkeys whose screaming and crashing around on corrugated-iron roofs took a certain amount of getting used to.[15] The city of Lucknow itself, once the cultural capital of north India, boasted palaces, gardens, street music and markets of all kinds, if one was prepared to put up with the bustle and the heat. Hoch was particularly impressed by a wedding procession, which featured a groom dressed in rich silk, clopping through the streets atop a white horse. A canopy of fragrant white flowers was held over his head while musicians dressed in red-gold uniforms walked out in front.[16]

Nur Manzil had opened in 1950, its name derived from Al-Nur, 'the Light': one of the ninety-nine names or attributes of Allah. It aimed to infuse modern psychiatric care with a Christian ethos. The clinic was available for all, and Hoch was relieved to find that there was no intention of using medicine as a means of evangelization. Instead, she had the happy, thought-provoking task of persuading Christian staff, alongside predominantly Hindu and Muslim patients, of the virtues of the modern mind sciences. Many of the people around her had grown up regarding mental illness as the work of the devil, spirits, magic, or the evil eye. Christians often attributed conditions like depression or anxiety to insufficient faith in a good and loving God.[17]

Where the challenge at Nur Manzil was the potential hostility of religious people towards secular psychotherapy, the situation across much of the West in the 1950s was the exact reverse. Some psychotherapists shared Freud's materialism, while others had found religious upbringings to be the cause of many of their clients' problems. Dr Rajan, Hoch's colleague at Nur Manzil, had experienced this antagonism first-hand, while undergoing a training analysis in the United States with the psychiatrist and psychoanalyst Frieda Fromm-Reichmann. She had suggested to him that his conversion to Christianity, some years before, was the result of neurosis. Rajan responded that God had used his neurosis as a means of reaching him. Fromm-Reichmann dismissed his explanation as a product of his 'oriental' background, but Rajan invoked the New Testament in his defence: 'While we were yet sinners, Christ died for the ungodly'.[18]

Fromm-Reichmann's attitude towards Rajan was a vestige of an earlier era when, under the combined influence of Darwinism and colonial ideology, 'culture' had been imagined in the singular: a trajectory of human civilization along which all societies travelled as they evolved. At one end were modern Europeans, taught to value purpose and the taking of responsibility in life. Taken to an excess, this left them vulnerable to anxiety and depression. Not so the Rousseauian 'noble savages' found across much of Africa and India. By virtue of living further back along that trajectory, they were less prone to neuroses. As late as the mid-1950s, the psychiatrist J. C. Carothers described Africans as 'lobotomised Europeans'.[19] This one-size-fits-all vision of culture, deeply racialized, made life difficult for Jung when he set out to laud 'primitive' societies for remaining uncorrupted by modern Western life. To educated Indian audiences, when he visited the subcontinent in 1938, 'primitive' sounded a lot like 'savage'.

Amongst those who helped to move Western thinking on towards a more pluralistic view of culture was Karen Horney, whose ideas influenced both Hoch and Watts. A psychoanalyst who practised first in Berlin, and then from the 1930s in Chicago and New York, she criticized Freud for having little to say about women: the idea of 'penis envy' revealed just how little he understood about women's responses to the challenges of living in a man's world. More broadly, Horney thought his emphasis on strengthening the ego – against the competing demands of bodily desires and social norms – was a serious mistake. Many Western patients, in her experience, suffered from trying to exert *too much* control. Brought up in a competitive culture, they pursued an 'idealized' or 'proud' self, to the point of grandiosity, artifice and unrelenting self-criticism.

Horney concluded that in order for psychotherapy to catch this false, idealized self in the act, and to allow a 'real self' – free, mature and fulfilled – to emerge in its place, her profession would have to get better at attending to a patient's present state of mind. Dipping into Aldous Huxley's *The Perennial Philosophy* almost every night during the last years of her life, and reading D. T. Suzuki's writings on Zen, persuaded Horney that Asian cultures possessed greater insight, here, than their Western counterparts.[20] On a brief visit to Japan in 1952, she encountered people who seemed able to pay wholehearted, self-forgetful attention to what was going on around them. She watched a single waiter serve around 200 guests, almost entirely by himself and without a single spill. 'Quite absorbed in his vocation,' she recalled, 'the whole man was nothing but eyes and hands.' This was not cold detachment, as critics of Buddhism and Japanese culture liked to suggest. It was utter receptivity to what was happening. Here, for Horney, was 'the very essence of Zen': a good way to work as a therapist, and an excellent way to live.[21]

Like Horney, Erich Fromm moved on from Freud with the help of Zen. In his experience, lots of people went to see therapists complaining of depression, insomnia or marital problems, when in fact they were suffering from a more fundamental 'maladie du siècle': alienation from nature and feeling, with too much value placed on 'having' – manufacturing things; owning property – and too little on just 'being'.[22] This, he thought, was a warped response to the profoundly difficult hand that human beings are dealt, waking up to an existence where they are both in nature and have a compelling sense of transcending it.[23]

With the Judaeo-Christian tradition increasingly unable to meet people in this difficult situation, Fromm saw two alternatives. One was to go backwards, to a point in humanity's past before a sense of separation from nature arose. As a German Jew who had fled Nazism in the early 1930s, he worried deeply about where such a search for 'prehuman unity with nature' might lead. In the case of Hitler, Himmler and Goebbels, he thought, it had led to the repudiation of higher human capacities like reason and love, resulting in orgiastic violence and 'ritual murder'.[24] The other option was to develop human capacities to their fullest, to the point where they fostered rather than frustrated an 'immediate, intuitive grasp of reality'.[25] While the mind sciences could help on the intellectual and therapeutic planes, Zen encouraged a direct, experiential form of self-knowledge. As a practitioner himself of *zazen* – seated meditation – Fromm found consolation in Suzuki's reassurances that the benefits could be felt even in the very early days of practice. For all the talk, in Zen circles, of *satori* – enlightenment – as the ultimate goal, Suzuki pointed out that if one is beginning with a pitch-black room, then even to introduce a single candle makes a difference.[26]

Horney did not live long enough to develop her ideas about Zen and psychotherapy, and Fromm was too wary of potential incompatibilities to push the connections very far. Hoch, by contrast, embarked on her work at Nur Manzil with both a professional and a personal stake in discovering how Christianity, Asian religions and the mind sciences might come together. Her major source of insight was her patients, whom intensive classes in Hindustani soon allowed her to begin to get to know: around sixteen in-patients, and a wide range of out-patients, young and old.[27] Over the course of compiling some 1,600 case studies during her time at Nur Manzil, Hoch encountered what she claimed were two unhealthy extremes. At one end were patients who suffered from having their sense of themselves so deeply embedded in family or caste community that they failed to develop a meaningful and responsible sense of self. At the other extreme were people whose existences were marred, thanks to a combination of British imperialism and Christian mission, by a shallow spirit of competition: 'an ambitious race for the unobtainable, marked by envy and anxiety, which often ends up in disappointment, failure or even a breakdown in complete exhaustion'.[28]

Hoch expected that more and more people would be drawn to the latter extreme, as India's increased contact with the West fostered individualism: first as a middle-class aspiration, and later as a widespread cultural norm. Hoch had met plenty of people in India who worried about this. When it came time for friends to settle a bill in a restaurant, they were horrified to find Europeans splitting it between them, where Indian friends might vie for the honour of settling it for all. Europeans struck these Indian critics as 'hard, selfishly calculating and without love'. Europeans' disdain for India's joint family system was likewise a mark against them.[29]

Presenting her ideas to predominantly Christian audiences at first, at conferences and in articles, Hoch argued that the kind of life embodied and taught by Jesus Christ offered a psychologically healthy middle way. He was the archetypal wise counsellor, under-standing the temptation to project one's own failings on to others, the importance of honest self-criticism as the basis for real love, and human beings' need to feel completely accepted by some higher authority before they will give up false ambitions and live a more authentic life. 'Love thy neighbour', Hoch suggested, was the ultim-ate expression of this middle way: a feat that a person could only manage if they possessed a strong, settled and realistic sense of themselves, allowing them freely to choose to act for the good of another.[30]

For colleagues in the mind sciences, Hoch attributed her progress at Nur Manzil to her Swiss mentor, Medard Boss, who was inter-ested in Indian culture and visited the clinic twice in the second half of the 1950s. Analysed by Freud himself, Boss had concluded that Freud's theories were wrong but that his therapeutic practice – and the personality of the man himself – pointed towards something true.

Boss' critique of Freud's ideas had its origins in one of the best-known philosophers of the era, Martin Heidegger. He worried that psychoanalysis was the extension into the inner life of a fundamen-tally mistaken attitude to the world, which had built up across centuries. Faced with that philosophers' favourite prop, a table, people would seek 'truth' by measuring its dimensions and place-ment in the room, and finding out what it was made of. Its significance might be acknowledged: this is the table where I eat; it is a little too low, or too close to the window. But such things would be regarded as secondary – and that, for Heidegger, was the mis-take. If physical and measurable objects were really the ultimate ground of everything, he argued, then we would find 'sorrow mol-ecules' and 'farewell molecules' in tears.[31]

Freud's great sin, for Heidegger, was reducing human beings to this 'object' view of the world. Significance was explained – or explained away – in terms of objects, real and imagined: brain, ner-vous system, ego, id and superego. Heidegger, on the other hand, wrote about human beings as Dasein: not just a 'being', but a 'being-*there*'. To be human was to be involved, all the time, in relationships of significance and meaning, to the world around and to one another. Whatever reality was – briefly a Jesuit novice, Heidegger now avoided speculating about God – it was a unified and meaningful whole; the relationships *between* people, and between people and their environment, were somehow more real than individuals and things themselves. People still knew this in their bones, he was sure, as the what-it's-like of being alive. Freud's outlook, steadily percolating through Western culture, threatened to persuade them otherwise.[32]

Drawing on Heidegger, Boss pointed out that modern psychology lacked any sense of freedom or of 'why we are here on earth'.[33] Freud's saving grace, as far as Boss was concerned, was that although he assumed that people were ultimately mechanical objects, in his warmth and kindness he treated them like Dasein: people for whom connection and significance were paramount. Boss' alternative to psychoanalysis, which he taught to Hoch on visits to Nur Manzil, was Daseinsanalysis. 'Illness', according to this outlook, being constricted somehow in one's relations with the world around. Where Freud required detachment from therapists, Boss encouraged them to engage authentically and lovingly with their clients, thus helping them to relate to the world in new ways.[34]

Having travelled to India because he didn't trust the translations that he was reading of Indian classics, Boss found corroboration for his ideas in the Sanskrit description of reality as *satcitananda*: existence (*sat*), consciousness (*cit*) and bliss (*ananda*). He thought that he saw, in *cit*, a concept very close to Heidegger's understanding of the what-it's-like of 'being'. For her part, Hoch discovered at Nur Manzil a certain quality to people's existences which attracted her, and which resonated with her reading of Indian philosophy. Inclined, as she was, to feel annoyed when anyone interrupted her, she was struck by the way that the gardener at Nur Manzil dropped what he was doing and attended to whatever task came his way. Hoch had read much about attending to the 'present moment', giving full attention to whatever life puts in front you. Here was a simple lesson in how it was actually done. The idea in Daseinsanalysis, that relationships are more real than individuals, was meanwhile illustrated for her by a Hindu patient, who claimed that gods and people 'impersonate' the Absolute. More than any single life or death, what mattered was – as Hoch put it – 'the continuity of LIFE written with capitals'.[35]

★

Erna Hoch found that what she started to learn at Nur Manzil only became fully clear after she was forced out, in 1961. From the outset, her relationship with Dr Stanley Jones had been frosty. He doubted her commitment to Christian fellowship at the clinic, and failed to discourage other staff from starting rumours and plotting against her – to the point where allegations of refusing to admit Christian patients were raised against Hoch.[36] After considerable acrimony, Hoch resigned. She left Lucknow in January 1962, making a 'long and at times perilous bus journey' northwards to the Himalayan town of Almora, close to India's border with Nepal.[37]

From Almora, Hoch was led for an hour on foot to her new, rented home: a small house atop a forested ridge. Arriving at night, she found it cold, dusty and thick with cobwebs. There was no running water, and no electricity. She would have to wait until the next day to find out who the owners were of the tiny feet pattering around above her as she tried to sleep, shivering in a hastily made bed and listening to a high wind and the howl of jackals.

With morning, everything changed. Hoch caught a first glimpse, through pine and cedar trees, of an enormous blue sky and the great snow-capped Kumaon peaks. It was a landscape into which, now and again over the next few months, Hoch was able to lose herself entirely – often at sunrise, out in her garden and wrapped in a shawl. Surely, she decided, the sages to whom the world owed the Upanishads had been inspired by solitude and solace like this.[38]

There was, Hoch soon discovered, an irony in coming to India's remote north in search of solitude: lots of other people had had the same thought. A number of the houses near hers were occupied by *sadhus* (religious ascetics): some real, some aspiring; some Indian, some foreign. The neighbourhood had acquired the nickname 'cranks' ridge'. Still, everyone seemed serious enough about the business of being alone that they rarely bothered one another. Hoch began to appreciate just how much her reliance, up to this point, on other people – family, school, work – had shaped her day-to-day thinking. It was all but impossible to have a thought that was not tied, in some way, to how others might react, or to what it might mean for her career. Inclined, as she was, to imagine 'authenticity' in terms of an absence of corrupting ideas and influences, Hoch felt that, up here by herself, authentic living might at last become possible.[39]

There was a reason, however, why Daseinsanalysis had appealed to her as the right direction for the mind sciences to take. The 'original and ultimate oneness' evoked in the Upanishads, and occasionally experienced in her Himalayan garden, was a deeply reassuring truth about reality. But it was a contemplative, poetic truth, which could hardly be sustained every minute of the day. Something was missing, for which the Christianity of Hoch's childhood had given her a taste. Christianity had come to lack meaning for her, Hoch concluded, because it seemed to hinge on the idea that believing a set of propositions about a third person – Jesus of Nazareth – would somehow change her life. It hadn't. Nor did Jung's approach help, of treating Christianity as a system of powerful symbols: wouldn't one myth be more or less as good as another, in that case?[40]

What Christianity did offer, and what the Upanishads, for all their brilliance, seemed to lack, was a sense of the cosmic importance of 'care' for others – an important concept for Heidegger and Boss, though Hoch used it in a simpler and more explicitly compassionate sense. A good, ethical life, as taught by Jesus Christ, was not merely an 'ought' or a nice-to-have for well-bred Europeans. Care complemented philosophy: to practise both was to find that each dug away at the other, steadily uncovering new layers of intellectual and felt meaning.

Hoch was sufficiently convinced of the truth of this to go searching in Indian literature for a compassionate ideal comparable with the gospels. She pursued it at the Ramakrishna Kutir, a religious centre in Almora established by disciples of Vivekānanda's teacher

Ramakrishna. The library there contained sacred Indian literature published in a mixture of English and Sanskrit, the latter rendered in the Devanagari script which Hoch could read. Confident that a psychiatrist, 'trained to observe and to interpret human behaviour', could find in these scriptures things that people more concerned with grammar and philosophy might have missed, she alighted on the *Bhagavad Gita*. Here were the seeds of a project which, in later years, Hoch would pursue together with Indian colleagues in India: reading the *Gita*'s celebrated account of a conversation between Krishna and Arjuna, the night before a great battle, both as a spiritual dialogue and an encounter between a compassionate therapist and his distressed client.[41]

Hoch would not have reached her conclusions about care and philosophy without the aid of people living nearby in Almora. Hearing that a doctor had moved into the area, they sought her out at all hours, sometimes in the forest, where she had tried to escape with her books. They struck her as 'clumsy and inarticulate', unused to the sorts of tests that a doctor might subject them to, and expecting instead that any decent medic would take one look at them and make a diagnosis. Some brought her flowers – picked, it turned out, from her own garden.[42]

The real gift, Hoch concluded, was having someone 'to get up for' in the mornings. True to Watts' worry about Christianity having degenerated into mere institutionalized pride, and to Bede Griffiths' discovery, 3,000 kilometres to the south of her in Kurisumala, of the creative power of humiliation and repentance, Hoch found deep value in having someone 'before whom to be ashamed'. Her pride in her qualifications and abilities had set her up well for this. It sharpened the shock of being able to do nothing for seriously ill patients but 'stand beside them as an equal partner . . . or at times even accept to serve them in all humility'.[43]

By the mid-1960s, Hoch seemed to have hit upon a creative combination of thought, contemplation and action. More broadly, she was starting to appreciate Westerners' need for what Erich Fromm described as a 'return to innocence on a higher level'. Here, Hoch thought, was a job for the mind sciences: distinguishing a higher level of innocence and oneness from counterfeit forms that might tempt people who were travelling a spiritual path. Someone with an immature form of connectedness would, like a child, be focused on receiving from the world around them. Mature forms would show themselves in a natural desire to give to the world: a selfless compassion, of the sort found in Christ and the Buddha.[44] Many Westerners, and growing numbers of Indian patients, were stuck in a mid-stage of development, thought Hoch. They had outgrown their immature, childhood sense of oneness, but had become mired in self-consciousness and a sense of distinction from the world. They valued qualities such as strength, firmness and consistency, whereas 'to the wise Indian [these were] a somewhat embarrassing limitation and separation'.[45]

These early conclusions were based on Hoch's work treating the psychological fallout, in Switzerland and India, from societies that failed to offer people convincing models of mature connectedness. She and others would build on these foundations in the years ahead, staking out shared terrain for transcultural psychiatry, psychotherapy, gurus and other religious leaders. For some in the West, however, particularly in the younger generation, this was all very nice – but it was too slow, and far too unambitious. The problem with pastoral care, whether therapeutic, religious, or some blend of the two, was that for all its professed interest in social pressures it still worked mainly with individuals. However implicitly, it was asking individuals to shoulder the burden of failed societies. The year of Hoch's arrival in India, 1956, a poem was published in America which promised – or threatened – a radically different approach:

I saw the best minds of my generation destroyed by madness, starving
    hysterical naked,
dragging themselves through the negro streets at dawn looking for an
    angry fix,

angelheaded hipsters burning for the ancient heavenly connection to

the starry dynamo in the machinery of night . . .[46]

Allen Ginsberg's 'Howl' was a furious denunciation of mainstream America's lifelessness, which launched the talented, the visionary, the sensitive and the desperate into all manner of escapist exploits, from the heavenly to the bleakly hopeless. Across the late 1950s, and into the 1960s, Ginsberg's Beat Generation began to accomplish something that Bede Griffiths had hoped, in vain, to see touched off by the Second World War: a revolutionary outpouring of disgust at the way Western society was headed, and a determination to try something else.

The Beats lacked Griffiths' quiet gentility, and they had more use for narcotics than either he or Hoch might have liked – the latter gave away her LSD in India, finding it unhelpful in therapy. But the likes of Jack Kerouac and Gary Snyder shared with Griffiths and Hoch an interest in what Asia might do for the West in its hour of need. The same was true of Timothy Leary, Harvard psychologist turned psychedelic scourge of the establishment.

During these same years, the stars finally aligned for a man whose long journey westwards from Chislehurst, Kent, saw him taking up residence in San Francisco shortly before that city found itself at the centre of the counter-culture. This would be one last hurrah for Alan Watts, a man ever determined to banish the dark shadows of Rowan Tree Cottage's chilly upper floor, and to make of his own mind a real home – a true palace of light.

Alan Watts, Timothy Leary, Allen Ginsberg and Gary Snyder, 1967.

19.

Liberation

Arriving with his family on America's West Coast in 1951, Alan Watts based himself at the new American Academy of Asian Studies. Its mission was to teach Asian languages, history, art, yoga, meditation and philosophy in a practically useful way, and to award master's and doctoral degrees to its students, who numbered around fifty in 1954. Alongside guest speakers including D. T. Suzuki and Watts' ex-mother-in-law Ruth Fuller Sasaki, the academy drew on the expertise in East Asian Buddhism that was available right on its doorstep, courtesy of San Francisco's Chinese and Japanese communities. The academy's location in San Francisco's Pacific Heights, overlooking the harbour, put it within a short drive of the city's Chinatown. A century old by this point, it owed its roots to America's first Buddhists: Chinese workers who migrated to California during the Gold Rush of the late 1840s.[1]

This was a dream job for Watts, but rather less so, as it turned out, for his family. His working hours, combined with time spent with friends and lovers, rendered him so neglectful that his daughter Anne took to standing outside in the rain, hoping to catch a cold and receive some sympathetic attention from her father. Watts' parents, Laurence and Emily, were sufficiently worried about Anne when they came to visit that they agreed to take her back with them to Rowan Tree Cottage and send her to a local school. Her elder sister Joan was sent to the ultra-progressive Happy Valley boarding school in the Ojai Valley, founded a quarter of a century earlier by Annie Besant, as a place where members of a 'new civilization' might be nurtured.[2]

By 1957, the toll of trying to administer as well as teach at the academy had become too much, and Watts resigned. The conventional suburban life desired by his long-suffering wife Dorothy was getting him down, too – 'mow the lawn, play baseball with the children', as he disdainfully recalled it.[3] He began an affair with a student whom he met at one of his talks in New York, Mary Jane Yeats. For a time, they carried on a long-distance relationship, turning a writer of dry, witty, self-consciously intellectual letters into a producer of love-struck poetry. He declared that he was with his beloved in his 'astral body', and signed off one of his missives: 'I love you again, and again, and again, and again, and again, and again!'[4]

Caught between two lives, and trying to keep up with a burgeoning career as a freelance writer, broadcaster and speaker on university campuses, Watts began relying on vodka to get him through the day. He once confessed to his daughter Joan that being drunk was the only time that he liked himself.[5] In 1960, he finally left his family, while Dorothy was pregnant with their fifth child. He moved in with Mary Jane, taking up residence on a century-old ferry-boat called the *Vallejo*, moored in Sausalito. It looked a little weathered on the outside, but inside its teak floors shone and a large window looked out over the bay. The *Vallejo* floated at high tide, and the sound of nearby ships' sails flapping in the wind was constant. Watts could imagine, when a fog came down from the hills, being out at sea.[6]

A model husband and father he was not, but Watts could at least claim to know, first-hand, something of what critics like William H. Whyte (*The Organization Man*, 1956) and Betty Friedan (*The Feminine Mystique*, 1963) were starting to say about the state of America. The country had emerged from the heroic period of the Second World War into a prosperous but notably less romantic everyday world shaped by consumer capitalism. Men shuttled back and forth between a company job and the meagre comforts of home and occasional holidays; women were forced to play happy housewives and mothers, with the help, if need be, of diazepam. The advent of television contributed to this grim picture, stoking fears of the Cold War turning hot and bringing the distress of the country's African-American population, especially in the south, into everyone's homes. The year of Allen Ginsberg's famous first performance of 'Howl', 1955, was also the year of the Montgomery bus boycott and of Elvis Presley being warned before concerts in Florida and San Diego that his signature hip-swing put him at risk of arrest for obscenity. Fears were rife that white music was being tainted by African-American culture.[7]

Watts had a front-row seat as San Francisco became a mecca for the discontented of this difficult decade, and for those determined not to relive their parents' lives. Forming the vanguard, the Beat Generation owed much to New York bebop – its sounds and rhythms, berets and goatees – as well as to Surrealist poetry and painting.[8] But they drew inspiration, too, from many of the same sources as Watts. American Transcendentalists like Emerson, Thoreau and Walt Whitman loomed large, as did Zen Buddhism. Gary Snyder, in particular, was a serious student of East Asian culture. He studied for a while with Watts at the academy, read a poem at the Six Gallery event in San Francisco where Ginsberg first performed 'Howl', and from 1956 he began to travel back and forth between California and Japan, working for a time with Ruth Fuller Sasaki. Watts remembered him as a 'wiry sage with high cheek-bones, twinkling eyes, and a thin beard . . . the recipe for his character requires a mixture of Oregon woodsman, seaman, Amerindian shaman, Oriental scholar, San Francisco hippie, and swinging monk.'[9]

Where Snyder learned East Asian languages and undertook formal Zen training, Jack Kerouac approached Zen as an alternative lifestyle. *The Dharma Bums* (1958) centred around a bunch of 'Zen lunatics', whose main character Japhy Ryder – based on Snyder – was respected amongst his friends for his understanding of Asia and for his simple way of life.[10] Watts found himself rather unflatteringly portrayed as the friendly but formal Arthur Whane. Still, he had long sympathized with Kerouac's view of higher education:

Nothing but grooming schools for the middle-class non-identity which usually finds its perfect expression on the outskirts of the campus in rows of well-to-do houses with lawns and television sets in each living room with everybody looking at the same thing and thinking the same thing at the same time . . .[11]

Alan Watts could also see something of himself in the romance and spontaneity of the alternative ideal: the rucksack wanderer and natural mystic, moving to 'the rhythm of the dance' and inspiring laughter and happiness wherever he went. And he was delighted to see Zen starting to attract so much attention. *Time* magazine carried a piece on it in 1957, the *Chicago Review* devoted a special section to Zen in 1958, and Watts himself, along with D. T. Suzuki, began to garner honourable mentions in magazines like *Vogue* and *Life*.[12]

Watts was cautious, however, about people's motives. He contributed a widely read essay entitled 'Beat Zen, Square Zen, and Zen' to the *Review*'s special section, in which he argued that devotees of Square and Beat Zen shared the same problem. They had rushed to embrace a new and exotic religion without first understanding the full impact on them of the Judaeo-Christian culture in which they had grown up, especially its emphasis on self-justification. This lack of reflection showed itself amongst practitioners of Square Zen, thought Watts, in an obsession with 'correct' Zen practice and 'correct' tests of success in achieving enlightenment (Watts was never fully reconciled either with *kōan* or with his mother-in-law, who practised a traditional form of Zen). Meanwhile, behind Beat Zen's 'Bohemian affectations' and the 'caprice' of its lifestyles and art forms lurked a strong element of self-justification – epitomized in a famous Kerouac comment: 'I don't know. I don't care. And it doesn't make any difference.' Real Zen, argued Watts, had no use for self-justification. It offered complete liberation from all such preoccupations.[13]

This was a neat way for Watts to position himself as the bringer, to the West, of the authentic Zen spirit, spurning the fussiness of scholars, the hidebound traditionalism of Japanese Zen and the excuse-seeking of idle dropouts – from whose numbers he generally excluded Snyder and Ginsberg, regarding both as serious about radically rethinking Western life. His years of learning and his British accent communicated an authority and authenticity of their own to American audiences, and his articulacy stood up well against Kerouc's prose, which quickly came to feel passé.[14] Strategy aside, Watts' portrayal of Zen as liberation was also very much in tune with his own temperament. As someone who had struggled with the discipline of *kōan* practice, the rigours of priesthood and the responsibilities of family life, he was deeply attracted to the idea that Western egocentrism was not a 'moral fault', requiring repentance or religious austerities, but rather a 'conceptual hallucination' of which one could be cured in an instant.[15] He much preferred the *wu-wei* – 'noninterference' – of Taoism to Confucius and his rules of conduct.[16]

In *The Wisdom of Insecurity* (1954), whose readers included Erna Hoch, and *Psychotherapy East and West* (1961), Watts sought to enlist quantum physics into his cause. It was now clear, he claimed, that the world is not made up of 'stuff'. Language and common sense might have yet to catch up, but reality was most accurately imagined as a field, or as shifting 'patterns of relationship'.[17] Get close enough to some 'thing', and you make three discoveries, he argued: it is made up primarily of movement, rather than anything solid; it is impossible to say where a given thing ends and the space around it begins; and to observe something is to participate in it.[18] One of the best visual metaphors, thought Watts, for the way reality really is could be found in a classic piece of Buddhist imagery:

A vast network of jewels, like drops of dew upon a multidimensional spider's web. Looking closely at any single jewel, one beholds in it the reflection of all the others.[19]

To feel the truth of this, argued Watts, was to enjoy a profound sense of interconnectedness with reality. It was the feeling of not being 'an agent, a doer of deeds'. Zen called it 'no-mind'; the *Bhagavad Gita* described it as the sense that 'I do nothing at all'. The common-sense view of a human being as a 'skin-encapsulated ego' was merely a vestige, Watts claimed, of the old Christian idea of a soul being carried along in its 'fleshy vehicle'. As people in Asia had understood for centuries, this view of human life was both false and damaging. Belief in a fixed and separate 'I', or ego, would constantly bump up against a reality of flux and interconnection. The result was pain: trying to hold on to things – people; possessions; the past – as part of a futile search for security. Buddhism taught this via the unreality of the ego, and the importance of compassion; Advaita Vedānta emphasized the unity of the field, of Self (*ātman*) with Brahman.[20]

Watts no longer saw much promise in Freud or even Jung in dealing with this modern predicament. Freud's caricaturing of a narrow and needy religious mindset had done little other than put Westerners off religion in general, to the detriment of Asian options. Jung's insistence, meanwhile, that human beings cannot reach beyond their mental world to make metaphysical claims struck Watts as both boring and circular: to assert the impossibility of making metaphysical claims was, in itself, to make a metaphysical claim. As for Jung's view of myth as a guide to life and source of healing, Watts had reached the conclusion that a myth only 'works' when a person believes it to contain a substantial element of literal truth.[21]

None of this meant that Watts had given up on the mind sciences. He hoped that human beings' deep-seated case of mistaken identity – falsely imagining themselves as an 'I', separate from the world – could be tackled by a new generation of psychotherapists inspired by Asian thought, Karen Horney and Erna Hoch's mentor Medard Boss amongst them. He expected that some people seeking liberation from mental illness would naturally be drawn to the ultimate, metaphysical source of their suffering. Show a degree of friendly curiosity towards a depressive mood, for example – 'invite it to come in and have a cup of tea' – and alongside the therapeutic benefit, of avoiding the pain associated with resisting that mood or trying to push it around, one might find a great philosophical boon.[22] It would become immediately, intimately clear that emotions and moods have their own *tao*, or 'way', and that the mind is more complex and mysterious than at first it might appear. This might end up becoming the first step in a philosophical search.

Another practical option, thought Watts, was to go looking for the 'I' of whose existence people tend to feel so convinced. Watts suggested reading a sentence in a book, and seeing whether it was possible, at the same time, to be aware of an 'I' who is doing the reading. Wasn't it in fact the case that the mind flits between the experience of reading and the experience of the thought 'I am reading'? The sheer speed of the transition creates the illusion of a reader, an 'I', who is doing the reading – where in fact there is *only* experience, pure and egoless.

Adapting a piece of Buddhist imagery, Watts likened this phenomenon to a burning stick being whirled in the air, creating the impression of a solid circle of fire.[23] He also enjoyed telling a famous story from the Chinese Chan (Zen) tradition. A man seeks peace, and asks a sage to pacify his mind. 'Bring out your mind [your 'I'], and I will pacify it,' answers the sage. 'I have searched for my mind this many years,' responds the man, 'and cannot find it.' 'There,' concludes the sage, 'it is pacified.'[24]

Western languages, suggested Watts, tend to complicate matters. In languages like English, most sentences require a subject: a do-er, or a done-to. In Japanese, it is perfectly normal to describe life in terms of things happening: rather than 'I am feeling anxious', a person might say *fuan ga aru* – 'There is anxiety.' In Taoism, meanwhile, the general divisiveness and deceptiveness of language was well-recognized: 'The Names that can be given / Are not Absolute Names.'[25] Here was a clue as to what 'liberation', as Watts understood it, might look like: not a privation, a cherished 'I' turning out to be unreal, but an opening up to each moment as 'utterly new and unique' – just look, suggested Watts, at the joy and liveliness of East Asian painting inspired by Zen.[26]

As the links with the mind sciences suggested, there was room, in this worldview, for the realities of suffering and pain. People were counselled to enter into them, rather than seek to resist. 'Having' pain, as the possession or affliction of an imagined separate entity, was terrible. 'Being' pain was both closer to the truth, and a little easier to endure. Such, for Watts, were the therapeutic benefits of his favourite phrase from the Upanishads: *Tat tvam asi* – 'You are that'. Pain, space, sea, sky: you don't have sensations of these things – you *are* these things.[27]

*

For growing numbers of young Americans in the early 1960s, conversations began with 'what Alan Watts said last night': on campus, on radio, or on television – the last including a twenty-six-part series called *Eastern Wisdom for Modern Life*, broadcast by National Educational Television.[28] Themes that had interested Watts since at least as far back as the 1940s were now major preoccupations for America's middle-class young. With lucidity and humour, and in an impeccably patrician accent, he revealed to them that they were being hoodwinked by their families, schools and wider society. The illusion of the ego derived much of its power, Watts argued, from the fact that it was a 'social fiction', sustained by societies in whose interest it was to raise purposeful, obedient and self-regulating citizens.[29]

Any truly helpful therapist, thought Watts, was therefore bound to double as a social critic. Too many Westerners imagined the aim of Advaita Vedānta and Buddhism as transporting an individual from one reality into another: from the everyday world of people, objects, death and rebirth into some separate, superior reality where all is one. Watts claimed never to have met an educated practitioner of either tradition who actually thought this way, or who believed in a literal cycle of death and rebirth. There was only one reality, and liberation was a matter of living in it with none of the usual distortions.[30]

For some, a brush with mental illness would help wake them up to this truth. For others, it would be disappointment at seeing their parents waste their lives or horror at the prospect of slowly rotting away in a prefab home of their own. In the late 1950s and early 1960s, a new kind of impetus altogether was starting to do the rounds: psychedelics. Aldous Huxley was amongst the pioneers, writing in *The Doors of Perception* (1954) of his experience of ingesting mescalin. Years spent exploring Eastern and Western mysticism persuaded him that what mescalin achieved was to suspend some of the filters on a person's experience of the world, which had evolved to help the mind focus on everyday necessities. In doing so, mescalin revealed reality to him in a new and profound way.

Huxley was cautious. 'I am not so foolish,' he wrote, 'as to equate what happens under the influence of mescalin . . . [with] Enlightenment, the Beatific Vision'. Still, he thought the experience akin to the 'Isness' of Eckhart's mystical philosophy; an exchanging of 'measures and location', in perceiving reality, for 'being and meaning'. Franz Mesmer had inspired people to experiment with hypnosis. The philosopher William James had used nitrous oxide to help him understand mystical experience. Huxley's generation had been gifted the most powerful tools yet for expanding consciousness: mescalin, LSD and psilocybin (the name given to the psychoactive element in certain species of mushroom).

Impressed by the way that psychedelics made Aldous Huxley and Gerald Heard appear 'more relaxed and humane', Watts tried LSD for himself in 1958 and again in 1959.[31] He discovered, the second time around, vivid vindication for the idea that the ego was unreal. 'I was no longer a detached observer, a little man inside my own head, *having* sensations,' he recalled, 'I *was* the sensations.'[32] Inside the house where Watts was conducting his experiment, everything was alive: 'tables are tabling, pots are potting, walls are walling'. Just as physicists of the day were claiming, this was a world not of things, but events. And just as India's philosophers had long taught, the universe was a place of play (*lila*). A game of divine 'hide-and-seek' was underway, in which the universe played at being lots of different things and people.[33]

Experiencing himself, at last, as part of that game was, for Watts, every bit the hoped-for liberation. Gone was the isolated creature who had once been convinced, in his bed upstairs at Rowan Tree Cottage, that terrible things were bound to befall him. Found, instead, was someone 'grow[ing] out from the rest of the universe like a hair from a head, or a limb from a body':

The 'myself' which I am beginning to recognise, which I had forgotten but actually know better than anything else, goes far back beyond my childhood, beyond the time when adults confused me . . . long before I was an embryo in my mother's womb, there looms the ever-so-familiar stranger, the everything not me, which I recognize, with a joy immeasurably more intense than a meeting of lovers separated by centuries, to be my original self. The good old sonofabitch who got me involved in this whole game.[34]

Watts regarded it as being entirely in keeping with the culture of the modern West that science would come up with solutions to problems which, in Asia, had been treated via religion, philosophy and the arts. Still, he did not regard psychedelics as a one-stop-shop for enlightenment. They provided an initial leg-up, to be complemented by therapy or spiritual practices like meditation: balancing out life in an 'overpurposeful civilization' with a regular period spent 'allowing the contents of consciousness to happen without interference'. Dancing and singing, too, would be a natural extension of the ego-free, connected feelings let loose by psychedelics. There was also an 'enormous spectrum of love' to be explored, 'between rather formal friendship and genital sexuality'.[35]

Anticipating objections to psychedelics, Watts argued that 'hallucinogens' was a very poor description: they heightened the senses rather than causing delusions. Nor were they any worse for the mind than the 'daily drivel' to be found on television.[36] He understood that their swift association with Beats and hipsters counted against them, in the eyes of some, as did the notion of spiritual experience being available from a bottle. But like Huxley he stressed that psychedelic experience only became meaningful and useful when it was integrated into people's everyday lives. Watts hoped that his own account of his experiences, *The Joyous Cosmology* (1962), would help people to understand the need to use psychedelics only in controlled settings, and with supervision.[37]

Watts could perhaps be accused of naivety where his fellow men and women were concerned. How many would, like him, pop a pill and then set themselves the task of contemplating the Mass, a particular work of art, or the relationship of Logos to Eros?[38] There was an element of disingenuous self-defence when he later blamed the disastrous abuse of psychedelics – 'afflict[ing] countless young people with paranoid, megalomaniac and schizoid symptoms' – on the outlawing of LSD, and the thwarting of proper research.[39] But to his credit, he never overestimated psychedelics. He insisted that much of the allure of *The Doors of Perception* was down to Huxley's skill as a writer – his powers of insight, and his talent for turning a phrase. Watts' own psychedelic writings emerged from thirty years of reading and reflecting on Asian philosophy. LSD brought confirmation and fresh force to his ideas, rather than any truly new insights.

The foreword for *The Joyous Cosmology* was written by Timothy Leary and Richard Alpert of Harvard University. Conducting research on psilocybin, they found that Asian philosophy – as found in the writings of Huxley, Watts and others – provided a better basis for interpreting their results than some of the standard psychological models of the day.[40] Harvard's decision not to renew their contracts in 1963 turned Leary and Alpert into free-wheeling evangelists for what Leary called 'applied mysticism'.[41] They continued their research together at a large mansion in Millbrook, New York, which doubled as a commune – complete with a 'Hindu room' covered in Indian furnishings and intended for meditation.[42] Leary, who described LSD to one reporter as 'modern yoga', travelled to India for his honeymoon in 1964, spending time in Calcutta and Erna Hoch's enclave of Almora.[43] He soon became famous – notorious – for his enthusiastic advocacy of psychedelics, handing them out to a range of writers including Allen Ginsberg and William S. Burroughs and urging people to 'Turn on, tune in, and drop out'.

Had this been the extent of it – fertilizing the creativity of a handful of people already living at the cultural margins – then research into psychedelics might have continued in America. Instead, university students began synthesizing their own LSD, while entrepreneurs tapped the growing market in cities like San Francisco. Ken Kesey, author of *One Flew Over the Cuckoo's Nest*, together with his band of 'Merry Pranksters', dished it out to anyone looking for the chance to be 'turned on' and to 'freak freely'.[44] Members of the Hell's Angels motorcycle club were amongst those to take him up on his offer.[45] Areas of San Francisco like Haight-Ashbury, around 8 miles south of Watts' houseboat in Sausalito, became home to people wandering around in bright clothing, high on marijuana or LSD (or both), and professing a hatred of war – America's involvement in Vietnam especially – and a love of Eastern and occult religion. The soundtrack, for an estimated one million doses of LSD being taken in America every year by the time that California banned it in 1966, was provided by Bob Dylan, 'British Invasion' bands like the Beatles, and local boys the Grateful Dead.[46]

As Watts fed the counter-culture, the counter-culture fed him. The stuffy, short-haired Englishman of the 1950s, whose irreverent ideas clashed with his decidedly formal personal style, turned – in Gary Snyder's estimation – into a blossoming flower child, sporting long hair, a goatee and a wardrobe that leaned heavily towards Asia, from kimono to sarong. Fans sought Watts out on his houseboat at all hours. One woman took to approaching him in restaurants and kissing his feet.[47] In 1966, he produced one of the best-loved popular distillations of his ideas on overcoming egocentrism: *The Book: On the Taboo against Knowing Who You Are*. And in January of the next year, he participated in the 'World's First Human Be-In', held in a field in San Francisco's Golden Gate Park.

On the morning of the great event, Snyder, Ginsberg and Watts performed a Hindu rite of circumambulation around the field. Later, some 25,000 people began arriving, turning out in tiaras, furs, feathers, beads, bells and bare feet. Gary Snyder got things started, blowing on a white conch shell to 'gather the tribes', which included Beats, hippies and veterans of the recent free speech movement at the University of California, Berkeley. Allen Ginsberg intoned mantras, the Diggers – an activist theatre group – handed out free sandwiches, and the Hell's Angels guarded the sound equipment while bands performed, including Jefferson Airplane and the Grateful Dead. Shunryū Suzuki, of the San Francisco Zen Center, meditated on stage and held up a flower – recreating the Buddha's wordless evocation of enlightenment. As the sun set, Gary Snyder blew once again on his conch shell, and brought the day to a close.[48]

★

In retrospect, the Be-In and the 'summer of love' that followed represented a high point for Watts, and for the brand of liberation that he offered. Whether one blamed drugs, or the media, or simply the passing of a moment, America's counter-culture was on the turn.

One day in 1967, Haight-Ashbury – 'Hashbury', as it had become known – received a very special visitor. He had played his final live concert in this very city the year before, having resolved to give up touring after it degenerated into an endless round of hotel incarceration, heavily policed motorcades and stints on stage where no music could be heard above the screaming. George Harrison had his limousine driver park a block away, so that he could stroll through Haight-Ashbury in his moccasins, paisley trousers and heart-shaped glasses, and – with luck – explore this fabled district in peace.

It wasn't to be. Harrison was quickly recognized, and a tide of hippies began to crash over him, his girlfriend Pattie Boyd, and their small group of friends. They offered weed, peyote and STP – a particularly powerful hallucinogen – and turned hostile when Harrison and co. declined. Awkward encounters with the public weren't especially new or alarming. Not long before, Harrison and Boyd had arrived home in Esher to find that two female fans had broken in and were hiding under their bed. What disturbed him about Haight-Ashbury was that he had been promised the capital of love, and had found instead streets full of rubbish, stoned children lying on benches and people begging for money.[49]

To Harrison, who had taken some LSD just before the visit to Haight-Ashbury, the fabled 'love generation' appeared like characters out of a Hieronymus Bosch painting – 'fish with heads, faces like vacuum cleaners coming out of shop doorways'. It would be the last time he took LSD, and he hoped the people he was leaving behind would soon have done with it too. As his limousine pulled away, he took from his pocket a picture of the yogi Paramahansa Yogananda – dark, flowing hair over ochre robes – and pressed it to the glass, to show the crowd outside. '*This*,' he is said to have told his friends in the car, 'is where it is.'[50]

George Harrison, John Lennon, Cynthia Lennon, Jane Asher and the Maharishi at Rishikesh, India, February 1968.

20.

Gurus

For anyone who longed to see Western life infused with the best of Asia, 1965 was a big year. It began on a beach in Bombay, where one January morning Ray Davies of the Kinks sat watching the sun rise and listening to the chanting of Indian fishermen as they prepared their nets. 'For some indescribable reason,' he recalled, the sound 'was immediately personal to me.'[1] He wrote a song, 'See My Friends', using a twelve-string guitar with gentle feedback to emulate the Indian drone, combining it with his trademark nasal whine. It became one of the first entries in a new musical mini-genre: 'Raga rock'.[2]

In February, work began on a film of whose plot Robert Southey would surely have approved. Where he had drawn inspiration from the great bone-crushing chariot of the Jagannatha festival, the film's writers borrowed from British tales of the Thuggee: a semi-legendary – perhaps entirely fictitious – cult of Indian robbers and murderers dedicated to the goddess Kāli. Members of the cult are about to sacrifice a woman to Kāli when they notice that she is not wearing the all-important sacrificial ring. She is, it turns out, a fan of the Beatles, and has sent the precious item to Ringo Starr.

A cinematic classic in almost no one's estimation – including the Beatles themselves, who were mostly stoned while making it – *Help!* was nevertheless a milestone in bringing Indian music to Western attention. It was while filming a scene at an Indian restaurant, mocked up in Twickenham Studios, that George Harrison got his first chance to play around with a sitar. He was fascinated by its weight, balance and sound, and bought a 'crummy' one of his own at a shop called Indiacraft on Oxford Street. Inspired by a recording of Ravi Shankar, and perhaps also the release of 'See My Friends' in the summer of 1965 – a loyal friend of the Kinks described the Beatles as 'vandals' for stealing their ideas – Harrison used the sitar to add a little something to a song that John Lennon had written about an extramarital affair. In the autumn, 'Norwegian Wood (This Bird Has Flown)' became the first Western pop song to feature a sitar. The Byrds and the Rolling Stones followed suit the next year, with 'Eight Miles High' and 'Paint It Black'.[3]

At the beginning of 1965 the relatively few Westerners who had heard a sitar would have associated it either with Shankar – if they were amongst his small but growing fanbase – or else with music halls and the ambience of Indian restaurants. By the early 1970s, the sound of a sitar scale hanging in the air was instantly capable of evoking some combination of dream, mystical vision, exotic journey and druggy haze. Shankar was amongst those who came to regret the fate of the sitar in the popular Western mind, suspended between inspiration and cliché. And yet while psychedelics ended up outlawed, and the hippy moment passed, the link forged in this short period between Asian spirituality and music – from ragas to chanting – lived on.

These years also marked a shift within the West's appreciation of Asian religion: away from an earlier, relatively intellectual focus on scripture, poetry and philosophy, and towards meditation and the subcontinent's *bhakti* (devotional) tradition. The Beatles, and George Harrison in particular, showed that in a collective search for meaning nothing quite matches music for democratic immediacy. At the same time, they became synonymous with the highs and lows of spiritual adventure, and with the charismatic figure of the guru.

*

George Harrison could claim to have heard the sound of the sitar before he was born. His mother Louise used to tune into a programme called 'Radio India' while she was pregnant with him, hoping that its music – sitars and tablas – would have a calming effect on her baby.[4] She brought her son up as a Catholic, but church interested Harrison little more than school. What moved him was seeing Lonnie Donegan play at the Empire Theatre in 1956, and hearing 'Heartbreak Hotel' on Radio Luxembourg. That same year, he successfully lobbied his mother for the £3 required to buy a guitar from a friend at school.[5] Harrison got talking to Paul McCartney on the top deck of the bus on the way to school – the latter lost in a haze of smoke – and they eventually joined John Lennon's Quarrymen: yet another band, in a city bursting at the seams with them.[6]

In 1962, Harrison and friends won a recording contract with EMI, and released 'Love Me Do'. The sound of screaming fans at their gigs – 'like pigs being slaughtered', noted one observer – heralded the arrival of Beatlemania, at whose peak in 1965 their manager Brian Epstein received a proposal for marketing their bathwater. Harrison underwrote his father's retirement, moved to London, began buying expensive cars, and started stepping out with a young model, Pattie Boyd.[7] But he was never happy with the sort of attention that The Beatles received, most of all during their world tour in 1966. Tokyo and Manila passed in a dispiriting blur of concrete, hotel rooms and armed police, and after their final date in San Francisco, in August 1966, he announced that he had had enough of touring.[8] He wanted to return to the man who had become his guru earlier that summer: Ravi Shankar.

Shankar agreed to take Harrison on as a student before hearing his attempt at the sitar on 'Norwegian Wood'. When enthusiastic nieces and nephews introduced him to the song, Shankar thought that it sounded 'terrible'. He resolved to say nothing about it.[9] Harrison learned his guru's expectations early on, studying with him at home in Esher and receiving a whack on the leg when he stepped over his sitar – a sacred object – to answer a phone call.[10] Besides disciplining his disciple, Shankar introduced Harrison to the basics of Indian classical music.[11] It favoured single notes rather than harmony, sung or played in an order capable of creating emotional and spiritual 'colour' – *ranga* in Sanskrit, from which the word 'raga' derives.

Music's religious connections went back centuries, to the chanting of the Vedas. Raga had developed from around the tenth century, and had come to be divided into a northern Hindustani style and a southern Carnatic counterpart.[12] There were thousands of ragas, each linked to different seasons, times of day and moods. 'My goal,' Shankar told Harrison, 'has always been to take the audience along with me deep inside, as in meditation, to feel the sweet pain of trying to reach out for the Supreme.' Harrison later recalled being ready, at that moment, to leave Esher behind, and 'take a one-way ticket to Calcutta'.[13]

After the concert in August 1966 Harrison flew to Bombay with Boyd for what would be his only extended period of training with Shankar. They relocated to a houseboat in Kashmir, after Harrison's new moustache failed to stop him being spotted by Indian fans at Bombay's Taj Hotel. During five weeks of training in India's far north, Harrison began to feel pain in his legs from prolonged periods of sitting cross-legged on the floor, supporting the sitar.[14] He tried to tackle the pain by practising Hatha Yoga, complementing it with a reading regime that included the *I Ching*, Swami Vivekānanda's *Raja Yoga* and Paramahansa Yogananda's bestselling *Autobiography of a Yogi* (1946) – this last a recommendation from Shankar.[15]

Born in 1893, the year of Vivekānanda's appearance at the World's Parliament of Religions, Yogananda's flowing hair, charismatic teaching style – always in his ochre robes – and keen sense of the burgeoning American market for Eastern spirituality had helped him to put together a lucrative yoga movement. He advertised his talks in newspapers and on billboards, and gave them titles like 'Recharging Your Business Battery'. He had now passed away, but Harrison was captivated by the photograph on the cover of his *Autobiography*. Yogananda's eyes, he recalled many years later, 'went right through me . . . to this day I have been under the spell of Yogananda.'[16] Reading the book, he encountered stories of saints and swamis who had gained extraordinary powers through yoga and other austerities. It reminded him of the world that LSD opened up: discerning God 'in every blade of grass . . . gaining hundreds of years of experience in twelve hours'.[17]

Turning his back on LSD for much the same reason as Alan Watts –

'when one has received the message,' wrote Watts, 'one hangs up the phone' – Harrison became serious about Indian spirituality.[18] He read about meditation and rebirth. He and Boyd travelled to Srinagar, Jaipur, Jodhpur, Delhi, Varanasi and Allahabad, taking in the sights: temples and holy men, pilgrims and a maharaja, elephants and peacocks. Then they returned home to England, Harrison a newly minted missionary for India.[19]

Harrison's music began to change. With the help of Ravi Shankar's tuition, Vivekānanda and Yogananda's writings, and session musicians drawn from the Asian Music Circle, his song 'Within You Without You' took on a meditative feel – musically and lyrically – that put it far from the jaunty sitar pluckings of 'Norwegian Wood' just two years before.[20] Both the track and Yogananda himself ended up on *Sgt. Pepper's Lonely Hearts Club Band* (1967), the latter's face appearing towards the top right of the famous throng. The era of the guru had opened, helped along by the relaxation of American immigration rules in 1965.

Swami Prabhupāda was one of the first Indian gurus to make the journey, founding the International Society for Krishna Consciousness (ISKCON) in New York in 1966. The *bhakti* tradition of which he was a part originated in Bengal, and his American followers soon became well-known for dressing in the style of medieval Vaishnavites (devotees of Vishnu as the supreme being), and for chanting and singing 'Hare Krishna' in the street.[21] Prabhupāda taught that Krishna was present in the pronunciation of his name, so that to chant it was to commune with God.[22] He had records made, featuring his followers chanting Vedic mantras, and one of these found its way into Harrison's hands. During a holiday cruise through the Greek islands in the summer of 1967 Harrison persuaded his bandmates to sing along while he strummed a ukulele. For six hours, stretching well into the night, the Beatles sailed the Aegean and sang 'Hare Krishna'.[23]

A few weeks later, Harrison, McCartney and Lennon found themselves in Wales, sitting alongside Mick Jagger at the feet of Maharishi ('great seer') Mahesh Yogi. His 'Transcendental Meditation' technique required twenty minutes, twice per day, of meditation with a mantra.[24] Harrison and Lennon were impressed both by the method and by the man himself, especially the compassion that the Maharishi showed them when news came in, while they were in Wales, of the sudden death of Brian Epstein. The two of them took up meditation as a regular practice, and in February 1968 the Beatles joined stars including Mike Love of the Beach Boys at the Maharishi's ashram in Rishikesh, funded by tobacco heiress Doris Duke and set amidst fourteen acres of land overlooking the Ganges.[25] Off came the 1960s fashion-wear, and on went cotton trousers (*churidars*) and long white shirts (*kurtas*), for a daily training regime that began with the call of peacocks and an al fresco breakfast, and continued with a combination of meditation and lectures from the Maharishi.[26]

The full three-month programme was not for everyone. Starr and his wife Maureen left after two weeks. McCartney lasted a month, returning home with his girlfriend Jane Asher and a trove of new songs written in between meditation sessions. Lennon stayed longer. The lingering pain of his mother's early death a decade before, and disillusionment in the wake of Beatlemania, had led him, of late, into a spiritual crisis of sorts. He read the Bible, the *Bhagavad Gita* and *The Tibetan Book of the Dead*, alongside Alan Watts and Timothy Leary. He even got down on his knees to pray for direction. Lennon wondered, while in Rishikesh, whether the Beatles might have a role to play in bringing Indian spirituality to a mass audience. Then he started to hear rumours, never substantiated, about the Maharishi making advances on one of his female disciples. Lennon returned home, and wrote a musical denunciation of his erstwhile guru whose title, with some effort, Harrison persuaded Lennon to change from 'Maharishi' to 'Sexy Sadie'.[27]

Lennon was clearly moved by his experience of meditation – captured in his song 'Across the Universe' – but when it came to religion he was, as Alan Watts said of himself, 'not a joiner'. Harrison, who left India along with Lennon, very much *was* a joiner: as the Beatles fell apart, he spent more and more time with ISKCON members in their makeshift warehouse-temple in Covent Garden.

Gathered around candles and garlanded brass statues, they sang and chanted while Harrison played the harmonium. He recorded 'Hare Krishna Mantra' with them in the summer of 1969, and released it as a single. It made it into the Top Twenty in the British and American charts, and viewers around Britain were treated to the sight of ISKCON devotees chanting amidst dry ice on *Top of the Pops*.[28]

*

Far from the set of *Top of the Pops*, Bede Griffiths spent 1969 settling into his new home at Shantivanam. Making the move from misty mountain-top to tropical Tamil Nadu in his early sixties, he looked forward to seeing out his days here: meditating for an hour at sunrise and sunset on the veranda of his little thatched hut, sunlight flickering through mango, coconut, palmyra and banana trees.[29] During the day, the woods were alive with squirrels, parrots, robins and woodpeckers going about their business, in temperatures that sometimes topped 40 degrees. At night, hot bustle gave way to a cool breeze and a pure, peaceful darkness, out of which shone – with extraordinary brilliance – the moon, the stars and what Griffiths thought might be the planet Venus.[30]

Established in the early 1950s by two French monks, fathers Jules Monchanin and Henri le Saux (who became better known as Swami Abhishiktananda: 'The Bliss of Christ'), the ashram consisted of no more than a few huts and a small chapel built in the style of a Hindu temple. With the help of an Indian friend and *sarvodaya* ('service of the people') activist, Stephen, who had made the journey with him from Kurisumala, Griffiths set about clearing overgrown areas of vegetation, constructing a new octagonal building to serve as a library and meditation centre, and installing electricity and running water – a pragmatic compromise with 'Babylon', as Griffiths put it to his old friend Martyn Skinner.[31] Stephen noted that even after more than a decade in India, Griffiths seemed to prefer English gardens to the sacred forests lauded in the Upanishads.[32]

Griffiths came to love Shantivanam, regarding it as the fulfilment of the Eastington experiment so many years before. The world beyond was another matter. Visiting Bangkok for a conference in December 1968, Griffiths encountered a city full of televisions, 'immense highways', and an atmosphere of 'utterly futil[e] . . . movement and noise'.[33] But just as Griffiths had given up on the men and women of his generation, their children came knocking on his door. Tens of thousands of young Westerners began heading out to India, using an overland route that would have been familiar, in parts, to Tom Coryate: Turkey, Iran, Afghanistan.[34]

Jack Kerouac's *On the Road* was an inspiration for this new generation of 'Legge-Stretchers', as was Yogananda's autobiography, Watts' *Way of Zen*, and Herman Hesse's *Siddhartha*: the natural successor to Edwin Arnold's *Light of Asia* as a romantic evocation of the Buddha's life. Some made spiritual discoveries in India almost by accident: as they had been in Coryate's day, religious sites like Agra were well connected by road, making them easy places to get to and hence natural stops on an itinerary. Others went actively in search of gurus like Sai Baba – revered alike by Hindus and Muslims – or ashrams where they might learn meditation or yoga.

Griffiths was well aware that some of the young Westerners who arrived at Shantivanam were into drugs. But he was happy, as he put it in letters to Martyn Skinner, to accept that 'various motives' might lead a person 'to discover the deep sources of life'. One young man from Cheltenham had begun living as a *sannyasin*, changing his name from Eric to Narayana. Like other Westerners who tried similar things, he found India's climate and people sufficiently hospitable that he was able to live off alms alone.[35] Griffiths was increasingly sympathetic, both to young Westerners in search of wisdom and to the Hindu philosophies – notably Advaita Vedānta – on which they alighted. 'Eastern wisdom gives the key to Christianity,' he told Skinner. 'I cannot conceive of Christ now except in terms of Vedānta.'[36]

Griffiths also had a talent for offering spiritual support, going back to his time as guest-master and then prior of St Michael's Abbey in Farnborough in the late 1940s and early 1950s. Back then, a fellow monk had disparaged his efforts as an 'apostolate of the parlour'. But it was perfectly suited to these new times. Griffiths had an intimate understanding of what it was like to live at the margins of Christianity – to be a dweller on the threshold – and he combined this with tremendous gifts as a confidant, listening to those who came in search of a guru and encouraging them to meditate.

Since the 1940s, Griffiths himself had been meditating with the 'Jesus Prayer', quietly repeating the phrase 'Lord Jesus Christ, Son of God, have mercy on me, a sinner'. At Shantivanam, he steadily changed the daily routine to allow monks and visitors more time for solitary silence. The elevated place of meditation in Hindu life and mythology had long impressed him. Shiva was said to have meditated for thousands of years at a time, and Hinduism was home to a rich range of associated practices: Patanjali's yoga, the living of everyday life with the minimum of attachment to self, the devotional strand that George Harrison was helping to popularize in the West, and innovative techniques like Transcendental Meditation, which Griffiths greatly admired.

Griffiths worried that Christianity was failing to keep up with Westerners' growing desire for spirituality of this kind: 'the Christian experience of God is of unfathomable depth' he wrote, 'but it is locked up in words and formulas, which have for many lost their meaning.'[37] He consoled himself with the thought that attempts were afoot to change this. The Catholic theologian Karl Rahner warned that 'the devout Christian of the future will either be a "mystic", one who has experienced "something", or he will cease to be anything at all'.[38] Meanwhile, the American Trappist Thomas Keating and the British Benedictine John Main were amongst those working to adapt monastic practices of meditation for the laity. Keating helped to develop a method called 'Centering Prayer', while Main taught a form of Christian mantra meditation, inspired by a technique which he had learned from an Indian *sannyasin*, Swami Satyananda Saraswati.

Despite the steep climb, Kurisumala, too, was now receiving its fair share of Western visitors. Many were attracted to its contemplative style of life, inspired by the vogue back home for Asian styles of meditation and by the writings of the American Trappist monk Thomas Merton, whose autobiography, *The Seven Storey Mountain*, had become a modern spiritual classic.[39] One visitor to Kurisumala, a young Floridian in his early twenties whom Father Mahieu referred to as 'Robert G', had come to India in 1971 in search of a guru and had stayed for a while at an ashram in Tiruvannamalai, established by Ramana Maharshi, one of the most revered Hindu teachers of the twentieth century. Robert hoped that although he had little in common 'with Christianity and Catholicism as it exists in the United States . . . Christ could be my guru'.[40]

Most people back in Florida would doubtless have found this a strange, even blasphemous notion. But it was in the nature of gurus that a person might meet theirs in physical form at just the right time in their lives – or else receive guru-like guidance from a 'cherished deity' by devoting themselves fully to that god. The idea could be found in Patanjali's Yoga Sutras, the writings of Ram Mohan Roy, the teachings of Ramana Maharshi and – most recently of all – in *Be Here Now* (1971) by the Harvard psychologist Richard Alpert, one-time colleague of Timothy Leary. He had visited northern India in 1967, found his guru – Neem Karoli Baba – and been utterly transformed by the experience: 'I cried and I cried and I cried . . . it felt like I was home. Like the journey was over.' He returned to America bearing a new name, given to him by his guru – 'Ram Dass'– and began writing and teaching.[41]

Staying for a while at Kurisumala, Robert G fell in love with the vast mountain ranges around him, and the 'feeling of brotherhood' that he found expressed in silence, communal work and worship. He had discovered a way, he said, of curing his sense of 'alienation from my own [Christian] culture', and a means of combining two things that he recalled as being mutually exclusive back home in America: devotional religion, and an 'intellectual yearning to know life as it is without colouring it up with fancy images of God'.[42]

Griffiths' sympathy with young Westerners who looked to Asia for answers in this way helped to draw him into the emerging movement for inter-religious dialogue during his early years at Shantivanam.

The advent of air travel, the launching of satellites, and images from space showing the earth as truly 'one world' were starting to render exclusive notions of 'truth' decidedly outdated.[43] Western Christian churches were well aware of the risk of responding to the challenge of religious pluralism by allowing a culture of relativism to develop. But as the Indian Christian theologian Paul Devanandan had put it, at a meeting of the World Council of Churches in 1961, Christians ought not to be blind to 'God's redemptive work with people of other faiths'.[44] Four years later, the Vatican had made a 'Declaration on the Relation of the Church with Non-Christian Religions', in which particular mention was made of Hinduism and Buddhism. 'The Catholic Church', it said, 'rejects nothing of what is true and holy in these religions,' and it called on Catholics to engage in dialogue and co-operation.[45]

Confident that things were moving in the right direction, Griffiths always sought official approval for his initiatives and innovations at Shantivanam. And yet quite what 'dialogue' ought to look like was unclear. In the early 1960s, Swami Abhishiktananda and Dr Jacques-Albert Cuttat – a philosopher interested in Asian spirituality, who was serving as the Swiss ambassador to India – had experimented with gathering people together, reading from Hindu and Christian scriptures, and engaging in meditation and reflection.[46] Griffiths followed in a similar vein. He attended inter-religious meetings across Asia, and in 1974 brought together a group of Hindus and Christians at Shantivanam for a three-day encounter featuring scripture readings, discussions, *bhajans* (Indian devotional songs) and hymns. The atmosphere, he reported to Martyn Skinner, was one of 'complete openness and friendship . . . meet[ing] as brothers seeking the one Truth'.[47]

Thomas Merton, too, became an early pioneer of inter-religious dialogue, with Buddhism in particular. Struck by the concern shown in Zen for technique and the use of the body in meditation, he began to study it in depth, reading and corresponding with D. T. Suzuki. He concluded that Zen had much in common with the Christian spirituality of the Desert Fathers in third-century Egypt, along with Meister Eckhart and St John of the Cross. In 1968, he travelled around Asia, learning about the Theravada and Tibetan traditions. In India, he met two prominent refugees from Chinese-controlled Tibet: Chögyam Trungpa and the fourteenth Dalai Lama.

Merton did not expect to find close philosophical parallels between Christianity, shaped by Greek thought, and Buddhism. He once said that comparing Christianity and Zen would be like 'trying to compare mathematics and tennis'.[48] He was more interested in the spiritual experiences to which different religious traditions gave rise. Buddhism, in its Zen and Tibetan forms especially, clearly had much to teach Christians about technique in prayer. It might also help to shift Christians away from the idea, which Merton traced back to Descartes, that the root of a person's identity is the everyday self. Merton came to believe that detachment from this 'superficial' self, modelled most clearly by Jesus Christ, made way for the emergence of a 'true self': similar, perhaps, to what Buddhists called 'no-self'.[49] As St Paul phrased it in his Epistle to the Galatians: 'It is no longer I who live, but it is Christ who lives in me.' Or as Merton himself put it, talking to people on one of his contemplative retreats: 'One thing [is] certain about heaven: there won't be much of *you* there!'[50]

There was much on which Merton and Griffiths might have agreed, had the two met in India, as planned, during Merton's Asian tour. It was not to be. Griffiths perhaps heard Merton speak (on Marx and monasticism) at the Bangkok conference in December 1968. But hours later Merton was dead, seemingly from accidental electrocution in the cottage where he was staying.[51] Griffiths would live another twenty-five years, facing the challenges of inter-religious dialogue without his might-have-been American ally.

Those challenges included the difficulty of distinguishing between learning from other religious traditions and edging towards syncretism. Griffiths thought it vital that people remain within a particular tradition rather than picking and choosing congenial elements from a variety of them. Eastern and Western religious traditions might well share a mystical core – Griffiths never renounced his commitment to the perennial philosophy – but the differences between them were profound, running deeper than most people would ever go in their spiritual understanding. He applied this rule to himself, turning down a number of opportunities to meet the Maharishi because he was afraid that it 'might draw me from my Christian basis, which is the deepest thing in my life'.[52]

This, in turn, raised the question, tackled three centuries before by Roberto de Nobili, of whether and how culture might be separated out from religion. How might aspects of Indian culture, from ritual to meditation, help Christianity to purify itself and bring disillusioned Christians closer to God without corrupting the gospel? Failure risked the charge, sometimes made against Griffiths, of developing a 'neo-Hindu Christianity'.[53] A third challenge was the range of potentially confusing contradictions that existed between religious traditions. The Christian concept of time was linear, running from Creation through the Fall of Adam and Eve and the coming of Jesus Christ, and moving ultimately into what St Paul called the 'new creation'. Hindus and Buddhists, by contrast, took a cyclical view of time. Christians who were drawn to the Upanishads and Advaita Vedānta also faced the question of how to reconcile their sense of a personal God, with whom one was supposed to be able to have a relationship, with advaitic 'non-dualism': the idea that all is ultimately one.

For Griffiths, as for the Indologist Bettina Bäumer, a young associate of Abhishiktananda, inter-religious dialogue ought to be grounded in personal experience, and in an openness to having that experience enriched. Christians could, thought Griffiths, learn from Hindus how to balance their inherited sense of living within a grand narrative with an awareness that God is an 'eternal reality . . . always there'.[54] On the question of a personal God, he shared with Alan Watts the view that a non-dual reality – though clearly impossible to conceptualize – must have room within it both for oneness *and* for plurality and relationship. As Bäumer pointed out, oneness could be found in John's gospel, while India's *bhakti* devotional tradition thrived on the idea of a relationship with God.[55]

With the help of two monks from Kurisumala, Amaldas and Christudas, who joined him in the early 1970s, Griffiths took dialogue a step further by working Indian – largely Hindu – elements into the ashram's liturgies. Shantivanam already possessed, as the centrepiece of its ornate gateway, a three-headed figure representing both the Christian Trinity – Father, Son and Holy Spirit – and the Hindu Trimurti: Brahma, Vishnu and Shiva. Elsewhere in the ashram, the Sanskrit symbol *Om* appeared inside a Christian cross, with a circle around the outside, representing the wheel of dharma in Hindu and Buddhist iconography. This striking inter-religious image was completed by a lotus leaf at its base. Griffiths created forms of worship that incorporated readings from the Vedas, Upanishads and *Bhagavad Gita*, alongside Sanskrit and Tamil *bhajans*. Prayer shawls, pastes, powders, incense, candles and ritual movements were all borrowed from Hindu tradition and integrated into Catholic liturgies, including the Mass.[56]

The early 1970s became years of discovery, too, for Erna Hoch. After going back and forth between Almora and temporary posts in New Delhi for a while, in 1969 she moved to Srinagar, in Kashmir, to take up the role of professor of psychiatry at its medical college and to oversee the city's mental hospital. The job had its challenges: staff who sometimes bunked off work to play cards in the attic, elderly Kashmiri patients who expected her to wield 'magical powers', and Western travellers whose quest for spiritual or narcotic highs had turned them into a mess of 'tangled, matted, long hair, teeming with vermin' (one had become convinced, by a combination of drugs and high altitude, that he was Jesus Christ). But Nigeen Lake was a saving grace: situated five minutes' walk away, and connected via a narrow stretch of water to Dal Lake, where Harrison, Shankar and Boyd had stayed a few years earlier. Hoch enjoyed taking boat rides, gliding past pink and white lotus blossoms, watching turquoise kingfishers skim the surface in their search for fish, and leaning back into the cushions – 'surrender[ing] to this paradisiacal landscape'.[57]

Grace found Hoch, too, in the form of a Kashmiri guru. Swami Gobind Kaul was a 'tall, dignified old man' of around seventy years of age, whom she encountered sitting cross-legged on the floor of his home dressed in a long white gown. When she confessed to 'the Swami', as she called him, her struggles with anger, he laughed, sympathized and reminded her that sometimes anger arises not from selfishness but from an inflamed sense of justice. He gave her some introductory yoga training, and took her through the initiations required to become his *chela* (disciple). Hoch sensed a 'transfer of energies' at this point, powerful enough to convince her that when the Swami died three years later it was worth listening out – in dreams, and during meditation – for guidance sent from his next life.[58]

The therapist had met her match. Hoch was struck by the ability of her guru to become whatever his *chela* needed at a given moment – 'father, mother, brother, friend'.[59] Exercises and disciplines would be offered to the *chela* until these needs faded away, one by one. The last to go was the need for the guru–disciple relationship itself, and this too had to be overcome.[60] For Hoch, it made one of the popular etymologies for 'guru', given in the Advayataraka Upanishad, seem especially apt:

The syllable *gu* signifies 'that which is dark'. The syllable *ru* signifies 'that which dispels'. It is on account of this power to dispel that darkness that the guru is so named.[61]

Hoch was less impressed with the Swami's circle of followers when she encountered them during *satsang*. Finding in these people all the usual human foibles, Hoch resolved to stick to the conviction that she had held since girlhood: the spiritual quest must ultimately be a solitary one.

Busy developing Shantivanam's communal life, and helping to open a new era of inter-religious dialogue across India and beyond, Bede Griffiths would no doubt have disagreed with Hoch's rather sceptical view of spiritual community. Alan Watts, meanwhile, appeared split on the matter. Though 'not a joiner', he enjoyed the company of people like Ram Dass after he returned to the United States from India dressed in a white robe and sporting a beard. Watts found Dass 'full of laughter and energy', a man who thrived – as Watts did – on 'thinking out loud with an appreciative and intelligent audience'.[62] Both men became gurus of a kind, positioning themselves alongside their readers and listeners as fellow dwellers on the threshold.

The danger of the guru role was that people came to expect too much. Watts enjoyed teaching at the Esalen Institute, home to an emerging Human Potential Movement, which drew on Asian thought and humanistic psychology. Esalen's roster of speakers included Aldous Huxley, Abraham Maslow, Susan Sontag and Timothy Leary. And he continued the writing and speaking that helped to pay his ever-increasing alimony bills. But fame of the kind that had would-be disciples scouring the waterfront in search of him was overwhelming.[63] In 1969, he and Jano – by this time the 'final and definitive Mrs Alan Watts', as he put it to his father – exchanged their houseboat for Druid Heights, a circular house built by their friend Roger Somers.

The *Vallejo* continued to serve as an office, from where Watts did his best to keep abreast of a vast correspondence with friends, fans, publishers and producers. He worked at a furious rate, steadily widening his audience to the point where it included readers of *Playboy*. 'Under the cover of lusty and curvaceous chicks (of whom I approve),' he told the magazine's editors in a letter, 'and of silly bunnies (of whom I disapprove), you have turned *Playboy* into the most important philosophical periodical in this country . . . by comparison, the *Journal of the American Philosophical Society* is pedantic, boring and irrelevant.'[64]

There was no doubting his influence, but Watts had become almost too accomplished a popularizer of Asian wisdom. He was capable of drinking prodigious quantities of vodka, yet remaining lucid at the lectern. When he fell asleep during the Q&A, audiences assumed that he had lapsed into gnomic silence.[65] The truth of his exhaustion was known only to close friends, family and the disappointed publisher of his autobiography. *In My Own Way* was clever and witty, but Watts either couldn't or wouldn't probe very deep.

As it dawned on Watts that he lacked the money to stop working and the strength to stop drinking, he took comfort in Taoism as the closest thing he had ever had to a creed. Moral striving and guilt, spending too much time in the past or the future, clinging to a small, anxious 'I': all these things, he concluded, keep us from the consolations of Life as it really is.[66] He thought and wrote about death. Would it be extinction – 'as if we had never been born'? Reincarnation? 'The disappearance of a particular pattern in the water?'[67]

★

The final song recorded by the Beatles before their break-up in April 1970 was George Harrison's 'I Me Mine'. It had the distinction of being jointly inspired by John Lennon, Paul McCartney and Swami Vivekānanda. From Lennon and McCartney, Harrison drew vivid illustrations of egocentrism. From Vivekānanda, he took the claim, found in *Raja Yoga*, that each person is potentially divine. In Harrison's experience, the challenge was to wrestle into submission his small 'I' – 'old blabbermouth', as he called it – so that he might feel a sense of the greater 'I', 'the complete whole universal consciousness'.[68] He sought that consolation, now and again, at Abbey Road studios, meditating in sound booths.[69] And he sought it in the *Bhagavad Gita*: a book that he loved so much he read it to his mother, Louise, on her deathbed in the summer of 1970.[70]

Towards the end of that year, Harrison provided musical consolation of his own for a Western world whose interest in Asian wisdom had reached a peak but which was in danger of having too many options: Zen, the Upanishads and the *Tao Te Ching*; East Asian poetry and painting; the books and broadcasts of Alan Watts, master raconteur; yoga courses, prayer courses and devotional chanting. Inspired by the gospel tradition of African-American Christianity, and in particular a recording of 'Oh Happy Day' by Edwin Hawkins, Harrison offered up 'My Sweet Lord'. It was a simple, unaffected expression of the yearning that drove the likes of Robert G out to India: 'I really want to see you, Lord, but it takes so long, my Lord.' The song's final refrain channelled the era's dawning inter-religious ideal, hinting that what Robert G was looking for might be found both far away and close to home: 'Hare Krishna . . . Hare Rama . . . Hallelujah.'

Amongst Harrison's fans was Alan Watts, who had initiated his daughter Joan into LSD by playing her the Beatles and Gregorian chant as the drug took hold.[71] At around 7 a.m. on the morning of Friday 16 November 1973, she received a phone call that began in the worst possible way: 'Are you sitting down?' Her father had died during the previous, stormy night, his heart failing at the age of fifty-eight.[72] A great gong nearby was said to have sounded of its own accord, and in the morning a group of Buddhists living nearby had arrived, offering to take Watts' body away for cremation. They knew he had died, they said, because he had visited them during the night. Jano, Watts' wife, believed that he had been experimenting with breathing techniques to achieve *samadhi* – absorptive contemplation of the Absolute – and had left his body without knowing how to come back. Joan concluded that he had simply 'had enough', and had 'checked out'.[73]

Alan Watts was given a Buddhist funeral, conducted by Richard Baker, dharma heir to Shunryū Suzuki and abbot of the San Francisco Zen Center. At a public memorial service held one hundred days after his death, his sometime student and long-time friend Gary Snyder read a poem:

> He blazed out the new path for all of us
> and came back and made it clear.
> Explored the side canyons and deer trails,
> and investigated cliffs and thickets.
> Many guides would have us travel single file,
> Like mules in a pack train and never leave the trail.
> alan taught us to move forward like the breeze, tasting the berries,
> Greeting the blue jays, learning and loving the whole terrain.[74]

Bede Griffiths conducting a service at Shantivanam.

21.

New Ages

Christopher Lasch had had it with hippies. Writing in 1979, one of America's most outspoken social critics argued that a 'culture of narcissism' had taken hold of his country. Disillusioned with politics, people had turned inwards:

> Having no hope of improving their lives in any of the ways that matter, people have convinced themselves that what matters is psychic self-improvement: getting in touch with their feelings, eating health food, taking lessons in ballet or belly-dancing, immersing themselves in the wisdom of the East, jogging, learning how to 'relate'.[1]

Where Lasch worried about a decline in American morals and mettle, the Palestinian-American writer Edward Said discerned longer-term harm to the 'East' itself as a result of the warping effect of Western interest. In *Orientalism* (1978), he charged that Westerners had a historical habit of conjuring the 'Orient' – Asia included, although he wrote mainly about the Islamic Middle East – in ways that served their own ends, and particularly those of imperial power. Such was the political and cultural clout of major Western countries that negative, often conflicting images of these parts of the world had gone global and threatened to become indelible: despotism, deviancy, dishonesty, erotic pleasure and luxurious excess.[2]

As this critique gathered pace across the 1980s, key figures in the modern encounter between East and West, such as Carl Jung, were singled out for sponsoring a combination of naïve, romanticized and racist views of the non-Western world. Alan Watts would no doubt have offered a spirited response to this fresh turn in the Western relationship with Asia. Ever-sensitive to shifting intellectual tides, he would probably have agreed with much of the criticism while defending the basic conviction that had shaped his life: people in the West were in crisis, and might usefully look farther afield for alternative ways of living.

Sadly, Alan Watts' many incarnations – precocious schoolboy, early adopter of Zen, Episcopalian priest and West Coast guru – never extended to the sage-like septuagenarian that he might easily have become. It fell to others to shape the 1980s and 1990s. These were decades of controversy but also great creativity, as Westerners sought to make a long-term home for Asian wisdom in their lives and societies. Some did so by looking for ways of helping particular Asian ideas – notably different strains of Buddhism – to take root in Western soil. Bede Griffiths and Erna Hoch were amongst those who contributed to the more eclectic approach of what became known as the 'New Age'. They set out to combine science, philosophy and religions East and West into a universal worldview – or, as Griffiths put it: 'a new vision of reality'.[3]

*

Christopher Lasch's concerns about Western infatuation with the East had an ancient Roman ring to them. Where Seneca and Cicero had fretted over the corrupting potential of spices and silk, Lasch worried about the impact that yoga and pseudo-philosophy might have. In both eras, an attraction to Asian wares was linked with a society's decline into laziness, self-seeking and loss of community feeling.

Edward Said's predecessors were rather more recent. Ravi Shankar had watched the sitar and Indian spirituality become indelibly associated with drugs and dropouts: 'Yoga, tantra, mantra, kundalini, ganja, hashish, Kama Sutra – they all became part of a cocktail that everyone seemed to be lapping up!' More than once, he abandoned a live performance – leaving the stage and taking his sitar with him – when he saw audience members drinking, smoking or talking while he played.[4] Here was an echo of the experience, a few years before, of African-American jazz musicians whose lives and music were embraced by Beats in search of something dangerous and marginal. Asian Americans knew the territory too. Japanese and Indian migrants who worked hard to integrate into American life were often distinctly unamused to find their religious traditions being linked with the outright rejection of society.

Carl Jung was no Beatnik. But he, too, was accused of having used and abused Asian ideas in his work. In an essay whose title got straight to the point – 'Jung: A Racist' (1988) – the psychotherapist Farhad Dalal accused him of 'pillaging' Sanskrit and Pali texts in the service of 'mystical notions', while writing off modern Indians as disorderly, deceptive and lacking a sense of history.[5] In time, prominent Jungians came to accept these claims.[6] Jung had offered a valuable critique of Western society's reliance on a narrow form of rationality. But his contrasting claim that non-Western minds were primarily mythical in their workings owed a great deal to the racialized thinking of the late nineteenth and early twentieth century.[7] Especially egregious was his equation of the modern African mind with that of prehistoric man. As the Indian psychologist Ashis Nandy pointed out, Western ideas about the non-Western world had a habit of lingering in the imagination long after empires retreated, corrupting the self-understanding and self-esteem of people in Asia and Africa.[8]

Narcissism, neo-colonialism and what some were starting to call 'cultural appropriation': Westerners who stuck with Asian wisdom, after others traded in their flares for suits and their campervans for sensible cars, found themselves with a challenge on their hands. And yet their strongest claim to legitimacy lay in just that: they were sticking with traditions or practices for which they had come to have great respect. Amongst them was George Harrison, who spent some of the early post-Beatles months converting the uppermost room of a neo-Gothic mansion in Henley-on-Thames into a meditation room, its floor covered with Persian rugs. He turned the wine cellar into an echo chamber for chanting. On good days, he flew a

Sanskrit *Om* flag from the roof. On bad days – meditation some-times left him low or angry, as did a copyright suit over 'My Sweet Lord' – passers-by might see a skull-and-crossbones fluttering in the breeze.[9]

Few Western fans of Indian wisdom described themselves as Hindus, connecting instead to particular philosophical or devo-tional strands like Advaita Vedānta or Krishna Consciousness. This was closer to the reality of religious life in India, where the colonial-era neologism 'Hinduism' was as much a political and cultural identity as a confessional term. Buddhism was different. A mission-ary religion from the start, it had a long history of adapting itself to new cultures. As the ever-popular Zen was joined by traditions from Tibet, Burma, South-East Asia and Japan – notably Sōka Gakkai (the Value-Creation Society), founded in the 1930s – it was clear that pluralism, democracy and psychology would have a hand in shap-ing Buddhism's Western incarnations. One might add 'celebrity', such was the role of figures like Richard Gere, Adam Yauch of the Beastie Boys, the Vietnamese monk Thich Nhat Hanh and the Dalai Lama in sparking a late-twentieth-century Buddhist boom that far outdid its Victorian predecessor a century before.

Students of Tibetan Buddhism, the offspring of Buddhist Tantra and indigenous Tibetan religion, liked to quote what they claimed was a thousand-year-old Buddhist prophecy, envisaging Tibet's modern travails and the dharma's journey westward: 'When the iron bird flies, and horses run on wheels, the Tibetan people will be scattered like ants across the World, and the Dharma will come to the land of the Red Man.'[10] Almost as striking as this prediction was the sheer breadth within late-twentieth-century Western Buddhism. In Arthur Schopenhauer's day, Buddhism was generally regarded as pessimistic, even nihilistic. Then came rational, scientific Buddhism, followed by the freedom and immediacy of Beat Zen. Towards the end of the counter-culture era, Tibetan Buddhism was embraced by those who associated it with mysticism, magic, mandalas – and prophecy. Chögyam Trungpa helped the tradition put down roots in Scotland, at Samye Ling, and in America, at the Naropa Institute (later Naropa University). The Dalai Lama toured the West with his signature blend of religion, politics and science. And teachers like Sharon Salzberg and Jack Kornfield began to offer *vipassanā* (insight) meditation, distinctly practical and psychological in its orientation. Salzberg became known in particular for her lovingkindness (*metta*) meditations, suggesting that people first develop this quality in themselves, via the gentle repetition of four phrases:

> May I be free from danger.
> May I have mental happiness.
> May I have physical happiness.
> May I have ease of well-being.[11]

Matching this broad range of options was the great diversity in Western engagement with Buddhism. One might actually become a Buddhist, or else read books, take up meditation, or go on retreats. Across the West in the 1990s, the interested but officially unaffiliated were estimated to run into the many hundreds of thousands, from Canada and the United States – the latter home to more than a thousand meditation centres, by this point – across to western Europe, eastern Europe after 1989, Australia and New Zealand.[12]

Where Asian-American migrants often sought to adapt their Buddhism to fit with America's Protestant mainstream – complete with Christian-style services and Sunday schools – Buddhist communities formed primarily from converts faced the challenge of balancing faithfulness to their new religion with necessary adaptations to Western life.[13] Amongst the first to tackle the problem in Britain was Hōun Jiyu-Kennett. Born 'Peggy Kennett' in southern England in 1924, she became involved with Christmas Humphreys' Buddhist Society and later trained at a Sōtō Zen monastery in Japan. After establishing Shasta Abbey in California and Throssel Hole Priory in Northumberland – Britain's first Sōtō Zen monastery – Jiyu-Kennett set herself the task of helping Zen to 'unfold' as naturally as possible in these new cultures.[14]

An accomplished musician in the classical tradition, who had

little time for what she regarded as Humphreys' fondness for Eastern exotica, Jiyu-Kennett translated Zen Buddhist sutras from
Japanese into metrical English and set them to plainchant and hymn
melodies.[15] It was a remarkable feat, but one of the difficulties of
adaptation was that cultures are always on the move. Jiyu-Kennett's
heavy use of the Anglican *Book of Common Prayer* helped to render
Zen familiar and intelligible for mid-twentieth-century British converts who had been brought up on its language. For later generations,
Buddhist liturgies replete with 'thine' and 'hail' would inevitably
require an update.[16]

Alongside language and liturgy ran the question of authority.
Ought the figure of the Asian monastic patriarch, set high over their
juniors, to be imported? While Shunryū Suzuki had been running
the San Francisco Zen Center (SFZC), this was not a major issue,
given his Japanese origins, the counter-cultural vogue for masters
and gurus, and the enormous respect in which Suzuki personally
was held. Discipline had been a priority for him: it was said that
people walking to the SFZC for morning meditation, shortly after
5 a.m., would wait on a deserted street corner until the light turned
green for them to cross the road.[17]

Suzuki's dharma heir, Richard Baker, was more entrepreneurial
than his predecessor, and more in sympathy – as Alan Watts had
been – with the freedom and emotional spontaneity that characterized much of American Zen. The SFZC was overseen by a board,
along lines borrowed from Protestant churches and Jewish syna-
gogues, and following rules required by American law.[18] But there
was little clarity about how an American abbot ought to behave,
and this ended up working against both Baker and his students. The
Zen practice of *dokusan*, a private interview between teacher and
student, turned into something resembling counselling. Students
shared the most intimate problems of their lives with Baker, many
of them beyond the scope of his gifts and training.[19]

By the early 1980s, some at the SFZC had come to resent Baker's
regular absences and his high-rolling lifestyle. They saw him
schmoozing with California's elite while the centre paid the bill,

from expensive dinners to a white BMW driven by one of his assistants.[20] From Baker's point of view, the money spent in this way was more than made up for by the donations that it brought in, amounting to millions of dollars during his time as abbot.[21] For disgruntled students living austere lifestyles – whether through choice or circumstances – it sat awkwardly with their ideal of Zen. The final straw was a series of revelations in 1983, about affairs that Baker had had with women connected to the centre. He resigned as abbot, and left the community.[22]

One of Baker's students, Katy Butler, had hoped to find in Zen a means to 'drop the games' that the everyday world forced her to play, and in Baker a 'wise and trustworthy teacher'. That had now been destroyed. She thought, in retrospect, that some of the norms imported into the centre from Japanese Zen had actually worked against it. The high value placed on silence, even outside meditation sessions, contributed to a contemplative atmosphere and discouraged people from being too preoccupied with themselves. But it also left students unable to voice their worries, and feeling alone when they struggled.[23] Added to this was the extraordinary authority and freedom that Baker enjoyed. Abbots in Japan were constrained by their peers – within the monastery and across the wider Zen establishment – and also by a culture of reserve, which discouraged any kind of informality between *rōshi* (master) and student.[24] American Zen, by contrast, was as yet too small, and perhaps too wedded to the figure of the freewheeling pioneer, for this to work.

To its credit, and to the great benefit of Buddhism in the West, the SFZC responded to this crisis by trialling new approaches to authority and community. Psychologists were brought in to help members communicate more freely with one another.[25] Provisions were introduced for electing the abbot every four years, and an ethics committee was established.[26] Respect for authority remained important: religious teachers taught – ideally, at least – from experience, and students might not immediately understand or particularly like what they had to say. As Annie Besant had discovered, courtesy of Madame Blavatsky, it can take someone with authority and insight to jolt you out of one way of being – for Besant, it was pride – and free you up to live another way. But that authority figure did not have to be a man, or even singular. In the 1990s, leadership of the SFZC was shared for a while between Blanche Hartman and Norman Fischer.[27]

A positive case could be made, too, for ritual and discipline. Far from being mere cultural incidentals, they were, in Zen at least, a means of encouraging the right atmosphere and attitude, conducive to taking a person beyond their everyday mind.[28] Ironically, as America and other parts of the West became more open and democratic – lacking in respect, conservatives might say – Zen became counter-cultural in a new way, its subversiveness marked now by the embrace rather than the rejection of strict standards. A similar trend could be found in American branches of Chinese (Taiwanese) Buddhism, including the 'City of Ten Thousand Buddhas' monastic community in California. Its members ate just one meal per day, and were required to sleep in a sitting position.[29]

*

Alongside a proliferation of Western groups and books linked to Hinduism and Buddhism, the 1980s and 1990s were home to a range of loosely religious phenomena that came to be grouped under the heading 'New Age'. This was a hoped-for epoch of spiritual revival: the 'Age of Aquarius,' popularized in the musical *Hair* (1967) – 'this is the dawning of the Age of Aquarius' – and taken up in the advertising for the Woodstock festival two years later. Quite what either the Age of Aquarius or the New Age meant, beyond better times for humanity, was hotly disputed. For its critics the term was so broadly applied as to be virtually meaningless: Tarot cards and crystals; alternative remedies and communities like Findhorn in Scotland; parapsychology and 'Mind Body Spirit' bookshelves; little shops where incense wafted around Asian woodcarvings, pendants and racks of brightly coloured cotton tie-dye skirts and shirts.

If the New Age was defined by anything, it was a casting

around – sometimes disciplined, sometimes casual – for ways of living and looking at the world that offered greater meaning than mainstream Western societies. Spiritual seekers of earlier times, many of them linked with Asia, provided inspiration: Ralph Waldo Emerson and the Transcendentalists, Madame Blavatsky and Carl Jung – there was no shortage of interest in séances, the 'channelling' of spirits and the psychology of dreams and myths. Alongside a search for meaning ran hope of integration: of different forms of knowledge – scientific, medical, religious, philosophical and sociological – into a single vision, holistic and healing.[30]

Late in life, Bede Griffiths came to be regarded as a leader – for some, the 'father' – of the New Age. Books like *The Marriage of East and West* and *Return to the Centre*, together with a growing reputation for saintliness, brought him an international celebrity that took him to Sri Lanka, Singapore, Pakistan, Israel, Egypt, America, Canada, Australia and all over Europe. People continued to visit him, too: during the 1980s, up to one hundred people at a time were staying at Shantivanam. Well into his seventies by this point, Griffiths met each person at the ashram gate as they arrived, and handed out the post each day as a way of maintaining contact. Everyone was offered spiritual guidance, though Griffiths tended to support more than teach. Many reported that simply spending time with him changed them.[31]

Not everyone was a fan. Griffiths' emphasis on meditation was regarded as suspect by some Christians, on the basis that it risked providing Satan with a gateway into the mind, or – as a 1989 Vatican document prepared by Cardinal Joseph Ratzinger put it – because some 'eastern methods' seemed to emphasize technique alone or else the conjuring of merely 'psychological experiences'.[32] Some Western Christians worried that Griffiths was trading orthodoxy for syncretism, while Indian critics, Christian and Hindu alike, accused him of meddling in their affairs. Writing about Shantivanam's architecture and liturgy, a local Christian journalist in Tamil Nadu accused Griffiths of using 'white skin and plenty of money' to do what he liked, resulting in 'tomfoolery' and 'gimmicks'. Griffiths' own bishop claimed, at one point, that he did not understand India and should go home and play at being a guru in the West.[33]

The harshest criticisms with which Griffiths was forced to deal came from Hindu nationalists, who regarded the religious pluralism of India's post-independence constitution as a cultural and political threat. In their eyes, Hinduism and India were synonymous, Islam and Christianity were foreign, and religion and culture were inseparable. One writer, Sita Ram Goel, described Roberto de Nobili as an 'abominable scoundrel', whose underhand missionary methods – wearing the *kavi* (ochre robes) and passing himself off as a *sannyasin* – had drawn 'unwary victims' into the faith of the despised Portuguese.[34] Griffiths, he charged, was cut from the same *kavi* cloth.

Another critic, Swami Devananda Saraswati, took offence both at Griffiths' presentation of himself as a *sannyasin* and the placing of the Sanskrit *Om* inside a Christian cross at Shantivanam.[35] For Griffiths, Hindu symbols and ideals such as *sannyasa* – renouncing the world and all attachments – were universal, pointing ultimately to reality itself.[36] Wearing the *kavi*, which he had been given back in the 1950s, ought, he thought, to be regarded as a matter of sincerity rather than identity. For Saraswati, these things were the property of a distinct religious tradition, and becoming a *sannyasin* involved an approved process.[37] Mere self-declaration was meaningless. 'I am surely a Hindu chauvinist,' Saraswati concluded, 'but you are the very worst kind of spiritual colonialist.'[38]

Griffiths regarded accusations of syncretism from some quarters, and appropriation from others, as the product of a misunderstanding about how culture and truth relate. He believed that any expression of ultimate truth must inevitably be culturally conditioned. Concepts were limited; silence ran deeper. One didn't have to take a mystic's word for this, or rely on suggestive similarities discovered across world religions. Reading the work of people like Fritjof Capra (*The Tao of Physics*) and Ken Wilber (*The Spectrum of Consciousness*) convinced Griffiths that the time had come for science and psychology to be recruited to his cause. He developed his thinking on these questions during talks that he gave at Shanti-vanam during the 1980s, and published them in the final book of his life: *A New Vision of Reality: Western Science, Eastern Mysticism and Christian Faith* (1989).

Quantum physics, Griffiths noted, had long ago dispensed with the idea of a universe made up of simple, solid 'stuff'. It described matter in terms of energy fields and profound interconnection.[39] The possibility of perfect objectivity had likewise been overturned by the finding that, at the level of quantum particles the very act of measuring affects that which is measured. The philosophical signifi-cance of such findings had been disputed since the 1920s. Albert Einstein cautioned against physicists introducing mysticism into their discipline. But for the theoretical physicist Werner Heisen-berg, the so-called 'observer effect' meant that science 'describes nature *as exposed to our method of questioning* . . . [making a] sharp separation between the world and the I impossible'. Wolfgang Pauli, a quantum physicist and one-time patient of Carl Jung, concluded that matter and consciousness may be two different aspects of the same reality beyond.[40]

Griffiths hoped that these ideas and debates would at least help to unsettle the common assumption that a person's inner life – the play of thoughts, feelings and experiences – is merely mechanical in nature: brain, nervous system, hormones and all the rest. He was encouraged by evidence in the Katha Upanishad that the human tendency to believe in the physical world as the full extent of reality was very old: 'Abiding in the midst of ignorance, thinking them-selves wise and learned, fools go aimlessly hither and thither, like blind led by the blind . . . "This is the only world," they say – "there is no other"; and so they go from death to death.'[41]

Inspired by his reading of Eastern and Western thought, and his own experience of prayer and meditation, Griffiths imagined reality in terms of three integrated aspects.[42] At the source of everything, claimed Griffiths, is 'transcendent reality'. This is the Tao, or 'uncarved Block' of Chinese thought.[43] It is Brahman in Hindu phil-osophy. And it is the Godhead or Ground of Being in the Christian tradition. Buddhists use concepts like emptiness (*sunyata*), nirvana, or 'the void': both a nothingness and an absolute fullness.[44] For Griffiths, the Buddhist insights were the most difficult, but also the most useful. They were a reminder that it makes no sense to talk about transcendent reality as 'existing' in the everyday sense. The clue is in the etymology. Exist: *ex-sistere*: to 'stand forth'. For things to exist means for them to stand forth, or come from, this transcendent reality: a process linked, in Hinduism, with the creator god Brahma.

What stood forth from transcendent reality, in Griffiths' view, was, first, a psychic or 'subtle' reality, as India's Advaita Vedānta philosophy referred to it. Next, at reality's 'outer fringe', came physical or 'gross' reality. Psychic reality, no less real than the physical world, was home to forces described in religious traditions around the globe: gods, goddesses, demons, saints and ancestors. Tibetan Buddhism had charted the terrain in particularly impressive detail, but the Judaeo-Christian tradition spoke of it too.[45] Moses had encountered a burning bush. St Paul had warned of 'elemental principles' and 'powers'. Theologians like Thomas Aquinas had written about angels as 'pure intelligences' who helped to order the universe – playing a role in everything, as Griffiths put it, from gaseous explosions inside a star to a person's shifting moods.[46]

People who accessed psychic reality sometimes gained new forms of influence over matter – controlling physical reality from within. Such powers had been wielded by shamans, prophets, seers and yogis the world over.[47] Jesus Christ had walked on water, stilled storms, healed the sick and turned a small quantity of loaves and fish into food for thousands of people.[48] Thinking, perhaps, of the demons Screwtape and Wormwood in C. S. Lewis' *The Screwtape Letters* – which he had read back in the early 1940s, and found 'perfectly brilliant' – Griffiths concluded that one of the most effective strategies employed by demonic forces was persuading human beings that psychic reality was an embarrassing superstition. Scholars and scientists, he noted, appeared particularly susceptible.[49]

Where Edwin Arnold had sought to redeem human evolution in his poetic life of the Buddha, more recent writers – including the philosophers Sri Aurobindo, Teilhard de Chardin and Ken Wilber – had discerned meaning in cosmic history as a whole. Griffiths embraced these ideas with enthusiasm, alongside cognitive archaeology – the study of the ancient human mind – and transpersonal psychology: the attempt to find a place for spiritual or mystical experience within modern psychology. The result was a portrait of reality marked by movement and purpose, with an important role played by the evolution of human consciousness: as a species, over enormous periods of historical time; and within the life of each person, as a key component of spiritual development.

Early or 'primeval' humans had enjoyed a sense of oneness with reality, of a type still known to babies in the womb and very young children. This 'oceanic' experience was best expressed, thought Griffiths, in Wordsworth: 'Heaven lies about us in our infancy'. As the human brain evolved, a more acute sense emerged of a separate 'I' and of the existence of past and future. Children, Griffiths noted, pass through something similar as they grow. This second stage in the evolution of human consciousness, which included the emergence of language, was characterized by the dominance of imagination and intuition. Awareness grew of the forces within psychic reality, and stories emerged of gods, goddesses, demons and great deeds.[50] Crucial to this view of human development, which owed a great deal to Ken Wilber in particular, was that when humanity reaches a new stage of consciousness, the previous ones are included – integrated – rather than lost: storytelling humans had not lost the earlier, oceanic sense of oneness with reality.

The supreme achievement of humanity thus far, thought Griffiths, had come during a third stage of development, between around 800 and 200 BCE – what the German philosopher Karl Jaspers called the 'Axial Age'. Capacities for logical and analytical thinking had emerged, becoming integrated with existing oceanic and intuitive capacities. Some of the world's greatest philosophical literature had been produced in this period: in Greece, the Middle East, India and China.[51] The essence of their greatness was the integration of three ways of knowing reality: direct experience, intuition and reflection using analytical concepts.

One found the results most clearly on display, thought Griffiths, in the early Upanishads, transmitted orally by the sorts of sages that Alexander the Great and his army may have encountered in the forests of northern India. Where they had given the name 'Brahman' to transcendent reality, later Upanishads, alongside the *Bhagavad Gita*, had revealed reality's personal and loving aspects. Arjuna calls out, fretting, the night before a great battle. With the voice of Lord Krishna, transcendent reality calls back: 'You are dear to me.'[52]

*

Far to the north, in a small house on a sunny hillside in Kashmir, Erna Hoch was doing much the same thing as Bede Griffiths: pulling together her ideas after twenty-five years of experience in India. Her contract at Srinagar Medical College had come to an end in 1980, and she had considered returning to Switzerland at that point, to teach or enter private practice as a psychiatrist. But Hoch shared with Griffiths an inclination towards holism. She could only pursue her deepest interests, she decided, by working across a broad range of disciplines, and the demands of professional life in Europe would make that impossible. Hoch resolved to stay in India for a few more years: reflecting, writing and providing an informal medical service to her neighbours – a useful spiritual exercise, she noted, for someone who struggled with 'impatience' and 'irritability'.[53]

Where Griffiths trawled widely in developing his picture of reality, Hoch continued to explore the ways in which religion and the mind sciences might relate. She concluded that India's ancient philosophers had been psychotherapists in the literal and best sense: 'carers for the soul', who had diagnosed and set out to tackle the 'separation anxiety' from which humankind suffered.[54] Most in her profession used the term to describe the suffering of a child at being apart from its parents. For Hoch, this suffering ran much deeper, to a sense of separation from reality itself. The mind sciences had a major role to play in tackling it: from treating people when they sought out and were let down by 'impermanent, destructible' forms of security, to understanding how a person's early years of life shaped their religious outlook. Considered vulnerable to sickness soon after she was born, Hoch herself had spent two or three months isolated in a 'glass box', in hospital. People in that era had not known how important it was for a baby to get an immediate sense of its mother's body. Those few months helped to explain, thought Hoch, the solitary existence that she had led, and the way that she was drawn to forms of spirituality that emphasized an impersonal reality over an 'I-Thou' relationship with the divine.[55]

The glory of Asia's religious traditions, for Hoch, lay in their ability to meet different people where they were. In the *Bhagavad Gita*, Lord Krishna laid out various practical paths to God for Arjuna: meditation, devotion, knowledge.[56] The Hindu *ashramas*, or four stages of life, recognized that a person's religious needs and capacities change across their lives. The first stage was the 'student', followed by the 'householder', a time when a person is most involved with the concerns of the everyday world. Hoch was now passing through the third stage, the 'retired person', preparatory to the full renunciation of the fourth and final stage.

The mind sciences too, thought Hoch, were capable of meeting people where they were and helping them on the spiritual path – steering them around common obstacles and pitfalls. Where the Dalai Lama likened religious syncretism to trying to 'put a yak's head on a sheep's body', for Hoch the problem with both syncretism and religious conversion was that they could become a way of avoiding the real *metanoia* – 'turning around' – that a person was being called to make.[57] Psychotherapy could help tease out mixed, sometimes unconscious motivations in the religious life. A therapist might also be able to spot, as Hoch believed that she had done while working at Nur Manzil, when people were seeking to overcome their ego-centred separateness by going backwards rather than forwards, regressing into an infantile dependence on others, on alcohol, or on something else that would prove equally futile in the end.

Hoch was not alone in starting to map out a role of this sort for the mind sciences in the 1980s. With Buddhist practice in mind, the American psychologist Jack Engler cautioned that 'You have to be somebody before you can be nobody': one could not lay aside the psychological challenges and pain of growing up on the basis that Buddhism denied the ultimate reality of a separate self. In *A Path with Heart* (1993), Jack Kornfield pointed out that moments of insight or grace would not wash away a person's problems, much though they might wish it. He noted, too, that most spiritual teachers were not qualified to help students with the psychological material that came up in meditation, from memories of child abuse to struggles with addiction.[58] When you were having a skull-and-crossbones day, a therapist might be your best bet.

Kornfield, Engler and Hoch all represented a step on from Alan Watts in this respect. Watts had been well informed about psychology and psychotherapy, but had tended to regard them as subordinate, in the end, to high philosophy. Perhaps because he preferred not to delve too deeply into his own psychology, he was tempted to make the very mistake about which Engler was warning.

When it came to the Christian cultures of their childhoods, however, a life spent immersed in Asian wisdom led Watts, Griffiths and Hoch to similar conclusions. All three thought, in common with members of an emerging Charismatic movement, that in the image of God as Trinity – Father, Son and Holy Spirit – the Spirit had long been underplayed. Griffiths understood the Spirit as pervading all of reality, guiding cosmic and human history. He wondered whether the work of his biologist friend Rupert Sheldrake might yield evidence of its operation in the physical world. Sheldrake speculated about the shaping of matter/energy by 'formative causes'. These were controversial ideas, but Griffiths saw promising parallels with Aristotle's idea of 'form'.

Watts, Griffiths and Hoch shared, too, a love of the portrait of the Spirit found in John's gospel, where it was sometimes referred to as the 'Comforter'. Hoch was struck by Jesus' words to his disciples: 'It is expedient for you that I go away: for if I go not away, the

Comforter will not come unto you.' She was delighted to find that Swami Abhishiktananda had spoken, with great reverence, of the 'Johannine Upanishads'.[59]

Hoch never returned to the full, all-embracing faith of her childhood. But her experience as a psychiatrist, and as disciple to a guru, inspired in her a fresh appreciation for Jesus Christ as a spiritual teacher of the first order. One of the responsibilities of a guru, she noted, was to protect disciples from the 'premature irruption of spiritual forces . . . shelter[ing them] from unaccustomed exposure to an overwhelming and blinding light'.[60] In a similar way, psychiatrists avoided burdening an unprepared patient with a highly technical account of their illness: the priority was to address it, not explain it. When one of his disciples asked him why he spoke in parables, Jesus had replied: 'Because they seeing, see not; and hearing, they hear not; neither do they understand.' He had known, Hoch reflected, how to blend 'revealing' with 'concealing'.[61]

As she prepared to return to Switzerland, finally packing her bags for the journey home in 1988, two parables in particular came to mind: the Lost Sheep and the Prodigal Son. Both, she insisted, were significant for their emphasis on the infinite value of the individual.[62] Both, her therapist might have noted, had she had one, were concerned with being alone, and with the prospect of being found.

★

While meditating on the veranda of his hut, early one morning in January 1990, Bede Griffiths felt a bomb go off in his brain. The combined effects of heart failure, pulmonary oedema and a mild stroke very nearly killed him. Instead, Griffiths found himself set free. The stroke, the loving care that he received from people at the ashram – 'washed and bathed and combed just like an old dog', as he put it – and a plunge into deep reflection on Christ's suffering on the cross combined to open him up to a love more profound than he had ever known.[63] Those around Griffiths noticed a change in him. His English reserve had been 'blasted away', reflected one observer.

He was less afraid, now, of physical touch, or of responding with tears to the pain of others.[64] His mind seemed to have taken on a new clarity.

Ever eager to speculate and to weave fresh ideas into the rich cloth on which he had been working since his youth, Griffiths noted that his stroke had felt like a blow to the head coming from the left side, impelling him towards the right. A line of thinking in modern neuroscience suggested that people's analytical capacities were associated with activity in the left hemisphere of the brain, and their intuitive capacities with the right. Griffiths wondered whether he had somehow been jolted into a better balance of the two. Raised in a patriarchal society, and heir to Carl Jung's ideas about the masculine and the feminine, he experienced his boosted intuition as a 'breakthrough to the feminine': an embrace from the 'divine mother'. 'Death, the Mother, the Void, all was love,' he recalled. Here was 'the "unconditional love" of which I had often spoken, utterly mysterious, beyond words'.[65]

This new experience of life stayed with Griffiths for the next couple of years, as he travelled the world giving talks and interviews. It became indispensable to reconciling the two loves of his life: Advaita Vedānta, with its sublime vision of cosmic unity, and Christianity, with its forceful insistence on God's grace and love for Creation. Beyond all intellectual gymnastics, Griffiths found the apparent contradiction resolved in his immediate experience of life: 'I never feel separated from the earth or the trees or people; it's all one, and yet the differences remain.' This, he thought, was the meaning of a mysterious phrase in John's gospel: 'I am in the Father, and the Father in me.'[66]

A Canadian bishop who went to hear Griffiths speak confessed that he had done so in part to test the orthodoxy of his ideas. He could find nothing wrong: for all that he walked a razor's edge, using language rarely heard in the pulpit, Griffiths never lost his orthodoxy.[67] An English Literature graduate, and a great lover of poetry, Griffiths had always been fascinated by the challenge of language in religion. For people of a literalist cast of mind, he realized, talk of Jesus Christ as part of 'God's plan' might conjure the image of an old-time deity, bearded and berobed, scribbling away on a piece of parchment. Instead, he talked about the birth of Jesus as the moment when reality had given rise to a human being who was capable of a unique degree of insight. He had known that he was related to transcendent reality, the Godhead, in love – as a son to a father ('Abba').[68] This moment in history rippled outwards through his disciples, who encountered the risen Jesus in a new form: psychic or 'subtle', capable as he apparently was of appearing and disappearing. At Pentecost, the disciples were 'filled with the Spirit', turning them from a group of ordinary people whose leader and friend had just been executed into missionaries of extraordinary courage and commitment.[69]

Griffiths hoped that with the help of India's still thriving sense of the sacred, Westerners might grasp the cosmic importance of these events. He did not expect that people would find it easy: he had spent enough time as a dweller on the threshold to know how the mind rebelled, made excuses, looked away. But ever since his boyhood experience of nature at dusk on the school playing fields, he had been convinced that the human urge towards self-transcendence was about more – as he put it – than 'climbing mountains and going to the moon'. That urge was a grace, a gift of a loving Spirit. So was faith, understood as an 'utter receptivity' to that Spirit. Its antithesis was not doubt, but rather sin: refusing the Spirit, closing oneself off to the evidence that mattered most, and clinging to the illusion of an independent, evidence-seeking ego – a villain whose unmasking had been most successfully accomplished in Buddhism.[70]

In December 1992, Griffiths suffered a second, far more serious stroke. He was taken to hospital, and found that he could no longer pray: 'All they were interested in was my body and the blood and the brain. I felt the absolute disappearance of God. It was a terrifying experience.' For much of the next few weeks, Griffiths was barely able to move, and was often in so much pain that he screamed.[71]

In quieter moments, love returned. Griffiths had come to know love in a new way, in recent years, thanks to an intense friendship with Russill and Asha Paul D'Silva. Russill had been a postulant at Shantivanam – 'God has given me a son,' Griffiths told Martyn Skinner, not long after he arrived – and had later met and married Asha. Griffiths' friendship with the couple was platonic, but in a letter to them he concluded that 'agape without eros simply does not work. It leaves our human nature starved . . . I cannot experience the divine love, unless it is united with my human love for you.'[72]

There were those at Shantivanam who had resented the amount of time that Griffiths spent with the couple. He sometimes went away on retreat with them and later visited them after they moved to America. But it was the love and care of all at the ashram and in hospital, especially those who looked after him towards the end, that helped Griffiths to experience the truth of what he had argued in *New Vision*: that everything really is connected, from a taste of transcendent reality in meditation to the touch of a fellow human being when you are lost in pain and hopelessness.

Philosophy, literature, science, politics: all these things had mattered deeply to Bede Griffiths across his life. He loved to talk, write and argue. But 'ultimately', he concluded, 'a religion is tested by its capacity to awaken love in its followers'.[73] He found that capacity in the devotionalism of the *Bhagavad Gita*, in Buddhist *karuna* (compassion) and in the gospel of John, which a close friend recalled reading to Griffiths as he lay in his hut, slowly dying, in the spring of 1993:

When I read the words 'This is my commandment, that you love one another,' he caught his breath, lifted his finger with emphasis and said: 'That is the whole gospel.'[74]

Bird on a Branch, by Unkei Eii.

Epilogue: Onward

What is real? Who says? How should we live? Much of the Western world's fascination with 'the East', across nearly two and a half millennia, has turned on these three questions. Asia had its material attractions: jewels and precious metals; spices and silk; the chance for invaders and colonizers to tax people and their produce. But while the rumour that India abounded in gold was clearly of interest to Herodotus, what fascinated him was the story of where that gold came from: dug from the ground by enormous ants, then hauled away on the backs of camels as swift as Greek horses.

Marvels multiplied in the writings of Scylax of Caryanda and Ctesias of Cnidus. They told of howling dog-headed men and of one-legged people who deployed their enormous feet as a sunshade. Whether or not such extraordinary creatures looked and behaved precisely as billed, reality was obviously larger and stranger than previously appreciated. Emperor Augustus felt it, perhaps, when he came face to face with an Indian tiger. Or Pope Leo X, when a white Asian elephant bowed to him and then doused him with water from its trunk.

Human limitations being what they are, in place of a full comprehension of reality, we make do with areas of understanding, degrees of certainty and a shadowy, shifting sense of what is plausible and what is not. Augustus and Leo X both presided over institutions – an empire and a Church – whose success rested, in large part, on the power to mediate what people imagined to be real, natural and true. For most Europeans in Pope Leo's day, the teachings of the Catholic Church were not simply one intellectual option amongst others. They were the air that people breathed, and the light by which they saw the world around them.

Entering Westerners' imaginative worlds in fragments at first – a tall tale here, an exotic creature there, a pinch of spice to amuse one's dinner guests – Asia added dashes of colour without threatening to redraw the picture. For Megasthenes, India made sense as terrain once trodden by Dionysus and Heracles, their imprint obvious to him in the country's architecture and festivals. For Cicero and Propertius, *sati* was evidence of a wifely devotion that they assumed to be a universal good – and which Roman women were at risk of letting slip. Medieval storytellers deployed the Indian adventures and misadventures of Alexander the Great to warn about human ambition and hubris. Into the mouth of a humble Indian philosopher, they placed a single, searing question: 'When you have seized everything, where will you take it?' Those same storytellers enlisted elephants, too: thousands of them, readied for war and arrayed along a riverbank, demonstrating that even for the kind of man capable of leading an army undefeated to the edge of the known world there would always be an unreachable farther shore.

Travel writers continued this general trend, offering their readers great wonders and horrors rather than radical new ideas about how the world might work. When Marco Polo's friends quizzed him on his deathbed, it was not about whether Christianity was true but about which of the incredible things Polo claimed to have witnessed in Asia had been invented. Likewise with England's early modern hustlers. Most journeyed eastward in search of trade deals or strategic advantage over rival countries. Thomas Coryate was a colourful exception, but though his accounts of 'superstition and impiety most abominable' were undoubtedly entertaining, their impact on Westerners' self-understanding appears to have been little greater than that of his oratory on Emperor Jahangir – who responded to his gabby foreign supplicant by throwing coins down to him from a high window, perhaps to make him go away.

And yet by the time Coryate's body was committed to India's soil in 1617, Christendom's hold on the European imagination was slipping, and the question 'What is real?' was attracting an ever-wider range of respondents: natural philosophers, publishers, rival Churches and theologians, and people vying for secular power. European discoveries about Asia, multiplying and deepening in the era of seaborne conquest and mission work, no longer resulted in mere novel extensions of reality's range. They began to strike at the heart of what was real, and to reshape Western notions about who might legitimately and plausibly venture a view on questions of such consequence.

For Voltaire, the antiquity and sophistication of Chinese civilization brought parts of the Bible into question, including its implied claims about the age of the earth and the ancestry of the human race. Placing the accomplishments of the Chinese alongside the genius of Isaac Newton, he concluded that knowledge of reality was rather less dependent than most Europeans supposed on the mediating power of Christian scriptures and clerics. Arthur Schopenhauer found in Asia a combination of inspiration and consolation, as he turned his back on Christianity and declared himself 'an irradiated manifestation of the supreme Brahme'.

For the likes of Goethe and Samuel Taylor Coleridge, the scholar-poet William Jones stood head and shoulders above the competition as a profound and highly plausible communicator of Asian wisdom. The essence of fascination, in this era at least, was familiarity seasoned with strangeness. William Jones experienced flashes of this in India, and shared it with his readers, combining Plato, Christianity and Idealism with what he regarded as the very best of Indian philosophy. Creation, Jones concluded, is 'rather an *energy* than a *work* . . . like a wonderful picture or piece of music' conjured in the minds of creatures by the divine. His poem 'Hymn to Náráyena' evoked the bliss of transcendent reality breaking in upon a person, as an experience at once intimate and without limit: 'My soul absorb'd One only Being knows'.

Western estimations of Asia, however, were always mixed and always on the move. Within a few short years of Jones' death, his enthusiasm for Indian philosophy and spirituality appeared to have fewer takers in England. For people like Jemima Kindersley and Thomas Babington Macaulay, 'What is real?' was outweighed by 'Who says?' Recent European achievements in science, industry, commerce and the projection of military power put India – and so, in their minds, much of Indian thought – in the shade. That darkness itself became an object of fascination. Robert Southey depicted India as a place of Gothic corruption. Critics of Edwin Arnold's paean for the Buddha asked why, if his presentation were accurate, the heirs of this great sage lived in such squalor across Asia.

It was during these important decades that the question 'How should we live?' also began to play a role in Western encounters with Asia. For some, including Samuel Taylor Coleridge, it was as much a case of 'How *can* I live?' An early attraction to India's contemplative wisdom lost out, in the end, to a voice inside him – inchoate, intermittent and a source of much struggle – that persuaded Coleridge he could not live without the God of Christianity and all that flowed from having a personal presence at the heart of reality: sin, responsibility, forgiveness and redemption.

Jones' 'Hymn to Náráyena', Coleridge's anguished disavowal of Advaita Vedānta as 'a painted Atheism', Arnold's depiction of the Buddha as a man forced to choose a religious path: each, in its own way, heralded a maturing of the West's fascination with Asia. Annie Besant blazed the trail, embarking on an extraordinary personal odyssey that helped pave the way for the likes of Alan Watts, Bede Griffiths and Erna Hoch in the twentieth century. The thrill of East and West meeting anew, in those and earlier eras, can never be recovered. But the three big questions on which that encounter has frequently turned remain pressing, animated now as much by technological as by geographical frontiers.

What is real? The more immersive and demanding that virtual and augmented realities become, the more difficult it will be to say why a world built from bytes is less 'real' than one composed of biological processes. These and future technologies may accomplish what Griffiths and Watts hoped that quantum physics might: releasing people from a deep-seated assumption that reality is reducible, in the end, to matter in motion. Such is the cultural power of science and technology that this idea could perhaps only effectively be overturned from within the natural sciences themselves.

Who says? As technology progressively removes the limitations to which we are accustomed – a brain with restricted capacities; a single, perishable body; machines that only do what they are told – we will find ourselves forced to ask ever more fundamental questions about what human beings are, or are for. Whose answers will command acceptance? Will the development of artificial intelligence be shaped by consensus of some kind, or simply by the people who win the race to control it?

How should we live? Since the death of Bede Griffiths in 1993, explorations have gathered pace regarding the links between mental health, spiritual or existential questions and the way that societies are set up – how, in particular, they encourage their members to live and think. Zen and *vipassanā* (insight) meditation fed into Jon Kabat-Zinn's 'mindfulness-based stress reduction programme', helping in turn to inspire a broader mindfulness movement across the late 2000s and 2010s. Medical research on psychedelics has restarted, focused on their potential in treating severe depression and investigating not just their impact on brain chemistry but the therapeutic value of psychedelic (or 'mystical') experience in itself. A wellness ideal is attracting ever more attention, moving beyond mere absence of illness to embrace a positive concept of wellbeing and incorporating Asian ideas and practices along the way, from Reiki to Ayurvedic medicine.

Quite where these trends are taking us remains too early to say. At their best, mindfulness and wellness represent the infusion of practical wisdom from across Asia into Western healthcare, businesses, schools and government policy. At their worst, they become dominated by markets and politics. Critics of the mindfulness movement point to the sidelining of the personal benefits of meditation in favour of its potential to improve efficiency in the workplace and to absolve governments of their duty to care for citizens – social injustices are all too easily recast as the problems of individuals, to be tackled in solitary silence or by mindful colouring-in. Critics of wellness point to elements of pseudoscience in its approach, alongside an excessively individualistic ethic – the 'we' in

'How should we live?' threatens to go missing entirely. There is also the danger of warping the question of 'What is real?', confusing what is true with what makes people feel better – healthy, happy or righteous.

As long as these three questions – what is real, who says and how should we live – retain their place at the heart of human life, odyssey and fascination will remain evergreen. By its very nature, personal discovery can never be passed on. But new generations always make use of the resources handed down by forebears, not least their autobiographical dos and don'ts. With that in mind, is there anything in the lives of Besant, Hoch, Watts and Griffiths from which we might learn? Anything – to borrow a phrase from Tom Coryate – 'worthy the observation'?

Firstly, dissatisfaction with what they had or what they knew proved a profitable place for their odysseys to begin. All had a strong sense that something was wrong in their lives, and that it had to do, in part at least, with the societies in which they had grown up. Modern Western success in commerce, conquest and industry – and perhaps something in Westerners' approach to life, which underpinned that success – had resulted in damage to people's souls. They had become like a garden left untended: dried out and weed-infested, its original pattern and glory obscured. Christianity had once been the keeper of that garden, but in its present state it no longer appeared a likely source of regeneration.

Next came the 'how' of the odyssey. What began as a purely intellectual search for Besant and Griffiths gave way to an experience of being seized from outside of themselves. Besant met Madame Blavatsky in Holland Park, and experienced 'a well-nigh uncontrollable desire to bend down and kiss her, under the compulsion of that yearning voice, those compelling eyes'. Griffiths encountered God in Bethnal Green: '[he] brought me to my knees, and made me acknowledge my own nothingness . . . I was no longer the centre of my life, and therefore I could see God in everything.'

Besant and Griffiths both recalled, in retrospect, that going it alone in high intellectual gear was useful for a while, but that it was ultimately rather safe and mundane – and also liable to be neverending, so vast was the stock of ideas to be considered. Nothing was really being ventured: Griffiths, especially, became mired in a kind of cultured procrastination – stasis with the illusion of movement. Pride played a role here, as George Bernard Shaw recognized in the case of his friend Annie Besant. But there was more to it than that. As one of Griffiths' intellectual heroes, John Henry Newman, put it: most people retain a 'corner' in their heart that they do not intend to give up, for fear that they will no longer be themselves. This made an armchair odyssey look all the more attractive, despite the fact, as Newman put it, that 'life is not long enough for a religion of [intellectual] inferences . . . we shall never have done beginning, if we determine to begin with proof.'[1]

Proof had its place in the kind of journeys that Besant and Griffiths were undertaking. But, alongside Watts and Hoch, they were cautious about defining that concept too narrowly. Early modern natural philosophers had resolved to focus their experimental efforts only on what was measurable or otherwise quantifiable. By the twentieth century, some appeared to have made a further philosophical leap: insisting that anything which was not measurable was not real – a proposition reinforced by the role of numbers in modern economies, technologies and everyday life. Where a constricted concept of proof ran culturally deep, Watts, Griffiths and Hoch were inspired by their contact with Asia to look elsewhere in exploring reality and justifying their conclusions. They effectively swapped 'proof' of something with 'grounds' for believing it: a broader notion, longer in gestation and less easily conveyed to others – but no less precious or consequential for all that.

Reason, too, required a rethink. Too exclusive a reliance on it, thought Watts, reinforced a person's false sense of being a separate, lonely, cogitating 'I'. Much as Hoch enjoyed philosophical speculation, she found that 'care' – directed, sometimes rather grudgingly, towards her patients – was its indispensable complement. Each dug away at the other, steadily revealing new layers to reality. Griffiths came to value the iconoclastic potential of reason. It could be used to tease out bogus or unhelpful ideas, patterns of thought, ingrained cultural biases and all manner of self-deception. Watts thrived on showing his audiences how the wrong root metaphors were holding them back. To be convinced, at some fundamental level, that reality is a machine is to foreclose on the possibility of experiencing it as 'immeasurably alive'. Too many Christians, claimed Watts, were lumbered with an image of God as a judge, or a father before whose face they had to dangle their achievements. Meanwhile Shiva danced, and Krishna played the flute.

This iconoclastic, subtractive element to spirituality – using the intellect as much to discredit false propositions as to forge new ones – helped Griffiths to create more space for his heart in discerning truth. As his letters to Martyn Skinner attest, this involved a great deal of trial and error. He would experiment with a new idea by committing himself to it completely, and seeing what resonated while he did so – dropping it or pursuing it further on that basis. For Griffiths, this method was to reality as a whole as the natural sciences were to the physical world.

What about the 'we' in 'How should we live?' Watts and Hoch both struggled with this. Watts used to hate it, as a child, when his mother kept probing for his emotions.[2] As an adult, he had declared himself to be 'not a joiner' – and no doubt his wives sometimes felt that this was also his philosophy of marriage. Hoch blamed the few days that she had spent in a glass box, soon after she was born, for her enduring sense of life as being a 'personal venture'.

And yet Watts found his outlook transformed by friendship, from Francis Croshaw – he of the dressing gown, dog whip and Burmese cigars – to Christmas and Aileen Humphreys in their Pimlico flat. Hoch had struggled to love, or even much like, some of her guru's followers when they met at *satsang*. But amongst the most profound of her experiences in India was finding in her patients – especially those who were gravely ill, and for whom she could do little – someone 'before whom to be ashamed'.

Griffiths had of course chosen community as a young man, when he became a Benedictine. But he, too, was changed by his encounters in India. The Syriac and Malayalam liturgies of the Thomas Christians seemed crafted to bring participants to tears, 'break[ing] down the barrier', as Griffiths put it, that prevented grace from entering a person's life.[3] George Harrison, in common with other devotees of Swami Prabhupāda and Krishna Consciousness, was gifted similar moments of release through music and communal chanting.

As some of the hippies who visited Griffiths at Shantivanam discovered, community offered plenty of other benefits besides: friendships that were at once critical and supportive; the deepening of devotion that comes from pursuing it with others; the chance to live a particular social and economic ideal, as Griffiths had first tried to do at Eastington. Community also offered structure and waypoints, whether for a spiritual odyssey or for life in general. A popular critique of the modern West in Griffiths' day, made by Carl Jung amongst others, was that it failed to offer these in the way that traditional societies had done. They had developed rituals to mark and make sense of childhood, adolescence, maturity and finally a readiness to mentor others or go it alone.

Finally, there was the question – fraught with difficulty and paradox – of where, if anywhere, an odyssey might be leading. Foundational for Griffiths, in answering this question, was his conviction – dating back to his numinous experience at dusk on the school playing fields as a child – that there is 'something' at the heart of it all: a dimension to reality, which is in some sense personal (or certainly not *less* than personal) and which grasps hold of a person in moments of grace. Myth, ritual, discipline, ethics, art and community all have parts to play, thought Griffiths, in opening a channel of communication between a person and this 'something'. Where he, and others like him, had grown up feeling removed from the natural and religious landscape in which their ancestors had lived, the power of a tradition – for Griffiths, either Hinduism or a Christianity refashioned by its light – lay in the ability to put people back into that landscape, and to let them smell its air once again.

Orthodox Christian critics of Griffiths regarded this approach to religion as a form of agnosticism – what Coleridge might have described as 'a painted Atheism'. Griffiths' response was shaped by Newman's observation that Christian doctrine offers but a 'dim view of a country seen in the twilight'.[4] He was inspired, too, by strands within Buddhism and Indian philosophy that recognized the profound influence of culture and personality on people's religious lives. Griffiths pointed out that we are always starting from somewhere when we consider an idea. Much depends on that 'somewhere', and on the kind of attention that we pay. He sympathized, as a result, with those who likened religious truth to a story or a Gothic cathedral: it can only really be appreciated from the inside.

Some who disposed themselves in this way to religious ideas might, like C. S. Lewis in the case of Christianity, end up concluding that a given religious tradition is a 'true myth': not just effective at opening up an encounter with transcendent reality – which can only ever *be* encountered, never comprehended – but possessed, too, of elements of historical truth that render it superior to other outlooks. Such was Griffiths' respect and affection for Hinduism, and his sense of the supremacy of silent encounter over words or images, that by the end of his life he viewed Christianity, Hinduism and Buddhism alike as 'true': either all the way down, or at least further down than most people would ever go in their lives.

Alan Watts was sceptical about this approach to religion. And yet he approved of one of its outcomes: suddenly everything is religious. Not in the narrow, sectarian sense that he encountered during his period as a clergyman, with its 'superficial effervescence of heartiness'. Rather, as a renewed way of seeing, exchanging – at least now and then – what Watts called the 'spotlight vision' of everyday, discriminating awareness for a more immediate and much more open 'floodlight' vision.[5] With luck, one became able to see tomatoes and raspberries as he had done as a child in his garden at

Rowan Tree Cottage: as 'glowing, luscious jewels'. It was the difference between looking at a piece of fruit while thinking about which
variety it might be or wondering what kind of smoothie to make,
and apprehending it instead as this particular, only-now bit of life,
right in front of you. The fathomless particularity and sheer gratu-
ity of it might suddenly grasp you: not *what* it is' but *'that* it is'.[6]

Friedrich Schleiermacher and Alan Watts saw that paying this
kind of attention would not in itself provide a person with a destination for their odyssey. Both men cautioned against confusing
meaning with information, and as a result seeking meaning in terms
of a fixed and final form of words. Griffiths, Hoch and Watts would
probably all, in the end, have regarded the very notion of a 'destination' as yet another unhelpful metaphor. They did not expect to
arrive somewhere and never leave; rather, just now and again to
gain a brief glimpse of a true home, before the everyday world reas-
serted itself.

Griffiths and Watts ended up with differing ideas about what
living in the everyday world might entail. Griffiths well understood
the perplexity experienced by Westerners, grappling with Asian
ideas which had appealed to them, initially, as both fascinating and
liberating. How does one practise meditation without clinging to a
hope of results? How does one work without attachment to its
fruits, as Krishna counsels Arjuna in the *Bhagavad Gita*? Griffiths'
conclusion seems to have been that human beings are built for both
liberation *and* commitment – a healthy, generative tension exists
between the two, though it may take time to understand and make
the best of it. Learning from Asian traditions how to commit himself to a Christian set of symbols, he eventually found liberation and
a love like no other.

Words like these remain empty, thought Griffiths, until you start
down the road for yourself. That road is best trodden in good company: balancing freedom with commitment, receiving the revelatory
gift of being seen and known by others, and gaining practical guidance along the way as life unfolds. Unless one expects reason to do
all the work, to encompass the world – and what a meagre world

that would be – then one can only go step by step: living fully in a new way, seeing how things look from that vantage point, and then setting a course from there.

For Watts, the ideal was for fleeting moments of realization, which occasionally came upon him, to infuse the rest of life with a sense of freedom and joy. He knew with sudden and complete certainty during those precious instants that his loneliness, felt most acutely as a boy abed on Rowan Tree Cottage's shivery upper floor, stemmed from a simple case of mistaken identity. The real Alan Watts was, and had always been, part of an immeasurably greater, glorious and inextinguishable whole.

Critics accused Watts, not without cause, of sometimes mangling Asian wisdom by insisting that Buddhism, Advaita Vedānta and Taoism all taught precisely this ideal. But Watts' greatest achievement remains: extending to people – shamelessly, in the very best sense – the invitation of a lifetime. Just thinking about the big questions raised by religion, philosophy and encounters across cultures is, he once said, like reading the menu while refusing the food. Whether it be ideas that have made their way westward from Asia, or counterparts closer to home upon which Asia has shed a little of its light, why not put down the menu at some point – and taste for yourself?

Acknowledgements

This project began when I encountered Bede Griffiths' autobiography, *The Golden String*. I remember, with great affection, beginning my archival work in Oxford with Griffiths' biographer, Shirley Du Boulay. Warm and wise, Shirley's belief that a project of this kind was worth undertaking gave me enormous encouragement early on. I regret very much that, after Shirley's passing in 2023, I shan't be able to place a copy in her hands.

Shirley put me in touch with a number of her friends, all of whom were equally generous in their support. My thanks to Hazel Eyles, for sharing the Griffiths-Skinner correspondence; to Adrian Rance, for allowing me to use his own collection of Griffiths' letters; and to Father Laurence Freeman, of the World Community for Christian Meditation, for sharing his memories of Bede Griffiths.

For supporting my research on Erna Hoch, I am grateful to the staff at the Gosteli Foundation in Switzerland, who hold most of her letters, and to Claudius Tewari and his colleagues at Nur Manzil in Lucknow, who hold an archive of their own and who made for wonderful hosts. Marjory Foyle, who worked for a time at Nur Manzil, was kind enough to grant me an interview, as were the Jesuit theologians Michael Amalodoss and George Gispert-Sauch. Thank you to Margaret Ries, for helping me to translate Hoch's letters from German into English, and to Renish Abraham for his assistance and great company in Kerala (including a memorable stay at Kurisumala Ashram, accessed via a terrifying bus climb up the mountain).

My research on Alan Watts benefitted enormously from the dedication of his children in collating and publishing their father's letters and talks – in print and also in podcast form, bringing that wonderfully patrician accent and hearty smoker's laugh to new generations. Many other people had a hand – directly or indirectly – in this project, including Chris Bayly, Crispin Bates, Judith Brown, Hephzibah Israel, Shruti Kapila, Richard King, Iain McGilchrist, Neil McGregor, Jackie Marsh, Gavin Miller, Alexander Mooney, Luke Mulhall, Liz Oldfield, Ptp and Mark Vernon.

Acknowledgements

My thanks to colleagues and students on our Global Connections course at Edinburgh University, from whom I have learned a great deal about the bigger picture that I try to sketch in this book. Thank you, too, to all the students who have passed through my year-long special subject course: for letting me drone on in class, but more especially for showing the kind of lively engagement with this subject matter that helped to convince me of its value.

Thank you to Robyn Read and everyone at BBC Radio 3, for letting me air my better ideas, for humouring my worse ones (while also steering me clear of using them), and for letting me play with the toys now and again, presenting episodes of *Free Thinking*. Thanks to Diane Banks, Matthew Cole, Martin Redfern and the whole team at Northbank Talent Management, for your support and sage advice. My editor Simon Winder has offered an unfailing combination of enthusiasm, patience and a judicious sense of when to crack the whip. Thank you, indeed, to all at Allen Lane, for your work on my books and your continued willingness to read what I send through. Thank you to Celia Mackay for help with image permissions, and to Louisa Watson for your great care in editing the manuscript (also for your lovely comments in the margins).

I never met Bede Griffiths or Erna Hoch, and Alan Watts passed away before I was born. I can, however, now claim to have had an email exchange with Gary Snyder. My thanks to him for granting permission for me to reproduce the poem that he read at Watts' funeral. Snyder tells me that he remembers Watts now with great fondness, having been saddened at the time, as many were, by his struggles late in life. For financial support in the writing of this book, thanks go to the Great Britain Sasakawa Foundation, the Daiwa Anglo-Japanese Foundation, the Wellcome Foundation, the British Academy and the School of History, Classics and Archaeology at the University of Edinburgh.

Finally, there is an irony to writing about the joys of adventure and discovery while leaving your children to sit in front of the television as you do so. To my wife Kae and our children Shoji, Yocchan and Hana: as politicians say when they lose an election – 'I get it, I'm listening, and I'll do better' (in my case, I mean it). Thank you, and also Mum, Dad, Elizabeth and Theresa, for all your love.

Notes

Introduction

1 Letter from Swami Vivekānanda to Alasinga Perumal, 2 November 1893, in *The Complete Works of Swami Vivekananda*, vol. 5 (Advaita Ashrama, 1947), pp. 16–21; John Henry Barrows (ed.), *The World's Parliament of Religions: An Illustrated and Popular Story of the World's First Parliament of Religions, Held in Chicago in Connection with the Columbian Exposition of 1893* (The Parliament Publishing Company, 1893), p. 62.

2 Stanley K. Hunter, *Footsteps at the American World's Fairs: The International Exhibitions of Chicago, New York and Philadelphia, 1853–1965: Revisited in 1993* (Exhibition Study Group, 1996), p. 24; Richard Hughes Seager, *The World's Parliament of Religions: The East/West Encounter, Chicago, 1893* (Indiana University Press, 1995), pp. 10–12.

3 Seager, op. cit., pp. 10–12.

4 Ibid., p. 43; Barrows (ed.), op. cit., pp. 62 and 66.

5 The 'devoted biographer' was Sailendra Nath Dhar, his words reproduced in John R. McRae, 'Oriental Verities at the American Frontier: The 1893 World's Parliament of Religions and the Thought of Masao Abe', *Buddhist-Christian Studies* vol. 11 (1991), p. 16. Vivekānanda gave his own recollection of events in his letter to Alasinga Perumal of 2 November 1893, describing himself as a 'fool' for arriving that first day with no ready-made speech to hand.

6 Swami Vivekānanda, 'Response to Welcome', 11 September 1893, in *The Complete Works of Swami Vivekananda*, vol. 1 (Advaita Ashrama, 1957), pp. 3–4.

7 Sailendra Nath Dhar, *A Comprehensive Biography of Swami Vivekananda*, Part One (Vivekananda Prakashan Kendra, 1975), p. 462. See also McRae, op. cit., pp. 12 and 34.

8 Frederick Douglass, 'The Reason Why', reproduced in Ida B. Wells-Barnett, *Selected Works of Ida B. Wells-Barnett* (Oxford University Press, 1991), pp. 51–2.

9 Ibid., pp. 52 and 58.

10 Ruth Harris, *Guru to the World: The Life and Legacy of Swami Vivekananda* (Harvard University Press, 2022), p. 118.

11 Swami Vivekānanda, 'Paper on Hinduism', 19 September 1893, in *The Complete Works of Swami Vivekananda*, vol. 1 (Advaita Ashrama, 1957), pp. 6–20.

12 Ibid., pp. 6–20.

Chapter 1: Barbaroi, Agrioi

1 Lucian, 'Herodotus and Aetion', translated in Dan Nässelqvist, *Public Reading in Early Christianity: Lectors, Manuscripts, and Sound in the Oral Delivery of John 1–4* (Brill, 2016).

2 This is the estimate given in Ian Oliver, 'Plataea Performed: The Impact of Audience on Herodotus's *Histories*', *The Classical Journal*, vol. 117/1 (2021), p. 24.

3 George Rawlinson, *History of Herodotus* (John Murray, 1862), pp. 14–15.

4 Tom Holland (trans.), *Herodotus: The Histories* (Penguin, 2014), p. xvii.

5 On Herodotus' portrayal of the Persians, see Erich Gruen, *Rethinking the Other in Antiquity* (Princeton University Press, 2010), pp. 9–52.

6 Ibid., pp. 9–52. On modern (mis)uses of Herodotus' *Histories*, see also David Kopf, 'A Macrohistoriographical Essay on the Idea of East and West from Herodotus to Edward Said', *Comparative Civilizations Review* 15/15 (1986).

7 Diarmaid MacCulloch, *A History of Christianity: The First Three Thousand Years* (Penguin, 2010), p. 36.

8 Susan Guettel Cole, ' "I Know the Number of the Sand and the Measure of the Sea": Geography and Difference in the Early Greek World', in Kurt A. Raaflaub and Richard J. A. Talbert (eds.), *Geography and Ethnography: Perceptions of the World in Pre-Modern Societies* (Blackwell, 2009),

pp. 197–214; Richard Talbert, *Ancient Perspectives: Maps and Their Place in Mesopotamia, Egypt, Greece and Rome* (University of Chicago Press, 2012), pp. 89–90.

9 Herodotus, *Histories*, Book 4, Chapter 45, in Holland (trans.), op. cit., p. 279.

10 See Herodotus, *Histories*, 4, in ibid., pp. 261–336.

11 See ibid. See also James Romm, 'Continents, Climates and Cultures: Greek Theories of Global Structure', in Kurt A. Raaflaub and Richard J. A. Talbert (eds.), op. cit., p. 220 and Cole, op. cit., p. 209.

12 Romm, op. cit., pp. 220–3.

13 On Scylax, see Grant Parker, *The Making of Roman India* (Cambridge University Press, 2008), pp. 14–15; Wilhelm Halbfass, *India and Europe: An Essay in Understanding* (State University of New York Press, 1988), p. 11; Daniela Dueck, *Geography in Classical Antiquity* (Cambridge University Press, 2012), p. 10; Dmitri Panchenko, ' "Scylax" ': Circumnavigation of India and Its Interpretation in Early Greek Geography, Ethnography and Cosmography', *Hyperboreus*, vol. 4 (1998), p. 213.

14 Parker, op. cit., p. 56.

15 A. D. Godly (trans.), Herodotus, *Histories: The Persian Wars*, vol. II: *Books 3 to 4*, Loeb Classical Library edn (Harvard University Press, 1921), Book 3, Chapter 98.

16 Herodotus, *Histories*, Book 3, Chapter 99, in Holland (trans.), op. cit., p. 235.

17 Herodotus, *Histories*, Book 3, Chapter 101, in ibid., p. 236.

18 Herodotus, *Histories* 3:104, Loeb Classical Library edition (1921).

19 See Michel Peissel, *Ants' Gold: The Discovery of the Greek El Dorado in the Himalayas* (HarperCollins, 1984).

20 Herodotus, *Histories* Book 3, Chapter 106, in Godly (trans.), op. cit.

21 Herodotus, *Histories*, Book 7, chapters 65 and 86, in Holland (trans.), op. cit., pp. 472 and 477; Parker, op. cit., p. 56.

22 See Richard Stoneman, *The Greek Experience of India: From Alexander to the Indo-Greeks* (Princeton University Press, 2019), p. 100; Parker, op. cit., p. 17; E. R. Bevan, 'India in Early Greek and Latin Literature', in Edward James Rapson (ed.), *The Cambridge History of India*, vol. 1: *Ancient India* (Cambridge University Press, 1922), p. 394.

23 Jan P. Stronk, 'Ctesias of Cnidus, A Reappraisal', *Mnemosyne* vol. 60 (2007), p. 27; Parker, op. cit., pp. 28–33; Stoneman, *Greek Experience of India*, p. 100; J. M. Bigwood, 'Aristotle and the Elephant Again', *American Journal of Philology* 114/4 (1993), 541.

24 Bigwood, op. cit.; K. Karttunen, 'The Reliability of the *Indika* of Ktesias', *Studia Orientalia Electronica* 50, 105–8. On the rust-resistant alloy, see Raoul McLaughlin, *The Roman Empire and the Silk Routes* (Pen & Sword History, 2016), p. 5.

25 A. Brian Bosworth, 'Aristotle, India and the Alexander Historians', *Topoi* 3/2 (1993), 421.

26 Richard Stoneman (trans., author of introduction and notes), *The Greek Alexander Romance* (Penguin, 1991), p. 2.

Chapter 2: Into India

1 Richard Stoneman (trans., author of introduction and notes), *The Greek Alexander Romance* (Penguin, 1991), p. 133.

2 Stanley Wolpert, *A New History of India* (Oxford University Press, 2000), p. 56; Grant Parker, *The Making of Roman India* (Cambridge University Press, 2008), p. 35.

3 Richard Stoneman, *The Greek Experience of India: From Alexander to the Indo-Greeks* (Princeton University Press, 2019), p. 68; Daniela Dueck, *Geography in Classical Antiquity* (Cambridge University Press, 2012), p. 14; A. Brian Bosworth, 'Aristotle, India and the Alexander Historians', *Topoi* 3/2 (1993), 423; Romila Thapar, *The Penguin History of Early India* (Penguin Books India, 2003), p. 157.

4 Quoted in Parker, op. cit., p. 36.

5 Plutarch, 'Alexander', in Bernadotte Perrin (trans.), *Plutarch's Lives* (Harvard University Press, 1919), Chapter 62. See also W. W. Tarn, *Alexander the Great*: vol. 2, *Sources and Studies* (Cambridge University Press, 2003).

6 Stoneman, *The Greek Alexander Romance*, p. 131. On the ancient sources for the encounters with 'naked philosophers', see Olga Kubica, 'Meetings with the "Naked Philosophers" as a Case Study for the Greco-Indian

Relations in the Time of Alexander', *Studia Hercynia* XXV/1 (2021), 72–81.

7 Stoneman, *The Greek Alexander Romance*, pp. 132–3.

8 Stoneman, *Greek Experience of India*, pp. 291–2. On who these naked philosophers might have been, including speculations about Pyrrho and Buddhism, see Stoneman, *Greek Experience of India*, pp. 346–56; Kubica, op. cit., 75–6.

9 See Stoneman, *Greek Experience of India*, pp. 100–137 and Parker, op. cit., p. 42. Some scholars, including Stoneman, question whether Megasthenes' work may reasonably be referred to as ethnography; see *Greek Experience of India*, p. 137.

10 Stoneman, *Greek Experience of India*, pp. 319–29; Richard Stoneman, *Megasthenes' Indica: A New Translation of the Fragments* (Routledge, 2021), pp. 43–4.

11 Stoneman, *Megasthenes' Indica*, pp. 143, 189, 198.

12 Cornelia Isler-Kerényi (trans. Wilfred G. E. Watson), *Dionysos in Archaic Greece: An Understanding through Images* (Brill, 2007), pp. 1–3.

13 For a brief discussion of this point, see Allan Dahlquist, *Megasthenes and Indian Religion: A Study in Motives and Types* (Motilal Banarsidass, 1977), pp. 9–11. See also Klaus Karttunen, *India and the Hellenistic World* (Finnish Oriental Society, 1997), pp. 27–8 and 89–91, and Stoneman, *Greek Experience of India*, pp. 80–98.

14 For Megasthenes' account of Indian social life, see Parker, op. cit., p. 46; Stoneman, *Greek Experience of India*, pp. 211–17; Stoneman, *Megasthenes' Indica*, p. 63; Donald F. Lach, *Asia in the Making of Europe*, vol. I: *The Century of Discovery* (University of Chicago Press, 1965), pp. 9–10.

15 Stoneman, *Megasthenes' Indica*, pp. 274–86.

16 Parker, op. cit., pp. 48–9; Stoneman, *Greek Experience of India*, pp. 377–401.

17 Thapar, op. cit., p. 254. See also Eivind Seland and Hakon Teigon (eds.), *Sinews of Empire: Networks in the Roman Near East and Beyond* (Oxbow Books, 2017).

18 Stoneman, *Greek Experience of India*, p. 417.

19 Shonaleeka Kaul, 'South Asia', in Craig Benjamin (ed.), *The Cambridge World History*, vol. 4: *A World with States, Empires, and Networks 1200 BCE–900 CE* (Cambridge University Press, 2015), pp. 485–98.

20 Christian Habicht, 'Eudoxus of Cyzicus and Ptolemaic Exploration of the Sea Route to India', in Kostas Buraselis, Mary Stefanou and Dorothy J. Thompson (eds.), *The Ptolemies, the Sea, and the Nile: Studies in Waterborne Power* (Cambridge University Press, 2013), p. 199. See also Matthew Adam Cobb, *Rome and the Indian Ocean Trade from Augustus to the Early Third Century* CE (Brill, 2018).

21 Parker, op. cit., p. 55.

22 Steven E. Sidebotham, *Roman Economic Policy in the Erythra Thalassa: 30 BC–AD 217* (Brill, 1986), p. 129.

23 See Franz Ferdinand Schwarz, 'Pliny the Elder on Ceylon', *Journal of Asian History* 8/1 (1974).

24 Warwick Ball, *Rome in the East: The Transformation of an Empire* (Routledge, 2000), p. 149.

25 Richard Saller, *Pliny's Roman Economy: Natural History, Innovation and Growth* (Princeton University Press, 2022), p. 95. The uncertainty over Pliny's sources for his figures is mentioned in Parker, op. cit., p. 189. See also Cobb, op. cit., pp. 274–7.

26 Ball, op. cit., pp. 143–50; Pliny the Elder, *The Natural History*, 6:26 (trans. John Bostock, Taylor and Francis, 1855).

27 For details of the Rome–India trade, see Parker, op. cit., pp. 157–76; Ball, op. cit., pp. 144–8; Buraselis *et al.* (eds.), op. cit., p. 203; Lach, vol. I: *The Century of Discovery*, p. 15.

28 Reproduced in Parker, op. cit., p. 173.

29 Parker, op. cit., pp. 151–3.

30 Paul Freedman, *Out of the East: Spices and the Medieval Imagination* (Yale University Press, 2009), p. 26.

31 Kelly Olson, *Dress and the Roman Woman: Self-Presentation and Society* (Taylor & Francis, 2012), p. 14.

32 Michael Loewe, 'Knowledge of Other Cultures in China's Early Empires', in Kurt A. Raaflaub and Richard J. A. Talbert (eds.), *Geography and Ethnography: Perceptions of the World in Pre-Modern Societies* (Blackwell, 2009), p. 79.

33 Henry G. Bohn (trans.), *The Epigrams of Martial*, Bohn's Classical Library (George Bell and Sons, 1897), Book XI, XXVII: 'To Flaccus'.

34 Parker, op. cit., p. 90.

35 Reproduced in ibid., pp. 90–91.

36 Ibid., pp. 107–8.

37 Quoted in ibid., p. 53.

38 Quoted in ibid, p. 216.

Chapter 3: Silk, Spice, Paradise

1 Quoted in Ken Curtis and Valerie Hansen, *Voyages in World History* (Wadsworth Publishing, 2016), p. 85.

2 Quoted in Victor H. Mair *et al.* (eds.), *Hawai'i Reader in Traditional Chinese Culture* (University of Hawaii Press, 2005), p. 170.

3 Valerie Hansen, *The Silk Road: A New History* (Oxford University Press, 2015), p. 5.

4 Ibid., pp. 14–17.

5 On the voyage of Gan Ying, see Li Feng, *Early China: A Social and Cultural History* (Cambridge University Press, 2013), pp. 280–81 and Edwin G. Pulleyblank, 'The Roman Empire as Known to Han China', *Journal of the American Oriental Society* 119/1 (1999), p. 78.

6 Reproduced in Han Xiaorong, 'The Role of Vietnam in China's Foreign Relations', in Clara Wing-chung Ho *et al.* (eds.), *Voyages, Migration and the Maritime World* (De Gruyter Oldenbourg, 2018), p. 123.

7 See Paul Freedman, *Out of the East: Spices and the Medieval Imagination* (Yale University Press, 2009), pp. 2–31.

8 Ibid., pp. 2–31.

9 Ibid, pp. 78–80.

10 Origen, *On First Principles* [trans G. W. Butterworth] (Ave Maria Press, 2013), pp. 383–4.

11 See 'Allegory', in John Anthony McGuckin (ed.), *The Westminster Handbook to Origen* (John Know Press, 2004).

12 Freedman, op. cit., p. 91.

13 Ibid., pp. 89–94.

14 Donald F. Lach, *Asia in the Making of Europe*, vol. I: *The Century of Discovery* (University of Chicago Press, 1965), pp. 20–21.

15 Ibid, pp. 24–6.

16 'Letter of Prester John', in Sir E. Denison Ross (trans.), 'Prester John and the Empire of Ethiopia', in Arthur Percival Newton (ed.), *Travel and Travellers of the Middle Ages* (Routledge and Kegan Paul, 1926), p. 175.

17 Love, truth and the magical mirror feature in a number of versions of the Prester John tale. See Keagan Brewer (ed.), *Prester John: the Legend and Its Sources* (Taylor & Francis, 2019).

18 See Romila Thapar, *The Penguin History of Early India* (Penguin Books India, 2003), p. 385; Sugata Bose and Ayesha Jalal, *Modern South Asia: History, Culture, Political Economy* (2004), p. 21.

19 See Robert Eric Frykenberg, *Christianity in India: From Beginnings to the Present* (Oxford University Press, 2008), p. 99.

20 Quoted in M. Uebel, *Ecstatic Transformation: On the Uses of Alterity in the Middle Ages* (Palgrave Macmillan, 2005), p. 123.

Chapter 4: Esplorati: *Polo and Columbus*

1 Marco Polo, *The Travels* (trans. and introduction, Nigel Cliff) (Penguin, 2015), p. 3.

2 On the Italian maritime republics, see John H. Pryor, 'The Maritime Republics', in David Abulafia (ed.), *The New Cambridge Medieval History* (Cambridge University Press, 1999), pp. 419–46.

3 Polo, op. cit., pp. xx–xxiii.

4 Ibid., pp. xx–xxxix. See also Jørgen Jensen, 'The World's Most Diligent Observer', *Asiatische Studien* LI (1997), 723–4; Paul Freedman, *Out of the East: Spices and the Medieval Imagination* (Yale University Press, 2009), p. 174; Surekha Davies, 'The Wondrous East in the Renaissance Geographical Imagination: Marco Polo, Fra Mauro and Giovanni Battista Ramusio', *History and Anthropology* 23/2 (2012), 215–34.

5 Polo, op. cit., p. xiii. Until relatively recently, it was thought that most medieval European readers were sceptical about Polo's claims, but that view has since been revised. See Kim M. Phillips, *Before Orientalism: Asian Peoples and Cultures in European Travel Writing, 1245–1510* (University of Pennsylvania Press, 2013), p. 37.

6 Donald F. Lach, *Asia in the Making of Europe*, vol. I: *The Century of Discovery* (University of Chicago Press, 1965), p. 38.

7 Polo, op. cit., pp. xiii–xiv; on 'Europe' as a cultural entity see Phillips, op. cit., p. 62.

8 Polo, op. cit., pp. xiii–xiv and 237.

9 Ibid., pp. 66–9 and 239.

10 Ibid., p. xxiv.

11 Ibid., pp. xxxii–xxxiii.

12 On the scholarly consensus, see, e.g., Hans Ulrich Vogel, *Marco Polo Was in China: New Evidence from Currencies, Salts and Revenues* (Brill, 2013); Na Chang, 'Kublai Khan in the Eyes of Marco Polo', *European Review* 25/3 (2017), 502–17.

13 Joan-Pau Rubiés, *Travel and Ethnology in the Renaissance: South India through European Eyes, 1250–1625* (Cambridge University Press, 2004), pp. 50–71.

14 Polo, op. cit., p. xxiv.

15 Ibid., pp. 93–4 and 270.

16 Ibid., pp. 247–8.

17 Ibid., p. 251.

18 Rubiés, op. cit., p. 68.

19 Polo, op. cit., pp. 252–79.

20 Ibid., pp. 227–8.

21 Ibid., pp. 228–32.

22 Ibid., pp. 228–31.

23 See Freedman, op. cit., pp. 173 and 190; Lach, vol. I: *The Century of Discovery*, p. 65.

24 Freedman, op. cit., pp. 179–81.

25 Valerie Flint, *The Imaginative Landscape of Christopher Columbus* (Princeton University Press, 1992), pp. 128 and 151–2. See also Markus Bockmuehl, 'Locating Paradise', in Markus Bockmuehl and Guy G. Stroumsa (eds.), *Paradise in Antiquity: Jewish and Christian Views* (Cambridge University Press, 2010).

26 Flint, op. cit., p. 115.

27 Lach, vol. I: *The Century of Discovery*, p. 98.

28 Freedman, op. cit., p. 204; Lach, vol. I: *The Century of Discovery*, p. 143; Stanley Wolpert, *A New History of India* (Oxford University Press, 2000), p. 140.

Chapter 5: God's Marines

1 See Robert J. Miller *et al.*, *Discovering Indigenous Lands: The Doctrine of Discovery in the English Colonies* (Oxford University Press, 2010).

2 Francis Augustus MacNutt, *Bartholomew de Las Casas: His Life, Apostolate and Writings* (2020), p. 197.

3 For an overview of the *Spiritual Exercises*, see Philip Endean, 'The Spiritual Exercises', in Thomas Worcester (ed.), *The Cambridge Companion to the Jesuits* (Cambridge University Press, 2008). On Ignatius of Loyola, see Lu Ann Homza, 'The Religious Milieu of the Young Ignatius', in ibid.

4 Donald F. Lach, *Asia in the Making of Europe*, vol. I: *The Century of Discovery* (University of Chicago Press, 1965), p. 345.

5 Alfonso de Albuquerque, *The Commentaries of the Great Alfonso de Albuquerque, Second Viceroy of India* ([trans. Walter De Gray Birch] Cambridge University Press, 2010), p. 171; Lach, vol. I: *The Century of Discovery*, p. 168.

6 On early modern European writings about India, see Donald F. Lach, *Asia in the Making of Europe*, vol. II: *A Century of Wonder*, Book 2: *The Literary Arts* (University of Chicago Press, 1977).

7 See Robert Eric Frykenberg, *Christianity in India: From Beginnings to the Present* (Oxford University Press, 2008); Leonard Fernando SJ, 'Jesuits and India', essay in Oxford Handbooks Online (2016); Donald F. Lach, vol. I: *The Century of Discovery*, pp. 236–48.

8 Lach, vol. I: *The Century of Discovery*, pp. 242–4.

9 Ibid., pp. 229–331; Ines G. Županov, ' "One Civility but Multiple Religions": Jesuit Mission among St Thomas Christians in India (16th–17th Centuries)', in *Journal of Early Modern History* 9/3, pp. 284–325.

10 Županov, op. cit.; Lach, vol. I: *The Century of Discovery*.

11 Županov, op. cit.; Lach, vol. I: *The Century of Discovery*.

12 Županov, op. cit., pp. 319–22.

13 João Vicente Melo, *Jesuit and English Experiences at the Mughal Court, c. 1580–1615* (Palgrave Macmillan, 2022), pp. 10–16 and 23; Sugata Bose and Ayesha Jalal, *Modern South Asia: History, Culture, Political Economy* (Routledge, 2004), p. 31.

14 Melo, op. cit., pp. 67–8 and 23.

15 Ibid., pp. 27–9; Lach, vol. I: *The Century of Discovery*.

16 Gauvin Alexander Bailey, 'The Truth-Showing Mirror': Jesuit Catechism and the Arts in Mughal India', in John W. O'Malley *et al.* (eds), *The Jesuits: Cultures, Sciences and the Arts, 1540–1773* (University of Toronto Press, 1999), pp. 381 and 392.

17 Melo, op. cit., p. 30; Lach, vol. I: *The Century of Discovery*, p. 278.

18 See Bailey, op. cit. and Gauvin Alexander Bailey, ' "Le style jésuite n'existe pas": Jesuit Corporate Culture and the Visual Arts', in O'Malley *et al.* (eds.), op. cit., pp. 38–89.

Chapter 6: The Challenge of China and the Promise of Japan

1 Jonathan D. Spence, *The Chan's Great Continent: China in Western Minds* (W.W. Norton & Company, 1999), p. 1.

2 Donald F. Lach, *Asia in the Making of Europe*, vol. I: *The Century of Discovery* (University of Chicago Press, 1965), pp. 730–31.

3 See David Mungello, *The Great Encounter of China and the West, 1500–1800* (Rowman & Littlefield, 1999); Lach, vol. I: *The Century of Discovery*, p. 740.

4 Ying Liu *et al.* (eds.), *Zheng He's Maritime Voyages (1405–1433) and China's Relations with the Indian Ocean World: A Multilingual Bibliography* (Brill, 2014), p. xxiii.

5 Spence, op. cit., p. 20.

6 Lach, vol. I: *The Century of Discovery*, pp. 733–7; Mungello, op. cit.

7 Lach, vol. I: *The Century of Discovery*, p. 737; Spence, op. cit., pp. 21–3.

8 Roderich Ptak, 'The Demography of Old Macao, 1555–1640', *Ming Studies* I (1982).

9 Lach, vol. I: *The Century of Discovery*, pp. 743–4.

10 Quoted in Lach, vol. I: *The Century of Discovery*, pp. 756–7.

11 Lach, vol. I: *The Century of Discovery*, pp. 738–81.

12 Lach, vol. I: *The Century of Discovery*, pp. 765–84; Spence, op. cit., p. 26.

13 Ricardo Padrón, *The Indies of the Setting Sun: How Early Modern Spain Mapped the Far East as the Transpacific West* (University of Chicago Press, 2022), p. 193.

14 Liam Matthew Brockey, *Journey to the East: The Jesuit Mission to China, 1579–1724* (Harvard University Press, 2008), p. 31.

15 Ibid., p. 32.

16 Franklin Perkins, *Leibniz and China: A Commerce of Light* (Cambridge University Press, 2008), pp. 16–19.

17 Brockey, op. cit., p. 421; Nicholas Standaert, 'Jesuits in China', in Thomas Worcester (ed.), *The Cambridge Companion to the Jesuits* (Cambridge University Press, 2008).

18 Lach, vol. I: *The Century of Discovery*, pp. 656–9.

19 Kirk Sandvig, *Hidden Christians in Japan: Breaking the Silence* (Lexington Books/Fortress Academic, 2019), p. 22–3.

20 Linda Zampol D'Ortia, Lucia Dolce and Ana Fernandes Pinto, 'Saints, Sects and (Holy) Sites: The Jesuit Mapping of Japanese Buddhism (Sixteenth Century)', in Alexandra Curvelo and Angelo Cattaneo (eds.), *Interactions between Rivals: The Christian Mission and Buddhist Sects in Japan (c. 1549–c. 1647)* (Peter Lang, 2021), p. 71.

21 Sandvig, op. cit., p. 26; D'Ortia *et al.*, op. cit., p. 72.

22 Lach, vol. I: *The Century of Discovery*, p. 661.

23 D'Ortia *et al.*, op. cit., p. 72; Lach, vol. I: *The Century of Discovery*, p. 661.

24 Alessandro Valignano's account, quoted in Jurgis Elisonas, 'Christianity and the Daimyō', in *The Cambridge History of Japan*, vol. 4: *Early Modern Japan* (Cambridge University Press, 1991), p. 309.

25 Ibid., p. 313.

26 Linda Zampol D'Ortia, 'The Dress of Evangelization: Jesuit Garments, Liturgical Textiles, and the Senses in Early Modern Japan', *Entangled Religions* 10 (2019).

27 Elisonas, op. cit.; Lach, vol. I: *The Century of Discovery*, p. 667.

28 Elisonas, op. cit., pp. 314–15; D'Ortia *et al.*, op. cit., pp. 73–4.

29 See Kevin Doak, *Xavier's Legacies: Catholicism in Modern Japanese Culture* (UBC Press, 2008), p. 1. Sandvig (op. cit.) gives a figure of 6,000 (p. 26).

30 On this trade route, see Cristina Castel-Branco and Guida Carvalho, *Luis Frois: First Western Accounts of Japan's Gardens, Cities and Landscapes* (Springer, 2020), pp. 23–40. The profit figure comes from Kiichi Matsuda, *The Relations between Portugal and Japan* (Junta de Investigações do Ultramar, 1965), p. 12.

31 Alexandra Curvelo, 'The Disruptive Presence of the Nanban-jin in Early Modern Japan', *Journal of the Economic and Social History of the Orient* 55 (2012), 581–602.

32 See D'Ortia *et al.*, op. cit., pp. 74–6; Lach, vol. I: *The Century of Discovery*, pp. 707–17.

33 D'Ortia *et al.*, op. cit., pp. 75–85.

34 See Lach, vol. I: *The Century of Discovery*, pp. 680–2; D'Ortia *et al.*, op. cit.

35 M. Antoni J. Üçerler, 'The Jesuit Enterprise in Sixteenth- and Seventeenth-century Japan', in Worcester (ed.), op. cit., pp. 158–9.

36 See Andrew C. Ross, 'Alessandro Valignano: The Jesuits and Culture in the East', in John W. O'Malley *et al.* (eds.), *The Jesuits: Cultures, Sciences and the Arts, 1540–1773* (University of Toronto Press, 1999), pp. 344–7; Luis Frois, S. J. (trans. Richard K. Danford, Robin D. Gill and Daniel T. Reff), *The First European Description of Japan, 1585* (Routledge, 2014).

37 Frois, op. cit., p. 15.

38 On Jesuit numbers in Japan, see Joseph Moran, *Alessandro Valignano and the Early Jesuits in Japan* (Continuum, 1992), p. 2. On *dōjoku*, see Haruko Nawata Ward, 'Jesuits, Too: Jesuits, Women Catechists, and Jezebels in Christian-Century Japan', in John W. O'Malley *et al.* (eds.), *The Jesuits II: Cultures, Sciences, and the Arts 1540–1773* (University of Toronto Press, 2005), p. 640.

39 Ibid., pp. 643–5.

40 Figures from Lach, vol. I: *The Century of Discovery*, p. 689.

41 On Oda Nobunaga grilling Luis Frois, see Frois, op. cit., p. 35. On armour stopping a bullet, see Stephen R. Turnbull, *The Book of the Samurai: The Warrior Class of Japan* (Gallery Books, 1982), p. 78.

42 Derek Massarella, 'Envoys and Illusions: The Japanese Embassy to Europe, 1582–90, *De Missione Legatorvm Iaponensium*, and the Portuguese Viceregal Embassy to Toyotomi Hideyoshi, 1591', *Journal of the Royal Asiatic Society* 15/3 (2005), 330.

43 Quoted in Lach, vol. I: *The Century of Discovery*, pp. 690–91.

44 Massarella, op. cit., 346.

45 Judith C. Brown, 'Courtiers and Christians: The First Japanese Emissaries to Europe', *Renaissance Quarterly* 47/4 (1994), 875.

46 On the boys' dress, and audience with King Philip II, see Michael Cooper, *The Japanese Mission to Europe, 1582–1590* (Global Oriental, 2005), p. 60. On presents, and the crowd size when approaching Rome, see Lach, vol. I: *The Century of Discovery*, pp. 693–5. On the journey, and the welcome into Rome, see Brown, op. cit., 890–98 and Massarella, op. cit., 333.

47 Massarella, op. cit., 333–5; Cooper, op. cit., pp. 88–91.

48 Ibid., 336 and Lach, vol. I: *The Century of Discovery*, p. 698.

49 Brown, op. cit., 889.

50 Massarella, op. cit., 336 and Lach, vol. I: *The Century of Discovery*, p. 700.

51 Brown, op. cit., 889; Cooper, op. cit., p. 51.

52 Massarella, op. cit., 335; Cooper, op. cit., p. 92.

53 Brown, op. cit., 893 and Lach, vol. I: *The Century of Discovery*, p. 697.

54 Massarella, op. cit., 343.

55 Quoted in Lach, vol. I: *The Century of Discovery*, p. 702.

56 Massarella, op. cit., 348–50; Cooper, op. cit., p. 158.

57 Üçerler, op. cit., p. 161.

58 Figures from David W. Kling, *A History of Christian Conversion* (Oxford University Press, 2020), p. 444. Exact figures are uncertain and disputed, both in the case of Japanese Christians and the Japanese population as a whole.

59 From Frois, op. cit., pp. 79–127.

60 Doak, op. cit., p. 1. Some of the main disciples of Sen no Rikyū, Japan's most influencial tea master, were Christians.

Chapter 7: England's Legge-Stretchers

1 Reproduced in William Foster (ed.), *Early Travels in India, 1583–1619* (Humphrey Milford/Oxford University Press, 1921), pp. 271–3.

2 Ibid., pp. 271–3.

3 Quoted in R. E. Pritchard, *Odd Tom Coryate* (The History Press, 2004), p. 19.

4 William H. Sherman, 'Stirrings and Searchings (1500–1720)', in Peter Hulme and Tim Youngs (eds.), *The Cambridge Companion to Travel Writing* (Cambridge University Press, 2002), p. 19.

5 Peter E. Pope, *The Many Landfalls of John Cabot* (University of Toronto Press, 1997), p. 14.

6 On cod, see James Evans, *Merchant Adventurers: The Voyage of Discovery That Transformed Tudor England* (Orion, 2013), p. 16. On game, see Pope, op. cit., p. 28.

7 Pope, op. cit., pp. 32–42.

8 Louis Sicking and C. H. (Remco) van Rhee, 'The English Search for a Northeast Passage to Asia Reconsidered', *The Mariner's Mirror* 105/4 (2019), p. 392.

9 See Lydia Towns, 'Merchants, Monarchs and Sixteenth-Century Atlantic Exploration: New Insight into Henry VIII's Planned Voyage of 1521', *Terrae Incognitae: The Journal of the Society for the History of Discoveries* 52/1 (2020).

10 Evans, op. cit., pp. 95–219.

11 Ibid., pp. 214 and 238; Sicking and van Rhee, op. cit., p. 388.

12 Evans, op. cit., pp. 194–216.

13 Ibid., pp. 62–3 and 253–4.

14 Donald F. Lach, *Asia in the Making of Europe*, vol. I (University of Chicago Press, 1965), p. 477; João Vicente Melo, *Jesuit and English Experiences at the Mughal Court, c. 1580–1615* (Palgrave Macmillan, 2022), pp. 109–10.

15 Foster, op. cit., pp. 1–8; Lach, vol. I: *The Century of Discovery*, p. 477–8; J. Courtenay Locke, *The First Englishmen in India: Letters and Narratives of Sundry Elizabethans Written by Themselves* (Taylor & Francis, 2004), p. 42.

16 Locke, op. cit., pp. 41–9; Foster, op. cit., pp. 3 and 16.

17 Pritchard, op. cit., p. 252.

18 Foster, op. cit., pp. 17–18; Courtenay Locke, op. cit., p. 54.

19 William Dalrymple, *The Anarchy: The Relentless Rise of the East India Company* (Bloomsbury, 2019), p. 14.

20 Courtenay Locke, op. cit., p. 54; Melo, op. cit., p. 113.

21 Quoted in Courtenay Locke, op. cit., p. 58.

22 Ibid., pp. 70–72; Lach, vol. I: *The Century of Discovery*, p. 215.

23 Dalrymple, op. cit., pp. 9–12.

24 *Coryat's Crudities: Hastily Gobled up in Five Moneth's Travells* (William Stansby, 1611), section entitled 'The Epistle to the Reader'.

25 Foster, op. cit., pp. 234–5; Mark Aune, 'An Englishman on an Elephant: Thomas Coryate, Travel Writing and Literary Culture in Early Modern England': doctoral thesis submitted to the Graduate School of Wayne State University, Detroit, Michigan (2002), p. 16.

26 M. G. Aune, 'Thomas Coryate versus John Taylor: the Emergence of the Early Modern Celebrity', *Cahiers Élisabéthains: A Journal of English Renaissance* Studies 101/1 (2020), p. 87.

27 '[S]weetmeats and Coryate' is quoted in Aune, 'An Englishman on an Elephant', p. 9. 'Try their wits' is quoted in Foster, op. cit., p. 234.

28 Aune, 'Thomas Coryate versus John Taylor', p. 90.

29 John Donne, 'Upon Mr Thomas Coryat's Crudities', in John Donne (Alexander Balloch Grosart (ed.), *The Complete Poems*, vol. 2 (Robson Books, 1873), p. 94.

30 Foster, op. cit., pp. 236–60.

31 Ibid., pp. 243–71.

32 Pritchard, op. cit., p. 228.

33 Foster, op. cit., p. 245.

34 Ibid., p. 246.

35 Ibid., p. 247.

36 Ibid., p. 262.

37 1614 is marked on the tombstone as Mildenhall's year of death. When exactly it was created and put in place is uncertain. In the early twentieth century, a fresh tablet bearing an English inscription was laid over it. Foster, op. cit., p. 51.

38 Hawkins, quoted in Foster, op. cit., p. 76; Melo, op. cit., p. 137.

39 On the Pathan warriors, see Katie Hickman, *She-Merchants, Buccaneers and Gentlewomen: British Women in India* (Virago, 2019), p. 32 and Foster, op. cit., p. 78. On English accounts of India in this era, see also Kate Teltscher, *India Inscribed: European and British Writing on India 1600–1800* (Oxford University Press, 1995).

40 Foster, op. cit., pp. 67 and 116. See also Nandini Das, *Courting India: England, Mughal India and the Origins of Empire* (Bloomsbury, 2023).

41 Joan Mickelson-Gaughan, *The 'Incumberances': British Women in India, 1615–1856* (Oxford University Press, 2014), p. 17. On Thomas Roe's career in India, see Das, op. cit.

42 Quoted in Pritchard, op. cit., p. 237.

43 Foster, op. cit., pp. 244–6; Das, op. cit.

44 Pritchard, op. cit., pp. 261–3.

45 Amrita Sen, 'Traveling Companions: Women, Trade, and the Early East India Company', *Genre* 48/2 (2015), p. 193.

46 On the Towersons and Mrs Hudson, see Foster, op. cit., p. 71; Sen, op. cit., p. 195; Mickelson-Gaughan, op. cit., p. 19; Hickman, op. cit., p. 29.

47 Hickman, op. cit., p. 29; Mickelson-Gaughan, op. cit., p. 4.

48 Sen, op. cit., pp. 198 and 206.

49 Sen, op. cit., pp. 206–8; Mickelson-Gaughan, op. cit., p. 20.

Chapter 8: In Search of Souls

1 Thomas Coryate, writing to his mother in October 1616. Reproduced in William Foster (ed.), *Early Travels in India, 1583–1619* (Humphrey Milford/Oxford University Press, 1921), pp. 261–70.

2 See Wayne Hudson, *The English Deists: Studies in Early Enlightenment* (Routledge, 2016), pp. 47–8; R. W. Serjeantson, 'Herbert of Cherbury Before Deism: The Early Reception of the De Veritate', *The Seventeenth Century* 16/1 (2001).

3 Jan Peter Schouten, 'A Foreign Culture Baptised: Roberto de Nobili and the Jesuits', *Exchange* 47 (2018), 186–7; Richard Stoneman, *The Greek Experience of India: From Alexander to the Indo-Greeks* (Princeton University Press, 2019), p. 229.

4 Francis X. Clooney SJ, 'Roberto de Nobili's *Dialogue on Eternal Life* and An Early Jesuit Evaluation of Religion in South India', in John W. O'Malley *et al.* (eds.), *The Jesuits: Cultures, Sciences and the Arts, 1540–1773* (University of Toronto Press, 1999), p. 405; Wilhelm Halbfass, *India and Europe: An Essay in Understanding* (State University of New York Press, 1988), p. 42.

5 Schouten, op. cit., 187–91.

6 Gita Dharampal-Frick, 'Revisiting the Malabar Rites Controversy: A Paradigm of Ritual Dynamics in the Early Modern Catholic Missions of South India', in Ines G. Županov and Pierre Antoine Fabre (eds.), *The Rites Controversies in the Early Modern World* (Brill, 2018); and Roberto de Nobili (trans. and introduction: Anand Amaladass SJ and Francis X. Clooney SJ), *Preaching Wisdom to the Wise: Three Treatises by Roberto de Nobili SJ, Missionary and Scholar in 17th Century India* (Institute of Jesuit Studies, 2000), pp. 17–19; Clooney, 'Roberto de Nobili's *Dialogue*', pp. 404–5; Robert Eric Frykenberg, *Christianity in India: From Beginnings to the Present* (Oxford University Press, 2008), p. 139.

7 Paul Collins, 'The Praxis of Inculturation for Mission: Roberto de Nobili's Example and Legacy', *Ecclesiology* 3/3 (2007), 325; Will Sweetman, 'Reading Jesuit Readings of Hinduism', *Jesuit Historiography Online* (2019).

8 Figures from Schouten, op. cit., 188.

9 Francis X. Clooney SJ, *Western Jesuit Scholars in India* (Brill, 2020), pp. 24–32.

10 Schouten, op. cit., pp. 191–3; Clooney, *Western Jesuit Scholars in India*, pp. 40–42.

11 See Clooney, 'Roberto de Nobili's *Dialogue*'; De Nobili, op. cit.; Schouten, op. cit.

12 On de Nobili and the 'divine descent' argument, see Clooney, *Western Jesuit Scholars in India*, p. 94.

13 Schouten, op. cit.

14 Schouten, op. cit.

15 See Michael Walsh, *The Jesuits: From Ignatius of Loyola to Pope Francis* (Hymns Ancient and Modern, 2022).

16 Liam Matthew Brockey, *Journey to the East: The Jesuit Mission to China, 1579–1724* (Harvard University Press, 2008), p. 421; Nicholas Standaert, 'Jesuits in China', in Thomas Worcester (ed.), *The Cambridge Companion to the Jesuits* (Cambridge University Press, 2008), p. 178; Matteo Ricci (trans. Timothy Billings), *On Friendship: One Hundred Maxims for a Chinese Prince* (Columbia University Press, 2009).

17 Quoted in Franklin Perkins, *Leibniz and China: A Commerce of Light* (Cambridge University Press, 2004), p. 20.

18 Donald F. Lach, *Asia in the Making of Europe*, vol. III: *A Century of Advance* (University of Chicago Press, 1965), p. 1652.

19 Quoted in Colin Mackerass, *Western Images of China* (Oxford University Press, 1999), p. 28. See also Perkins, op. cit., pp. 9–10.

20 See David Mungello, *The Great Encounter of China and the West, 1500–1800* (Rowman & Littlefield, 1999); Raymond Dawson, *The Chinese Chameleon* (Oxford University Press, 1967), pp. 46–7.

21 Brockey, op. cit., p. 34.

22 Catherine Pagani, 'Clockwork and the Jesuit Mission to China', in John W. O'Malley *et al.* (eds.), *The Jesuits II: Cultures, Sciences, and the Arts 1540–1773* (University of Toronto Press, 2005), p. 660.

23 See ibid., pp. 660–61; Brockey, op. cit., p. 32; Standaert, op. cit., p. 173.

24 On Ricci's map, see Qiong Zhang, *Making the New World Their Own: Chinese Encounters with Jesuit Science in the Age of Discovery* (Brill, 2015).

25 Ibid, p. 38; Brockey, op. cit., p. 68.

26 Brockey, op. cit., pp. 71–98.

27 Ibid, pp. 76–115; Standaert, op. cit., pp. 175–8.

28 Mungello, op. cit.

29 Toby E. Huff, *The Rise of Early Modern Science* (Cambridge University Press), p. 204.

30 See Mungello, op. cit.

31 Standaert, op. cit., p. 173.

32 Brockey, op. cit., p. 106.

33 Quoted in Brockey, op. cit., p. 107.

34 Standaert, op. cit., p. 173; Pagani, op. cit., p. 658; Friederike Biebl, 'The Magnificence of the Qing: European Art on the Jesuit Mission in China', in *MaRBLe Research Papers* (2014).

35 Pagani, op. cit., p. 663.

36 Standaert, op. cit., p. 170; Brockey, op. cit., p. 141.

37 Huff, op. cit., p. 209.

38 Brockey, op. cit., pp. 128–30; Mungello, op. cit.; Standaert, op. cit., p. 170; Zhang, op. cit., p. 158.

39 On astronomy in this respect, see Yunli Shi, 'Chinese astronomy in the time of the Jesuits: Studies following *Science and Civilisation in China*', in *Cultures of Science* 3/2 (2020).

40 On the heliocentrism controversy and its repercussions in China, see Richard J. Blackwell, *Galileo, Bellarmine and the Bible* (University of Notre Dame Press, 1991); John Patrick Donnelly SJ, Review of *Galileo, Bellarmine and the Bible*, in *The Journal of Modern History* 65/4 (1993); Nicholas Spencer, *Magisteria: The Entangled Histories of Science and Religion* (Oneworld Publications, 2023); Chapter IV, 'Copernicus in China', in Nathan Sivin, *Science and Ancient China: Researches and Reflections* (Variorum, 1995); Han Qi, 'Between Science and Religion: Antoine Thomas (1644–1709, SJ) and the Transmission of the Copernican System During the Kangxi Reign', in Alexandre Chen Tsung-min (ed.), *Catholicism's Encounters With China: 17th to 20th century* (Ferdinand Verbiest Institute, 2018); Shi Yunli, 'Nikolaus Smogulecki and Xue Fengzuo's *True Principles of the Pacing of the Heavens*: Its Production, Publication, and Reception', *East Asian Science, Technology and Medicine* 27 (2007).

Chapter 9: China in Europe

1 Matteo Ricci, quoted in Markman Ellis, Richard Coulton and Mathew Mauger, *Empire of Tea: The Asian Leaf That Conquered the World* (Reaktion Books, 2015), p. 21.

2 Alessandro Valignano, quoted in Morgan Pitelka, 'The Tokugawa Storehouse: Ieyasu's Encounter with Things', in Paula Findlen (ed.), *Early Modern Things: Objects and Their Histories (1500–1800)* (Routledge, 2021), p. 371.

3 Ellis *et al.*, op. cit., pp. 23 and 31. On Dutch interest in Mughal art, see Sanjay Subrahmanyam, *Europe's India: Words, People, Empires, 1500–1800* (Harvard University Press, 2017), pp. 34–6.

4 On early European traders in China, see Jonathan D. Spence, *The Search for Modern China* (W.W. Norton & Company, 1990), pp.119–21.

5 Donald F. Lach, *Asia in the Making of Europe*, vol. III: *A Century of Advance* (University of Chicago Press, 1965), p. 1583.

6 Ibid., pp. 1588–1618 and 1709–10.

7 John Ovington, *An Essay Upon the Nature and Qualities of Tea* (R. Roberts, 1699).

8 Ellis et al., op. cit., pp. 76–88.

9 Helen Clifford, *Chinese Wallpaper: An Elusive Element in the British Country House* (2014): https://blogs.ucl.ac.uk/eicah/chinese-wallpaper-case-study/.

10 Raymond Dawson, *The Chinese Chameleon* (Oxford University Press, 1967), pp. 110–11; Michael Keevak, *Becoming Yellow: A Short History of Racial Thinking* (Princeton University Press, 2011), p. 66.

11 See Richard J. Blackwell, *Galileo, Bellarmine and the Bible* (University of Notre Dame Press, 1991).

12 See Steven Shapin and Simon Schaffer, *Leviathan and the Air-Pump: Hobbes, Boyle, and the Experimental Life* (Princeton University Press, 1989).

13 See Chapter 2 in Dorinda Outram, *The Enlightenment* (Cambridge University Press, 2019). The words of Robert South are reproduced in Nicholas Spencer, *Magisteria: The Entangled Histories of Science and Religion* (Oneworld, 2023), p. 173.

14 Quoted in François Rigolot, 'Curiosity, Contingency and Cultural Diversity: Montaigne's Readings at the Vatican Library', *Renaissance Quarterly* 64/3 (2011), 857.

15 'Each man' is quoted in Franklin Perkins, *Leibniz and China: A Commerce of Light* (Cambridge University Press, 2004), p. 11.

16 Miranda Fricker, 'Styles of Moral Relativism: A Critical Family Tree', in Roger Crisp (ed.), *The Oxford Handbook of the History of Ethics* (Oxford University Press, 2013), p. 796.

17 Gregory M. Reihman, 'Malebranche and Chinese Philosophy: A Reconsideration', *British Journal for the History of Philosophy* 21/2 (2013), 266.

18 Alexander J. B. Hampton, 'An English Source of German Romanticism', *Heythrop Journal* 58/3 (2017), 420.

19 Perkins, op. cit., p. 21.

20 Gregory M. Reihman, 'Malebranche's Influence on Leibniz's Writings on China', *Philosophy East & West* 65/3 (2015), 847.

21 Reihman, 'Malebranche's Influence', 852–4; Gregory M. Reihman, 'Constructing Confucius: Western Philosophical Interpretations of Confucianism from Malebranche to Hegel': doctoral thesis submitted to the University of Texas at Austin (2001).

22 On critics of Malebranche, see ibid. and Reihman, 'Malebranche's Influence'.

23 On Leibniz and China, see David E. Mungello, 'Leibniz's Interpretation of Neo-Confucianism', *Philosophy East & West* 21/1 (1971), 20; Perkins, op. cit.

24 Johnson Kent Wright, 'Voltaire and the *Lettres Philosophiques*', in Christopher Nadon (ed.), *Enlightenment and Secularism: Essays on the Mobilization of Reason* (Lexington Books/Fortress Academic, 2013).

25 '[I]nnate ideas' is quoted in John Bennett Shank, *The Newton Wars and the Beginning of the French Enlightenment* (University of Chicago Press, 2008), p. 313. '[New] world' is quoted in Ian Davidson, *Voltaire: A Life* (Profile Books, 2012).

26 See Outram, op. cit., Chapter 9.

27 Quoted in Raymond Dawson, *The Chinese Chameleon* (Oxford University Press, 1967), p. 54.

28 Quoted in Colin Mackerass, *Western Images of China* (Oxford University Press, 1999), p. 30.

29 Quoted in David Allen Harvey, *The French Enlightenment and Its Others* (Palgrave MacMillan, 2012), p. 42.

30 Quoted in ibid., pp. 48–9.

31 Ibid., p. 57; Edwin J. Van Kley, 'Europe's "Discovery" of China and the Writing of World History', *American Historical* Review 76/2 (1971), 361–3.

32 Quoted in ibid., 374.

33 Dawson, op. cit., pp. 118–19.

34 Harvey, op. cit., p. 54.

35 Ibid., pp. 44–5.

36 Quoted in Dawson, op. cit., p. 112.

37 Reproduced in Caroline Frank, *Objectifying China, Imagining America: Chinese Commodities in Early America* (University of Chicago Press, 2011), p. 73.

38 Harvey, op. cit., pp. 62–3.

39 Lach, vol. III: *A Century of Advance*, pp. 1568–9 and 1621–49.

40 Dawson, op. cit., p. 44; Mackerass, op. cit., p. 29.

41 Harvey, pp. 60–64.

42 Quoted in Rolf J. Goebel, 'China as an Embalmed Mummy: Herder's Orientalist Poetics', *South Atlantic Review* 60/1 (1995), 116.

43 Quoted in Kate March, *India in the French Imagination: Peripheral Voices, 1754–1815* (Routledge, 2016), p. 119.

Chapter 10: *Calcutta*

1 On Calcutta's layout, see William Dalrymple, *The Anarchy: The Relentless Rise of the East India Company* (Bloomsbury, 2019); Michael J. Franklin, *Orientalist Jones: Sir William Jones, Poet, Lawyer and Linguist, 1746–1794* (Oxford University Press, 2011), pp. 9–10.

2 Letter LXV (Calcutta, June 1768), in Jemima Kindersley, *Letters from the Island of Teneriffe, Brazil, the Cape of Good Hope and the East Indies* (J. Nourse, 1777). The population estimate comes from Dalrymple, op. cit., p. 70.

3 Letter LXV (Calcutta, June 1768) in Kindersley, op. cit.

4 Letters LXV (Calcutta, June 1768), XXI (Calcutta, April 1766) and LXVII (Calcutta, September 1768) in ibid.

5 Dalrymple, op. cit., p. 75.

6 'Pucker fever' is in Letter XXI (Calcutta, April 1766), in Kindersley, op. cit. The two-thirds figure is given in Dalrymple, op. cit., p. 76.

7 Letter LXVII (Calcutta, September 1768), in Kindersley, op. cit.

8 See Dalrymple, op. cit., pp. 50–52. On Asian agency in the rise of the British Empire, see David Veevers, *The Origins of the British Empire in Asia, 1600–1750* (Cambridge University Press, 2020).

9 Farhat Hasan, 'Indigenous Co-operation and the Birth of a Colonial City – Calcutta, *c.* 1698–1750', *Modern Asian Studies* 26/1 (1992), 66–8; Dalrymple, op. cit., p. 25.

10 Letters XL (Allahabad, August 1767), XLI (Allahabad, August 1767), XLIII (Allahabad, August 1767) and XLV (Allahabad, August 1767), in Kindersley, op. cit.

11 Letters XLV (Allahabad, August 1767) and XLVIII (Allahabad, September 1767), in Kindersley, op. cit.; Dalrymple, op. cit., p. 25.

12 Letter XLIII (Allahabad, August 1767), in Kindersley, op. cit.

13 Letters XXX (Allahabad, July 1767), XXXIII (Allahabad, July 1767) and XXXIV (Allahabad, July 1767), in ibid.

14 Letter XXXIV (Allahabad, July 1767), in ibid.

15 Letter XXXI (Allahabad, July 1767), in ibid.

16 Franklin, op. cit., pp. 206–16; Garland Cannon, *The Life and Mind of Oriental Jones: Sir William Jones, the Father of Modern Linguistics* (Cambridge University Press, 1991), pp. 200–208; Dalrymple, op. cit., p. 238.

17 Jessica Patterson, 'Enlightenment and Empire, Mughals and Marathas: The Religious History of India in the Work of East India Company Servant, Alexander Dow', *History of European Ideas* 45/7 (2019).

18 See Cannon, op. cit., pp. 5–48; Franklin, op. cit., pp. 1–2.

19 William Jones, 'Essay on the Poetry of Eastern Nations (1777)', in Lord Teignmouth (ed.), *The Works of Sir William Jones*, vol. 10 (Cambridge University Press, 2013), p. 359.

20 Quoted in Franklin, op. cit., pp. 3–4. See also Cannon, op. cit., p. 194.

21 Franklin, op. cit.

22 Ibid., pp. 22–8 and 206–40.

23 Ibid., pp. 206, 210, 240; Cannon, op. cit., pp. 205–6.

24 Jan Peter Schouten, *The European Encounter with Hinduism in India* (Brill, 2020), pp. 65–70.

25 Ibid., p. 82.

26 Wilhelm Halbfass, *India and Europe: An Essay in Understanding* (State University of New York Press, 1988), p. 48.

27 Ibid., p. 67.

28 Franklin, op. cit., p. 240.

29 Cannon, op. cit., pp. 285–97.

30 Franklin, op. cit., p. 35.

31 Ibid., pp. 36–7; Cannon, op. cit., p. 245.

32 Robert S. P. Beekes (revised and corrected by Michiel de Vaan), *Comparative Indo-European Linguistics: An Introduction* (John Benjamins, 2011), p. 12.

33 Cannon, op. cit., p. 244.

34 Franklin, op. cit., pp. 38 and 224–8.

35 Cannon, op. cit., pp. 318–39.

36 P. J. Marshall (ed.), *The British Discovery of Hinduism in the Eighteenth Century* (Cambridge University Press, 1970), p. 36.

37 William Jones, 'On the Gods of Greece, Italy and India', reproduced in ibid., pp. 200–222.

38 Cannon, op. cit., pp. 246–7.

39 William Jones, 'On the Hindus', in Marshall (ed.), op. cit., p. 254.

40 In Lord Teignmouth (ed.), *The Works of Sir William Jones*, vol. 13 (Cambridge University Press, 2013), pp. 301–9.

41 Franklin, op. cit., pp. 216–27.

42 Cannon, op. cit., p. 239.

43 'Indian Shakespeare' is quoted in Franklin, op. cit., p. 253.

44 Sanjay Subrahmanyam, *Europe's India: Words, People, Empires, 1500–1800* (Harvard University Press, 2017), p. 21.

45 Richard King, 'Orientalism and the Modern Myth of "Hinduism"', *Numen* 46/2 (1999), p. 162.

46 On Hinduism, see ibid.; Robert Eric Frykenberg, 'The Emergence of Modern "Hinduism" as a Concept and as an Institution: A Reappraisal with Special Reference to South India', in Gunther Sontheimer and Hermann Kulke (eds.), *Hinduism Reconsidered* (Manohar, 1989); Arvind Sharma, 'On Hindu, Hindustan, Hinduism and Hindutva', *Numen* 49/1 (2002).

47 Cannon, op. cit., pp. 268–9; Franklin, op. cit., pp. 212–13.

48 William Jones' introduction to *A Hymn to Náráyena*, in Lord Teign-mouth (ed.), *The Works of Sir William Jones*, vol. 13 (Cambridge University Press, 2013), pp. 302–5. Emphases on 'energy' and 'work' appear in the original.

49 Ibid., p. 309.

50 William Jones, 'On the Mystical Poetry of the Persians and Hindus', in Lord Teignmouth (ed.), *The Works of Sir William Jones*, vol. 4 (Cambridge University Press, 2013), p. 216.

51 Ibid., pp. 219–20.

52 Marshall, op. cit., p. 5.

53 Warren Hastings, 'Letter to Nathaniel Smith', in ibid., pp. 188–9.

54 Charles Wilkins, *The Bhagvat–Geeta, or Dialogues of Kreeshna and Arjoon; in Eighteen Lectures with Notes* (C. Nourse, 1785).

55 Hastings noted the likelihood of Westerners struggling with practical difficulties like these in his prefatory letter to Wilkins' translation. See Hastings, op. cit.

56 Franklin, op. cit., p. 233; Simon Ferris, *New Illustrated Lives of Great Composers: Ludwig van Beethoven* (Omnibus Press, 2018).

57 Hastings, op. cit., p. 187. On Hastings' view of the potential of Indian literature, see Joshua Ehrlich, *The East India Company and the Politics of Knowledge* (Cambridge University Press, 2023), Chapter 1.

58 Alexander Dow was amongst the first to make this case. See Patterson, op. cit., 983–4.

Chapter 11: Germany's Oriental Renaissance

1 Quoted in Azade Seyhan, 'What is Romanticism and Where Did It Come from?', Nicholas Saul (ed.), *The Cambridge Companion to German Romanticism* (Cambridge University Press, 2009), p. 6.

2 Quoted in E. Backhouse and J. O. P. Bland, *Annals and Memoirs of the Court of Peking* (William Heinemann, 1914), pp. 322–31.

3 Sarah Schneewind, 'Clean Politics: Race and Class, Imperialism and Nationalism, Etiquette and Consumption in the Chinese and American

Revolutions', *The Asia-Pacific Journal* 7/45 (2009); Colin Mackerass, *Western Images of China* (Oxford University Press, 1999), pp. 40–41; Jonathan D. Spence, *The Search for Modern China* (W. W. Norton & Company, 1990), p. 121.

4 Estimate of opium addiction in China comes from Spence, op. cit., p. 129.

5 Alexander J. B. Hampton, 'An English Source of German Romanticism: Herder's Cudworth Inspired Revision of Spinoza', *Heythrop Journal* 58/3 (2017), 421; Elías Palti, 'The "Metaphor of Life": Herder's Philosophy of History and Uneven Developments in Late Eighteenth-Century Natural Sciences', *History & Theory* 38/3 (1999), 332.

6 Hamilton, op. cit., 426.

7 Johann Gottfried Herder, quoted in Wilhelm Halbfass, *India and Europe: An Essay in Understanding* (State University of New York Press, 1988), p. 70.

8 Herder, quoted in ibid, pp. 70–71.

9 See Michael J. Franklin, *Orientalist Jones: Sir William Jones, Poet, Lawyer and Linguist, 1746–1794* (Oxford University Press, 2011), pp. 252–60.

10 Stephen Cross, *Schopenhauer's Encounter with Indian Thought: Representation and Will and Their Indian Parallels* (University of Hawaii Press, 2013), p. 21.

11 Quoted in Franklin, op. cit., p. 262.

12 Seyhan, op. cit., p. 13; Halbfass, op. cit., p. 81.

13 Quoted in Seyhan, p. 17.

14 Ibid, p. 17; Michael Dusche, 'Friedrich Schlegel's Writings on India', in James Hodkinson *et al.* (eds.), *Deploying Orientalism in Culture and History* (Cambridge University Press, 2013), p. 37; Halbfass, op. cit., p. 81.

15 Dusche, op. cit., pp. 32–4.

16 Robert Cowan, *The Indo-German Identification* (Cambridge University Press, 2010), p. 113.

17 Dusche, op. cit., p. 38.

18 Dusche, op. cit., pp. 40–44.

19 Halbfass, op. cit., p. 75; Dusche, op. cit., p. 35; Cowan, op. cit., p. 107; Cross, op. cit., p. 12.

20 '[A]n opinion' is quoted in Cowan, op. cit., p. 120. See also ibid., pp. 116–17; Halbfass, op. cit., pp. 76–7.

21 The French writer Maurice Blanchot, commenting in 1993. Reproduced in Paolo Diego Bubbio and Paul Redding (eds.), *Religion after Kant: God and Culture in the Idealist Era* (Cambridge Scholars Press, 2012), p. 27.

22 Quoted in Halbfass, op. cit., p. 101.

23 This is Schelling's own metaphor. See Andrew Bowie, *Aesthetics and Subjectivity: From Kant to Nietzsche* (Manchester University Press, 2003), p. 104.

24 Quoted in Halbfass, op. cit., p. 102.

25 See Louis Dupre, 'The Role of Mythology in Schelling's Late Philosophy', *The Journal of Religion* 87/1 (2007).

26 On Hegel and India, see Halbfass, op. cit., pp. 85–105.

27 Schopenhauer delivered this verdict when commenting on Schlegel's conversion to Catholicism. Quoted in Cross, op. cit., p. 12.

28 Ibid., p. 15.

29 Bryan Magee, *The Philosophy of Schopenhauer* (Clarendon Press, 1997), p. 12.

30 Cross, op. cit., pp. 20–22.

31 Bart Vandenabeele, *A Companion to Schopenhauer* (Wiley, 2015), p. 267.

32 See Cross, op. cit., pp. 29–35.

33 Quoted in Cross, op. cit., p. 115. See also pp. 52–4.

34 Quoted in Urs App, 'Schopenhauer and the Orient', in Robert L. Wicks (ed.), *The Oxford Handbook of Schopenhauer* (Oxford University Press, 2020), p. 93.

35 Cross, op. cit., p. 96.

36 Quoted in Halbfass, op. cit., p. 87. See also Cross, op. cit., pp. 112–13.

37 Magee, op. cit., pp. 20 and 24.

38 Halbfass, op. cit., p. 110.

39 See Magee, op. cit., pp. 199–200; Cross, op. cit., pp. 209–10.

40 Cross, op. cit., p. 38.

41 App, op. cit., p. 914.

42 Quoted in ibid., p. 101.

43 Quoted in ibid., pp. 94–5.

44 Quoted in Cross, op. cit., p. 13.

45 Quoted in Christopher Ryan, *Schopenhauer's Philosophy of Religion: The Death of God and the Oriental Renaissance* (Peeters, 2010), p. 142.

Chapter 12: Intuiting India: From the Vile to the Vast

1 On the birthday party, and the chant, see Friedrich Schleiermacher (trans. Frederica Rowan), *The Life of Friedrich Schleiermacher: As Unfolded in His Autobiography and Letters*, vol. 1 (Smith, Elder & Co, 1860), p. 163; Steven R. Jungkeit, *Spaces of Modern Theology: Geography and Power in Schleiermacher's World* (Palgrave MacMillan, 2012), pp. 41–2.

2 On the size of the East India Company army at this point, see William Dalrymple, *The Anarchy: The Relentless Rise of the East India Company* (Bloomsbury, 2019).

3 Friedrich Schleiermacher (ed. Richard Crouter), *On Religion: Speeches to Its Cultured Despisers* (Cambridge University Press, 1996), pp. 23–5 and 99.

4 Ibid., p. 49.

5 Quoted in Diarmaid MacCulloch, *A History of Christianity: The First Three Thousand Years* (Penguin, 2010), p. 832.

6 Schleiermacher, op. cit., p. 53.

7 MacCulloch, op. cit., p. 859.

8 Robert Williams, 'Schleiermacher and Feuerbach on the Intentionality of Religious Consciousness', *The Journal of Religion* 53/4 (1973).

9 Lynn Zastoupil, *Rammohun Roy and the Making of Victorian Britain* (Palgrave Macmillan, 2010), p. 25; Noel Salmond, *Hindu Iconoclasts: Rammohun Roy, Dayananda Saraswati, and Nineteenth-Century Polemics against Idolatry* (Wilfrid Laurier University Press, 2006), pp. 48–50.

10 Ibid., p. 48; Kenneth W. Jones, *Socio-Religious Reform Movements in British India* (Cambridge University Press, 1994), pp. 31–2.

11 Salmond, op. cit., p. 45.

12 Ram Mohan Roy, 'Introduction', *Translation of the Moonduk Opunishud of the Uthurvu-Ved* (Times Press, 1819); Salmond, op. cit., p. 59.

13 Roy, 'Introduction', op. cit.

14 Roy, op. cit., pp. 4–5.

15 Zastoupil, *Rammohun Roy and the Making of Victorian Britain*, p. 28.

16 Salmond, op. cit., pp. 51–61.

17 Ibid., p. 46; Lynn Zastoupil, 'Defining Christians, Making Britons: Rammohun Roy and the Unitarians', *Victorian Studies* 44/2 (2002), 226;

Rammohan Roy, *The Precepts of Jesus* (The Unitarian Society, 1824), p. 328.

18 Zastoupil, *Rammohun Roy and the Making of Victorian Britain*, p. 73. Roy had advised against government action to abolish *sati*, but supported the governor-general, nevertheless, once he had gone ahead with a ban.

19 Salmond, op. cit., p. 45.

20 David J. Neumann, 'The Father of Modern India and the Son of God: Rammohun Roy's Jesus Christ', *Journal of Religious History* 45/3 (2021), 372.

21 '[N]ation' is Salmond, op. cit., p. 47. On political radicals of this era, see C. A. Bayly, 'Rammohun Roy and the Advent of Constitutional Liberalism in India, 1800–30', *Modern Intellectual History* 4/1 (2007).

22 Neumann, op. cit., 388.

23 Salmond, op. cit., p. 47.

24 Roy's encounter with Owen is reported in Mary Carpenter, *The Last Days in England of Rajah Rammohun Roy* (R. C. Lepage, 1866), p. 111.

25 Zastoupil, *Rammohun Roy and the Making of Victorian Britain*, pp. 1–3.

26 Carpenter, op. cit., pp. 126–32.

27 Timothy Larsen, *A People of One Book: The Bible and the Victorians* (Oxford University Press, 2011), p. 166.

28 Carpenter, op. cit., pp. 140–2.

29 Carol Bolton, *Writing the Empire: Robert Southey and Romantic Colonialism* (Taylor & Francis, 2007), p. 18.

30 Samuel Taylor Coleridge, 'Consciones Ad Populum', in Samuel Taylor Coleridge (eds. Lewis Patton and Peter Mann), *The Collected Works of Samuel Taylor Coleridge*, vol. I (Princeton University Press, 1971), p. 58.

31 Samuel Taylor Coleridge, 'Lectures on Revealed Religion, Its Corruptions, and Political Views', in ibid., p. 226.

32 Quoted in Bolton, op. cit., pp. 28–9.

33 'Envy, Rapine, Government, and Priesthoood' is Coleridge, 'Lectures on Revealed Religion', in *The Collected Works of Samuel Taylor Coleridge*, vol. I, p. 227. '[I]nspired Philanthropist' is Coleridge, 'Lecture on the Slave-Trade', in ibid., p. 248.

34 Simon Schama, *A History of Britain*, vol. III: *The Fate of Empire, 1776–2000* (Bodley Head, 2009).

35 Anne Janowitz, 'Rebellion, Revolution, Reform: The Transit of the Intellectuals', in *The Cambridge History of English Romantic Literature* (Cambridge University Press, 2009), pp. 359–61.

36 Quoted in Alison Hickey, ' "Coleridge, Southey and Co.": Collaboration and Authority', *Studies in Romanticism* 37/3 (1998), 312.

37 Carol Bolton, 'Debating India: Southey and *The Curse of Kehama*', in Claire Lamont and Michael Rossington (eds.), *Romanticism's Debatable Lands* (Palgrave MacMillan, 2007), pp. 198 and 207.

38 Edward Meachen, 'History and Transcendence in Robert Southey's Epic Poems', *Studies in English Literature, 1500–1900* 19/4 (1979), 595; Nigel Leask, '*Kubla Khan* and Orientalism: The Road to Xanadu Revisited', *Romanticism* (Edinburgh) 4/1 (1998); Stuart Andrews, *Robert Southey: History, Politics, Religion* (Palgrave MacMillan, 2011), pp. 39–40.

39 Claudius Buchanan, quoted in Andrew Rudd, 'India as Gothic Horror: Maturin's *Melmoth the Wanderer* and Images of Juggernaut in Early Nineteenth Century Missionary Writing,' in Lawrence J. Trudeau (ed.), *Nineteenth Century Literature Criticism* 347 (2018).

40 Reproduced in *The Complete Poetical Works of Robert Southey* (D. Appleton & Company, 1846).

41 Bolton, *Writing the Empire*, p. 221.

42 Quoted in Krishna Dutta, *Calcutta: A Cultural and Literary History* (Signal, 2003), p. 198.

43 Michael Dusche, 'Friedrich Schlegel's Writings on India', in James Hodkinson *et al.* (eds.), *Deploying Orientalism in Culture and History* (Cambridge University Press, 2013), p. 31.

44 Reproduced in *The Poetical Works of Samuel T. Coleridge* (Ward, Lock & Co, 1880), pp. 91–2.

45 Jeff Strabone, *Poetry and British Nationalisms in the Bardic Eighteenth Century: Imagined Antiquities* (Palgrave MacMillan, 2018), p. 249; Peter Vassallo, 'Voyaging into the "Vast" ', *Romanticism* (Edinburgh) 24/1 (2018), 80.

46 See Deirdre Coleman, 'The "Dark Tide of Time": Coleridge and William Hodges' India', in David Vallins *et al.* (eds.), *Coleridge, Romanticism and the Orient: Cultural Negotiations* (Bloomsbury, 2014).

47 Vassallo, op. cit., p. 80.

48 *The Poetical Works of Samuel T. Coleridge*, pp. 91–2.

49 Reproduced in Ernest Hartley Coleridge (ed.), *Letters of Samuel Taylor Coleridge* (Houghton, Mifflin and Company, 1895), p. 228.

50 *The Poetical Works of Samuel T. Coleridge*, pp. 91–2.

51 Reproduced in Coleridge (ed.), *Letters*, pp. 228–9.

52 John Drew, *India and the Romantic Imagination* (Oxford University Press, 1987), p. 193; Natalie Tal Harries, ' "The One Life Within Us and Abroad": Coleridge and Hinduism', in David Vallins *et al.* (eds.), op cit, pp. 114–5. Coleman, op. cit., points out that Coleridge may also have encountered an illustration showing Vishnu on the ocean in Thomas Maurice's *The History of Hindostan*, vol 1 (1795).

53 See Andrew Warren, 'Coleridge, Orient, Philosophy', in ibid.

54 Ibid.; Drew, op. cit., pp. 186–7.

55 Quoted in Coleman, op. cit, pp. 53–4.

56 On Coleridge's outlook here, see Rosemary Ashton, *The Life of Samuel Taylor Coleridge: A Critical Biography* (Wiley-Blackwell, 1995), p. 257.

57 See ibid., pp. 174, 206, 258.

58 Ibid., p. 257.

59 For India as gothic horror, see Rudd, op. cit.

60 Phyllis Cole, 'A Legacy of Revolt, 1803–1821', in Jean McClure Mudge (ed.), *Mr Emerson's Revolution* (Open Book, 2015), pp. 24–36.

61 Ralph Waldo Emerson (ed. Kenneth Walter Cameron), *Indian Superstition* (Cayuga Press, 1954).

62 Alan Hodder, 'Asia in Emerson and Emerson in Asia', in Mudge (ed.), op. cit., p. 378.

63 Quoted in Arthur Versluis, *American Transcendentalism and Asian Religions* (Oxford University Press, 1994), p. 53.

64 See Alan D. Hodder, 'Emerson, Rammohan Roy, and the Unitarians', *Studies in the American Renaissance* (1988), 142; Versluis, op. cit., p. 53.

65 Hodder, 'Emerson, Rammohan Roy, and the Unitarians', 143–4; Hodder, 'Asia in Emerson and Emerson in Asia', p. 378; Zastoupil, *Rammohun Roy and the Making of Victorian Britain*, pp. 49–50.

66 See Wesley T. Mott, 'Becoming an American "Adam", 1822–1835', in Mudge (ed.), op. cit., pp. 60–69.

67 Versluis, op. cit., p. 54.

68 Ralph Waldo Emerson, 'Address', in *Emerson's Complete Works*, vol. 1 (Houghton, Mifflin and Company, 1888).

69 Emerson, 'Address', in ibid.

70 From Ralph Waldo Emerson, 'Nature', reproduced in Jay Parini (ed.), *The Oxford Encyclopedia of American Literature* (Oxford University Press, 2004), p. 486.

71 Ralph Waldo Emerson, 'The Over-Soul', in *Emerson's Complete Works*, vol. 1 (Houghton, Mifflin and Company, 1888).

72 Ralph Waldo Emerson, 'Self-Reliance', in *Emerson's Complete Works*, vol. 2 (Houghton, Mifflin and Company, 1876).

73 Quoted in Hodder, 'Asia in Emerson and Emerson in Asia', p. 386.

74 Ibid., pp. 380–81; David M. Robinson, 'The "New Thinking": Nature, Self, and Society, 1836–1850', in Mudge (ed.), op. cit., p. 99.

75 Hodder, 'Asia in Emerson and Emerson in Asia', p. 382.

76 Ralph Waldo Emerson, 'Brahma', *Atlantic Monthly* vol. 1 (1857), p. 48.

77 Samuel Taylor Coleridge, 'Human Life: On the Denial of Immortality', in *Sibylline Leaves: A Collection of Poems* (Rest Fenner, 1817).

Chapter 13: The Light of Asia

1 Edwin Arnold, 'The Light of Asia', in *Poetical Works of Edwin Arnold* (John B. Alden, 1883), pp. 21–2.

2 Diarmaid MacCulloch, *A History of Christianity: The First Three Thousand Years* (Penguin, 2010), pp. 856–61.

3 Gary B. Ferngren, 'Christianity and Science', in James W. Haag *et al.* (eds.), *The Routledge Companion to Religion and Science* (Routledge, 2013), p. 64.

4 Arnold, ibid., p. 22.

5 '[S]cribbled on shirt-cuffs' comes from Brooks Wright, *Interpreter of Buddhism to the West: Sir Edwin Arnold* (Bookman Associates, 1957), p. 71.

6 Philip C. Almond, *The British Discovery of Buddhism* (Cambridge University Press, 1988), pp. 15–62.

7 Sebastian Lecourt, 'Idylls of the Buddh": Buddhist Modernism and Victorian Poetics in Colonial Ceylon', *PMLA* 131/3 (2016), p. 670; Almond, op. cit., pp. 9–12; J. J. Clarke, *Oriental Enlightenment: The Encounter between Asian and Western Thought* (Routledge, 1997), pp. 74–5.

8 Lecourt, op. cit., p. 670.

9 Ibid., p. 670; Judith Snodgrass, *Presenting Buddhism to the West: Orientalism, Occidentalism, and the Columbian Exposition* (University of North Carolina Press, 2003), pp. 94–9.

10 The point about Buddhism's 'idolatry' is in Patrick Grant, *Buddhism and Ethnic Conflict in Sri Lanka* (SUNY Press, 2009), pp. 54–5.

11 David McMahan, *The Making of Buddhist Modernism* (Oxford University Press, 2008), pp. 52–3.

12 Max Müller, *Lectures on the Science of Religion* (Scribner, Armstrong & Co, 1874), pp. 12–13.

13 Almond, op. cit., p. 35.

14 J. Jeffrey Franklin, 'The Life of the Buddha in Victorian England', ELH 72/4 (2005), 941; Douglas Ober, 'Translating the Buddha: Edwin Arnold's *Light of Asia* and Its Indian Publics', *Humanities* 10/1 (2021), 1–2.

15 Snodgrass, op. cit., p. 89; Almond, op. cit., p. 72.

16 Amongst the earliest and most influential makers of this case was the Unitarian minister James Freeman Clarke, in a piece for *The Atlantic*: 'Buddhism; Or, the Protestantism of the East' (June 1869).

17 Franklin, op. cit., 943.

18 Sales estimate and *Huckleberry Finn* comparison given in Wright, op. cit., p. 75.

19 Arnold, op. cit., p. 13.

20 On Arnold's professional background, see Wright, op. cit., p. 88; Ober, op. cit., 3.

21 Arnold, op. cit., pp. 12–13.

22 Franklin, op. cit., 964.

23 Arnold, op. cit., p. 36.

24 Arnold, op. cit., pp. 148–57.

25 C. Clausen, 'Sir Edwin Arnold's *Light of Asia* and Its Reception, *Literature East and West* 17 (1973), 56.

26 Arnold, op. cit., p. 153.

27 Ober, op. cit., 1–2; Wright, op. cit., p. 83.

28 Clausen, op. cit., 14.

29 William Cleaver Wilkinson, *Edwin Arnold as Poetizer and as Paganizer* (Funk & Wagnalls, 1884), p. 91.

30 Clausen, op. cit., 31–5; Franklin, op. cit.; Almond, op. cit. pp. 126–7.

31 Samuel Kellogg, *The Light of Asia and the Light of the World* (MacMillan, 1885), pp. 176–87.

32 Quoted in Almond, op. cit., pp. 84–5.

33 See ibid., pp. 88–90.

34 Wilkinson, op. cit., p. 93.

35 Ibid., p. 128.

36 Ibid., pp. 83–4.

37 Ibid., pp. 8–16.

38 Clausen, op. cit., 35.

39 Edwin Arnold, *Seas and Lands* (Longmans Green, 1891), p. 163.

40 Isabella Bird, *Unbeaten Tracks in Japan* (Dover Publications, 2005), pp. 22–5 and 45.

41 Estimated in Jonathan D. Spence, *The Search for Modern China* (W. W. Norton & Company, 1990), p. 149.

42 Wright, op. cit., p. 141.

43 Lafcadio Hearn, *Glimpses of Unfamiliar Japan*, vol. 1 (H. O. Houghton and Company, 1894), p. 9.

44 Edwin Arnold, *Seas and Lands* (Longmans Green, 1891), pp. 494–506.

45 Christopher Harding, *Japan Story: In Search of a Nation, 1850–the Present* (Allen Lane, Penguin Books, 2018), pp. 106–7.

46 Ibid., pp. 96–101.

47 On Arnold's life in Japan, see Wright, op. cit.

48 Clausen, op. cit., 43–4.

49 Ibid., 25.

Chapter 14: Experiments in Truth

1 Annie Wood Besant, *Annie Besant: An Autobiography* (T. Fisher Unwin, 1893), pp. 13, 24–5, 52–7 and 89.

2 Ibid., pp. 117, 136, 147, 159 and 167–8.

3 Ibid., pp. 199–207.

4 Ibid., p. 330.

5 On Besant's pioneering enrolment, see Janet Oppenheim, 'The Odyssey of Annie Besant', *History Today* (September, 1989), p. 14.

6 Annie Wood Besant, *Why I Became a Theosophist* (Freethought, 1889), pp. 8–11.

7 Paola Bertucci, 'Sparks in the Dark: The Attraction of Electricity in the Eighteenth Century', *Endeavour* 31/3 (2007), 88–93; Daniel Cohen, 'Jan 18, 1803: Giovanni Aldini Attempts to Reanimate the Dead', at Odd Salon.com, see https://oddsalon.com/jan-18-1803-giovanni-aldini-attempts-to-reanimate-the-dead/, accessed 13 June 2023.

8 Wouter J. Hanegraaff, *Western Esotericism: A Guide for the Perplexed* (Bloomsbury, 2013), pp. 175–87.

9 Ibid., p. 220; Joy Dixon, *Divine Feminine: Theosophy and Feminism in England* (Johns Hopkins University Press, 2001), p. 26.

10 Dixon, op. cit., p. 17.

11 On Blavatsky's writings, see Hanegraaff, op. cit., pp. 221–2; Dixon, op. cit., p. 47; Richard M. Eaton, *The Lotus and the Lion: Essays on India's Sanskritic and Persianate Worlds* (Primus Books, 2022), pp. 67–8.

12 Hanegraaff, op. cit., pp. 213–14.

13 Besant, *Annie Besant: An Autobiography*, p. 341. See also Arthur H. Nethercot, *The First Five Lives of Annie Besant* (University of Chicago Press, 1960), Chapter 4: 'Building the Kingdom'; Dixon, op. cit., pp. 21–5.

14 Nethercot, p. 286.

15 Besant, *Annie Besant: An Autobiography*, p. 346.

16 Nethercot, p. 283.

17 Besant, *Why I Became a Theosophist*, pp. 21 and 27; Besant, *Annie Besant: An Autobiography*, pp. 345–6.

18 Nethercot, p. 305.

19 Besant, *Annie Besant: An Autobiography*, pp. 346–7.

20 M. K. Gandhi, *The Story of My Experiments with Truth* (Navajivan Press, 1927), pp. 144 and 164–6.

21 Martin Bevir, 'Theosophy and the Origins of the Indian National Congress', *International Journal of Hindus Studies* 7 (2003), pp. 106–10.

22 Nethercot, p. 360.

23 Dixon, op. cit., p. 50.

24 Gandhi, op. cit., p. 169.

25 Dadabhai Naoroji, *Poverty and Un-British Rule in India* (Swan Sonnen-schein & Co, 1901).

26 W. J. Hanegraaff, 'Western Esotericism and the Orient in the First The-osophical Society', in H. M. Krämer and J. Strube (eds.), *Theosophy across Boundaries* (SUNY Press, 2020), p. 30.

27 Max Müller, 'The Parliament of Religions in Chicago, 1893', 1894, in Jon R. Stone, *The Essential Max Müller: On Language, Mythology and Religion* (Palgrave MacMillan, 2002), pp. 343–5.

28 Stefanie Syman, *The Subtle Body: The Story of Yoga in America* (Farrar, Straus and Giroux, 2010), p. 42.

29 Reproduced in John Henry Barrows (ed.), *The World's Parliament of Religions: An Illustrated and Popular Story of the World's First Parliament of Religions, Held in Chicago in Connection with the Columbian Exposition of 1893* (Chicago: The Parliament Publishing Company, 1893), p. 444.

30 Testimony from another of the Japanese delegates to the WPR, reported in Judith Snodgrass, *Presenting Buddhism to the West: Orientalism, Occidentalism, and the Columbian Exposition* (University of North Carolina Press, 2003), p. 191.

31 In Barrows, op. cit., pp. 448–50.

32 Snodgrass, p. 183.

33 'The greatest art ... fine, intelligent, mobile face ... fascinating personality ... the little sarcasms thrown into his discourses are as keen as a rapier ... his courtesy is unfailing, for these thrusts are never pointed so directly at our customs as to be rude' all feature in *Critic* (7 October 1893); 'white teeth ... well-chiselled lips' in *Boston Evening Transcript* (30 September 1893). See *The Complete Works of Swami Vivekānanda*, vol. 3 (Advaita Ashrama, 1946). The Napoleon comparison is reported in Syman, op. cit., p. 44.

34 Swami Vivekānanda, 'Paper on Hinduism', 19 September 1893, in *The Complete Works of Swami Vivekānanda*, vol. 1 (Advaita Ashrama, 1957).

35 Ibid.

36 Ibid.

37 On Vivekananda's short time teaching yoga in the United States, see Syman, op. cit.

38 Quoted in ibid., p. 54.

39 Ibid., pp. 55–6.

40 Shaku Sōen, 'The Law of Cause and Effect, As Taught by Buddha', in Barrows, op. cit., pp. 829–31. See also Larry Fader, 'Zen in the West: Historical and Philosophical Implications of the 1893 Chicago World's Parliament of Religions', *The Eastern Buddhist* 15/1 (1982), 125–6.

41 Okakura Kakuzō, *The Ideals of the East with Special Reference to the Art of Japan* (London, 1903), p. 5.

42 Ibid., p. 5. See also Stephen N. Hay, *Asian Ideas of East and West: Tagore and His Critics in Japan, China and India* (Harvard University Press, 1970), pp. 39–40; Partha Mitter, 'Rabindranath Tagore and Okakura Tenshin in Calcutta: The Creation of a Regional Asian Avant-garde Art', in Burcu Dogramaci *et al.* (eds.), *Arrival Cities* (Leuven University Press, 2020).

43 On Okakura and Tagore, see Hay, op. cit., pp. 38–9 and Mitter, op. cit.

44 Sister Nivedita, 'Introduction', in Okakura Kakuzō, *The Ideals of the East with Special Reference to the Art of Japan* (London, 1903). On Okakura and Sister Nivedita, see John Rosenfield, 'Okakura Kakuzō and Margaret Noble (Sister Nivedita): A Brief Episode', *Review of Japanese Culture and Society* 24 (2012); Inaga Shigemi (trans. Kevin Singleton), 'Okakura Kakuzō and India: The Trajectory of Modern National Consciousness and Pan-Asian Ideology across Borders', *Review of Japanese Culture and Society* 24 (2012).

45 Sister Nivedita, Letter 488, *Letters of Sister Nivedita* (ed. Sankari Prasad Basu), vol. 2 (Advaita Ashrama, 1982).

46 John R. McRae, 'Oriental Verities at the American Frontier: The 1893 World's Parliament of Religions and the Thought of Masao Abe', *Buddhist-Christian Studies* vol. 11 (1991), pp. 26–7.

47 Rabindranath Tagore, 'The Message of India to Japan', lecture delivered at the University of Tokyo (University of Tokyo, 1916), pp. 6–10. See also Hay, op. cit., pp. 42–3.

48 Quoted in ibid., p. 107.

49 Annie Wood Besant, *The Future of Indian Politics: A Contribution to the Understanding of Present-Day Problems* (Theosophical Publishing House, 1922), p. 47.

Chapter 15: Two Worlds

1 Reproduced in Alan Watts, *In My Own Way: An Autobiography* (New World Library, 1972), p. 35. For Watts' memories of Rowan Tree Cottage, see ibid., pp. 23–33. On Watts' family, see Monica Furlong, *Zen Effects: The Life of Alan Watts* (Skylight Paths, 2001), pp. 1–4.

2 Watts, op. cit., p. 35.

3 Ibid., pp. 58 and 84; Alan Watts (Joan and Anne Watts, eds.), *The Collected Letters of Alan Watts* (New World Library, 2017), p. xiii.

4 Watts, *In My Own Way*, pp. 7–11, 26 and 37.

5 Ibid., p. 63.

6 Ibid., pp. 7–22.

7 Ibid., pp. 48–53; Furlong, op. cit., p. 27.

8 Watts, *In My Own Way*, pp. 67–9.

9 Furlong, op. cit., p. 35.

10 Lafcadio Hearn, *Glimpses of Unfamiliar Japan*, vol. 1 (H. O. Houghton and Company, 1894), p. 7.

11 Watts, *In My Own Way*, p. 69.

12 On Watts and nirvana, see Furlong, op. cit., p. 35.

13 Christmas Humphreys, *Both Sides of the Circle: The Autobiography of Christmas Humphreys* (George Allen & Unwin, 1978), pp. 31–66.

14 Watts, *In My Own Way*, p. 68.

15 On Arnold's armchair, see Humphreys, op. cit., p. 64.

16 Watts, *In My Own Way*, pp. 73–80.

17 Ibid., p. 71; Furlong, op. cit., pp. 36–9. Watts mentions passing around his reading materials in a letter to his mother and father on 13 March 1932, reproduced in Watts (eds.), *Collected Letters*, pp. 10–11.

18 Watts, *In My Own Way*, p. 80.

19 Furlong, op. cit., p. 40.

20 Ibid., pp. 57–8. On Krishnamurti and his British connections, see Mick Brown, *The Nirvana Express: How the Search for Enlightenment Went West* (C. Hurst & Co., 2023), pp. 57–72.

21 Quoted in Ellen F. Franklin and Peter J. Columbus, 'Jung Watts: Notes on C. G. Jung's Formative Influence on Alan Watts', in Peter J. Columbus (ed.), *The Relevance of Alan Watts in Contemporary Culture* (Routledge, 2021), p. 6.

22 C. G. Jung, 'Commentary', in Richard Wilhelm, *The Secret of the Golden Flower: A Chinese Book of Life* (Taylor & Francis, 2013), p. 82.

23 Watts wrote to Jung on 17 October 1936. Reproduced in Watts (eds.), *Collected Letters*, pp. 12–13.

24 J. J. Clarke, *Jung and Eastern Thought: A Dialogue with the Orient* (Routledge, 1994), pp. 6 and 59.

25 Reported in a letter from Alan Watts to his mother and father [hereafter 'AW to M&F'], 3 January 1940. Reproduced in Watts (eds.), *Collected Letters*, pp. 45–6.

26 See C. G. Jung, 'The Difference between Eastern and Western Thinking', in *Collected Works*, ed. and trans. Gerhard Adler and R. F. C. Hull (Princeton University Press, 1969), vol. XI, pp. 475–93.

27 Santanu Biswas, 'Rabindranath Tagore and Freudian Thought', *International Journal of Psychoanalysis* 84 (2003), 718.

28 Ibid., 722.

29 For overviews of Jung's thinking here, see J. J. Clarke, op. cit. and Joseph Campbell, 'Introduction', in C. G. Jung (ed. Joseph Campbell; trans. R. F. C. Hull), *The Portable Jung* (Penguin Books, 1971).

30 Alan W. Watts, *The Legacy of Asia and Western Man: A Study of the Middle Way* (John Murray, 1937), pp. 20–21 and 157.

31 Clarke, op. cit., p. 98. Martin Buber's interest in Taoism is mentioned in Elizabeth Harper, 'The Early Modern European (Non) Reception of the Zhuangzi Text', in *Journal of East-West Thought* 9 (2019), 34.

32 '[C]entral psychic facts' is in Jung, 'Commentary', in Wilhelm, op. cit., p. 85.

33 Watts made this comment when writing to his publisher on 30 April 1940. Reproduced in Watts (eds.), *Collected Letters*, pp. 51–3.

34 Watts, *The Legacy of Asia*, pp. 18–20.

35 Ibid., p. 80.

36 Ibid., pp. 80–81.

37 Joseph Laycock, 'Yoga for the New Woman and the New Man: The Role of Pierre Bernard and Blanche DeVries in the Creation of Modern Postural Yoga', *Religion and American Culture: A Journal of Interpretation* 23/1 (2013), p. 106.

38 Ibid., p. 114.

39 Ibid., pp. 118–9.

40 Ibid., pp. 105–6.

41 Syman, *The Subtle Body*, p. 94.

42 Quoted in ibid., p. 98.

43 Laycock, op. cit., p. 108; Syman, op. cit., pp. 80–99; Hugh B. Urban, 'The Omnipotent Oom: Tantra and its Impact on Modern Western Esotericism,' *Esoterica* 3 (2001).

44 Watts, *In My Own Way*, pp. 120–25; Isabel Stirling, *Zen Pioneer: The Life and Works of Ruth Fuller Sasaki* (Catapult, 2007), p. 11.

45 Watts, *In My Own Way*, p. 77; Watts (eds.), *Collected Letters*, p. 20; Furlong, op. cit., pp. 63–8.

46 Watts, *In My Own Way*, p. 128.

47 AW to M&F, 21 September 1938 and 29 May 1939, in Watts (eds.), *Collected Letters*, pp. 21 and 33–6; Watts, *In My Own Way*, p. 132.

48 AW to M&F, 21 September 1938 & 4 October 1938, in Watts (eds.), *Collected Letters*, pp. 21 and 22–4.

49 Tim Pallis, 'Review of Mary Farkas (ed.), *The Zen Eye: A Collection of Zen Talks by Sōkai-an*', *The Eastern Buddhist* 29/2 (1996), pp. 291–7.

50 Watts, *In My Own Way*, p. 136. Watts' realization that he knew little about Zen: AW to M&F, 18 October 1938, in Watts (eds.), *Collected Letters*, p. 25.

51 '[A]fter a few months' is in Furlong, op. cit., p. 75.

52 AW to M&F, 26 November 1939, in Watts (eds.), *Collected Letters*, pp. 38–40.

53 Alan Watts, 'Newsletter #2', reproduced in ibid., pp. 40–42.

54 Watts, *In My Own Way*, pp. 139–42.

55 Ibid., p. 147.

56 AW to M&F, 15 April 1941, in Watts (eds.), *Collected Letters*, pp. 70–72.

57 AW to M&F, 21 March 1941, in ibid., pp. 68–70.

Chapter 16: God? Brahman? Nirvana?

1 Alan Watts, *In My Own Way: An Autobiography* (New World Library, 1972), pp. 140–41.

2 Letter from Alan Watts to his mother and father [hereafter 'AW to M&F'], 24 August, 28 September and 7 December 1941, in Alan Watts (Joan and Anne Watts, eds.), *The Collected Letters of Alan Watts* (New World Library, 2017), pp. 85–7, and 95–9. See also Joan Watts' commentary in ibid., p. 88.

3 Monica Furlong, *Zen Effects: The Life of Alan Watts* (Skylight Paths, 2001), p. 78.

4 Key authors for Watts in this era included Etienne Gilson, Jacques Maritain and Dom John Chapman.

5 Letter from Alan Watts to Lillian Baker, 9 August 1943, in Watts (eds.), *Collected Letters*, pp. 139–40.

6 AW to M&F, 1 December 1942, in ibid., pp. 118–20.

7 Letter from Alan Watts to Mrs Leggett, 2 August 1943, in ibid., pp. 130–32.

8 Ibid., p. 131.

9 AW to M&F, 24 October 1943, in ibid., pp. 149–54.

10 AW to M&F, 1 November 1942, in ibid., pp. 114–8.

11 '[C]ourthouse furniture' is in Alan Watts, *Behold the Spirit: A Study in the Necessity of Mystical Religion* (Pantheon Books, 1971), p. xxi. '[A]pologizing' and 'jurisprudence' appear in Watts, *In My Own Way*, p. 182.

12 Watts, *Behold the Spirit*, p. xvii. Italics are in the original.

13 AW to M&F, 14 June 1939, in Watts (eds.), *Collected Letters*, pp. 36–8.

14 Watts, *Behold the Spirit*, p. 179.

15 Alan W. Watts, *The Meaning of Happiness: The Quest for Freedom of the Spirit in Modern Psychology and the Wisdom of the East* (Harper & Row, 1940), p. 51.

16 The references to Krishna and Shiva appear in Watts, *Behold the Spirit*, p. 167. The one mentioning Bach appears on p. 178, ibid.

17 '[S]tuffy' features in AW to M&F, 28 September 1941, reproduced in Watts (eds.), *Collected Letters*, pp. 95–8. '[L]umberjacks and hillbillies' appears in AW to M&F, 14 January 1942, reproduced in ibid., pp. 100–102. A 'superficial effervescence of heartiness' is in Watts, *Behold the Spirit*, p. 182.

18 AW to M&F, 1 November 1942, in Watts (eds.), *Collected Letters*, pp. 114–18.

19 Ibid.

20 Alfred, Lord Tennyson, quoted in Alan W. Watts, *The Supreme Identity: An Essay on Oriental Metaphysic and the Christian Religion* (The Noonday Press, 1957), p. 79.

21 Letter from Alan Watts to Clare [Cameron Burke], 19 February 1944, in Watts (eds.), *Collected Letters*, pp. 164–7. For Watts on Martin Buber, see Watts, *In My Own Way*, p. 170.

22 Watts, *The Supreme Identity*, pp. 75–9.

23 Reproduced in ibid., p. 83. Watts uses the spelling '*atma*'. For the sake of clarity and consistency, this has been changed to '*atman*' in the present text.

24 Ibid., pp. 83–4.

25 Letter from Alan Watts to Mrs Burch, 9 February 1944, in Watts (eds.), *Collected Letters*, pp. 162–4.

26 '[B]un-fights, bazaars and whist drives' features in a letter from Alan Watts to Adolph Teichert, 7 December 1944, in Watts (eds.), *Collected Letters*, pp. 192–5. '[S]piritual gymnastics' appears in Watts, *Behold the Spirit*, p. 149.

27 Watts, *The Supreme Identity*, p. 72.

28 For Watts' view of his new role, see Watts, *In My Own Way*, p. 175.

29 On Watts' soirées, see Joan Watts' commentary in Watts (eds.), *Collected Letters*, pp. 175 and 199–200; Watts, *In My Own Way*, pp. 176–7; Furlong, op. cit., p. 98.

30 Watts, *In My Own Way*, p. 191.

31 Joan Watts' commentary in Watts (eds.), *Collected Letters*, p. 219.

32 Furlong, op. cit., pp. 116–18.

33 Letter from Alan Watts to 'My Dear Friends', August 1950, reproduced in Watts, *In My Own Way*, pp. 193–9.

34 Ibid.

35 Letter from Canon Bernard Iddings Bell to Alan Watts, 30 August 1950, reproduced in ibid., pp. 199–200.

Chapter 17: The Hill of the Cross

1 Letter from Bede Griffiths to Mary Allen and Mary Dunbar [hereafter 'BG to MA/MD'], 10 February 1957, in Adrian B. Rance (ed.), *Falling in Love with India: From the Letters of Bede Griffiths* (Saccidananda Ashram, 2006), pp. 251–2.

2 Letter from Bede Griffiths to Martyn Skinner [hereafter 'BG to MS'], 20 July 1958. Lark song reminding Bede of England is in BG to MA/MD, 1 June 1958, in Rance, *Falling in Love with India*, pp. 315–17.

3 Bede Griffiths, *The Golden String: An Autobiography* (Fount Paperbacks, 1979), pp. 92–3.

4 Shirley Du Boulay, *Beyond the Darkness: A Biography of Bede Griffiths* (Rider and Co., Pocket edn, 1998), pp. 18–31.

5 Griffiths, op. cit., pp. 65–82; Du Boulay, op. cit., pp. 48–9.

6 Du Boulay, op. cit., pp. 45–59.

7 Griffiths, op. cit., p. 9.

8 Ibid., p. 37.

9 Letter from BG to MS, 30 May 1932.

10 See Griffiths, op. cit., pp. 48–64 and Du Boulay, op. cit., pp. 32–59.

11 Griffiths, op. cit., p. 104.

12 Ibid., p. 107.

13 Ibid., p. 108.

14 See Mary Rahme, 'Coleridge's Concept of Symbolism', *Studies in English Literature, 1500–1900* 9/4 (1969).

15 Quoted in Alister McGrath, *C. S. Lewis: A Life* (Hodder & Stoughton, 2013).

16 Ibid.

17 Letter from C. S. Lewis to Bede Griffiths (undated). Du Boulay Archive, 2/1.

18 G. K. Chesterton, *Orthodoxy* (Bodley Head, 1908), p. 20.

19 On 'Tollers', see McGrath, op. cit., p. 200.

20 Ibid., p. 157.

21 BG to MA/MD, 3 April and 17 April 1955, in the Adrian Rance Collection.

22 BG to MA/MD, 24 August 1955, in the Adrian Rance Collection.

23 Ibid.

24 BG to MS, 16 November 1961.

25 Bede Griffiths, *Christ in India: Essays Towards a Hindu-Christian Dialogue* (Charles Scribner's Sons, 1966), p. 13.

26 Ibid., p. 26.

27 BG to MS, 7 October 1966.

28 Griffiths, *Christ in India*, pp. 26–8.

29 BS to MS, 25 September 1940.

30 Ibid.

31 BG to MS, 13 April 1940.

32 Letter from Bede Griffiths to Mary Allen, 22 August 1946, in the Adrian Rance Collection; Griffiths, *The Golden String*, p. 173.

33 BG to MS, 16 January 1942.

34 Griffiths, *Christ in India*, p. 10.

35 Du Boulay, op. cit., p. 133; BG to MS, 20 July 1958; Griffiths, *Christ in India*, p. 42. The Helvellyn comparison features in BG to MS, 19 November 1961.

36 On these early months, see BG to MA/MD, 23 March 1958 and 28 September 1958, in Rance, *Falling in Love with India*, pp. 307–8 and 332–3; Du Boulay, op. cit., p. 135; BG to MS, 26 March 1959.

37 BG to MS, 19 November 1961; BG to MA/MD, 6 July 1958, in Rance, *Falling in Love with India*, pp. 317–20.

38 BG to MA/MD, 1 June 1958, in Rance, *Falling in Love with India*, pp. 315–17; 'Kurisumala Ashram: Monastery of the Mountain of the Cross': short typescript history, in the Kurisumala Ashram Archive (Kurisumala Ashram, Kerala, India).

39 On pineapples, see BG to MS, 20 July 1958; BG to MA/MD, 1 June 1958, in Rance, *Falling in Love with India*, pp. 315–17. On the expansion of the ashram, see Du Boulay, op. cit., pp. 134 and 142; Griffiths, *Christ in India*, p. 45.

40 Du Boulay, op. cit., p. 141.

41 BG to MS, 20 July 1958 and 19 November 1961.

42 BG to MS, 19 November 1961; Griffiths, *Christ in India*, pp. 43 and 52–3; Du Boulay, op. cit., pp. 136–7.

43 Du Boulay, op. cit., p. 139.

44 BG to MS, 24 August 1955.

45 Bede Griffiths, *The Marriage of East and West* (Medio Media, 2003), p. 6.

46 See both letters and commentary in Rance, *Falling in Love with India*.

47 Letter from Bede Griffiths to Mary Allen, 13 May 1946, in the Adrian Rance Collection.

48 BG to MA/MD, 25 March 1957, in Rance, *Falling in Love with India*, pp. 255–8. Italics in the original.

49 Griffiths, *The Golden String*, p. 159.

50 Letter from Bede Griffiths to Mary Allen, 21 January 1962, in Rance, *Falling in Love with India*, pp. 382–5.

51 For Griffiths' growing fame, see Du Boulay, op. cit., Chapter 13.

52 Shirley Du Boulay, interview with Father Francis Mahieu. In the Du Boulay Archive.

Chapter 18: The Palace of Light

1 Letter from Erna Hoch to her family, 12 April 1956. In 'Privatarchiv Erna Hoch', Gosteli-Stiftung, Worblaufen, Switzerland [hereafter 'Erna Hoch Archive'].

2 Quoted in Roy Porter, *Madness: A Brief History* (Oxford University Press, 2002), p. 186.

3 Christopher Harding, 'The Emergence of "Christian Psychiatry" in Post-Independence India', CSAS Working Paper, November 2011.

4 Letter from Erna Hoch to Dr Norell, 26 November 1955, in Erna Hoch Archive; Erna M. Hoch, *Hypocrite or Heretic* (The Christian Institute for the Study of Religion and Society, 1983), pp. 9–10.

5 Ibid., pp. 10–11.

6 Ibid., pp. 5–10.

7 Ibid., pp. 8–18.

8 Ibid., pp. 16–20.

9 Ibid., pp. 19–27.

10 Ibid., p. 25.

11 Ibid., pp. 25–9.

12 Ibid., p. 31; Letter from Erna Hoch to Dr Norell, 26 November 1955.

13 Hoch, *Hypocrite or Heretic*, p. 71.

14 Letter from Erna Hoch to her family, 12 April 1956.

15 Ibid.; Letter from Erna Hoch to her family, 15 April 1956, in Erna Hoch Archive.

16 Letters from Erna Hoch to her family: 15 April 1956 and 15 July 1956, in Erna Hoch Archive.

17 Hoch, *Hypocrite or Heretic*, pp. 58–9.

18 Quoted in Harding, op. cit.

19 Quoted in Amima Mama, *Beyond the Masks: Race, Gender and Subjectivity* (Taylor & Francis, 2002), p. 31.

20 On Horney's reading of Huxley, see Susan Quinn, *A Mind of Her Own: The Life of Karen Horney* (Summit Books, 1987), p. 403.

21 'Quite absorbed' and 'the very essence' are quoted in Marcia Westkott, 'Karen Horney's Encounter with Zen', in Janet L. Jacobs (ed.), *Religion, Society and Psychoanalysis: Readings in Contemporary Theory* (Routledge, 1997), p. 83.

22 Maladie du siècle' appears in Erich Fromm, D. T. Suzuki and Richard De Martino, *Zen Buddhism and Psychoanalysis* (Harper & Row, 1960), p. 86. 'Just "being"' is ibid., pp. 78–9.

23 Ibid., pp. 86–7.

24 Ibid., p. 93.

25 Ibid., p. 94.

26 Ibid., p. 138. Fromm's own practice is reported in Alan Roland, 'Erich Fromm's Involvement with Zen Buddhism: Psychoanalysis and the

Spiritual Quest in Subsequent Decades', *The Psychoanalytic Review* 104/4 (2017), 505–7.

27 Letters from Erna Hoch to her family: 12 April 1956 & 28 July 1956, in Erna Hoch Archive.

28 Hoch, *Hypocrite or Heretic*, p. 70.

29 Ibid., pp. 159–60.

30 Ibid., pp. 48–59; 159–60.

31 Quoted in Richard Askay and Jensen Farquhar, *Of Philosophers and Madmen: A Disclosure of Martin Heidegger, Medard Boss, and Sigmund Freud* (Rodopi, 2011), p. 116.

32 Ibid., pp. 114–5.

33 Medard Boss, *A Psychiatrist Discovers India* (Oswald Wolff, 1965), p. 10.

34 Ibid., pp. 126–9.

35 Hoch, op. cit., pp. 45–52. On Boss' motivations for travelling to India, and his introduction there to *satcitananda*, see Boss, op cit., pp. 13–4 & pp. 126–9.

36 Kannu V. Rajan, 'Administrative Report, 1 July 1960–18 May 1961', in Erna Hoch Archive.

37 Letters from Erna Hoch to her family: 19 May 1956 and 1 July 1956; Hoch, *Hypocrite or Heretic*, p. 71.

38 Ibid., pp. 76–9.

39 Ibid., p. 79.

40 Ibid., p. 81.

41 Ibid., p. 83.

42 Ibid., pp. 84–5.

43 Ibid., pp. 86–93.

44 Ibid., pp. 100–101.

45 Ibid., p. 106.

46 From Allen Ginsberg's 'Howl', quoted in David Stephen Calonne, *The Spiritual Imagination of the Beats* (Cambridge University Press, 2017), p. 93.

Chapter 19: Liberation

1 Monica Furlong, *Zen Effects: The Life of Alan Watts* (Skylight Paths, 2001), pp. 132–40; Letter from Alan Watts to 'Jacquie', 22 July 1954, in Alan Watts (Joan and Anne Watts, eds.), *The Collected Letters of Alan Watts* (New World Library, 2017), pp. 311–12; Letter from Alan Watts to his mother and father [hereafter 'AW to M&F'], 4 November 1952, in ibid., p. 298–300; Joan Watts, commentary in ibid., p. 288; C. S. Prebish, 'Introduction', in C. S. Prebish and Kenneth K. Tanaka (eds.), *Faces of Buddhism in America* (University of California Press, 1998), p. 3.

2 Furlong, op. cit., pp. 134 and 140. On Annie Besant's school, see Annie Besant, 'The Happy Valley Foundation': www.besanthill.org/annie-besant-1927-happy-valley-foundation-announcement/.

3 In Furlong, op. cit., p. 143.

4 Letters from Alan Watts to Mary Jane, 5 May 1959 and 14 May 1959, in Watts (eds.), *Collected Letters*, pp. 346–9.

5 Anne Watts, commentary in ibid., pp. 354–5.

6 Furlong, op. cit., pp. 149–51; Joan Watts, commentary in Watts (eds.), *Collected Letters*, pp. 394–5; Letter from Alan Watts to his father, late November 1961, in ibid., pp. 410–11.

7 Christopher Gair, *The American Counter-Culture, 1945–1975* (Edinburgh University Press, 2007), pp. 31–2.

8 Ibid., pp. 57–64.

9 Quoted in Furlong, op. cit., p. 136.

10 See Michael Masatsugu, ' "Beyond This World of Transiency and Impermanence": Japanese Americans, Dharma Bums, and the Making of American Buddhism during the Early Cold War Years', *Pacific Historical Review* 77/3 (2008), 'Zen lunatics' is quoted from p. 440 of ibid.

11 Jack Kerouac, *Dharma Bums* (Penguin Books, 1990), p. 39.

12 Jane Iwamura, *Virtual Orientalism: Asian Religions and American Popular Culture* (Oxford University Press, 2010), pp. 47–8.

13 Alan W. Watts, *Beat Zen, Square Zen, and Zen* (City Lights Books, 1959).

14 Iwamura, op. cit., pp. 47–50.

15 Furlong, op. cit., p. 136.

16 Alan W. Watts, *Psychotherapy East and West* (Penguin Books, 1973), pp. 69–70.

17 Ibid., p. 14.

18 Ibid., pp. 14–15 and 84.

19 Ibid., p. 65.

20 'I do nothing' is in ibid., p. 42, 'fleshy vehicle', p. 20. On humankind's futile search for security, see Alan W. Watts, *The Wisdom of Insecurity* (Rider & Co., Pocket edn, 1983), p. 18. On Vedānta, see Watts, *Psychotherapy East and West*, pp. 57 and 66.

21 Ibid., p. 22; Watts, *The Wisdom of Insecurity*, p. 18.

22 '[C]up of tea' is in Alan W. Watts, *The Meaning of Happiness: The Quest for Freedom of the Spirit in Modern Psychology and the Wisdom of the East* (Harper & Row, 1940).

23 Watts, *The Wisdom of Insecurity*, p. 78.

24 Ibid., p. 76.

25 Quoted in Watts, *Psychotherapy East and West*, p. 68.

26 Watts, *The Wisdom of Insecurity*, p. 86; Watts, *Psychotherapy East and West*, p. 26.

27 Watts, *The Wisdom*, p. 99.

28 Peter J. Columbus and Donadrian L. Rice (eds), *Alan Watts – Here and Now: Contributions to Psychology, Philosophy and Religion* (SUNY Press, 2012), p. 3. '[W]hat Alan Watts said' is in Furlong, op. cit., p. 174.

29 '[S]ocial fiction' is in Watts, *Psychotherapy East and West*, p. 75.

30 Ibid., pp. 17 and 91–2.

31 'More relaxed' is in Alan Watts, *In My Own Way: An Autobiography* (New World Library, 1972), p. 323. Huxley's cautionary comments about mescalin are reproduced in Nicholas Murray, *Aldous Huxley: An English Intellectual* (Little, Brown, 2002).

32 Furlong, op. cit., p. 166.

33 Alan W. Watts, *The Joyous Cosmology: Adventures in the Chemistry of Consciousness* (Pantheon Books, 1962), pp. 63–9.

34 Ibid., pp. 49–50 and 65.

35 Ibid., pp. 12 and 84–92.

36 Ibid., p. 20.

37 Watts, *In My Own Way*, p. 326.

38 Watts, *The Joyous Cosmology*, pp. 20–1.

39 Watts, *In My Own Way*, p. 326.

40 Ibid., pp. xii–xiii.

41 Stephen A. Kent, *From Slogans to Mantras: Social Protest and Religious Conversion in the Late Vietnam War Era* (Syracuse University Press, 2001), p. 14.

42 Damon R. Bach, *The American Counterculture: A History of Hippies and Cultural Dissidents* (University Press of Kansas, 2020), p. 54; Stefanie Syman, *The Subtle Body: The Story of Yoga in America* (Farrar, Straus and Giroux, 2010), p. 215.

43 Ibid., p. 215.

44 Quoted in Gair, op. cit., p. 134.

45 Bach, op. cit., p. 81.

46 Syman, op. cit., p. 217. The estimate of one million doses comes from *Life* magazine, 25 March 1966.

47 Furlong, op. cit., pp. 175–9.

48 On the World's First Human Be-In, see ibid., pp. 181–2; Bach, op. cit., pp. 1 and 101.

49 Joshua M. Greene, *Here Comes the Sun: The Spiritual and Musical Journey of George Harrison* (Bantam Books, 2006), pp. 75 and 120–21; Gary Tillery, *Working-Class Mystic: A Spiritual Biography of George Harrison* (Quest Books, 2011), pp. 53–4.

50 Greene, op. cit., p. 121.

Chapter 20: Gurus

1 Ray Davies, *X-Ray: The Unauthorized Autobiography* (ABRAMS Press, 2007).

2 Jonathan Bellman, 'Indian Resonances in the British Invasion, 1965–1968', *The Journal of Musicology* 15/1 (1997), p. 120.

3 George Harrison, *I, Me, Mine* (W. H. Allen, 1982), p. 52; Peter Lavezzoli, *The Dawn of Indian Music in the West* (Continuum, 2007), p. 173; Steve Hamelman, 'Leaving the West Behind: the Beatles and India', in

Kenneth Womack (ed.), *The Beatles in Context* (Cambridge University Press, 2020), p. 280.

4 Joshua M. Greene, *Here Comes the Sun: The Spiritual and Musical Journey of George Harrison* (Bantam Books, 2006), p. 16; Gary Tillery, *Working-Class Mystic: A Spiritual Biography of George Harrison* (Quest Books, 2011), p. 33.

5 Greene, op. cit., p. 26; Tillery, op. cit., p. 12; Lavezzoli, op. cit., p. 172.

6 Greene, op. cit., p. 26; Craig Brown, *One Two Three Four: The Beatles in Time* (Fourth Estate, 2020), pp. 32–3.

7 The analogy with pigs being slaughtered appears in Greene, op. cit., p. 55 and in John Macmillian, *Beatles vs. Stones* (Simon & Schuster, 2014), p. 85. The bathwater offer is Greene, op. cit., p. 80 and Brown, op. cit., p. 240.

8 On the Asia tour, see Harrison, op. cit., pp. 48–51.

9 Lavezzoli, op. cit., p. 176. 'Terrible', and Shankar's decision to 'keep my mouth shut,' as he put it, come from Al Weisel, 'Ravi Shankar on his pal George Harrison and "Chants of India"', *Rolling Stone*, 15 May 1997.

10 Lavezzoli, op. cit., p. 177; Harrison, op. cit., p. 55.

11 Greene, op. cit., p. 92.

12 Lavezzoli, op. cit., pp. 19–21.

13 Quoted in Keith Badman, *The Beatles Off the Record: Outrageous Opinions and Unrehearsed Interviews* (Omnibus Press, 2001), p. 191.

14 Harrison, op. cit., p. 55; Ravi Shankar, *Raga Mala: the Autobiography of Ravi Shankar* (Genesis Publications, 1997), pp. 189–93.

15 Harry Oldmeadow, *Journeys East: 20th Century Western Encounters with Eastern Religious Traditions* (World Wisdom, 2004), p. 271; Shankar, op. cit., p. 189–93.

16 Quoted in Greene, op. cit., p. 103; Tillery, op. cit., p. 56.

17 Robert Love et al (eds), *Harrison: By the Editors of Rolling Stone* (Simon & Schuster, 2002), p. 34.

18 '[W]hen one has received the message' is from Alan Watts, *In My Own Way: An Autobiography* (New World Library, 1972), p. 327.

19 Tillery, op. cit., pp. 56–8.

20 On the involvement of the Asian Music Circle, see Kathryn B. Cox, '"Swinging London", Psychedelia, and the Summer of Love', in Womack (ed.), op. cit., p. 276.

21 Jeffery D. Long, *Hinduism in America: A Convergence of Worlds* (Blooms-bury, 2020), pp. 223–4.

22 Tillery, op. cit., p. 58.

23 Greene, op. cit., pp. 117–8; Tillery, op. cit., pp. 58–9.

24 Long, op. cit., p. 223; Tillery, op. cit., p. 58.

25 Lavezzoli, op. cit., p. 180; Hamelman, in Womack (ed.), op. cit., p. 284.

26 Tillery, op. cit., p. 63.

27 On Lennon, see Tillery, op. cit., p. 35. On the Beatles in Rishikesh, see Brown, op. cit., pp. 443–53.

28 Stefanie Syman, *The Subtle Body: The Story of Yoga in America* (Farrar, Straus and Giroux, 2010), p. 201; Tillery, op. cit., p. 71; Greene, op. cit., p. 177.

29 Shirley Du Boulay, Interview with Father Augustine, in Shirley Du Boulay Archive.

30 Shirley Du Boulay, *Beyond the Darkness: A Biography of Bede Griffiths* (Rider and Co., Pocket edn, 1998), p. 158; Letters from Bede Griffiths to Martyn Skinner [hereafter 'BG to MS'], 25 December 1968 and 6 April 1969.

31 BG to MS, 18 December 1969 and 19 January 1971.

32 Du Boulay, op. cit., p. 160.

33 BG to MS, 25 December 1968.

34 Sharif Gemie and Brian Ireland, *The Hippie Trail: A History, 1957–78* (Manchester University Press, 2017).

35 BG to MS, 22 July 1970.

36 BG to MS, 19 January 1971 and 1 December 1973.

37 Quoted in Du Boulay, op. cit., p. 183.

38 Quoted in Harvey D. Egan, 'The Mystical Theology of Karl Rahner', *The Way* 52/2 (2013), 51.

39 Kurisumala Scrapbook, 'Monastic Contact with Hippies and Spiritual Seekers from the West', Kurisumala Ashram Archive.

40 Quoted in ibid.

41 Christopher Key Chapple, 'Raja Yoga and the Guru', in Thomas A. Forsthoefel and Cynthia Anne Humes (eds.), *Gurus in America* (SUNY Press, 2005), pp. 16–17.

42 Quoted in Kurisumala Scrapbook, 'Monastic Contact'.

43 Gregory Alles, 'The Study of Religions: The Last 50 Years', in John R. Hinnells, *Routledge Companion to the Study of Religion* (Routledge, 2009), p. 40.

44 Quoted in Douglas Pratt, 'Interreligious Dialogue: A Case Study Approach in Respect to the Vatican and the World Council of Churches', in Martha Frederiks and Dorottya Nagy, *World Christianity: Methodological Considerations* (Brill, 2020), p. 185.

45 Quoted in Du Boulay, p. 168.

46 Shirley Du Boulay, *The Cave of the Heart: The Life of Abhishiktananda* (Orbis Books, 2005), pp. 173–87.

47 BG to MS, 24 January 1974.

48 Quoted in Jaechan Anselmo Park, *Thomas Merton's Encounter with Buddhism and Beyond* (Liturgical Press, 2019).

49 Ibid.

50 Quoted in Thomas Keating, *Spirituality, Contemplation and Transformation* (Lantern Books, 2009), p. 74.

51 Rembert G. Weakland, 'Thomas Merton's Bangkok Lecture of December 1968', *Buddhist-Christian Studies* 28 (2008), pp. 91–9.

52 Quoted in Du Boulay, *Beyond the Darkness*, p. 196.

53 Judson B. Trapnell, *Bede Griffiths: A Life in Dialogue* (SUNY Press, 2001), p. 118.

54 Quoted in Du Boulay, *Beyond the Darkness*, p. 198.

55 See Du Boulay, *Cave of the Heart*, p. 184.

56 Du Boulay, *Beyond the Darkness*, pp. 169–70.

57 Erna M. Hoch, *The Madhouse at the Lotus Lake* (self-published, 2000), pp. 26, 42, 124 and 221–6.

58 Erna M. Hoch, *Hypocrite or Heretic* (The Christian Institute for the Study of Religion and Society, 1983), pp. 117–24.

59 Erna M. Hoch, 'Ancient Indian Philosophy and Western Psychotherapy', in Erna M. Hoch (ed.), *Sources and Resources: A Western Psychiatrist's Search for Meaning in the Ancient Indian Scriptures* (Book Faith India, 1993), p. 22.

60 Ibid., p. 22.

61 Quoted in Patricia Walden, 'Take an Action', in Kofi Busia (ed.), *Iyengar: The Yoga Master* (Shambhala, 2007), p. 47.

62 Alan Watts, *In My Own Way: An Autobiography* (New World Library, 1972), p. 332–3.

63 Monica Furlong, *Zen Effects: The Life of Alan Watts* (Skylight Paths, 2001), p. 186. On Esalen, see Jeffrey J. Kripal, *Esalen: America and the Religion of No Religion* (University of Chicago Press, 2007).

64 Letter from Alan Watts to *Playboy* magazine [undated], in Alan Watts (Joan and Anne Watts (eds.), *The Collected Letters of Alan Watts* (New World Library, 2017)), pp. 506–7.

65 Furlong, op. cit., p. 200.

66 Alan W. Watts, *The Supreme Identity: An Essay on Oriental Metaphysic and the Christian Religion* (The Noonday Press, 1957), p. 178.

67 '[A]s if we had never been born' is in Watts (eds.), *Collected Letters*, p. 556; '[r]eincarnation?' is in Furlong, op. cit., p. 216; 'The disappearance' is quoted in ibid., p. 207.

68 Harrison, op. cit., p. 158.

69 Tillery, op. cit., p. 10.

70 Ibid., p. 79.

71 Joan Watts' commentary is in Watts (eds.), *Collected Letters*, p. 500.

72 Joan Watts' commentary is in ibid., pp. 553–4.

73 '[W]ithout knowing how to come back' is reported in Furlong, op. cit., p. 213. '[H]ad enough', 'checked out' and the visit from a group of Buddhists is featured in Joan Watts' commentary in Watts (eds.), *Collected Letters*, pp. 553–4.

74 Reproduced in Watts (eds.), *Collected Letters*, p. 554.

Chapter 21: New Ages

1 Christopher Lasch, *The Culture of Narcissism: American Life in an Age of Diminishing Expectations* (W. W. Norton & Company, 1979), p. 4.

2 Edward Said, *Orientalism* (Pantheon Books, 1978).

3 Bede Griffiths, *A New Vision of Reality: Western Science, Eastern Mysticism and Christian Faith* (HarperCollins, 1989).

4 Peter Lavezzoli, *The Dawn of Indian Music in the West* (Continuum, 2007), p. 181.

5 Farhad Dalal, 'Jung: A Racist', *British Journal of Psychotherapy* 4/3 (1988).

6 See, for example, 'Open Letter from a Group of Jungians on the Question of Jung's Writings on and Theories about "Africans"', *British Journal of Psychotherapy* 34/4 (2018).

7 For an influential argument to this effect, see Ronald Inden, 'Orientalist Constructions of India', *Modern Asian Studies* 20/3 (1986), 403.

8 Ashis Nandy, *The Intimate Enemy: Loss and Recovery of Self under Colonialism* (Oxford University Press, 1983), p. xi.

9 Gary Tillery, *Working-Class Mystic: A Spiritual Biography of George Harrison* (Quest Books, 2011), pp. 67–8 and 90–91.

10 Quoted in C. S. Prebish, 'Introduction', in C. S. Prebish and Kenneth K. Tanaka (eds.), *Faces of Buddhism in America* (University of California Press, 1998), p. 6.

11 Sharon Salzberg, *Lovingkindness* (Shambhala, 1995), p. 40.

12 Thomas A. Tweed, 'Who is a Buddhist? Night-Stand Buddhists and Other Creatures', in Charles S. Prebish and Martin Baumann (eds.), *Westward Dharma: Buddhism beyond Asia* (University of California Press, 2002), p. 20; Martin Baumann, 'Buddhism in Europe: Past, Present, Prospects', in ibid., pp. 92–3; Richard Hughes Seager, 'American Buddhism in the Making,' in ibid., p. 109.

13 Gil Fronsd, 'Insight Meditation in the United States', in Prebish and Tanaka (eds.), op. cit., p. 169.

14 Quoted in Robert Bluck, *British Buddhism: Teachings, Practice and Development* (Taylor & Francis, 2006), pp. 65–6.

15 Reverend Helen Cummings, 'Adapting Western Chants and Hymn Tunes to Buddhist Texts', *The Hymn* 60/2 (2009). Jiyu-Kennett on Humphreys and exotica appears in Bluck, op. cit., p. 85.

16 Ibid., p. 70.

17 Rick Fields, *How the Swans Came to the Lake: A Narrative History of Buddhism in America* (Shambhala, 1999), p. 231.

18 G. Victor Sōgen Hori, 'Japanese Zen in America', in Prebish and Tanaka (eds.), op. cit., p. 65.

19 Helen Tworkov, *Zen in America: Five Teachers and the Search for an American Buddhism* (North Point Press, 1990), p. 232.

20 Jason C. Bivins, ' "Beautiful Women Dig Graves": Richard Baker-roshi, Imported Buddhism, and the Transmission of Ethics at the San Francisco Zen Center', *Religion and American Culture: A Journal of Interpretation* 17/1 (2007), 78; Katy Butler, 'Events Are the Teacher: Working through the Crisis at San Francisco Zen Center', *Coevolution Quarterly* (Winter, 1983).

21 Tworkov, op. cit., p. 236.

22 Bivins, op. cit., 79.

23 Butler, op. cit.; Tworkov, op. cit., p. 233.

24 Hori, op. cit.

25 Butler, op. cit.; Tworkov, op. cit., p. 243.

26 Sandra Bell, 'Scandals in Emerging Western Buddhism', in Prebish and Baumann (eds.), op. cit., pp. 226 and 238.

27 David McMahan, *The Making of Buddhist Modernism* (Oxford University Press, 2008), p. 243.

28 Hori, op. cit., pp. 57–8.

29 McMahan, op. cit., p. 248.

30 See Wouter J. Hanegraaf, *New Age Religion and Western Culture* (State University of New York Press, 1998), pp. 1–23.

31 Shirley Du Boulay, *Beyond the Darkness: A Biography of Bede Griffiths* (Rider and Co., Pocket edn, 1998), pp. 205–20 and 260.

32 Congregation for the Doctrine of the Faith, 'Letter to the Bishops of the Catholic Church on Some Aspects of Christian Meditation', 15 October 1989, see https://www.vatican.va/roman_curia/congregations/cfaith/documents/rc_con_cfaith_doc_19891015_meditazione-cristiana_en.html.

33 Quoted in Du Boulay, op. cit., pp. 176–9.

34 Sita Ram Goel, *Catholic Ashrams: Sannyasins or Swindlers?* (Voice of India, 2009), pp. 16–17.

35 Ibid., p. 123.

36 Bede Griffiths, *Return to the Centre* (Collins, 1978), p. 10.

37 Klaus Klostermaier, 'Hindu-Christian Dialogue: Revisiting the Tannirpali Trinity's Original Vision', *Journal of Hindu-Christian Studies* 16 (2003).

38 Goel, op. cit., p. 129.

39 Bede Griffiths, *A New Vision of Reality: Western Science, Eastern Mysticism and Christian Faith* (HarperCollins, 1989), pp. 17–18.

40 Bede Griffiths, *The Marriage of East and West* (Medio Media, 2003), pp. 24 and 49; Iain McGilchrist, *The Matter with Things: Our Brains, Our Delusions, and the Unmaking of the World* (Perspectiva Press, 2021), pp. 1050–52.

41 Reproduced in Griffiths, *Return to the Centre*, pp. 69–70.

42 Ibid, p. 94.

43 Ibid, p. 68; Judson B. Trapnell, *Bede Griffiths: A Life in Dialogue* (SUNY Press, 2001), p. 162.

44 Griffiths, *A New Vision*, p. 11; Griffiths, *Return to the Centre*, pp. 22–3.

45 Griffiths, *A New Vision*, pp. 264–8.

46 Ibid, pp. 51, 191, 199 and 271; Griffiths, *Return to the Centre*, p. 55.

47 Griffiths, *A New Vision*, pp. 191 and 265–6; Griffiths, *Return to the Centre*, p. 100.

48 Griffiths, *Return to the Centre*, pp. 54–5.

49 Ibid, p. 56. '[P]erfectly brilliant' is in BG to MS, 24 May 1942.

50 Griffiths, *A New Vision*, pp. 33–5; Griffiths, *Return to the Centre*, p. 99.

51 Trapnell, op. cit., p. 143.

52 Griffiths, *A New Vision*, pp. 131–2 and 151; Griffiths, *The Marriage of East and West*, p. 60.

53 Erna M. Hoch, *Hypocrite or Heretic* (The Christian Institute for the Study of Religion and Society, 1983), p. 131.

54 Erna M. Hoch, 'Ancient Indian Philosophy and Western Psychotherapy', in Erna M. Hoch (ed.), *Sources and Resources: A Western Psychiatrist's Search for Meaning in the Ancient Indian Scriptures* (Book Faith India, 1993), p. 16.

55 Hoch, *Hypocrite or Heretic*, p. 147.

56 Ibid., p. 144.

57 Ibid., p. 140. '[P]ut a yak's head' is from His Holiness the Dalai Lama, *The Good Heart: A Buddhist Perspective on the Teachings of Jesus* (Wisdom Publication edn, 1998), p. xii.

58 Jack Kornfield, *A Path with Heart* (Random House, 1993), pp. 246–7.

59 Hoch, *Hypocrite or Heretic*, pp. 148–51.

60 Hoch, *Sources*, p. 22.

61 Hoch, *Hypocrite or Heretic*, pp. 153–4.

62 Ibid., pp. 158–60.

63 'Washed and bathed' is quoted in Du Boulay, op. cit., p. 245.

64 Author interview with Father Laurence Freeman, 2013.

65 Quoted in Du Boulay, op. cit., pp. 248–9.

66 Griffiths, *A New Vision*, p. 169.

67 Author interview with Father Laurence Freeman, 2013.

68 Trapnell, op. cit., p. 151; Griffiths, *A New Vision*, p. 124.

69 Griffiths, *The Marriage of East and West*, pp. 180–85.

70 Griffiths, *A New Vision*, pp. 172 and 222.

71 Du Boulay, op. cit., p. 281.

72 Quoted in ibid., p. 243.

73 Trapnell, op. cit., p. 191.

74 Quoted in Alan Jones, *Common Prayer on Common Ground: A Vision of Anglican Orthodoxy* (Church Publishing Incorporated, 2006), p. 64. The close friend in question was Fr Laurence Freeman.

Epilogue: Onwards

1 Quoted in Ian Ker, *John Henry Newman* (Oxford University Press, 2010), p. 95.

2 Alan Watts, *In My Own Way: An Autobiography* (New World Library, 1972), p. 7–8.

3 Letter from Bede Griffiths to Mary Allen, 21 January 1962, in Rance, *Falling in Love with India*, pp. 382–5.

4 Ker, op. cit., p. 211.

5 David L. Smith, 'The Authenticity of Alan Watts', in Gary Storhoff and John Whalen-Bridge (eds.), *American Buddhism as a Way of Life* (SUNY Press), p. 25.

6 On 'what it is' versus 'that it is', see David Bentley-Hart, *The Experience of God: Being, Consciousness, Bliss* (Yale University Press, 2013), p. 293–332.

Index

Index

Index

Olcott, Colonel Henry Steel 210
Old Testament 40, 171
Olympia 11
Olympics 11–12
Om symbol 318, 328, 334
'Om the Omniscient' (Pierre Arnold
    Bernard) 236
Ōmura, Lord of 81
'On the Mystical Poetry of the
    Persians and Hindus' (Jones) 157
On the Origin of Species (Darwin)
    190
*On Religion: Speeches to Its Cultured
    Despisers* (Schleiermacher) 169
On the Road (Kerouac) 312
On Truth (Herbert) 106
'One-eyes' (legendary people) 27
One Flew Over the Cuckoo's Nest (Kesey)
    301
Onesicritus 24, 26, 61
The Open Door to Hidden Heathenism
    (Rogerius) 143
The Organization Man (Whyte) 292
Oriental / Orientalist 12–13, 145, 155, 163,
    167, 179, 184, 197, 237, 238, 325
Orientalism (Said) 325
Origen 39–40, 166, 190
Ormuz 54, 2, 93
Orwell, George 268
Osaka 80, 84
Otoliknoi 17
Ottoman Empire / Ottomans 51, 55, 95,
    213
Ōuchi Yoshitaka, Lord 75, 76
Oupnek'hat (Anquetil-Duperon) 144,
    164
Ovington, John 122
Owen, Robert 174
Oxford (town) 259–60
Oxford Street (London) 305

Oxford, University of *see* University
    of Oxford

Pacific Heights (San Francisco) 291
Pacific Ocean 53, 57, 84
'Paint it Black' (Rolling Stones) 306
Pakistan 333
'Palace of Light' (Nur Manzil) 274
Pali language 166, 192
Pali scriptures / texts 192, 327
Pali Text Society 192
Panama, Isthmus of *see* Isthmus of
    Panama
Pandaea, Queen 25
Pandava brothers 147
Panipat, Battle of 64
'Pantisocracy' 176, 258
Papacy 59
Papal bull (1715) 133
Papal states 82
Paravas 62, 109
Paris 94, 132–3, 160, 167, 183
Parliament 174, 207, 212
Parthian Empire 36
Pataliputra 25, 27
Patanjali 216–17, 313, 314
A Path with Heart (Kornfield) 340
Pathans 98
Paul, apostle / saint 39, 108, 117, 316, 317,
    336
Pauli, Wolfgang 335
Pearl Fishery Coast 62
Pearl Harbor attack 244
Pearl river 71, 72
Peking 70, 73, 112–13, 114, 116, 122, 130,
    157 *see also* Beijing
Pentecost 343
pepper 31, 38, 41, 49, 50, 53, 63, 92, 176, 257
The Perennial Philosophy (Huxley) 244,
    280

441

Tantrik Order 237–8

The Tao of Physics (Capra) 334

Tao Te Ching 235, 244, 247, 258, 260, 266, 321

Taoism 2, 78, 112, 114, 15, 228, 234–5, 236, 245, 247, 295, 297, 321, 335, 358

'Taprobane' (Sri Lanka) 30

'*Tat tvam asi*' (Upanishads: 'You are that') 243, 249, 297

Tattuwa-Bhodacharia Swami 108–9

Taxila 21, 24

tea 47, 72, 78, 79, 82, 86, 121–3, 144, 232, 257, 296

Telegraph, the 201

Tenjiku 75

Tennyson, Alfred, Lord 189, 193, 202, 249

Thames river 258

Thar Desert 16

Thelwall, John 180

Theosophical Society 210, 213, 228

Theosophy 205–6, 209–12, 219–20, 228, 234, 241, 260

Theravada tradition 191–2, 316

Thermopylae, Battle of 12

Thich Nat Hanh 328

Thina 37

Thomas, apostle/saint 42–3, 63, 72, 74, 89

Thomas, Dylan 307

Thomas Christians 63–4, 106, 257, 268, 354–5

Thoreau, Henry David 183, 185, 226, 293

Throssel Hole Priory (Northumberland) 329

Thuggee cult 305

Tianxue ('Celestial Teachings') 113

Tibet 191, 209, 210, 241, 247, 316, 328, 336

The Tibetan Book of the Dead 310

Tibetan language 166

Tiger (ship) 92

Tigris river 40

Time magazine 294

Tiruvannamalai 314

Titianus, Maes 37

Tokugawa Ieyasu 84–5

Tokugawa shogunate 85, 200

Tokyo 199, 200, 307

Toledo 81

Toleration, Edict of *see* Edict of Toleration

Tolkien, J. R. R. 262, 263

Tolstoy, Leo 196, 260

Top of the Pops 311

Tordesillas, Treaty of (1494) 52, 53, 57

Tower of Babel 131

Towerson, Gabriel 99, 100

Towerson, Mariam 99, 100

trade/commerce 26, 43, 45, 57, 58, 69, 73, 82, 85, 90, 91–2, 200, 214, 221, 348, 349, 352

China's trade with England 157

China's trade with Europe 70, 121–2, 134, 157

China's trade with Japan 76–7

China's trade with Mesopotamia 36

China's trade with Roman Empire 36, 37–8

China's trade with South Asia 36

and East India Company 94, 97, 98, 99–101, 122

in horses 50

India's internal trade 28–9

India's trade with Egypt 29

India's trade with England 89, 92, 98, 99–101, 138, 175–6

India's trade with Europe 40–1, 42, 53, 54

India's trade with Graeco-Roman world 29, 30

India's trade with Portugal 53–4

BOTHNIA

AVSSIA ALBA

Dsuidna fl.

Abij S

Colmogora
regio

Alani Scythæ

Auzacitis
regio

MOSCOVIA

Rha fl.

Aspã sti montes

Tapuri

mons

Iaxartes

Massagetæ

Auzacia

Aftotæ

Saccæ

Mare Caspiū

Sogdiana

Cassia

Bilthe

Oxus fl.

MEDIA

Hyrcania

Bactri
ana

Emodij mo

PERSIS

Tolaius monter

PARTHIA

Aria

Arachosia

INDIA

Gāges

citra Gāgem

Dragiana

Reg

Sinus Persicus

Carmania

Cambaia

Indus fl.

Narsingæ
regnum

ARABIA

Ormus

Goa

Sinus Gangeticus

Aden

Sinus Guzerat

Canonor

Mare Rubrum

Calicut

Aethiopiæ
pars

Zaylon

TAPRO
BANA
Suma

Christiana

Mare
Praffodum

Madagaftar

Zanzibar